THE CLASS

A MEMOIR OF A PLACE, A TIME, AND US

KEN DRYDEN

McCLELLAND & STEWART

Hardcover edition published 2023

McClelland & Stewart and colophon are registered trademarks of
Penguin Random House Canada Limited.

Library and Archives Canada Cataloguing in Publication data
is available upon request.

ISBN: 978-0-7710-0923-5
ebook ISBN: 978-0-7710-0924-2

Excerpt from *Until the End of Time: Mind, Matter, and Our Search
for Meaning in an Evolving Universe* by Brian Greene, © 2020 by
Brian Greene. Used by permission of Alfred A. Knopf, an imprint
of the Knopf Doubleday Publishing Group, a division of Penguin
Random House LLC. All rights reserved.

Front jacket art: page from *The Etobian*, courtesy of Etobicoke
Collegiate Institute; photograph of Ken Dryden by Bev Best
Typeset in Janson Text by M&S, Toronto

Printed in Canada

McClelland & Stewart,
a division of Penguin Random House Canada Limited,
a Penguin Random House Company

www.penguinrandomhouse.ca

1   2   3   4   5   27   26   25   24   23

To The Class

We shared a time together.

Until we write our own stories, we won't know who we are.

—April De Angelis, *My Brilliant Friend*
(play, from the novel by Elena Ferrante)

I had been thinking of writing this book for about thirty years. I have always been drawn to "why" questions. Why am I as I am? Why are you? Why is this place or that thing the way they are? There are always reasons, I had come to learn, often weird, impossible-to-predict reasons, where some seemingly insignificant choice or action makes some other seemingly insignificant choice or action more likely to happen, then some other, until you have in front of you, or in you, something *very* significant. Maybe life-transforming.

We had been classmates for five years at Etobicoke Collegiate, in a suburb of Toronto, a very long time ago. We had written special exams, and from among many others we had been chosen. A few left our class during these years, a few came in, but of the core there were thirty-five of us. I was one. I have memories of us then. I have feelings about us. We went through an awkward, exciting, difficult time together, near children at the beginning, near adults at the end, on the way to somewhere. I liked these people, some of them a lot, though not enough, it turned out, to have stayed in close contact in the years since (another "why" question), but enough to wonder: How are you doing? How's life? What have all these years been like for you?

I also thought this would be a book I'd never get around to writing. And to ask questions like this of others, I'd have to ask them of myself, because, as a fellow classmate, I'm part of this story too. I had been asked many of these same questions before because of the work I've done in sports and politics, but in fifteen-second or even fifteen-minute clips it's not hard to get away with only saying what's easiest to say. Faced with the black-and-white of your own page, it's harder. Yet I was coming to an age where, if your mind isn't busy thinking about things you need to do, questions like this ambush you. If this was happening to me, I thought, it might be happening to my classmates. Maybe we were all trying to figure out the same things. Maybe it was time to talk.

I decided to try to find them. I knew where some were, and they led me to others. Especially difficult to locate were the girls who might have married and taken on a husband's last name. I had heard that two of us had died. I didn't know that two others had as well. Our conversations began in early January 2020. I told them what I was hoping to do. A few were enthusiastic. Most, like me, weren't sure. The more we talked, the more it seemed right to do. Soon Covid-19 became the central fact of all our lives. But Covid also gave us more time, more need and reason to talk with others, and more things to talk about. It sent us into our basements and attics to do things we had put off doing. There we culled, we threw away, and we also discovered: old photos, old essays, projects, and report cards, old treasures of all kinds. Things we had forgotten, and forgotten about ourselves, feelings we didn't know we had. Covid put death, and life, into our minds. It made us quieter, more introspective. It slowed us down. It was a great time to talk.

We spoke one-on-one, for about two hours at a time. The number of conversations ramped up as I found more people, and for a period of seven or eight months, each weekday I talked to one classmate in the morning and one in the afternoon, ten conversations a week, and at the end of each one I'd say, "Same day, same time, two weeks from now?" And two weeks later we picked up where we'd left off. It was exhausting. It was exhilarating. I loved it. Almost all the conversations were by phone. Only twice, pre-Covid, did I talk with anyone in person. Only one person I spoke with regularly by Zoom. I asked everyone to send me photos of themselves from different stages of their lives, so as we were speaking about that time I could see the person we were talking about. The people whom I'd known as teenagers I could see in their younger, then slightly older, then middle-aged selves, but I could see only traces of them in our now seventy-plus-year-old faces. What stunned me was their voices. Every person I spoke with was instantly recognizable. The words they chose, their laugh, their pauses. Voices I hadn't heard for decades. Maybe voices more than eyes are the mirrors of our souls.

I spoke to twenty-six of us in all. I talked to each person, on average, for about ten to twelve hours in total. I also spoke to family members, friends, and co-workers of five of the six who had passed away. One had died in his early twenties, and I could find no one who had been close to him at that time. One other classmate I couldn't find. Another decided not to participate. Writing our own stories in our own minds is one thing, but helping someone else to write their version of our story is risky. All of us have memories we are used to recalling, stories we've often told, often in the same words for decades, so much so that our kids and friends, with a roll of their eyes, can recite them back to us. As a result, our life stories can come to become whatever we say they are, and, comfortable with the way they come out, we come to become what they are. But after talking with my classmates for that first hour or so, after we felt less need to impress each other, when we began to seek out and puzzle through towards answers we didn't know, when we discovered that we knew each other better than we thought and wanted to know each other better still, in the last ten hours or so, it was great.

I write about some in the class more than others. I thought it would turn out this way, but when I started I didn't know who they would be. Sometimes, because we were each going through many of the same things, telling one person's story about something was telling others' as well. But every one of us is here, all thirty-five, because we were all part of the class, we are all part of its story, and we are all part of each other's story. And at that time, at least, I might have been any of them and they might have been me. Why I wasn't and why they weren't become two more of those "why" questions. We were the same age, we had grown up in the same place at the same time, which made the differences I heard, our "whys," so interesting and surprising.

I don't know how things really were then. I know what I remember, and what I feel. All I can do—all any of us can do—is take all that we've experienced, all we've come to understand, all we remember, all we feel, and try to make sense of it. It's not about being right. It's about finding coherence.

I

THE
EARLY
YEARS

CHAPTER ONE

We were twenty-one girls and fourteen boys. There were three Marilyns, three Joans, three Margarets, two of whom were called Peggy, two Judys, and two Kathys. Among the boys, there were two Kens. Otherwise our names were Cheryl, Penni, Wayne, Gord, Murray, Lisa, Diana, Daryl, Bruce, and lots of others common to the time. All but three of us were born in Canada, in Ontario. Twenty-eight were born in 1947, seven in 1946. A few left the class for other classes at the school, or moved away before they had come to seem like real members of the class. Two who entered later seemed as if they had always been there. But almost all of us were together for five years, from 1960 to 1965, at Etobicoke Collegiate Institute, or ECI, the oldest and biggest high school in Etobicoke, then a suburb of about 150,000, the most western of Toronto, at the time the second-largest city in Canada.

We were 35 among 347 grade 9s at ECI. Which means we were 35 of about 21,000 grade 9s in Toronto, of 210,000 in Canada, 2.1 million in the U.S.

Our formative roots—our parents—extend back almost to the beginning of the last century, and our life-affirming, life-sustaining branches—our children and grandchildren—now extend well into this one. Our parents were born as early as 1904 and as late as 1923—except for one father, who was born in 1886. Some of them were old enough that their own parents' lives, and in some ways theirs, had been changed by the First World War and the Spanish flu epidemic. All of them were old enough to have experienced the Great Depression directly, and to have had their lives hurried up, or put on hold, by the Second World War before being thrust into mature adulthood by the war and by a rush into marriage and parenthood at its end. It was into the uncertainty, then the excitement, of this post-Depression, postwar world that we, all thirty-five of us, were born.

We lived through the explosion of everything new—houses, schools, churches, playgrounds, suburbs, cars, TVs, household appliances. Freed from the urgencies of the present, it was a time when the future *finally* could be thought about, planned for, dreamed of. When everything in the Western world, in Canada, in Etobicoke, felt possible. We lived through a time when our parents also wrestled with the questions and doubts that followed: As the incredibly lucky beneficiaries of this never-before opportunity, what *should* they, and we, their children, reach for? What is worthy of this time, this place, this bounty? What should we—Canada, Etobicoke, *us*, their children—be?

In the 1950s, we lived through "the bomb," polio, and the Cold War, through a time of Brownies (now called Embers), Cubs, Kiwanis, Rotary, the Y, and kids' leagues for hockey and baseball. Through a time when, our parents believed, a village was needed to raise a child, a rising tide raised all ships, and we were better together. When soon-to-be universal health insurance offered the freedom of mind and security, and education the fuel, to make any future. When big government, doing big things, was a good thing.

We then lived through the big doubts in the decades that followed, when the promise of the immediate postwar years became difficult to realize, and the world that was becoming, became.

Now we are seventeen women and twelve men, twenty-nine in all. Or we might be twenty-eight; I haven't been able to find one girl from the class. Most of us are seventy-six years old, a few are seventy-seven, a few seventy-five. Almost all of us married, a few divorced. We have sixty-two kids and eighty grandkids between us (and no great-grandkids). Born when our life expectancy was 64.6 years for men, 69.6 for women, we should be gone by now. And after all the days we spent together in high school, through the confusion of our "one step forward, three steps sideways" teenage years, very few of us have had more than accidental contact with each other in the decades since. Only two who were close friends then are still close friends now.

We were the Brain Class, as other students called us. We were together, except during holidays or illness, from 9:00 in the morning until 3:20 in the afternoon, Monday to Friday, September to June. In math and science classes, in history, geography, phys ed—the girls with the girls, the boys with the boys—in music or art, in industrial arts for the boys or home economics for the girls, in English, French, Latin, either German or Russian, with many good teachers, a few inspiring ones, and some who weren't, through good days and really bad ones, during a time when we were becoming teenagers, young adults, when at different paces and in different ways we were growing up.

Almost sixty years have now passed. Almost none of us have lived the lives we imagined.

How did we get from there to here?

CHAPTER TWO

"The pupils selected for this class are the ones who ranked in the first thirty to thirty-five of those applying, based on a test written on May 11th [1960] and on Grade 8 standing."

The letter informing us of our acceptance, dated June 17, 1960, was addressed to our parents. It was signed T.D. Boone, Superintendent of Secondary Schools for Etobicoke. Officially, we were called the "Selected Class."

We had attended one of four elementary schools in central Etobicoke: Lambton-Kingsway, Islington, Rosethorn, or Humber Valley. I was at Humber Valley. Most of us had been in "accelerated" classes at those schools, taking grades 4, 5, and 6 in two years. We were the ones born in 1947. The others, whose parents didn't believe they should be separated from kids their own age, or as more often was the case, who had moved to Etobicoke after grade 4, and too late to join one of these classes, were a year older, born in 1946. For historians, this was the Atomic Age. Our lives and futures would be determined by scientists, spies, and bomb builders in the East and the West. But in Toronto and Etobicoke, in cities and suburbs across Canada and the United States, in the day-to-day, for our parents and for us, this was the age of building. Of construction, not destruction. This was the Education Age.

In North America, education systems had built up randomly, haphazardly over the previous century. Schools had begun as places where kids went for a few years to learn a few basics, mainly to read, until they were old enough—around fourteen—to join the adult world. To help out the family. It was early in the twentieth century, when families began leaving the farm for the cities and European immigrants arrived in these same cities in big numbers, that things began to change. Kids now needed to learn city things to do city jobs, and began staying in school longer, not necessarily to graduate from high school, which at the time wasn't considered essential, but to get one or two more years of learning. And university? For almost everybody, even for the rich, that wasn't in their minds. Only a small percentage of our parents' generation went to university, to be doctors, lawyers, engineers, professors, and that's about it. University wasn't needed for anything else. To become a teacher, a high school education was enough. The same to be a businessman, or to work in a store or an office. You started at the bottom and worked your way up, and learned your way up as you went. It was the same on farms and in factories, where most people worked. University took years, and it cost money. You needed to get on with your life, your family needed you to get on with life, so you could earn your keep.

While big national dreams were beginning to simmer in Canada and the U.S. in the early 1900s, with education and progress at the centre, for our parents, those dreams got shut down by the hard times of the Depression years and the wartime realities a decade later. But in the late 1940s, as we were being born, those tough times were mostly over and done with. And if Canada and the U.S. were truly to fulfill those big dreams, to become more than anything had ever been, it would be because of more people learning more and better for longer. That meant university. And that meant better elementary schools and high schools to get us there.

To our parents, this was obvious: *Look at the world we've created,* they said to themselves, *and with no more than a high school education. Imagine what our university-educated sons and daughters might create?*

To our parents, the answer was clear: we have to give our kids the chance to be smarter. We have to identify the smart ones earlier, separate them from the pack, give them special teachers with special training, surround them with kids who are just like them to challenge and push them, and give them every opportunity to be as special as they are, and as special as the future, as Canada, needs them to be. Then send them out into the world. See what they might do.

Most of our parents had no idea how smart they were. They were only high school graduates, or dropouts. Smart to them meant a university degree, being a university graduate, a completely different category of person who wasn't them or anyone they knew, and never would be them. Those people were *educated*. They were smarter than everyone else, and their diplomas proved it. They held the most respected positions. That's what our parents wanted for us. If only we could go to university, imagine Canada, imagine the world, imagine our futures.

Imagine the excitement our parents felt. They didn't say much about this to us, not about the As on our report cards, not about getting into the Brain Class. It wasn't their way, it wasn't the times. They were practical people. They had seen too much. They knew that no matter how good things were or seemed to be, the first lesson, drilled into them by their parents, and into us by them, was: never get too full of yourself. Everything's going great . . . until *boom*, the Depression. *Boom*, the war. They had come from families of modest means and modest achievements. It's who they were. But that didn't mean they didn't dream for us.

In the 1950s, special programs in schools were created everywhere in Canada. If smarter was possible, why not give more kids the chance to be smarter? But while school boards knew what they wanted, they weren't sure how to achieve it. They weren't looking to uncover prodigies. The questions on the tests they gave us suggested that they were looking for broad general knowledge, and some indication of our capacity to learn. This was the era of the "all-rounder," the all-round achiever in every field, in school, in sports—ultimately, they believed, in life itself. Future prime ministers played hockey and future presidents played baseball. Educators believed—and because they believed, parents believed—that kids should be given lots of different experiences, in school, church, sports, other activities, with other kids, with other adults, all so they could learn about lots of things, about people, about themselves, about life. They believed that the way to learn specific things better and become expert in them was not to do them over and over, but to do many other different things as well.

That way of thinking was applied to every field. If you played sports, the highest compliment at the time was to be called an "all-round athlete." In the first half of the twentieth century, Babe Ruth, who dominated the most dominant sport more than anyone ever had, wasn't considered America's greatest athlete. Jim Thorpe was, an outstanding football player, a good baseball player, and an Olympic decathlete. The greatest Canadian athlete wasn't Maurice Richard or Howie Morenz but Lionel Conacher, a football, hockey, baseball, and lacrosse player, a boxer and wrestler, who wasn't anywhere near the best in any of those sports. Kids who played sports at the time played every sport, and not just because sports were played outdoors and baseball wasn't suited for winter or hockey for summer. It was because, the thinking went, each sport made you better in every other sport in ways, and to dimensions, that specializing in one could not.

It was the same in the classroom. Our educational leaders taught us English, math, science, and history because they believed that an educated person needed to know all these subjects, because they were all important in themselves, and more so because they offered ways to learn other things better, at that moment and also later in life. Because learning English somehow made you a better math student, which made you a better science student, which, together with all the other things you learned along the way, inside and outside school, made you a better learner. So the best student wasn't the math nerd or science genius, but the best all-round student. It's why education experts at the time decided that if you failed one course, you failed the year. After all, if a student was supposed to learn something about everything, then education's purpose was only fulfilled if you passed a year's worth of courses. Only that showed whether you were becoming an educated person or not.

So the test we were given on May 11, as well as our grade 8 standing, was looking to determine this: Out of those who applied, who were the best thirty to thirty-five all-round students from these four elementary schools?

Wayne Yetman was one of those kids. He lived close to ECI, in a small bungalow on Mabelle Avenue, a short street that dead-ended at a small factory near the railway tracks. He had no brothers or sisters. His parents were older—they had little education and had grown up in Newfoundland before it had become a province of Canada. Wayne was good enough at school to be near the top of his class every year. But ECI was high school. It had many hundreds more kids than Islington, his elementary school, did. The kids at ECI were older. Bigger. Smarter. They knew what was going on, and how things worked, and Wayne had never been good at figuring out stuff like that, even with kids his own age. He watched, he listened as everyone else did, then said something, and somehow others turned their heads towards him and looked a certain way. He'd missed something, and he didn't know what or why. Eventually this wasn't a problem. The other kids got to know him and like him. He was funny and interesting. This was just Wayne being Wayne, they learned. But all that takes time.

Some of the kids in his new ECI class had also been at Islington, but he didn't know them well. There weren't any school teams there, or a yearbook to work on. He hadn't been on student council or in the choir, where he might meet other kids. He and his parents went to one church, the other kids and their parents went elsewhere. But more than that, he wasn't "accelerated" like they were. They had been identified early by their teachers and put into a different stream, taking three grades in two years. So while he was one of the best students at Islington, he wasn't really, and if others didn't know that, he did. The best were in the accelerated class. It had taken him one more year to get where they were.

Now he was about to enter a high school class so special that even most of the kids in Islington's accelerated class hadn't been chosen for it, one where the best of the best from *four* elementary schools, Islington included, would be his classmates. He didn't know how he'd keep up. His parents didn't know either. A big part of him, and a big part of them, wondered: Who does he think he is? Who do we think we are?

Cheryl Beagan (married name LaFrance)* knows Wayne from Islington, but not very well. She was in the accelerated class. And unlike Wayne, who is now rushing around not quite ready for this school year to begin (something his parents had noted), Cheryl has had her notebooks and pens and what she's going to wear organized and ready since last week, if not last month. At Islington, Cheryl was always one of the first to put her hand up in class, not only to answer a question or to ask one but to volunteer to do this or that. When something needs to be done, or an adult or even another kid asks you to help, why wouldn't you say yes. And she did say yes, to anything, with a big toothy smile.

Cheryl didn't know much about ECI. Like Wayne, she didn't have older brothers or sisters who had gone there. But she knows lots of kids there, from Islington, from her church, and from all the neighbourhood street games they play. She's excited, because Cheryl gets excited. She likes to do lots of different things, but school is *her* world, and she can't wait to get there.

Lisa Sweeting likes school too, but she also likes after school, and weekends, and holidays, and summers. She likes to read, and think, and get lost in things. To go down to the creek not far from her house to wander along its banks, to jump from rock to rock, especially with her friends. One of those friends, Kathy McNab (Brankley), will be in her new class at ECI. The creek is almost wild there, or a kid

---

* All but two of the women in our class changed their last names when they got married. Where they are first introduced, I include their married name.

can pretend that it is, the trees angling over it from both sides, the brush uncleared, the water burbling, sometimes rushing, frozen in winter, the ice along its edges brittle enough to stomp on and crack and crunch, yet in its middle, only a few shuffle-steps away, solid and smooth, a great first place to skate.

At ECI Lisa will be with the older kids again. In grade 8, being among the oldest in her elementary school was fine, it's the way it was, but older kids, especially boys, do so many more interesting things, she thinks, and now she'll have kids around her who are years older, real teenagers, who think about stuff, talk about doing stuff, and sometimes do it. And they'll let her be around them because older boys are comfortable with her, and because girls, older or younger, aren't threatened by her. Because she's nice to people.

Pat Gregory lives in a small one-time mill worker's house, tucked away and almost invisible at a bend in the Humber River below a railway and car bridge that not many decades earlier had brought the city of Toronto to Etobicoke. Pat likes the river. He loves to explore. When he sees random-strewn rocks on its banks, he imagines what's under them. Newts, salamanders, and if he's really lucky, snakes. He comes down here in the spring and fall after school and on weekends, and in summer he might be here anytime. All day. Sometimes with friends who, if not to find snakes, like to explore as much as he does. Other times he comes alone. The river is not much more than a stone's throw from his house, and when he's here his mother knows what he's doing, and doesn't worry.

Daryl Browne's house backs onto the fourteenth hole of Islington Golf Club. In late fall, all winter, and early spring, even in summer after the last golfers of the day reach the fifteenth tee, Daryl and his older brothers and friends use the course as their backyard. Its hills are their toboggan runs, especially the elevated, steep sixteenth tee, its creek their hockey rink, its fairways their own personal course to hit a few furtive balls in the summer's late darkness. Like Pat, Daryl likes to discover whatever nature he finds, even if it's hardly off the fairways and in the woods where there are many more golf balls than snakes.

But especially if it's on the other side of Kipling Avenue, the club's and ECI's western boundary, where suburb turns to country, where there's no one to bother you and everywhere to explore. Where you can ride your bike, cover forbidden distances, feel freedom, feel older.

Daryl too was in an accelerated class, at Rosethorn, along with Ken Church, Craig MacGregor, and Diana Boylen (Hiller), all of whom will be his classmates again at ECI. They live only minutes apart, and some of their parents know each other a little, but outside school Daryl doesn't see them much. Nor does he know any of his other new classmates. He does know ECI pretty well because he has three brothers who went there, his next-older brother having graduated the year before. He also knows ECI's basketball coach, who lives down the street. A year ago, the coach needed somebody to act as scorer for his team's games. Daryl is small for his age, too small to play on organized teams, but he loves sports, loves to get involved in almost anything. So he said yes. He's a good student and a good learner—his mind takes him to places well beyond what he learns in class, to math's puzzles and quirks, to George Bernard Shaw as well as the Hardy Boys. Yet he doesn't assume anything about what's next. He's that way about everything. He knows he will need to work hard and find his way again in his new school. And it will be clear to his teachers and his classmates that he has found his way, far sooner than it will be to him.

I'm not looking forward to school. That doesn't have much to do with going into a special class in a new school with kids I don't know. It has much more to do with not liking the first days of almost anything I've done before. Something that's *entirely* new, I love. That's adventure. Something new that I've done before—a new school year, a new hockey or baseball season, where I need to show again that I can do what I've done before—I don't love. Months have passed and I have no way of knowing whether whatever worked the last time won't have left me just as mysteriously as it came. That's what every new school year feels like to me, what every Labour Day weekend in anticipation of it is like. Years from now, I still won't believe I can do something before I try, but I'll have learned not to believe that I *can't*, and just do it, and find out, and realize most of the time I can. But that's not now. Today, all these decades later, Labour Day remains my least favourite day of the year.

Like Lisa, I like being around older kids. I play on teams with kids who are two years older, and play ball hockey with my brother and his friends, and he's six years older than I am. Like Lisa, I liked elementary school a lot until my friends left for high school. Now at ECI, I'll be around older kids again. Like Daryl, I got to know the school a little through my brother. We went to his band concerts, I read about the football team in the local newspapers, sometimes even in the Toronto papers, and knew, and was proud, that Gerry Doucette, the Toronto Argos backup quarterback and punter, had played at Etobicoke. But mostly what I feel about ECI now is that I don't want to be there. I like all the freedoms of summer. I'll get over how I feel, but not right away.

Six of us. Not much different from the rest. Maybe.

CHAPTER THREE

Gord Homer was a star. He was good-looking, tall and athletic, and had the kind of red hair, not too light or too bright, that punctuated his looks but didn't dominate them. At Islington, in the accelerated class, and in sports, he had been a star. In school, there is something new to learn every day in every subject, and if Gord, even fleetingly, didn't understand something, it was never obvious. He would rivet his attention on whatever he didn't know until he had an answer, his face never changing, making it seem to the rest of us as if the answer had always been there. He was the same in sports. He played hockey and baseball, as most of the boys did, but even more he played basketball, and participated in gymnastics and track and field. He wasn't just a player. He was an athlete. Nothing seemed beyond him.

Yet he didn't strut like a star, or talk loud like a star. He could have commanded the attention of any room, but he didn't. He seemed shy, and a little awkward, but mostly it was what he was doing that got our attention, and his own; he didn't look for it himself. His brother, Chuck, had the same red hair and athletic good looks, but two years older and able to do what Gord did in school and in sports two years better, it seemed he, not Gord, had the right to be a star. More than that, their father, Jim, was very accomplished. They knew this not because he had told them, because he never talked much about himself, or because his trophies covered their living room mantelpiece like a shrine, because his trophies were still at their grandmother's house. It was their grandmother who had told them.

Jim's father, Charles—Gord's grandfather—had grown up on a farm near Erin, northwest of Toronto, his own father a butcher. Wanting a different life for himself, Charles moved to the big city, to Toronto. He got a job at Canadian Rogers Eastern Ltd. (or CREL), a sheet metal roofing company that had started up only a year earlier. This was in the early 1900s. CREL soon asked Charles to move to Winnipeg to work on a large new project, the construction of a copper roof for the Fort Garry Hotel, one of the grand château-style hotels being built across the country by the railroads. In Winnipeg, Charles met Bella, who worked in a tobacco shop at the nearby railway station. She was twenty, Métis, and had spoken only French until about the time she met Charles. One of her ancestors, Jean Baptiste Charette, had come from Quebec in the early 1800s, a voyageur with the North West Company. Before railroads, the only east–west route through the Canadian Shield's thicket of forest and bush was by water. Charette had trained as a carpenter, and with the North West Company he built and repaired the canoes and boats that were the country's lifeline. On a homestead a little south of Winnipeg, near present-day St. Norbert, he built a log cabin for himself, married an Indigenous woman, and raised a family. On the cabin's site today, opened to commemorate one of the earliest Métis families in the area, is Parc Charette.

The Fort Garry Hotel was completed in December 1913. It was the tallest building in Canada between Toronto and Vancouver. Soon after, Charles and Bella married, and three years later Jim was born. (At that same time, my father, Murray, was five years old, living with his family on a farm in Domain, less than forty kilometres south of the Fort Garry, less than twenty-five kilometres from the Charette cabin.) In 1920, Charles, Bella, and Jim settled in Toronto. They moved into a small house in the St. Clair Avenue–Dufferin Street area, not far from the CREL plant. The neighbourhood was crowded with families like theirs, the men holding working-class jobs like Charles's, the women at home with their young children like Bella, in

the now fast-industrializing city. A second son, John, was born soon
after. The 1920s were good years for CREL, but the '30s got harder.
The Homers, with only four mouths to feed, a smaller family than
most at the time, adapted.

Jim went to high school at Vaughan Road Collegiate, a good student and a better athlete. He played football. In track and field he
was a sprinter—the 100-yard dash and 4×110-yard relay were his spe-
cialties—and he threw the shot put as well. In 1930, the first British
Empire Games (now the Commonwealth Games) had been held in
Hamilton, Ontario. Four years later, the first Intra-Empire Schoolboy
Games were held in Melbourne, Australia. High school athletes from
Australia, New Zealand, and Canada would compete. There were
provincial meets, then national trials, from which the twelve best
schoolboy athletes in Canada were chosen, providing, of course, that
"their scholarship is also commendable," as the regulations stipulated.
Jim was one of the twelve. A shoulder injury he had suffered playing
softball the summer before limited him to the sprints. He was also
Canada's team captain. Two others on the team were John Loaring,
who two years later, in the 1936 Berlin Olympics, won a silver medal in
the 400-metre hurdles, and Sam Richardson, who in the same Games
competed against Jesse Owens in the long jump and relay.

They travelled by train to Vancouver and on to San Francisco,
then by ship, making stops at islands on their way, at Tahiti, where
they tried out their high school French with mixed success, and at
Rarotonga in the Cook Islands, where they visited a "native" school,
as they called it, tried out native canoes, and ate native food. Then on
October 13, they crossed the international dateline and lost a day. It
was Jim's eighteenth birthday. In Melbourne, the Canadian team won
most of the events. On their way back home, they had further competitions in New Zealand, put in at Fiji and Hawaii, and spent Christmas
on board the ship, before arriving in Vancouver. They were gone four
months in all. Jim returned with boomerangs, a grass skirt, and a toy
koala bear, a prized companion of Gord's when he was young, but with
very few stories that he passed down to the family.

Jim had graduated from Vaughan Road the previous June. It was the middle of the Depression. The school's motto, from Virgil, which described the behaviour of bees, embodied the modest spirit of the age: *In medium quaesita reponunt*, "They lay up in store for common use whatever they have gained." It was now time for Jim to get on with his future. He had a chance to go to the University of Western Ontario (now Western University) and play football. His father had now been with CREL for more than twenty years, having worked his way up to become owner Edward Rogers's right-hand man. Jim's decision seemed to him like no decision at all. He started at CREL as an apprentice. Gord has a photo that was taken just after his father joined the company. It shows nineteen of CREL's workers in front of their plant. Most are in overalls, and in the middle of the first row, four are in ties and vests, their white shirtsleeves rolled up. Jim's father, Charles, is one of them. Directly behind him, same face, same black hair, one generation younger, and taller, is Jim. He would work his way up too.

Five years later, in 1940, Jim met Enid Kirby at a young people's group at the YMCA. She had grown up in Toronto, had moved to Montreal, and was back in Toronto again. She was three years younger. Her father, Gordon, had come to Canada in 1906 from Wales, where he had been the city engineer for Newport, not far from Cardiff, and joined the CPR, as an older brother had done a few years earlier.

People at the time stayed in their jobs longer, often for their whole career. So you "joined" the bank, the insurance company, the CPR—just as you joined the army. Enid's father became head of the CPR's signals department for Toronto, then was transferred to Montreal in 1930. By this time they were a family of five. Four years later, he died. Enid was fifteen. With little money and no pension from the company, Enid's mother decided to move back to Toronto and into the house they had bought years earlier and had rented out while they were in Montreal. She got a job as a sales clerk at Eaton's, at that time Canada's largest department store. Enid had been a good student in Montreal, but the Quebec education system was different from Ontario's, and in Toronto she was put back a grade. She would later graduate from a secretarial course at Northern Vocational School (now Northern Secondary School). When she and Jim met, she was a secretary at General Electric. A few years later, she was secretary to the president of the *Toronto Star*.

It was now wartime. CREL had several defence contracts, and Jim's contribution to them was considered important enough to the war effort that he stayed on in Toronto. He and Enid married; they moved into an apartment in Toronto. Their first-born, Chuck, was named after Jim's father; Gord was named after Enid's.

With the kids gone, Charles and Bella, looking to escape their congested city neighbourhood, bought a house in Etobicoke, on Kipling Avenue, almost across the road from the fifteenth hole at Islington Golf Club, near to what would become Daryl Browne's favourite toboggan hill two decades later.

Kipling, today a busy north–south street that runs almost from the airport to the lake, was then basically a country road. Charles and Bella had a little English Tudor cottage on a double lot, where they could grow vegetables and flowers, and have around them, to the west and north, for farther than the eye could see, the market gardens of Etobicoke that fed the grocery stores and restaurants of Toronto. A few years later, in 1950, Jim, Enid, Chuck, age five, and Gord, age three, moved from their Toronto apartment to Etobicoke, to Holloway Road, about halfway between Jim's parents' house on Kipling and Etobicoke Collegiate.

When he was starting at ECI, Gord didn't know much about his grandparents, or even about his mother and father. He knew a few details, but they hadn't really pieced themselves together into some kind of story. Certainly not anything that mattered to Gord in any big, life-affecting way. It was the same for all of us. Only later, only as we got older and more details began to accumulate, as we got old enough to see connections and patterns and logic, as we began to wonder about enough things we didn't understand and began searching for answers, did our pasts become important. And even then, all we had were guesses, sometimes very bad ones, *mis*understandings that might send us down a very wrong path. Besides, we were all too busy to live our lives through a rear-view mirror, and so much that was so much more interesting was right there ahead of us. But we did come from somewhere, our kids and grandkids came from somewhere. Our cities and towns and country. All this, it turned out, did matter.

And if we didn't know our own family's story, we certainly didn't know the backstories of our classmates. Stories that might have explained, or at least hinted at, a lot. But nor would those backstories have seemed significant to us then. Gord was Gord. Wayne was Wayne. They were who they were.

Like Gord, Marilyn Cade was a star, in the way that girls at the time could be stars. Which meant they had to be almost perfect.

They had to be capable in almost everything, able to handle almost anything, emotionally, intellectually. But not with too obvious ease. That would be showing off. In class, they had to know almost every answer, but not put their hand up every time. They had to have a sense of humour, but not be funnier, or louder, than the boys. Being better at answers was mostly acceptable, being better at opinions was not. They had to be better than boys in everything in school *except* in those subjects that boys were supposed to be better at, math and maybe science—where they could be as good or slightly less good—and definitely phys ed. But in being nearly perfect, they had to be unaware of being nearly perfect, or certainly never act as if they knew, or insist on being it, or want to be it, because what could be less perfect than that. There's high maintenance and low maintenance, and girl stars had to be no maintenance. Boy stars could get things wrong and remain stars. Girl stars couldn't. It's the way it was.

Marilyn's parents had also come from working-class backgrounds. They were almost the same age as Gord's parents, both of them born in 1918. One side of her mother's family had come to Toronto from Horsforth, near Leeds, in Yorkshire, a family of blacksmiths. On the other side, a daughter, only eighteen years old, had come "all by herself," as family stories related with pride, from Beith, near Glasgow, to a farm in remote Manitoba, before heading east to Toronto, where many years later, her daughter Gladys, Marilyn's mother, grew up.

Marilyn's father, Don, was one of eight kids in a family from Singhampton, Ontario, a village south of Georgian Bay, not far from Collingwood, one that was small enough to have had a general store, which his father operated, just as he'd operated other general stores in other villages in rural Ontario. In the early years of the Depression, the family made its way to Toronto, into a neighbourhood not far from, and not much different from, that of Gord's parents. Ontario's high schools at the time had two streams, the academic, which had thirteen grades and was *not* for everyone, and the more common commercial, business, and technical, which had twelve grades and was for the rest. Don went to Central Commerce, a four-year school. Gladys was in the academic stream at nearby Oakwood Collegiate, but then transferred to Central Commerce. It's not clear if this is where they met, or whether it was through youth groups at church or through their parents or their parents' friends. But it was at A.E. Wilson Insurance, in their first jobs, on the paths open to men and women at the time—Don in sales, Gladys a secretary—when they really got to know each other.

They were not yet twenty. Their lives at this point weren't much different from those of tens of thousands of other twenty-year-olds across the country. Like them, their families had arrived in Canada from the Old World, crossing an ocean, then, just as daunting, crossing a hard, snow-swept land to somewhere, taking a shot at a different future, knowing there was little for them where they'd been. Sometimes what seems heroic is only an absence of choice. Then, generations later, as it was for Marilyn's parents, they somehow find themselves in the same school, or in the same office, with not much special on which to base and build a future except some general skills, some way of seeing and doing things, some ethics and values that had come from those around them, a love for each other, and underpinning it all, youth. And in that youth, a cautious hope and a cautious fear, shaped by, but not scarred by, the Depression. This, as it was for most of our parents, they had going for them. And also, importantly, they did not have much that would stand in their way.

Then the war came. Marilyn's father enlisted right away, as most of his able-bodied male friends did, and in 1940 was sent to Hagersville, near Hamilton, for his RCAF training. He and Gladys got married. They were twenty-two. She continued at A.E. Wilson for a while, but as the urgency of wartime set in, she went to work at Moffat, a large appliance maker that had been pressed into manufacturing war matériel. Don was sent to Fort Macleod, near Calgary, and Gladys went with him, but when he was sent to Sainte-Agathe, Quebec, she returned home to Toronto. Eventually Don was shipped out of Halifax and ended up in Yorkshire. He was in the RCAF, but colour-blindness kept him out of the air and he was assigned to intelligence. For the rest of the war, he watched his buddies take off into the darkness, drop their bombs, and return. Except almost every night, a few didn't. The next day, he and others analyzed what had gone wrong and right, and what to do next—it was a job you had to take very personally and couldn't take too personally. Years later, he told Marilyn and her brother and sister stories about the crazy, fun stuff they used to do in their barracks. He showed them pictures of these tough, war-hardened guys, himself included, their own father, in aprons—washing dishes. They *had* done crazy, fun stuff, and Don had loved the bonding of it, the closeness they had, the bigness of purpose they felt. Gladys, at these same family moments, who knew at least some of the story, didn't want to talk about any of it. Don took in the war the way he needed to. He couldn't not see, and he couldn't not feel, what had happened. But each new day was another day, and those who were flying out into that night deserved the best from him. He had no right to give them anything less. So, you carry on, don't dwell, and do the right thing.

When the war ended, he received a telegram from A.E. Wilson himself. It read, "You're expected back here."

Hundreds of thousands of troops were still in Europe at war's end and ships of all kinds, even luxury liners, were brought in to transport them back. Don didn't get home until early 1946. He and Gladys moved in with her parents in the city. They were twenty-nine years old. It was time to begin the future. Not much housing was available, even as new units for war vets were going up fast. They found a small semi-detached house on Allanbrooke Drive in Etobicoke, a few football fields away from ECI. They moved in six weeks before Marilyn was born.

Kathy McNab was fun. She had a face that was fun, and a laugh that was fun and a way about her that was even funnier. Years before Annie Hall, she was Annie Hall, as if she might have worn big floppy hats and big floppy clothes, as if she might have said, "Oh well, la dee da, la dee da," which she didn't. She was a little scattered—it seemed. A little flighty—it seemed. Not to be taken seriously—that would be a mistake.

Like Wayne, she was an only child. Her mother, Betty, was from Toronto, her father, Cam, from Acton, a small town about an hour northwest of the city. Although Cam spent most of his childhood and adulthood in Toronto, he always described himself as "Cam McNab from Acton." He and Betty were both good students, and he was on the football team. If they had been born a generation later, they both would have gone to university, and he might have played football. But they weren't and he didn't. So when Cam graduated from Western Tech in 1933, and Betty from nearby Western Commerce, he got a job with the Ontario Department of Highways on its surveying crews, and she found a job as a secretary at Toledo Scales. A lot of things came to a halt during the Depression, but building roads and bridges, infrastructure of all sorts, could employ lots of people, keep what money there was circulating, and keep others elsewhere in the economy working as well. Infrastructure projects, which are mostly taken on with the future in mind, at this time were meant to help sustain whatever present they could. Their even larger importance would come later.

Ontario is vast, as big as Maine, New Hampshire, Vermont, Massachusetts, Rhode Island, Connecticut, New York, New Jersey, Pennsylvania, Delaware, Maryland, Virginia, West Virginia, Ohio, and Michigan—fifteen states in all—*combined*. To exist even as an idea, Canada needed to be connected east and west. For it and Ontario to function as economic entities, they needed also to be connected north and south. So in the 1930s, Cam McNab worked on the construction of the Queen Elizabeth Way, the QEW, to connect Toronto and Buffalo. He started as a surveyor, later he was chief of his survey crew, then supervisor of all of the province's survey crews, working on countless other roads and highways, travelling all over the province. He did dog-team surveying in Geraldton, north of Lake Superior. He went into small remote towns and smaller villages and saw how their own economies worked, how their goods were grown and products were made, and how all those goods and products had to get to market, to bigger places far away and to others not so far, but which, without proper roads, were inaccessible. He saw how communities worked. How governments work, where and how they are needed, how they fit in.

The Conservative Party had governed Ontario throughout his childhood, the Liberals during his early adult years, and now the Progressive Conservatives were in power again, as they would be through most of his adult working years, into his retirement and beyond, for all but nine years between 1923 and 1985. The bedrock of Conservative support was in these towns and villages. Rural Ontario needed to be connected into the province's life. The power figures inside the party, its premiers and its most important cabinet ministers in its most important departments, Highways included, represented ridings outside the province's biggest cities. For decades, more of Ontario's budget was spent on highways and roads than on anything else except education. (Later, most would be spent on health care.) Cam McNab was able to see all this up close, in his late teens and twenties. He could see its importance. This was his education. It was the same lesson the Chinese had learned. As Le Yucheng, the country's vice-minister of foreign affairs, later put it: "We Chinese often say that if you want to get rich, build roads first."

Cam enlisted when the Second World War began and was assigned to the artillery, but soon was seconded into the British Army to survey and build, urgently and overnight, roads where they had never existed, in Italy, Belgium, and the Netherlands. When he got back home, armed with his new learning about roads, big projects and governments, he was ready to take on more. Until the war, he had been laying the groundwork for his career and, literally, for the province's future. He wouldn't be surprised at what came next, but much of it he couldn't have imagined. How the building of each piece of road and highway, as they had been doing, stretch by stretch, would finally come together to become Highway 401, linking Detroit and Montreal, and how the 401 through the city of Toronto would some-day become a busier route than I-405 through L.A. and I-75 through Atlanta. How the 401 would become the world's busiest truck route, and come to connect the economies of the U.S. Midwest to eastern Canada, as the Great Lakes and St. Lawrence Seaway had done, but this time by pavement, not water. And how all those other roads they had built, that fed into the 401, like creeks feeding a great river, would come together and open up the north economically, its mines and mills, and open it up recreationally, its uncountable lakes, to those looking to escape the cities in the south. The north, where his daughter, Kathy, would make her future.

All through her childhood, Kathy would be surrounded by maps and stories of other places. Also by an attitude, and an outlook, about building and growing and the future. Later, during her high school and university years, her father held the province's second-top job for highways and roads, for twelve years the deputy minister of what would come to be called the Ministry of Transportation and Communications.

Before the war ended in 1945, there were not that many cars or trucks or travellers on these roads. The roads were there in readiness for the right time and the right circumstances; for the explosive growth of the cities, Toronto especially, and the suburbs in particular.

Bruce McLeod's family got to Etobicoke a different way. Bruce's father, Alex, got his B.A. from Queen's University and a Ph.D. from

Harvard. His mother, Rosalind, had a B.A. from Queen's. She was one
of only two mothers in our class who had a university degree. She had
grown up in Chatham, New Jersey, and Alex in Regina. Alex's father,
Norman, had come from Glengarry County, a rural area populated
by Highland Scots in far eastern Ontario, about 100 kilometres from
Montreal. In the McLeod family nobody had ever gone to university, but everyone could see Norman was special, so sacrifices were
made. But when he graduated from Queen's in 1906 he didn't go back
home, to teach and inspire the next generation of kids, to make the
community that had supported him stronger and better. Instead, he
went west, to the newly created province of Saskatchewan. Only five
years earlier, the population of what would become Saskatchewan was
less than 100,000; by 1911, almost half a million. In the next decade
it nearly doubled, and kept rising dramatically during the 1920s, with
immigrants who were arriving from rural Soviet Russia, Ukraine, and
Poland settling in even more rural and remote parts of the province.
Between 1911 and 1941, Saskatchewan was the third-most populous
province in Canada, after Ontario and Quebec.

Saskatchewan's incredible growth meant incredible growth in
almost everything, including education. Norman landed a job as
a teacher in Arcola, a small town near Regina, in a "continuation"
school, as it was called, which offered instruction beyond elementary
age but not to the end of high school because so few parents were
interested in their kids staying in school that long, because if their
kids' future was on the farm, what was the point of all that schooling?
A few years later, he got a job teaching at Regina Collegiate Institute,
then became principal of the new Scott Collegiate, the city's second
high school.

Because Saskatchewan was a new province, and Regina a new
capital, a whole new infrastructure of government, business, everything, had to be created, and as a schoolteacher and principal, Norman
became one of its creators. He was friends with M.J. Coldwell,
later a co-founder of the Co-operative Commonwealth Federation
(or CCF), precursor of the NDP. He knew Tommy Douglas, who as

Saskatchewan's premier would bring universal health care to the province and inspire its implementation across the country. Everything and everyone was interconnected. This was the childhood world of Alex, Bruce's father.

Bruce's mother, Rosalind, was the daughter of a Presbyterian minister, a force in a not so different way in his own community in New Jersey. Education, religion, politics, community service—they were at the centre of the lives of both families, a fact that was never more telling than early in the 1930s, when Alex and Rosalind were still teenagers, when New Jersey got hit hard by the Depression and Saskatchewan got hit even harder, its problems compounded by drought. This was a time for deep beliefs, forceful actions, and formidable people. People with substantial backgrounds that had been built on top of substantial backgrounds. Alex saw the Depression as the turning-point experience of his life, the beginning of what he later described as his lifelong Quest (which he always wrote with a capital *Q*). Its misery had so transformed life that he needed to know why it had happened, what could be done about it, and what *he* could do about it, so it would never happen again. It's why he got his Ph.D. in economics, why he worked for the Department of Finance in Ottawa during the Second World War, and why after the war, he, Rosalind, and their new young son, Norman, moved to Washington, D.C., where he worked for the International Monetary Fund, then in its infancy. And where they were living when Bruce was born.

Not many others in our class had parents who went to university. Three of our fathers who did were lawyers, two others were engineers, one was an accountant, another a teacher, two were businessmen. With Bruce's dad, ten fathers in all. And four of our mothers (one of whom, Joan Boody's, got her degree at forty-four, after her kids were grown up), and a few other mothers who spent a year at Normal School, another who trained as a dental hygienist, and another as a physical and occupational therapist. Out of seventy parents. And only a few parents, like Bruce's mother, who were born outside Canada.

Judy Clarke's father had come to Canada as a teenager from Crawley, in West Sussex, after the First World War. Ted and Steve Whistance-Smith's father, despite their hoity-toity hyphenated last name, was from, as he put it, a "shithole" coal mining town somewhere in England. Pat Gregory's father was from Bilston, near Birmingham, his mother from Le Havre, France, the two meeting first as pen pals in high school, then in real life in Paris during the war. The father of Barbara Vaughan-Parks (Zaccai) was from England's West Country, her mother from Surrey. All those born in Europe having experienced the war up close. Wayne's parents were also born outside Canada, in Newfoundland before it became a province. None of our parents or their ancestors had come from southern or eastern Europe, or anywhere else in the world.

But wherever our parents were from or whatever they ended up doing, almost all of them had working-class beginnings. They had working-class ancestors who had working-class educations, did working-class jobs, had working-class attitudes and expectations about the present and the future and their role in them. As the war ended and we were about to be born, with only one exception (one father was fifty-nine), they were as old as forty and as young as twenty-one. But they were all at the same stage in their lives. They all now had the opportunity to live more than working-class lives and have a chance at more than working-class futures.

The war had slowed down their lives, but the postwar was about to speed them up. There was pent-up demand for everything—jobs, marriage, kids, cars—and time was a-wastin'. To any laggard who would waste it, as my grandmother would admonish, "This won't buy the baby a shirt." Everything was about to take off. Our parents, most of their lives spent in crowded cities, were ready to move up. But in order to move up, they had to move out. To the suburbs.

CHAPTER FOUR

I was born in Hamilton, but I was an Etobicoke kid. I was a year old when we moved there in 1948—my father, Murray, my mother, Margaret, my grandmother, whom we called Bam, and my brother, Dave, who was six years older than me. My sister, Judy, would come along three years later. For my father, things were just starting to come together.

Murray Dryden was born in Domain, Manitoba, in 1911, the oldest of eight kids. His great-grandparents, Andrew Dryden and Janet Cairns, with their nine grown children, many with spouses, had come to Canada in 1834 from Teviotdale, near Hawick, in the Scottish Borders. Andrew was then fifty-five, Janet forty-nine. Andrew had been a wheelwright, as had his father, and the family were tenant farmers. The future for them in Scotland would be what the past had always been—the oldest son would stay on the land, the others would leave and need to find their own way. When I travelled to Scotland in 2014 to write about the Scottish referendum, I went back to the house my ancestors had inhabited and talked to the man who was living there. He was a dyker, a person who repairs the centuries-old dry stone walls that snake across the hills and dales everywhere in the area. He was tenant in the house. His landlord was the Duke of Buccleuch, the largest private landowner in Scotland, just as an earlier Duke of Buccleuch had been when my ancestors lived there 180 years earlier.

Andrew and his family found their way to a patch of scrub near to what is now Cambridge, Ontario, about 100 kilometres west of Toronto. A generation later, his grandson, also an Andrew, and as a second son also needing to seek his own future, went west again, to another patch of land, this one south of Winnipeg. Manitoba, the "Gateway to the West," as it came to describe itself, and the West meant opportunity, just as it had for Gord Homer's and Marilyn Cade's ancestors. It was 1879. Two years later, my grandfather Will was born. And thirty years after that, in 1911, my father.

My father, as the oldest son, might have stayed on the farm, but he had someplace else in mind. He always had someplace else in mind. When the harvest was done in 1929, he left, first for Winnipeg, then Regina, then back to Winnipeg. He went wherever he hoped some-one might buy whatever it was he was selling. But this was now 1930, and nobody was buying. The problem couldn't be that he was selling the wrong products, or his own sales skills, but that he had the wrong territory. So he did what any salesman would do: often ticketless, he rode the rails east, to Hamilton. A few years later, he met my mother, Margaret Campbell, and they were married.

During the 1930s, a lot happened for him, but not much changed. He was still selling, and too few were buying. Then the war came. He wasn't eligible for military service, the rheumatic fever he'd had as a child having damaged his heart, so he got a job with the YMCA, which was providing supports for soldiers training on bases near Toronto. In 1941, my older brother was born. When the war ended, the Y sent my father overseas to Hilversum, in the Netherlands, to run a centre called the Maple Leaf Club for those soldiers who, without transport home, still remained. In 1946, he arrived back in Hamilton. He was thirty-five years old, seventeen years off the farm. He had a son, five, and I was about to be born. Because of the Depression and war, he had not yet begun to live his life. And selling was all he knew.

But one big thing had changed. Now he had the right territory. In postwar Canada, *everywhere* was the right territory. And one more big thing: now, he definitely had the right products to sell. No more

silk stockings or Masculine Mask—"Turns your pimples to dimples."
He was selling cement blocks and bricks, and everybody wanted them
in Hamilton. But even more wanted them in Toronto. So we moved.
He was ready. He was about to be the overnight success decades in
the making.

He had energy. He believed in everything he did, in every product he sold, in every person he worked with, in every place he lived.
In Winnipeg, he loved everything Winnipeg. He loved the West. He
loved its big blue, wide-open skies, its frigid winter sunshine. He loved
the Bombers—the Winnipeg Blue Bombers of the CFL. In Hamilton,
he loved everything Hamilton, except in Grey Cup games, it was the
Bombers all the way. From the age of nineteen until he died at ninety-
two, he never lived in the West again, but in his mind he was always
a westerner.

When he started selling cement blocks and bricks, there was nothing like Argo Block, nothing like Booth Brick or Storrar Dunbrik.
Nothing. Later, when poured concrete became the construction rage,
when he would pass by a worksite and see a poured concrete basement
in the excavated ground, he would, theatrically, hold his nose between
his fingers and scowl, and we'd laugh and make fun of him, and he'd
only hold his nose more. If you don't believe in what you're selling,
why should anyone else?

And if you don't believe in yourself, it's the same. He spent his
days driving around to jobsites on mucky rutted ground that wasn't
yet paved, while my mother would be home in the office on the phone,
taking orders from the contractors, calling the orders in to the plants.
At Argo Block, she always spoke with Vic. I never knew his last name,
I never met him, but ten times a day Vic would get those orders from
my mother. My father believed he had to be on-site, with the builders,
with their workers, to see for himself, to watch, to listen, to know his
customers, to know their needs, to make sure those needs were met,
exactly, and to make sure that what he'd ordered had arrived when he'd
promised it, when they needed it. He always drove a Ford, two-tone
blue, a dark blue roof with a light blue body with a dark blue flashing

that ran along each side of the car from the headlights to the back of
the front doors. He wanted his customers to know that when they
looked up from what they were doing and saw that car with that flashing, it was Murray Dryden and he was on the job.

No matter how much he believed in the companies he worked
for, he was far more a customer man than a company man. Most of
the builders were from southern or eastern Europe, with thick accents
and garbled vocabularies. He had their backs, their fronts, their tops
and bottoms. Whenever he was home, I would hear him on the phone,
talking to the plant offices. "Where's that order of brick?" he'd say.
"I promised it for this afternoon." Never abusive, but very, very insistent. If the brick wasn't there, that wasn't right, it had to be righted.
My mother would pass on the same message later in the day, but more
nicely. Those at the offices *knew*. When I was three or four, on my
toy phone, and before I could pronounce my ells, I even had my own
imaginary friend who was also my imaginary customer, whom I named
Mr. Cunchunch. "More bocks today, Mr. Cunchunch?"

He never stopped. He was always selling. He had pens made
up with his name and phone number on them, key chains, multi-
page brochures printed up properly, professionally. Everything had
to look right, be right. Including him. You had to look sharp to be
sharp. Dress for success to be a success. He always wore a suit and
tie, even on worksites, even at night and on weekends—you never
knew; you had to be ready. And a fedora. The car always had to be
spotless, even with mud-splattering days on the road ahead. And each
year he bought a new one, same Ford, same colours, same flashing.
He put about fifty thousand kilometres on it each year, and on those
roads. And above all, you had to sell, sell, sell. One summer when my
younger sister, Judy, was about two and getting used to walking, if not
always to where she should go, to give her some freedom, but only to
a point, my parents put her into a harness, attached a long tether to
it, and attached it to a cement block, so she could wander the front
lawn, under my mother's and grandmother's surveillance. My father
took a picture of her and put it in his brochure. The cement block had

printed on it in big capital letters "ARGO," and the caption underneath it read, "Another use for an Argo Semi-Solid." An opportunity not taken is an opportunity missed.

Years later, after he'd retired from work, he didn't retire from selling. One day, when my first book, *The Game*, had just come out, my father had some banking to do. He knew there was always a line for a teller, so he took along one of my books and read it while he waited. Except he wasn't reading it. He had it open, and others could see it was open, but he had already read it. He waited a minute or two, then said something, anything, it didn't matter what, to the person standing in front of him, then to the person behind him. Sooner or later, he knew, they would ask him what he was reading. And he would tell them. Then, after a suitable pause, he'd say, "Oh, and my son wrote it," and there would be more talk, and soon others in the line, and soon the whole line, would overhear. Oh, and he always just happened to have a box of my books in the car. "I sold twelve in that line," he told me later that day.

His company was called Murray Dryden Limited. On his brochure he put his phone number and the hours that people could call, from 7 a.m. to 10 p.m. But if they called later, it didn't matter. And if they called before seven and woke him, he'd clear his throat and answer, and after the person identified himself, he'd say, "Joe! Hey, how are ya! Great! Great!" as if he'd been up for hours, as if he was already well into his day—no point making the customer feel stupid— as if he'd never stopped. Because he never had.

He loved to sell, and he loved to believe. And he believed in himself. He knew he was a great salesman. He knew he could sell anything to anybody anytime. Of course, he'd never say that, or even allow himself to think that. That would mean having a "swelled head," something which he and our mother reminded us kids again and again never *ever* to have. As my father also liked to say, "Self-praise stinks."

He was a "grade 11 dropout," he would always say, and a "peddler." Two things that most people aren't proud to say, but he was proud of both. In a way, it was part of his shtick, part of him and what he was peddling. But being both a dropout and a peddler also said something about him, and *to* him, that mattered. He was a hard-working guy. Look at what he'd made of himself. Look at what he'd done. Or, more accurately, look at what he was making, and doing, because he knew the job was *never* done. And while he was a high school dropout, he was a lifetime learner. When you're a salesman, you have to be. You have to know your product, and the market, but most important, you have to know your customer, what he wants, what she's thinking, how their mind works. Today, not yesterday. And because almost all of his customers were immigrants who had come from hard times and broken countries, he had to know what that felt like. And every night, he brought what he'd learned home to us, never in the form of big object lessons, just somehow in what he said and did. In later years, he would have other Masculine Masks and silk stockings. Failures and embarrassments. But he was never embarrassed. Why would he be? A salesman's got to try, always, and there's nothing better, nothing more exciting, than a new "line" to sell.

When the war ended, my father was a blank slate, and so was Etobicoke, and so was Canada. Each with all sorts of possibilities. My father was made for this time. It was a time for makers and doers. And it was time to get on with the making.

In today's conventional wisdom, the suburbs of the 1950s were a void of energy, interest, meaning, and purpose. That's *not* how our parents felt.

Etobicoke was on the other side of the Humber River from Toronto. In school, we studied the great rivers of the world. The Nile ran almost the length of a continent and for millennia was the lifeblood of civilizations. The Amazon's waters came from a thousand different places and defined a landscape, uncountable cultures, and biological life itself. The Mississippi was the inspiration for the mythology of a nation. From it came the idea of the West—the *other* side of the Mississippi—the frontier, of new frontiers always to seek, always ahead, of ideas that were even mightier than the river. The Nile, Amazon, and Mississippi—*those* were *rivers*. But the Humber?

In distant years past, the Humber had been part of water routes that one way or another connected Lake Ontario to Georgian Bay in the west, and to the Ottawa River and Montreal in the east. These lands were first the domain of Indigenous peoples, the Algonquins, Iroquois, and Mississaugas. ("Etobicoke" is a derivation of a Mississauga word meaning "place where the alders grow.") Then, in the 1700s, the French built a fur-trading post near the mouth of the Humber and operated it until so much land had been cleared by the settlers that the animals they trapped disappeared. To me, the Humber was either out of mind or just there, its tributaries, the Mimico and Etobicoke Creeks, nuisances that got in the way, took extra minutes to get across, and had no apparent purpose, except at Central Park, where we played baseball and where, because there were no big league–like fences, if you hit the ball into Mimico Creek, it was a home run. Then you could do your home run trot. Something that did matter.

Yet the Humber River was also wide enough to be a boundary. When Toronto was growing in the nineteenth and early twentieth centuries, it did so along Lake Ontario until it was stopped by the Humber on the west and by the Don River on the east. So the city developed north instead, then farther north, until there was enough reason and enough money to build bridges to spread the city west and east, to the other sides of the two rivers. On the west, that meant to Etobicoke.

Before that time, on maps at least, Etobicoke was mostly wide-open spaces. In real life, it was farms and market gardens with occasional clusters of houses, a few general stores, churches, a mill or two, a post office, maybe an inn, later an elementary school, all scattered about to support each other. One such cluster was the village of Islington, the core of which ran along Dundas Street West, one of the main east–west routes of Toronto then and now. Years later, new houses went up in Islington, just north and south of Dundas, where Wayne, Cheryl, Gord, Marilyn Adamson, and Marilyn Cade came to live, and where ECI, Etobicoke's first high school, was built. It was along Dundas, and along another main east–west route, Bloor Street West, about a kilometre south, that in the 1920s bridges were built that were substantial enough to support the growth that might come.

For Etobicoke, the first big change came in the late twenties, with the development of Kingsway Park, a plot of densely treed land on the west side of the Humber between the Dundas and Bloor bridges. Its developer was Robert Home Smith, a remarkably capable person who held an even more remarkable array of positions in a life that spanned less than sixty years. He made his first fortune in ore-rich northern Ontario, developing some of the biggest of the early mines. Later, he spurred the introduction of tobacco growing in Norfolk County in southwestern Ontario. He was part owner of a fleet of steamships on the Amazon. As well, among other things, he was president of Algoma Steel, chairman of the Niagara Falls Parks Commission, chairman of the Toronto Harbour Commission, and president of the Algoma Eastern, Algoma Central, Mexico Northwestern and Rochester, Lockport and Buffalo railways. But it was the development of Kingsway Park that helped shape the formative years of our parents, our family lives, and us.

Kingsway Park was inspired by the garden city movement in England in the late 1800s. The Industrial Revolution had made a few people very rich and many others better off, and for everyone, it had made the inner cities of where they lived almost uninhabitable. So those who could afford to leave left, to homes in areas as lush and green as the countryside but still close enough to their jobs in the city. Model towns were built. Among the first were by Cadbury and Lever near their massive factories in Birmingham and Liverpool. At Kingsway Park, Home Smith wanted to create, as its motto stated, *Angliae pars, Anglia procul*—"A little bit of England far from England." He wanted to create an oasis of space and trees, of refined living away from the grit and disease of the city, something that had the look and feel of a park that had houses in it, rather than a gathering of houses that also had trees. And that's what he did. Kingsway Park had no sidewalks; its roads were more like paths, winding, following the contours of the land; no high fences were permitted. Houses had to be made of stone, brick, or stucco, their designs approved by Home Smith's own architects, and buyers signed covenants to bind themselves. Most houses were constructed in Tudor or English cottage style. Many of the tradesmen who built them—carpenters, plasterers, bricklayers—were Scots who lived in what had been millworkers' cottages near the river under the new Dundas bridge, where Pat Gregory and his family came to live many years later. About one-third of our class lived in Kingsway Park, or in smaller Kingsway-Park-design-inspired houses on smaller lots nearby. The parents of one class member, Margaret Silvester (Cooke), moved into Kingsway Park right after they were married in 1933 and lived there until they died, one week apart, in 1990.

By the early 1930s, Kingsway Park had been mostly built out, the Depression was worsening, Home Smith died, the war soon came, and the development of other company lands near the Humber were put on hold. Next up for development would be Humber Valley Village, but not until the early 1950s, and this time not with houses that wanted to look much older than they were, but with houses that wanted to look modern and futuristic in every way. That wanted to look *suburban*. After we'd moved from Hamilton, we lived for a few years on Brentwood Road North, in a small house outside the boundaries of Kingsway Park. We moved to Humber Valley Village when I was six.

In 1941, before nearly all of our families had moved to Etobicoke, its population was 19,000. In 1951, with almost all of us there: 54,000. A decade later, in our first year at ECI, it was 156,000. Etobicoke's development plan, written in 1947, had imagined a population in 1975 of between 60,000 and 62,000. By then, it was actually almost 300,000.

All of this happened so fast. We, the members of that ECI class, were separated by only one generation, maybe two, from the old world, from the farm, from working-class lives, from futures that for centuries had been no different from presents and pasts. Etobicoke was about to become a suburb. This is the Etobicoke we grew up in.

CHAPTER FIVE

And this is the Canada we grew up in.

This was the postwar world. Our soon-to-be fathers and soon-to-be mothers were barely adults as the war years began. Most weren't more than twenty-five years old. They had lived in their parents' world, in their same neighbourhoods, sometimes even under the same roofs. They were doing what their parents were doing, learning what their parents had learned and knew, just as generations and centuries of parents before them had done. They were living in the Toronto, in the Canada, in the world, in the circumstances, in the times, with the attitudes and understandings, expectations and horizons of their parents. They had known no other life. Now, at war's end, at this moment, and from this moment on, this would be *their* life. Our soon-to-be fathers and soon-to-be mothers were now their own men and women. All this energy. What to do, what to be? What was next? First came anxiety, the fearful unknown before the exciting unknown.

The Depression had ended only because of wartime jobs in wartime industries making wartime things. Now that the war was over, with Europe and Japan decimated and the great empires of the world crumbling, the Depression would surely return. The old world order would surely become the new world disorder. For the first several months after the war, everyone held their breath. Things weren't that bad, news commentators acknowledged, not as bad as we've been expecting, but surely this won't last. Then a few more months passed, and a few more, and things were *still* not bad, but . . .

In some ways, the war that was over really wasn't over. The enemy of my enemy is my friend. But when my enemy is vanquished, is my friend still my friend? What about the Soviet Union? It had never felt like a friend. We had fought the same enemy, but had never felt we were on the same side. The wartime photos at Yalta we saw in school showed the great Allied leaders, Roosevelt, Churchill—and, oh yeah, Stalin. The Soviet Union stood for something different. Communism. A different way of life. Like a religion, something that could spread, take over your mind, not just your land. It took over eastern Europe. Who's next? Italy? Greece? Yugoslavia? Austria? Who's next after that? Africa? South America? India? The haunting image of the time: dominoes falling, *everywhere*, one after another, faster and faster. Inevitably. And now, shockingly, unthinkably, two years after we were born, the Soviets had the bomb too.

These were the big worries, but there were others that seemed inconsequential yet weren't. What about those who didn't go away to fight, who because of childhood disease or medical conditions had been rendered unfit, or who were too old, or who, it was determined, could fight the war better at home making what was needed for the war to be won? What did this coming-home time feel like to them? They had different war stories, from the *home* front, that now didn't seem like war stories at all. Did they even have the right to think of them that way now that the real warriors were home? Were they embarrassed not to have gone? At work, with people they met on the street, did they fear the question: "And what did *you* do in the war?" They had missed the party of their generation, and now it was Monday morning at the office and in all the noise and laughter at the water cooler they had nothing to say. Nothing they wanted to have to say.

Now came the really uncomfortable part: How could those who had stayed home justify the jobs they had? The things they'd learned? The three rungs up the ladder they'd climbed in the absence of, on the backs of, those who were away? The lives they had been able to live at home? The wives they'd married? The kids they'd had? The head start on life they'd been given? What right had they to those, to anything? Never having gone to war, they'd never graduated from boot camp. They'd never been a grunt, they'd never had to earn their way. Years later, when their own kids asked: "What did you do in the war, Daddy?" what would they say? They'd come up with an answer that sounded all right to their kids, but what about to themselves? Everybody had a role to play, everybody did their part. If only they believed that entirely. For the big life-shaping, life-defining experience of their generation, they hadn't been there. Now that all our dreams had been fulfilled, now that everyone was home, how would this work itself out?

Those of us in our ECI class were born at the beginning of *something*: for our parents, for Toronto, for Canada, for the world, for postwar times. The question was: What was the *something*?

For a year or two after the war, our parents still lived with their parents, or in small houses, apartments, or rooming houses on their own. It's only when they felt they had the beginnings of an answer to what that *something* was, when post-Depression, postwar times were becoming their *own* times, when they'd settled into their jobs, their families, their lives, into their own selves, that they moved to Etobicoke. Etobicoke was the place where this life, their life, this *something*, would be lived.

This is why the suburbs mattered so much. The suburbs were the answer, or at least the beginning of the answer, to the "what now?" question. As Steven Spielberg later put it, "The suburbs were my religion." They were that literal "green field," a blank slate to make of whatever you wished. The suburbs would offer people in working-class jobs that paid middle-class wages a middle-class life of houses and cars and TVs and washing machines and better schools, longer lives, and more time and more opportunity. But in this green field, on this blank slate, what would we grow, what would we write? We had more time, and more opportunity, for what? Our parents didn't know, or need to know. *Everything* became the answer. But what did that mean?

For generations, life had been about survival. Now it was about possibility. By 1947, about the time we were born, our parents began to breathe. Then dream.

For its January 1, 1950, issue, *Maclean's*, Canada's national magazine, chose Lister Sinclair to write its cover story on the state of the country at the end of the first half-century and on the verge of its second. Sinclair went on to an immensely varied career as a playwright, actor, and, as the long-time host of the radio series *Ideas*, CBC's resident intellectual. But at the time of the article, he was only twenty-eight years old. "The last 50 years has been the Age of Science," he wrote in his opening paragraph. "The things we think of as most typical of the modern world: radio, automobiles, movies, airplanes, birth control, to say nothing of the Kinsey Report and the Gallup Poll, surgery, public education and atomic energy—all these things have become universal in the Western world since 1900." He also characterized the first half-century as "the Age of Speed," "the Age of Universal War," "the Age of Propaganda," and with the diminished role of religion and the loss of faith and belief more generally except in times of war, as the "Age of Doubt." Science, Sinclair said, has become "the new religion." But unlike other religions, which are about things eternal, with science everything is relative, everything can change, nothing is absolute and forever.

Sinclair may have been right or he may have been wrong about our parents' world on the cusp of the 1950s, but in most ways it doesn't matter. In this time before TV, the internet, and social media, magazines were important, and *Maclean's* was the most widely read publication in the country, with more subscribers than any other magazine or any of the largest daily newspapers. And unlike them, it was national. Journalism often is referred to as "the first rough draft of history," and like all first drafts can be overwritten. But it does reflect the mood and thinking of a time. Many of our parents, including my own, subscribed to *Maclean's* and read such national voices as Ralph Allen, Pierre Berton, Peter Gzowski, and Peter C. Newman. Busy with piecing together their postwar lives, many of our parents didn't have the time to think about what these writers were thinking, but the writers' thoughts were all around them. From this article, the big question for our parents, and soon for us, was that the next fifty years would be the "Age of" what?

In the same issue of *Maclean's* was another article that did forecast these next fifty years. But it did so with gentle satire, focusing not on the dramatic changes ahead but, using the national in-jokes of the time, on what our parents and every Canadian knew would *never* change. John Largo, the article's author, wrote that in the first year of these next fifty, the CBC would announce that "television will still be 18 months away," the new Toronto subway "will be two feet nearer completion," a bridge will be built across the Strait of Canso to connect Cape Breton Island with the rest of Nova Scotia, the "St. Lawrence Seaway project will be reopened, considered, then deferred for a short time," and that the "country's population, now about 13 millions, will—owing to immigration, emigration, births, deaths and sheer exhaustion—increase to about 13 millions." Further, Largo wrote, with even greater godlike certainty, someone in Ottawa will say, "The 20th century . . . belongs to Canada." And that, on Monday, January 1, 2000, another voice in Ottawa will speak to the whole nation, "(now thanks to immigration, about 13 millions)," and say, "The 21st century . . . belongs to Canada."

What made this funny to *Maclean's* readers was that now, finally, there was more to Canada's story. This was no longer a moment for historians' certainties and backward glances. Who cared what we had been? There was a new story to write. This was a new, hopeful, high-minded time. A week before I was born, in its August 1, 1947, edition, *Maclean's* published an editorial about the newly formed United Nations, stressing that whatever we, as Canada, were now doing, we had to do more.

"We shall have to feed hungry peoples, even if it means rationing at home," the editors wrote, each sentence beginning "We shall," each one set off in its own paragraph, as if a commandment or proclamation.

We shall have to lend to destitute peoples, even if it means
stiff taxation at home.

We shall have to shelter the homeless of Europe, and defy
the fear and jealousy that would keep them out.

Hardest of all, we shall have to give the economy of the
free world a chance to function—in freedom. That calls for a
willingness to forgo regional protections, a readiness to buy
as well as sell, an end to some of our dearest prejudices.

And while doing all this, we shall have to maintain toward
the Soviet Union a firmness that must not sour into enmity,
a patience that must not weaken into appeasement . . .

Maybe it can't be done. Maybe we shall have war after all.
But surely this is no time to quit.

World War III is no more inevitable than was defeat after
Dunkirk.

Lofty aspirations like this were no longer unthinkable. Or inex-
pressible. And why would they be? As a *Maclean's* editorial noted a
year later, unemployment was the lowest in our history, investment
the highest, and the best was yet to come—the oil fields of Alberta,
the iron mines of Quebec and Labrador were still at their beginnings. Even the bad news—power outages that parts of the country had experienced, housing supply that was tight—was because of
good news: the outages had been because the demand for electricity
was even higher than it had been during the war, housing was limited because more people had more money to get married and to
buy or rent a place of their own. In the summer of 1948, after five
different parties had won power in five different provinces, did this
mean the country was tearing itself apart? Not at all, an editorial in
Saturday Night, the country's other major magazine, answered. After
a war, people are supposed to want a change of government—even
Churchill had been turfed out—and these five different governments
had all won re-election. "By and large," *Saturday Night* concluded,
"we have a contented country." And because the war hadn't been

fought on our territory, we didn't feel the need to rectify the past. For us, it could be "moving on," not "never forget." We could focus on, and make, the future.

The ads in both magazines told this same story. Companies, often in big, full-page displays, sold their products using nation-building messages. O'Keefe's, a popular beer of the time, ran a series of ads under the theme "Canada Unlimited." One told the story of northern Ontario—its pulp and paper and vast power resources, its gold, silver, and copper mines, its mines in Sudbury that produced 90 percent of the world's nickel—not once mentioning beer. Molson's ads told the story of the newcomer. Of Louis Fischl, who escaped from Czechoslovakia in 1938 at the age of fifty and now had factories in Prescott, Ontario, and Saint-Tite, Quebec, where he manufactured thousands of pairs of high-fashion gloves. "Canada is the most desired of countries," the ad stated. For immigrants, "it represents hope and opportunity. It is where they want to be," and concluded, "One of a series presented by Molson's in the interests of a greater Canadian appreciation of Canada's present greatness."

Calvert Distillers also focused on new Canadians—"Men of Vision," it called its series of ads. "Canada, land of opportunity, owes much of its strength and vitality, and the rich quality of its democracy, to the blending of racial and cultural heritages from many lands." An INCO ad reminded us that "the nickel man" needs "the lumberman," "the railwayman," and "the steelworker," that we all need each other, that "no matter how we earn a living, we are one family, each depending on the others." Weston's Bakeries focused on the role of women in our national life. In one ad, a woman is standing in her kitchen, in her apron, looking like everybody's mother, slicing a loaf of Weston's bread. In another, she's making a deposit in a bank wearing a smart coat and stylish beret-like hat. "Today the Canadian woman has many roles to play," the ad declared. "In national affairs, there are 3,750,000 Canadian women who are eligible to vote . . . In business, she is assuming more and more responsibility in executive, managing, directing and buying capacities. In the home, she is nurse, teacher,

wife, purchasing agent, housekeeper and cook . . . She is promoting
the kind of thought and action needed to keep Canada sound, sane
and progressive."

Insurance companies offered their own sound, sane messages.
An ad for London Life showed an on-the-way-up but mature-looking
young man in his late thirties in a suit jacket and bow tie, holding a
pipe, gazing slightly upward, the caption reading, "Dreams can come
true . . ." Above the drawing, in three thought bubbles, images of
the man in the future: in a new car, in a boat fishing on a lake, and,
with his wife, at their son's university graduation, a mortarboard on
the boy's head. Our parents, and all their ancestors before them, had
never had the luxury of thinking about the future. The possibilities
of having a different future now brought to them the fear of losing
it, and the need, in buying insurance, to plan for it. This was part of
nation-making too.

The 1951 Canada census offers numbers that fill out the nar-
rative. This was the country's first census after Newfoundland had
joined Confederation two years earlier, and it revealed (finally) that
Canada had exceeded the "13 millions" that John Largo had claimed
was our forever national destiny. Barely. On June 1, 1951, Census Day,
Canada's population was 14,009,429. (Thank you, Newfoundland.)

Our population had grown more than 20 percent since the previous census, in 1941. Over 90 percent of that had come from natural
increase—births over deaths—and less than 10 percent from immigration—in over out. The 1951 census also revealed that almost 85 percent of our population had been born in Canada, and another 7 percent
in the U.K. or Commonwealth countries. The rest, only 8 percent,
were from everywhere else. Among those considered visible minorities, 165,607 identified as, in terminology that was used at the time,
"Native Indian or Eskimo"; 32,528 as being of Chinese origin (four-
fifths of whom were male); 21,663 as Japanese; 2,148 as "East Indian,"
almost all of whom lived in B.C.; and 18,020 as "Negro"—a number
that had remained almost unchanged since the country's first census,
in 1871, and more than 80 percent of whom lived in Nova Scotia and

Ontario. On Census Day 1951, only a small percentage of a population of 14 million didn't have white skin.

The country's population growth had not been uniform. Ontario and B.C. had grown significantly, while the populations of Quebec, the Maritimes, and the Prairie provinces had become smaller. But after 1945, with the war done, Canadians everywhere were raring to go. They got married in numbers almost double those in the 1930s, had more kids, wanted more housing of their own, and, their lives shaped by their experiences of depression and war and seeking more security, bought their homes more often than they rented. They were buying more of almost everything: retail sales in general had tripled since 1941, car sales quadrupled. To afford this, in 1951, 82 percent of males and 24 percent of females age fourteen and over were in the workforce. A closer look at the numbers provides an even more revealing story. For eighteen- and nineteen-year-olds, 81 percent of males and 56 percent of females were in the workforce. For those twenty to twenty-four, it was not much different. But for those who were twenty-five to thirty-four, as marriage and children intervened, the number stayed roughly unchanged for men, but for women it dropped dramatically, to 24 percent, and it remained at that level for women aged thirty-five to forty-four—the age of most of our class's parents—before dropping even further for those who were older. Once married, especially when they had children, few women, as the census put it, were "gainfully employed."

What Canadians were doing in the workforce was also changing. The number of mining and mechanical engineers increased threefold between 1931 and 1951, civil and electrical engineers much less so. There were now many more draftsmen and designers, more doctors but not many more dentists, more male schoolteachers but not many more female, and barely more lawyers and judges at all. There were fewer barbers and more hairdressers. More butchers but fewer bakers, tailors, and shoemakers. There were many more motor vehicle mechanics, woodworkers, and metalworkers—welders, fitters, toolmakers, repairmen—and many fewer blacksmiths and coopers.

In short, many more Canadians were now employed in manufacturing, and many fewer in agriculture.

In construction, there were many more plumbers, electricians, and carpenters, and not many more painters. In transportation, there were more train engineers, conductors, and brakemen, fewer seamen and deckhands, more than twice as many taxi drivers, bus drivers, and chauffeurs, and three times as many truck drivers—more than 150,000, all of them male. In fact, truck driving was by now one of the largest job categories in the country.

In stores, there were now fewer male salesclerks and more female. Many more men were janitors, guards, watchmen, policemen, and detectives. As people moved to the cities, many more women were waitresses and cooks, but with fewer extended families now living together, there was less need for bigger houses, resulting in fewer housekeepers and maids as well. For men, the top five jobs in the country, numerically, were farmers and stock raisers (by far), labourers, farm labourers, office clerks, and truck drivers. Carpenters were next. For women, the top jobs were stenographers and typists (by far)—in fact almost one-third of all women "gainfully employed" were stenos and typists—then came office clerks; salesclerks; hotel, café, and private household workers; and teachers. Bookkeepers and cashiers were next. In the jobs that women most commonly held, they dominated. More than 95 percent of nurses, telephone operators, and housekeepers were women, and over 72 percent of teachers. These were our mothers in their younger years. Women did what was considered "women's work." Yet all of these job numbers together still added up to the only 24 percent of women who were in the workforce. For the rest, for the great majority, 64 percent described what they did, their "activity," as "keeping house."

Our family structures remained largely unchanged. In 1951, 64 percent of Canadians age fifteen and over were married, 30 percent were single, 6 percent widowed, only 0.3 percent divorced. Our families were now slightly smaller, not so much because the number of childless or one-child families had increased, but because more

Canadians were living in cities, cities were expensive, and while in a rural economy a bigger family might be an economic advantage, in an urban economy it wasn't. The 1951 census also showed just how close we were to our distant past and to our future in how we lived. In 1941, almost 90 percent of all households were heated either by wood (46 percent) or coal (42 percent), only 3 percent by oil. Ten years later, coal usage had remained largely the same, wood dropped to 28 percent, while oil, at 23 percent, was more than seven times higher. Yet the biggest change to daily life arrived with electricity. In the 1940s, the number of households with electric or gas refrigerators, washing machines, and vacuum cleaners increased by 50 percent or more, and in some agriculture-based provinces, by double or more. Women, increasingly, had new and different ways of "keeping house" and, with electricity's added conveniences, in theory more time to do other things.

Families still went to church. The largest denomination in the country in 1871 was Roman Catholic. Eighty years later, that was still the case, the percentage of its adherents having barely changed: 43.9 percent in 1871, 43.3 percent in 1951. Nor had the percentages changed much for Protestant churches. The largest Protestant denomination in 1871 was Methodist, followed closely by Presbyterian and Anglican. The Methodists, Congregationalists, and most Presbyterians came together in 1925 as the United Church of Canada, and for seventy years, from 1871 until 1941, the total membership of these churches remained slightly higher than that of the Roman Catholics. But the 1941 and 1951 censuses showed that the Roman Catholic Church was larger. A small change in numbers, maybe, but to a country sensitive to religious differences, a big change in what those numbers represented. Yet even more noteworthy, even as the country grew from 3.7 million in 1871 to 14 million in 1951, even with massive immigration, especially in the early 1900s, and from many different countries, the percentages of Protestants and Catholics in the country didn't change much. Those who came to Canada, it turned out, had similar religious beliefs to those already here. The United Church itself, in every province, had more members than the Roman Catholic Church, except in Quebec, where more than 87 percent of churchgoers were Roman Catholics. The 1951 census showed something else as well: Catholics married Catholics; United Churchers might marry Presbyterians or Anglicans, but very few married Catholics. Nineteen years later, in 1970, I, a United Churcher, married a Catholic.

In 1951 more kids were staying in school longer. For fifteen- to nineteen-year-olds, for the first time in any Canadian census, there were slightly more boys than girls in school. And for those twenty to twenty-four, 6.5 percent of boys were at university (the college system was still more than a decade away from being created), but only 3.3 percent of girls. More telling is that, of *all* the grade 5 to grade 9 students in Canada in 1941, ten years later, their high school years then over, less than 5 percent were in university. Our parents were slightly older, but this was their story too.

As for ours, in 1951, we were four or five years old. Our parents may have had in their heads dreams of us going to university a decade or so later, but this was the mountain they, and we, were up against.

The census, the articles and ads, the numbers and words—on paper, in 1951, everything ahead seemed possible. Our parents were hopeful but cautious, and they had reason to be. Reality is a mix of what is and what we imagine will be. To most of our parents in 1951, reality felt pretty good.

CHAPTER SIX

For our parents, the 1940s was a time of settling in, settling in to whatever postwar adult life was. For our fathers, this meant finding "steady" jobs that could support this life and this "steady" future. They had no perfect jobs in mind, and employers had no perfect candidates in mind to fill them. Few Canadians had gone to university, or been trained in any specialty, or had fathers whose jobs had seemed like a family calling and that they would naturally follow. If a job seemed good enough to the job seeker, and the job seeker looked eager enough to an employer, they'd make it work.

Almost all these companies, no matter what they'd done before or during the war, were also on their way to becoming something else, because Toronto, Canada, and the postwar world were on their way to something else. These companies would change, and they needed workers who they would come to know and trust, who would learn, day after day, as they learned, adapt as they adapted, see possibility as they saw it, change as they changed.

These companies, and our fathers, weren't looking for something *dramatically* better in their futures. Dramatically better had never been part of their life experience. They knew depression and war. What would "dramatically better" even look like? Better to them meant a little more, and then a little more, and if someone did hire you, that meant you were good enough to do the job, or would be, or might be, and if you were, you stayed, because why change? The grass that was greener was *up* the ladder, not somewhere else. My father worked for Argo Block and Booth Brick for more than twenty years, until he retired. Gord's father was with CREL all his working life, and his father's father the same before him. Kathy McNab's father worked for the Department of Transportation and Communications for more than forty years, Wayne Yetman's for Ontario Hydro, Judy Clarke's as a typesetter and Peggy Clarke's as a lawyer, both for the *Toronto Star*, for all their working lives. It was the same for most men at the time. Ships were rising because the tide was rising, everywhere.

If the 1940s were about settling in, the 1950s were about settling down. As kids, that meant settling down into our neighbourhood schools—Lambton-Kingsway,* Islington, Rosethorn, and Humber Valley. As families, it meant settling into our neighbourhood churches—Kingsway-Lambton United, Islington United, Royal York United, Humber Valley United, St. George's-on-the-Hill Anglican, All Saints Anglican (no Catholic churches, no synagogues)—and into our neighbourhoods themselves—our parents looking to be surrounded by the right parents, and for us by the right kids, because the right or the wrong ones, our parents knew, would affect our lives. We settled down into our activities—Cubs, hockey, and baseball for the boys, Brownies and music lessons for the girls, our parents sometimes our pack leaders or coaches. We settled down into weekday routines—breakfast every morning with the whole family at the kitchen table, except in the few families where the fathers had to leave early for work; dinner every night with the whole family at the dining room or kitchen table, every father there. This was family time. After dinner, every night, after the dishes were washed and dried— no electric dishwashers—after a few minutes in the living room, fathers reading their newspapers, mothers tidying up, kids doing

---

* The elementary school was named "Lambton-Kingsway"; the nearby church "Kingsway-Lambton."

who knows what, it was office work for our fathers, housework for our mothers, homework for us. A few nights a week, it was the church, the Y, Kiwanis, Rotary—because our parents believed church and the community were all part of family life, because they all made life for the family better. For some, bridge club acted as a community-bonding experience, a chance once a month for our parents to spend time with their neighbours, whose kids spent a lot of time with us, to get to know their neighbours better, and therefore their kids better, and for them to know us better as well.

We settled down into weekend routines too. There were chores to do around the house—lawns to cut, gardens to care for, leaves to rake, driveways to shovel, and always rooms to clean up—everything the week hadn't left time for. There was shopping to do—for weekly or monthly needs there was the Kingsway, a line of shops along Bloor Street West just south of ECI, where there was a store for almost everything—part of Home Smith's master plan for the area: Kingsway Cycle for bikes and hockey sticks, McCracken's Men's and Boys' Wear, Mainprize Drugs, who sponsored my brother's first baseball team, Genova's for fruits and vegetables. There was Ed's Barber Shop for my once-a-month buzz cut; more than sixty years later Ed is long gone but the barbershop is still there. Knox Shoes, which had this amazing boxlike machine that, when we stood on its platform base, the shoe salesman and our parents could look down through a scope at the top and see an X-ray image of our feet (so we were told) inside our shoes, to determine if they fit properly—another miracle of "Canada Unlimited." There was also a women's shop, a bakeshop, and a jewellery store. And just off Bloor, on Wendover Road, Pop's smoke shop, which sold cigars, pipes, and pipe tobacco to our fathers and cigarettes to our fathers and mothers, most of whom smoked, and to us, candy and pop and best of all, black balls the size of marbles, long-lasting and cheap, that changed colour as we sucked them and which we'd take out of our mouths to show to our friends. Stores where there really was a Mr. Knox, Mr. Mainprize, Mr. McCracken, Mr. and Mrs. Genova, a Pop and an Ed. And there was Kresge's five-and-dime for everything else.

For "big shopping," a few times a year, there were day-long excursions downtown, especially to Eaton's and Simpson's, Toronto's two big department stores, which really did have everything. But not on Sundays—no Sunday shopping was allowed in Ontario until 1992. Each trip was anticipated and planned for, with treats anticipated and planned for, and promised, to lighten the step and mood when the slog of the day set in. For me, the slog of the day set in before we left home. On Saturday nights, sometimes on Fridays, our parents had friends over for dinner, usually neighbours, sometimes people from the office, or parents of kids we knew from school. They'd talk, laugh, smoke, drink, listen to music on the record player. We'd make an appearance, then, happily for them, happily for us, make ourselves scarce the rest of the night. On other Saturdays, in rotation, they'd do the same at the others' houses.

Then Sundays, which for almost all of us, when we weren't certifiably on the verge of death, meant church. Which meant getting dressed up, going, some fathers helping with ushering or the offering, some mothers in the choir, then coming home, changing out of our good clothes, doing something, getting dressed up again, then picking up our grandparents if they lived nearby, for Sunday dinner—ham, mashed potatoes, and casseroles of all kinds, colours, and shapes—in the dining room. What we didn't do much of on Sundays, what was left mostly for Saturdays, was the busy, organized stuff, games and practices for the boys, music lessons for the girls. Sunday was quieter. In the brief open times we had, we'd drift off on our bikes or into our rooms or to somewhere else in the house on our own, to read, play house, play with our trains or Meccano sets, to pretend, imagine, dream, do our homework; and our parents might do the office work or housework that just wouldn't wait. Then Monday again.

In summer we had our routines too, and that meant being outdoors, which to our parents mattered more than whatever it was we *did* outdoors. Outdoors was sun, fresh air, moving, doing, looking healthy, being healthy. It was Pat exploring for all things amphibian and reptilian by the Humber River, Lisa, Kathy McNab, and

Joan Cliff (Milloy) finding whatever they could find in the scrub along Mimico Creek. It was Daryl, Ken, and Diana wandering through vacant fields and ravines on the other side of Kipling. For me, it was playing baseball. Playing a pickup game at the park or playing catch with my brother or with anyone else I could find. And if there wasn't anyone else, to play catch with myself, by throwing a lacrosse ball or tennis ball up against any wall and chasing after it, in my mind "going into the hole" between short and third, and with a long throw, nipping the runner at first to win the World Series. We took swimming lessons at the new pool near the high school, and ate its earth-brown french fries when we were done, covered in salt, vinegar, and grease that I can smell and savour to this day. It mattered a lot to our parents that we learned to swim. Water was fun, and water was danger. Cars, trains, and water—to our parents those were the big things in our preteen years that could go wrong, and go wrong in a flash, when they weren't around.

For most in the class, the best summer routine was "going north," to go camping for a few days with the family, or to an overnight camp for a week or more as we got older, or later, for many, as our families settled into their middle-class incomes, to go to a cottage by a lake. There we would do all the unscheduled, unorganized, unnecessary things we didn't do on weekends at home the rest of the year, and swim and boat with our summer-cottage friends.

Solid jobs, good schools, nice neighbourhoods. That was life in the fifties for most of us living in the suburbs. It didn't mean there weren't things to worry about—life was never what we hoped it would be. For our parents, having lived through the Depression and war, money was never not a concern, and war never not a threat. The bomb was everywhere in our newspapers, but by the mid-1950s it felt less immediate, less transfixing. There were big childhood diseases to be concerned about—scarlet fever, rheumatic fever, measles, chicken pox—that could shut down a family for weeks or months of a year, and sometimes change futures. Some of our fathers, mine included, had been turned down for military service because of the permanent effects of diseases like this. For some years polio was on our minds. The fathers of both Judy Tibert (Morgan) and Steve and Ted Whistance-Smith had had polio as children. But for most of us, and for most of our parents, tomorrow, it turned out, was as good as the day before, and maybe a little bit better. In the 1950s we were nicely, if cautiously, settled down in Etobicoke, into busy lives— "Idle hands are the devil's workshop"—on the verge of becoming less cautious.

Whether we were on the verge of more, or a lot more, depended on the jobs our fathers had, and on their personalities and backgrounds. There were jobs, solid jobs, and there were jobs that could grow. This was a good time for most, and a great time for some. The father of Penni Harcourt (Mansour) worked as a projectionist, and Sandie Barnard's as the manager, at the Westwood Theatre; Pat's father was a truck driver for Direct-Winters Transport, Marilyn Steels's a teacher, Cheryl's a cop, Wayne's a clerk at Ontario Hydro: solid jobs, but jobs that offered little room for financial growth. Ken's father was an accountant, Daryl's an engineer, both with aviation companies; Bruce's was an economist, Marilyn Cade's, Judy Tibert's, and Ted and Steve Whistance-Smith's were in insurance, Joan Cliff's in hardware supplies, Gord's in sheet metal, Doug Little's in industrial kitchens, my father in building materials, all of them in growth industries, many of them in big-growth areas in those industries. In a self-defining time, they had self-defining jobs. And nothing was more self-defining than sales.

Lew Tibert, Don Cade, Murray Dryden—none of them were more than high school graduates. All of them were smart, all of them had boundless energy. They were self-starters, go-getters. In sales, they could all make themselves what they wanted to be. A salesman is a believer, a dreamer—and this was a time to believe.

For our parents and us, nothing embodied the excitement of the times more than cars. Before the 1950s, cars were utilitarian in design, colour, and function. "Plymouth owners will tell you that Plymouth is a great car—in performance, economy, long-life, safety, and reliability," the car company's ad in *Saturday Night* told our parents in 1948. From Dodge, another Chrysler Corporation product: "Year after year Dodge engineering improvements gave Dodge owners extra thousands of miles of trouble-free operation . . . You will be happy with a dependable Dodge!" Not even a decade later, the pitch had changed: "Like the sleek tautness of the supersonic jet," a Chrysler ad exclaimed, "there's a bold new feeling of motion, power, and stability . . . in every poised-for-action line . . . from the smoothly contoured hood to new skyward-soaring rear fenders." Its cars are described as "an invitation to adventure," offering "the styling trend of tomorrow," and a "look of airborne beauty." As Chrysler's slogan proclaimed, this was "The Forward Look." In less than ten years we'd gone from what we could afford to what we wanted. From the utilitarian to a life statement.

In 1954, *Maclean's* offered this "Dominion Day Message" to Canadians:

> Canadians squander a good deal of their patriotic fervor proving that this is the second-best country in the world.
>
> Canada has the second-highest standard of living. That means the second-largest number of washing machines and deep freezes and automobiles and radio sets per capita, second-smallest work week and second-biggest take home pay.*
> We haven't looked it up, but we'd guess that Canada has also the second-highest incidence of stomach ulcers. Toronto is almost as modern a city as New York. Montreal is almost as Parisian as Paris.
>
> The purpose of these reflections is not to urge that the nation pull up its socks and start buying the *most* deep freezes, making the *most* money and collecting the *most* ulcers. Nor is

---

* *Maclean's* never feels the need to say *which* country has the biggest, largest, and highest.

it to issue a brave reminder that material things aren't everything. Our sole message for this Dominion Day is: let's relax.

The editorial goes on to make another point, almost as an afterthought, though it is anything but an afterthought: "Canada, we firmly
believe, is approaching that critical stage that in individual humans is
called the change of life. A silent earthquake is at work in the hidden
fastnesses of the body and the soul. Youth is disappearing and every
cell is protesting against age. The future of the whole organic structure rests on the success with which it makes the adjustment." By this
time our parents were in their mid-thirties; we kids were six or seven.
Reality isn't only what is, but is what we imagine will be.

The Dominion Day message talked about Canada coming to a
"change of life" moment, but the editorial didn't complete its own
thought. Over the next several years, *Maclean's*, and other magazines
and publications in Canada and the U.S., came to ask an even bigger
question: Now that we have what we say we want, is this all there is?

CHAPTER SEVEN

By the mid-1950s, doubts began to set in, among Canada's commentators at least. For our parents, who didn't have much time to doubt, it was more a creeping uncertainty.

As Canadians, we now had more than we'd ever had before. For most of history, most of humanity had only what kept them alive, and often just barely, and not for long. Then, in the early years in this past century, more of us, our grandparents and parents included, had a little more, and with that a chance to think about not only today, but about having even more in the future. Then the First World War came, then the Depression, and our parents could see how things might not always get better, but might get worse, and remain that way. Then the Second World War. But when it was over, better came. And better and better. Average people like them didn't need to live in rundown neighbourhoods anymore. They could move to somewhere spacious and green, to live lives that might be excitingly, unimaginably different, and better still. These were our growing-up years.

And the real miracle of this: these new houses and cars and appliances could be paid for out of *one* paycheque, because in this postwar world fathers were making more money and mothers didn't need to be "gainfully employed" at all. Fathers could focus on their work, on "getting ahead." On being better "providers." On being better fathers. Mothers could stay at home and focus on their families, on being better homemakers, nurturers, family-makers. On being better mothers. Kids could focus on learning, doing, developing, on "getting ahead" in our own world. On being better kids. What an unbelievable opportunity for everyone! For fathers, mothers, kids, for Canada, the U.S., the future. In all of history, nothing had ever been like this before.

Of course, all these material things were really so much more than that. New and bigger houses offered a chance for kids to have their own room. For twelve-year-olds to live as twelve-year-olds, to stay up later, have more time and space for homework, read, listen to the radio, to live in their own twelve-year-old's mind and not have a nine-year-old brother or sister in the same room ruining everything. For nine-year-olds to live their own best nine-year-old lives and have a room of their own too. Nice new cars offered a chance for fathers to get to work a few minutes faster and home a few minutes earlier to have more time for their families. Nice new fridges, stoves, and washing machines offered mothers a chance to spend more time helping their kids with their homework, being at their schools to get to know their teachers, the principal, the woman who ran the office.

These were good things, weren't they?

Father Knows Best, *Leave It to Beaver*, *Ozzie and Harriet* were on our TV screens to show us what life could be. To us, and to millions of other viewers, the Andersons, Cleavers, and Nelsons weren't living suffocating, stifling lives, the way we now think of those lives. These were fathers, mothers, kids, families having a chance to be more than and better than what they had been, were supposed to be, and wanted to be. These weren't the rich, those to the manner born who had no connection to the rest of us. This was *us* on our TV screens.

All this for fathers to be better fathers, mothers to be better mothers, kids to be better kids, people to be better people, families to be better families. This was a good thing, wasn't it?

We did get our new houses in our new suburbs, and they were nice and clean. And we did get our new schools, and our new churches and playgrounds and cars and fridges and stoves. And we got new TVs too, this miracle *thing* that allowed us to see real people in a different place at the same time—what could possibly be next? But then, by the late 1950s, came the question that until then not many commentators felt they had the right to ask: How come this new house of yours is the same as my new house? How come your new suburb/school/church/playground/car/fridge/stove is the same as my new suburb/school/church/playground/car/fridge/stove? How come when new *and* different finally are possible, we get new and *not* different? Why, when unimaginable and exciting are possible, don't we get either? And how come, with all this *more* we have, it seems we're only as happy and unhappy, satisfied and unsatisfied, fulfilled and unfulfilled as we were before? How come as fathers and mothers and kids, with all this time and opportunity to get ahead, we seem no more ahead? And when all of us and all of this is supposed to be better, but isn't, why, in some ways, does it feel worse?

This *was* a good thing, wasn't it?

Our parents were turning forty, we were turning ten. It was becoming a "yes . . . but" time. There were now more stories in newspapers and magazines about divorce and broken homes. The numbers were rising. Not by much, but rising. What was going on? Many of our grandparents and parents thought they knew why. They had lived through hard times, they had learned to do without and to help others as they in turn had been helped by others. But in these times, as more had become more possible, *things* had become more important, and people, and families, less. There were also more articles about kids—the scourge of "juvenile delinquency," the clothes they wore, the music they listened to, the way they talked, their basic, well, lack of respect. The way they seemed to think that life should be handed to them on a silver platter.

There were more articles about religion, about its place in this world of candy-store satisfactions, about how, after millennia of tough times, these good times, these possibilities, this gift from God had, for some reason, somehow, been bestowed on us. Yet how do we show our gratitude? We build beautiful new churches, we attend them more often, we seek religious meaning and inspiration wherever we can find it. In 1955, between September 18 and October 16, night after night, for almost a whole month, Billy Graham preached to Toronto audiences. More than 356,000 people in all! More than half as many as would watch the Toronto Maple Leafs in Maple Leaf Gardens that entire season. My parents were there, and, age eight, I was too. Yet theologians and commentators saw something else. They looked at how we lived on non-Sabbath days and asked: Yes, but do we *truly* believe? Or, in this time of science that had given us new cars and stoves and other ways of explaining the origins of our good fortune, do we go to church simply because we think we're supposed to, because others do? And really, truly, all this *more* that we have, what is it for?

And really, truly again, what is the *more* that we think is there, that must be there? Instead of cars with big fins, Levittowns, Etobicokes, and Elvis, is it more Shakespeare, more Mozart, more of everything great, where all of us exposed to great come to love great, can't get enough of great, and become great? What is within human possibility? What can we be?

Two words came to be heard often in the 1950s: "conformity" and "hypocrisy." Conformity: having the chance for the new and different but settling for only the new. Hypocrisy: knowing what can be and should be done but not living up to it, saying we are when we aren't. What is wrong with us—with society, with Canada, with the Western world? Why is *this* more, *our* more, only more of the same? With all this time and opportunity, with all this more and better education, for all these people, for us, why can't it be a different kind of more? Higher, loftier, better. And why, when we fall short, aren't we angrier?

A few years later, in the mid-1960s, Pierre Berton, the most widely read popular historian in the country, wrote about the loss of deep-seated religious belief within the established churches in his bestseller *The Comfortable Pew*. I didn't read the book at the time and I'm not sure my parents did either, but we knew about it. Our minister at Humber Valley, Reverend Arthur Steed, talked about it from the pulpit, and there were discussions and debates in all the newspapers. The book brought to focus this disquiet that had been building since the fifties, not only about the state of the church establishment but about our parents and us in the congregation. What Berton wrote was wrong, our parents wanted to believe. No pew *could* be comfortable when so much wasn't right in the world. This was just the provocative Berton being Berton.

But, our parents feared, maybe our pew *was* comfortable. Maybe *everything* was too comfortable. Maybe this *more* wasn't always a good thing.

In *Maclean's*, Lister Sinclair had described the century's first fifty years as the Age of Science. Left hanging was the bigger question: The *next* fifty years would be the Age of *What*? By the early 1950s, the answer was evident.

It is easy for us today to sneer at that time and that place—the suburbs, the appliances that slice and dice. But to most people then, our parents among them, what was wrong with more of us in more places living the way only the few ever had? What was wrong with more and nicer? To some philosophers and commentators at the time, and to many more who came later, the 1950s seemed an opportunity missed. Even wasted. Given the chance to be more in some history-changing way, we instead chose to be more in the same way. The answer to Sinclair's unasked question: this was the Age of the Common Man. To many philosophers and commentators, the Age of the Common Man was too common.

My classmates and I were three and four years old in the early 1950s, and teenagers by the end of the decade. During that time we grew and learned, discovered things we liked and loved and didn't like or love. Whatever had gone right in our lives until then would continue to go right tomorrow, it seemed, because why not? Whatever hadn't— mothers who didn't understand us, teachers who weren't nice, kids who were mean—might be different tomorrow, because why not? We weren't optimistic or deluded, we were kids, and from all we had lived and knew, that's what life was like.

We didn't see these as idyllic years when we lived them. We probably saw our life to be mostly as good as anyone else's, if we ever even thought about it at all, which we might when some other kid was allowed to do something our parents said we couldn't. And always there was some kid who had something better and nicer—new clothes, a new bike, new skates—which we *did* notice, but I don't think many of us felt hard done by, at least not for long. We went to good schools, played in nice parks and playgrounds. Only two of us had a parent who died during these years, and only one had parents who separated or divorced. If there were family troubles—marital, health—we didn't know about them, or if we did they didn't seem so bad they couldn't be overcome. Our parents were adults—they would find an answer. Most of us felt cared for and loved, if we ever thought about that too. Whatever we had, however we lived, was all we knew. It was normal to us, so it was normal, period. Very few of us experienced the kind of big trauma that throws life off the rails, gets into us and stays in us and never leaves us the rest of our lives. And if some of us had lived these traumas, we didn't know that they mattered so much. Not then. We were eight or ten or twelve years old, and things that seemed the end of the world, in a few days or few weeks weren't. We had decades of our lives ahead of us, decades to get over whatever had happened. We were getting smarter and stronger, and no one person, no one event, none of this would define us.

As for Canada, the breathless energy of the postwar decade was abating. Lots of big new resource projects continued, but there were fewer of them. Lots of immigrants still wanted to come to Canada, but the war-decimated countries of Western Europe had rebuilt themselves and were creating exciting futures of their own, and more of their citizens decided to stay. Things were good in Canada, and were going to get better, but maybe not as much as we had thought. Ads in magazines and newspapers now were more about lifestyle, about the products themselves, about how *they* would make our lives better, not about how Canada would. "Canada Unlimited"? Maybe Canada limited a bit.

As fast as we were growing, and as big as we were becoming, our smallness as a nation was becoming more obvious to us now, or again. Canada's population in 1960 was less than 18 million, many more than the "13 millions" John Largo saw but so much smaller than the United States, which was our true forever destiny. Sometimes when you focus on tomorrow, as we did, you don't see what's right in front of you. And while we Canadians of the 1950s had seen massive new developments, and all the riches that were coming out of the ground, *our* ground, we didn't see so clearly the U.S. companies that owned these riches and controlled our livelihoods, that had in *their* hands the health of our communities, the well-being of our families, our very independence. In the late 1950s, something happened that opened our eyes, at least a little. The Avro Arrow.

Daryl Browne's father, Eric, worked for De Havilland, a large aviation company that served as a subcontractor for A.V. Roe, which built the Arrow. He was an engineer, as his own father had been. Canadian engineers had a reputation internationally in mining and resources, in those fields most central to our economy. But they also had a history in aviation, one that had been enhanced during the Second World War. As kids, especially us boys, we had grown up mesmerized by stories of Spitfires and Messerschmitts, F-86 Sabres and MiGs, and of the fearless test pilots who in postwar years had broken the sound barrier. Every Labour Day weekend as a child I went to the Air Show (the best thing about Labour Day) at the Canadian National Exhibition to see a flypast of the fastest, sleekest, loudest, most awesome new planes, including our own CF-100, which, we knew, had broken the sound barrier. The threat in these Cold War years was Soviet nuclear bombers; the answer was high-speed interceptors. As the arms race escalated, better, faster interceptors were needed. The CF-100 evolved into the CF-103, and when that wasn't enough, design work began in 1953 on the CF-105, which would become the Avro Arrow.

In its first test flight, in 1958, the Arrow soared to an altitude of over fifty thousand feet and reached a speed of Mach 1.98, almost *twice* the speed of sound. On the same day the Soviets launched Sputnik.

Not only did Sputnik get all the news attention that day, but more significantly, it would change a way of thinking. Bombers go fast, missiles go faster. The future was intercepting missiles with missiles.

More successful test flights of the Arrow followed. But then, on February 20, 1959, Prime Minister John Diefenbaker announced its cancellation. On Black Friday, as it was called in the aviation industry and beyond, nearly fifteen thousand workers lost their jobs. One of them was Daryl's father.

He loved being an engineer, the challenge and puzzle of it, often having to create something that neither he nor anyone else had even thought of before. In Canada at that time, the Arrow was the highest of high tech for any engineer. This wasn't the flash and bling of big-finned cars, this was pure best-wins-the-day engineering, and he was doing it, and Canada was doing it, and it mattered, militarily and eco-nomically, and he was proud of that. At the time of Black Friday, he had been with De Havilland for almost twenty-nine years. He'd never been out of work before, even during the Depression. He was fifty years old. In the days, weeks, and months that followed the cancel-lation, he didn't know what to do. Eventually, he had to earn some money and took what employment he could find. But these were *jobs*, they weren't what he was trained for, what he was. It was almost a year before he found something steady. Daryl's mother, Marion, hadn't worked outside the house since Daryl's oldest brother was born in 1935. She got a job as a cashier at Grand Union, a local supermarket. Later, she trained to be a teacher. Daryl was ten when the Arrow was cancelled, old enough to know that something had happened, that something was wrong, to see his father unhappier than he had ever seen him.

The cancellation of the Arrow took on huge symbolic meaning in Canada, and the stories surrounding it have only grown with time. The plane that had flown at almost twice the speed of sound was dis-mantled, its plans were destroyed, as if all traces of it had to be wiped away. Why? One story that circulated was that the Americans didn't want the Arrow's technology to fall into the "wrong hands," and with

Cold War allegiances ever shifting, anybody's might be the wrong hands. Even Canada's own allies were suspect. That was just one story. And with all the theories, the conspiracies, it quickly became hard to know just how advanced the Arrow was, how important it might have been, what really had happened. But in many ways, it didn't matter, and doesn't matter, how much about the Arrow was fact and how much was myth. What was, and is, important is how the Arrow story came to be understood. This was Canada's giant leap into the engineering and technology of the future, from which more and more would be learned, from which we would get better and become more important players on the world stage, from which we would realize all that promise and possibility of the postwar years. The Arrow is what we had in us to be. Now it was gone. Because of the Americans.

The cancellation of the Arrow shook Daryl's father's confidence. It shook Canadians' confidence. It brought home some realities.

Yet most of our parents were unaffected by it, at least then. Life, a pretty good life, went on. By the end of the 1950s, as we were about to enter ECI, lots of things about us may not have been what we wanted them to be, but when seen through the eyes of our now seventy-plus-year-old selves, we had nothing to complain about. Everything was ahead of us. We were ready.

II

THE HIGH SCHOOL YEARS

CHAPTER EIGHT

None of us remembers the first day we were together at ECI. It is likely that most of us walked to school that day, maybe with an older brother or sister, maybe with a friend or two from elementary school. We would have worn something nice—not Sunday-nice, but next best, first-day-of-school nice. We would've been anxious, and excited, and would have tried very hard not to appear either. Once we got to school, we must have been directed to some classroom, assigned our lockers and our locker mates, introduced to our new homeroom teacher.* But no one remembers anything else. Except Wayne.

What Wayne Yetman remembers he remembers vividly, dramatically, and forever. He was then only a few weeks from his fourteenth birthday. A good student at Islington but not in the accelerated class, he'd now have around him the best students from *four* elementary schools. So, on this first day he was trying very hard to appear as though he knew what he was doing, and trying even harder to persuade others, and himself, that he felt confident.

---

* In high school, Joan Cliff's father, a high-energy, impossible-to-classroom-train student, had a young teacher just out of teachers' college. More than thirty years later, Joan met that teacher, our bluish/purplish-haired homeroom and English teacher, Mrs. Gemmell. Whenever Joan saw Mrs. Gemmell, she always felt the need to explain to her that she wasn't her father's daughter in every way.

There was an assembly for all the grade 9 students in the auditorium, Wayne remembers. ECI's principal, Mr. Durrant, was there.
Mr. Durrant was a shy, genial man once you got to know him—he
and my father were members of the same Kiwanis club—but in his
proper dark suit and rimless glasses he appeared formidable and aus-
tere. He stood at the podium on the auditorium stage and said a few
words that Wayne didn't quite take in, then introduced someone
Wayne didn't recognize. She was one of our fellow grade 9s, there to
represent all of us, to say something appropriate as a student new
to the school. Her name was Joan. She came onto the stage from the
wings, and though in his introduction Mr. Durrant had mentioned
that she was in 9G, our class, Wayne didn't know who she was—
which just goes to show, he thinks now, how much of a daze he was in
in those first few days. Now, more than sixty years later, talking about
the moment Joan appeared, it's as if Wayne transports himself back
to his almost fourteen-year-old self, all capital letters and exclamation
marks: "She was a fully mature woman! She came across the stage,
beautifully dressed, fully confident. And there was a gasp! I gasped,
the whole auditorium gasped. I was a very, very innocent child from
a sheltered, low-income, uneducated, very prudish, very dour, very
unfunny background. And to suddenly see this essence of maturity,
it was a very, very scary thing!" Whatever confidence Wayne had
wanted to project was gone.

Welcome to the Brain Class.

There were ten grade 9 classes in all, each designated by a letter,
9A through 9K, with no 9I because that would be too easily misread.
Each class had about thirty-five students, and most in ours were on
average a year younger than those in the rest of the grade, but at this
age some kids look ten and others look sixteen anyway, so in our class
photos that year we appear indistinguishable from those in others.
A few boys were really tall—Gord, Ken, Pat, me—and a few girls—
Barbara Vaughan-Parks, Lorna Casey (Walkling), Marilyn Steels—
and a few boys and girls were really small—Wilf Wallace, Daryl,
Judy Tibert, Peggy Clarke, Cheryl. We didn't seem much different

academically to what we were used to in our accelerated classes, at least not at first. Maybe Pat stood out a little—nobody any of us had ever known was fascinated by snakes, yet he played ball hockey too, and for some reason liked the Detroit Red Wings, so mostly he was normal. Even Marilyn Cade, who seemed to know the answer to every question in every subject, and about whom our yearbook, the *Etobian*, said that year, "And the one with the highest mark is . . . ," didn't look or sound smarter than anyone else, and there's always someone like that in every class.

As for the designation itself, the *Brain Class*, when someone called us that, most of us felt a little squirmy, and maybe more than a little bit proud. Like the TV comedian who appears embarrassed by the applause and holds up one hand to stop it, while with the other, out of camera, motions it on. And when all else failed in changing the subject from the Brain Class, we'd often say, "But what about Russell Hann?" Everyone knew how smart he was, and he wasn't in the class.

I don't remember the early weeks and months at ECI as uncomfortable, after I got over my first-day dread. We had more homework to do, but this was high school and we expected that. Wayne remembers never feeling he belonged in that class. There were just so many smart kids that there seemed no place for him. Daryl's memory is much the same, but his response was different. He recalls all these strong-minded, really bright students, especially the girls, and decided he just had to work harder. So every day after school he worked at his homework until it was done, however long that took. Lorna had grown up with two brothers who were ten and twelve years older, and now having older kids in the other classes and other grades around her, she remembers how "young" our class felt, not something she was happy about. But for most of us, our start in 9G was good days, bad days, and not many really bad ones.

Our lives were organized around school. We had to be in class before the first bell at 9; school ended after the PA announcements and bell at 3:20. In between, apart from lunch, there was a different subject, and a different teacher, in a different classroom every forty minutes. Then it was Friday, then it was Monday. We had exams at term ends in December, March, and June. Then it was summer. Then it was a new year and a new grade, but with the same classmates.

At the time, what happened one year or the next meant a lot to us. In memory, the years smudge together. We recall random, odd, sometimes weird things. Like nicknames. The initials for our principal, J.E. Durrant, spelled the nickname Jed, and ECI became Jed's Shed. The vice-principal, Mr. Evanson, was the Romper, and the Latin teacher, Mr. Miller, was Dusty, for reasons I don't remember, Mr. Miller's nickname all the better because it was our geography teacher, Mr. Rout, who called him that. Mr. Jackson, the math teacher, was Peepers and Mr. Hughes, the guidance counsellor, Porky—both for obvious reasons. Amongst ourselves we called the others by their first names—Vern, Ian, Jeannie, Doris, Harry, Wilfrid—which to us felt very subversive.

The moments we remember are random too: the day Murray played his violin in class—solo. *Anybody* playing the violin was amazing, but a *boy*, and Murray looked so stricken, as if this was show-and-tell and he was the show. And the time Mr. Hagerman threw Roger out of English class—nobody in our class ever got thrown out—and when Sandie Barnard announced to the class in her Sandie-like way that we didn't *have* to get Mr. Hagerman a Christmas gift if we didn't really like him. Or when Penni Harcourt, having fallen in love (again) with some Jewish boy she'd met, announced she was converting. Then there was Wayne's prize green leather ECI jacket with the chenille crest on it that he'd earned by winning the Etobicoke high school midget boys one-mile run (that, and by coughing up the forty bucks it cost) and how he always wore it—frigid cold or stifling hot—with the zipper undone, because he thought it made him look more manly. And the May morning when Bruce was racing to school on his bike to avoid getting a detention. He was near the school, a train had just passed, the railway gates were coming up, there was a long line of cars in both directions impatient to get going. Bruce dodged between

the cars going his way but didn't see the lead car going the other and
ended up with a broken thigh bone, tibia, and fibula and in the hospital in traction for ten weeks. Which was the last we saw of him that
year. And the time one winter when Wayne, minding his own business on his way back to school after lunch, walked over the pedes-
trian bridge that connected the park and the school, which he'd done
a thousand times, looked down and spotted, as he described it, "a tiny
mole-like animal on the ice," which, of course, he tried to catch and
which, of course, bit him, and because we had a chemistry test the
next period, led him to tell Mr. Relf, our chemistry teacher, about
it, who then, worried Wayne might have rabies, let him out of his
test to get medical treatment, which led Doug Little to accuse Wayne
of staging the whole thing to get out of the test. (Why are so many
stories about Wayne?)

And the stuff we'd say. Ken, in one of his rare heated moments:
"I'm angry, I'm not mad," a Brain Class distinction. And Bruce, at anything: "I disagree, sir." And Daryl: "It's a collection of terms, sir." And
Mary McIntyre, the year she was the UN Club's president, after every
global outrage: "Ah, racial prejudice rears its ugly head." And the way
Kathy McNab just talked. It didn't matter what she said. In the *Etobian*
one year, the blurb next to her name read: "But sir, I wasn't talking."
The next year: "When Kathy isn't talking, she's thinking of what to
say next." All this routine stuff that seemed funny to us because that
was just Bruce and Kathy and Daryl and Wayne.

Yet, oddly, it's our teachers we remember most. Mrs. Coupe,
Jeannie, had come to ECI as a first-year teacher in 1928, the year the
school opened. She had co-written our grade 12 English textbook.
In it, to introduce each poem, short story, or prose excerpt, she had
written something about the author and about the time. She knew
that every work was part of its own larger story and she needed us
to know that, to help us understand the work itself. Sometimes she
read portions of the works aloud, her hands on the podium in front
of her, and as she read, more even than acting out her stories she
became them, sometimes with tears in her eyes. Cheryl later became an

English teacher and to this day still has Mrs. Coupe's textbook, filled with Cheryl's own notations from that time.

Miss McKinnon taught us grade 9 French—talk about a thankless job. If any of us had taken French before it was an hour a week in elementary school taught by an itinerant language teacher. For Miss McKinnon, it must have been like giving first-day violin lessons, day after day. I thought of French as a game; maybe most of us did. It was funny little words and phrases. It was the *Canadiens* and *Alouettes*, *oui*, *merci*, *bonjour*, and *tout de suite* ("toot sweet"). My grandmother, with affection, I think, used to call me *mon petit crapaud*. I found out later it meant "my little toad." French, it seemed to me, was just English words translated—*crayon*, curiously, was "pencil," *bouche* was "mouth," which was fun to know because while my parents wouldn't let me say "shut up," I could say *fermez la bouche* to my heart's content. So right from our first day in class we expected Miss McKinnon to play this game called French with us. She'd say a word in English, then give us the word in French, and at dinner that night we'd dazzle our parents with our brilliance. Except she talked French. Only French. From the moment we walked in the door. She had to be able to see, in my eyes, in *our* eyes . . . nothing. I didn't understand a word. Yet she kept going, on and on, as if we understood everything. Same energy, same pleasant, expressive face. She was tireless, relentless. She never gave up. Eventually I'd hear some word in her yammering that sounded like an English word, that I understood. Then another. But together nothing made sense. Until later, a little.

And Mr. Watson in history. He was older, tall and stately looking, with a dark moustache and thick dark hair, each with the right amount of grey. He was very proper, but he had a twinkle in his voice and his eyes. Enough of a twinkle that in the midst of teaching us about kings and queens, wars and the bloodshed of Europe, he also had us read *1066 and All That*. Each day when we'd arrive in class he had written on the board a new question or proposition. Unlike in the other subjects we took, English being the other exception, opinion was allowed in history, and Mr. Watson encouraged it. Algebra, geometry, trigonometry, physics, chemistry, biology were about facts, right and wrong. Most of us were good at facts, but we hadn't had much practice at opinion, except at home, where our opinions were mostly tolerated, or at least not challenged, except with an eye roll that we didn't see. It wasn't always that way at school, with teachers or other students, and Bruce in particular had a hard time with that. He was young, even for our class. His father had held high positions in financial institutions, his mother was a force in the church, his older brother, even with a severe hearing disability, was for several years the leader of the school's UN Club. Bruce would have to find his own way at his family's dinner table, and to our well-brought-up ears, in pursuing his point he sometimes came across as a little pushy, his "I disagree, sir," too aggressive. But not to Mr. Watson's ears.

Jazz trumpeter Al Hirt was often called the "round mound of sound." To us at ECI, that was Mr. Orton, who taught English. He was very big, very loud, very bald, and very theatrical. His classroom was his stage, and all of us mere players—well, not really. But he was a character. He would do weird stuff. One morning he came into class as always with his old battered briefcase, stood in front of his desk, held his briefcase upside down over his head, his arms stretched up, all the time saying nothing. Then he opened the briefcase. As Steve Whistance-Smith recalls, "His books, pens, magazines, lunch, a whole cascade of stuff came flying out and hit his desk and went all over the floor." This wasn't performance, it was how he felt that day. And the way he talked: when Steve pushed things too far, which he often did, Mr. Orton would say, calmly, no anger, no malice, "Hey, Smith, wanna go see the boys in the office?" None of our other teachers referred to Mr. Durrant and Mr. Evanson as "the boys in the office."

Not everybody liked Mr. Orton—we weren't used to teachers having loud voices, and his could be scary. But like Mrs. Coupe, each in their own way, he brought English to life. Steve loved him. Later he majored in English and became an actor. He remembers another Orton day. "We were studying a D.H. Lawrence poem called 'The Snake,'" he says, "and he asked a question, and I put my hand up. And I stand up and start making what I consider is a marvellous explication of the poem. And he had these long arms, he was a big guy, and this one long arm comes out from his side, and his fingers stick straight out from his wrist, and his hand starts quivering, and his arm starts making an arc in the air, going up over his head, almost up to the ceiling. And I'm still talking, and I'm watching him, and when I stop talking, he says, 'As the sun slowly sets in the west.'" Steve begins to laugh. "He's just told me everything I said was complete nonsense, but I'm in tears of laughter. I was so lucky to have this guy," he says.

Mr. Thom in physics, KT we called him, was older, he parted his pitch-black hair squarely in the middle and wore a bow tie. He had the clear, uncluttered mind of a physicist. His approach as a teacher was: "This is what observation, experiment, and rigour have shown is the way things are. Learn this. It isn't rote. Know it." So his teaching notes one year were the same as his teaching notes had been five and ten years earlier. Some in our class saw this as KT being lazy. They wanted things always to be able to be different, so why not physics? Why not Mr. Thom and his notes?

He also coached the senior boys' basketball team. Basketball is messy, very unlike physics and a lot more like life. Yet, with the same quiet command that he had in the classroom, he was as good a coach as he was a teacher. ECI's biggest sports rival was Richview, the new snooty school with all the rich kids who lived in newer, bigger sprawling houses, some of them with swimming pools. Richview had taken over from ECI in football and mostly in track and field, but we still dominated them in basketball. Gord and I were on the team. And because KT was such a good coach, and because he was from the Ottawa Valley and still had a Valley accent, we'd make fun of him when he wasn't around. Just as everyone at the time who couldn't do impressions could do Ed Sullivan, we could all do KT: "Ya get the ball, and then ya bahrrull down the key, er-nelss-uh-corss yer covered, and then ya bahrrull to the outside . . ."

Mr. Relf, in chemistry. He must have still been in his twenties, light brown hair, tall, lean, upright, in profile all Adam's apple. He looked like a scientist, wore a white lab coat and talked with authority, and was at the same time both conscientious and pleasant. I think of him mostly in connection with one incident. It was a Friday, the last period of the day, we were in grade 12, it was November 22, 1963. I was sitting beside Barbara Vaughan-Parks in the back right corner of the class-room, where we shared a lab desk. The announcements came over the PA. It was 3:20. It was Mr. Evanson, who was now the principal. He told us that President Kennedy had been assassinated. The room, which had been growing louder in anticipation of the weekend, went silent. Barbara started sobbing. Each of us remembers certain moments during our five years together. This one we all remember.

The Latin teachers we had, Mr. Miller (Dusty) and Mr. McHaffie. Both were young. Mr. McHaffie in particular liked to act younger than he was. We found out somehow he had a girlfriend, a blonde, who wasn't much older than we were, and whom he later married, the whole thing as close to a scandal as our minds could manufacture about any of our teachers. He was a Scot, with a rich, learned accent, presence and flair, wavy, swept-back Hugh Grant–like hair and a slight cleft lip that gave character to his face. Sometimes he wore a kilt. In other words, we wondered why the heck he was teaching us high school Latin.

Mr. Miller, on the other hand, didn't try to be one of us, but with his quirky and funny demeanour he was kind of like us. He drove a blue Volkswagen Beetle, which was different enough at the time that some of the class decided to pool some money and buy him a big rub-ber wind-up key with a suction cup on the end of it, to stick on the back of his car where, in Latin, he had written *"cimex caerulum,"* meaning "blue bug." Mr. Miller also left ingrained in all of us a phrase we would remember for life. In a class early in the year, he wrote on the board *"semper ubi sub ubi"* and asked us to translate it. Then he watched us as we thought, consulted our textbook, *Living Latin*, mouthed the words to ourselves in English, mouthed them again, nothing register-ing, until finally we heard what we were saying: "Always where under where." A few of us laughed, then everybody. With both our own kids, and with our granddaughter, who is now taking Latin, I've done the same, telling them the Latin, watching them, watching them hearing themselves, the light finally coming on.

There is one other Latin phrase that still has meaning to me, thanks to Mr. Miller and Mr. McHaffie. When I was playing with the American Hockey League affiliate of the Canadiens, the Montreal Voyageurs, our coach was Ron Caron. Because Ron had been a teacher, *un professeur*, at a high school in Quebec, his hockey nickname was Prof. The team wasn't doing well, but we'd played three games in four nights, so after our latest loss he announced in the dressing room that the next day's practice would be optional. Then he added, "But remember, 'optional' comes from the Latin *opto optare*, meaning 'Be there!'" I've also used that on our kids and grandkids. I think it's funnier than they do.

And Mr. Smith. I never had Mr. Smith but I heard lots about him. In grade 11 we were given the option (*opto optare*) of taking German or Russian. I chose German, I don't know why. Our teacher was Mr. Steels, Marilyn's father. Mr. Smith taught Russian. Everything Russian at the time was mysterious, suspicious, subversive—maybe even *Mr. Smith*. A likely name. Where did he learn Russian? Doing what? Why? What is he doing here? And because everyone else, his fellow teachers included, thought he must be different because he had learned Russian, well, to Mr. Smith, why not *be* different? So he taught differently. Everybody in his classes loved him. In every other class, you had to raise your hand, be called upon, stand up, and ask your question. Mr. Smith thought that was a militaristic waste of time— just raise your hand and ask away. He gave all his students Russian names and titles, which they remember to this day: Daryl was Stepan Semionovich, "Head Collector of Party Propaganda (homework)." Bruce was Boris Alekseivich ("Official Party Mouthpiece"), Joan Boody was Sophia Grigorieva ("Exemplary Party Member"), Kathy Vodden was Katerina Karlovna, one of two "Chief revolutionaries and under-miners of party spirit." Mr. Smith himself was Grigori Grigorievich ("Supreme Dictator and Censor"). And when Mr. Smith called upon them in class, that's what he called them, and that's what they called him.

He started an after-school Russian Club, and many of its members were from our class. One year around Christmas, he decided to teach his class Russian carols. He also decided that if he taught them the carols, *everybody* should hear them. But the "boys in the office" didn't think that holding several school-wide assemblies to accommodate him was warranted, so if Napoleon couldn't go to Moscow, Moscow would go to Napoleon. Mr. Smith took his class out into the hall and they marched through the school singing, and they would have for longer, if, after hearing the commotion, word hadn't come down from the office that they didn't think this was a good idea either.

There were some teachers who weren't particularly memorable except for one thing (and to them we weren't always so kind). In grade 10, our music teacher had an accent, so that when he said the letter *h*, he pronounced it "etch." So the goal of every music class, for some of the boys at least, was to get him to say "etch" as often as possible. "Sir, sir, the names of the lines in the treble clef are E, G, B, D, F, right? Isn't there an H?" "No, of course not," he'd say. "There's no 'etch.'" Bingo! Or in grade 9, in industrial arts, which the boys took, our teacher taught us, among other things, to solder. Except instead of pronouncing the word as "sodder," like everyone else in Canada did, he always made a point of saying "soul-der," as if he was on a mission to educate the world that it had the letter *l* in it.

Some teachers we got to know better outside the classroom, especially those who were coaches, KT and others, who travelled with their teams to different schools, and in KT's case to Christmas basketball tournaments as well. Also teachers who were staff advisors to the various school clubs. Pat was the Science Club's president from grade 10 until the end of high school, and Mr. Walters, who taught biology, was its staff advisor. Every ECI student had to take his course, but not every student liked science, and very few loved it like Pat. There weren't many in the club. They met for an hour or so a week, watched science films, had discussions, and occasionally went with Mr. Walters on field trips to explore the creeks and riverbeds near the school. A few times, Mr. Walters took Pat to Saturday-evening talks downtown given by the Royal Society of Canada. It was Pat's introduction to the University of Toronto and to research scientists. "I didn't understand fully what research science entailed," Pat said years later, "but this was a start." Mr. Walters wasn't a warm and fuzzy guy. It wasn't until years later that Pat understood the effect Mr. Walters had on him.

Sometimes we got to know teachers in ways that had nothing to do with school. Mrs. Botterell was one of our history teachers, small, blond, very direct, and, as Cheryl remembers, wore pearls and cashmere sweaters. She was kind, though not many of us had the chance to know that about her. When Lorna was in grade 13, her father died. When she walked into his visitation at the funeral home, the first person she saw was Mrs. Botterell. They hadn't known each other in any special way. She was simply Lorna's history teacher. Ten years later, Lorna was living in Gravenhurst, about two hours north of Toronto, when her husband died. She was twenty-seven, a widow, and the mother of a five-month-old child, and she was beside herself in a hundred different ways. Who should arrive at her door but Mrs. Botterell.

Mr. Rout was crusty, snarly, and short, and far too old to have a brush cut, a white one at that. He was from Australia—the caption underneath a yearbook photo of him read, "Nobody goes anywhere until I get my boomerang back." He taught geography and coached the junior football team. He was also, as almost everyone knew, a total softy. Every Sunday afternoon he would go downtown to the pool at Beverley School and teach his son and other "mentally retarded" kids, as they were then called, to swim. One year, Joan Boody (Medina) went with them. Joan would later become a teacher. She traces her interest in special needs kids to those Sunday afternoons and Mr. Rout.

Then there was Mr. Jackson. He taught us for almost every one of our high school years, more than any other teacher, one year algebra, another geometry, another trigonometry, then algebra again. He was probably in his late forties, and he had taught my brother, which he would mention at least a few times every year. In my memory, he always wore a grey suit, the *same* grey suit, it seemed, every day. And though the suit was medium-grey, mostly it was shiny, wherever it wasn't covered in chalk dust. He was always at the board, writing equations, erasing them, writing more of them. The chalk got on his hands—his hands touched his suit. One day's chalk dust got layered onto another. He also wore thick glasses—thus his nickname, Peepers—which never seemed thick enough because he was always squinting.

There was something else curious about him. We sat in rows in his class, as we did in every class, five desks across, seven desks in each row. Some kids always liked to sit in the front row, they wanted to be immersed in the teacher and wanted the teacher immersed in them. Then there were the back-corner kids, who wanted nothing to do with a teacher or anyone else except other back-corner kids. They were the fun, occasionally annoying life of the party. Yet to be the "shit-disturbers" they wanted to be, because disruption is all about timing, they also had to listen to the front of the room, to the teacher, at least a little, to know the best time to disrupt. Someone like Roger might sit at the back, and maybe Ted and Steve, maybe Lisa or Kathy Vodden, or sometimes somebody who couldn't quite bring themselves to be the life of the party but loved having the party around them, like Ken. For those who didn't sit at the front or in the back corners but in the broad middle, which is most students in every class, they weren't much interested in the teacher or the other students, or really in being there at all. But they had to be there, so in their body posture and blank stares, they shrank into invisibility. In our Brain Class, however, our back-corner kids were less loud, our middle-of-the-class kids less disengaged, and our front-row kids, well, there just weren't enough desks to accommodate them all. As for me, I'd sit in the second row when I could, maybe a little to one side of centre, where I could take in everything and be just outside the teacher's main focus.

But in Mr. Jackson's class, we had no choice. At the start of each new term, he would rearrange our seating so that beginning with the row to his far right, the top student the previous semester would sit in the front seat, the second in the second, and so on, so the worst student was in the row farthest to his left, in the back corner. I don't remember

Mr. Jackson doing this, but Peggy Clarke does. She remembers sitting in the second row, nearer to the back, but immediately behind me, and because she was very short and I was tall, she could never see Mr. Jackson or the front board, or so she says. This seems doubtful. She was that short, and maybe I was that tall, but there's no way I got higher marks in math than Peggy. Mary McIntyre also remembers Mr. Jackson's strategy. She remembers it because she sat in the last row, not at the very back, she's quick to say, but close enough that she knew, clearly, where she stood. It was then, she says years later, after having been a teacher herself, that she began to hate math and believe she couldn't do math.

Mr. Jackson did this, he told us, so he could pick out at a glance those who needed help, which made sense to him, and maybe even to us—then. In any event, whatever his sometimes curious ways, when the subject of special teachers comes up among our class, Mr. Jackson is the one most often mentioned.

He clearly cared—about algebra and geometry, sure, but mostly about us *individually*. This was shown not in any pat-on-the-back or showy way—it would be hard to imagine him doing anything showy—but instead by being always attentive, always knowing you were there, always noticing when you weren't and wondering how you were when you came back. Always knowing how you did on the last test, and whether it was better or worse than the ones before, and always having in mind how you were doing against a standard he had in his head of how you should do. He was that way for each of us. He would be the easiest teacher in the world to make fun of—his suits, the chalk, the way he squinted, the way when he talked to you one-on-one, his body angled away, his eyes only occasionally willing to glance back at you. Teachers can never know the impact they have because when they teach you it's too soon to know, and when we know ourselves years later, we don't go back and tell them. Teaching is that act of faith. You do it right, and somehow, somewhere, with someone, you have to believe good things will happen, though as a teacher you'll never really know. Maybe, just maybe, there should be a rule that after we've left our adolescent and young adult years behind, when we reach our middle years and finally know for sure, that we have to go back and find that teacher that meant so much to us and tell her or him so.

The fact is, with teachers and other adults, most of us in the class weren't good at trouble. We didn't know how to do it, we hadn't had much practice at it, we couldn't pull it off. Mostly, we couldn't deal with the consequences of it. And we didn't like how it made us feel. In grade 8 at Humber Valley, there was a kid I didn't like much, and we got into a fight on the playground. Nothing serious. I wrestled him to the ground, got his arms over his head, held his wrists, and put my knees on his upper arms and pinned him. The next day over the PA system, "Would Ken Dryden please come to the office?" Our principal, Mr. Davy, asked me to sit down. He was about six four and looked twice that tall. He said, "Ken, I'm disappointed in you." I didn't hear anything else. At ECI, almost none of us got detentions for some behavioural lapse or another. The fact that we remember Roger being thrown out of class six decades later speaks for itself. For us, trouble mostly wasn't worth the trouble. Our parents, teachers, and coaches mostly liked us, rewarded us, greeted us with smiles and approval. We had a stake in doing right. We didn't want to let them down.

Several years ago, I watched a profile of former Duke University basketball coach Mike Krzyzewski on *60 Minutes*. It focused mainly on the question of how someone who didn't scream at his players or throw tantrums or chairs could win so often as a coach. The interviewer asked the question of Krzyzewski's wife. She seemed surprised that he even asked. His players play the way they do, and win, she said, because if they didn't, they know they would break his heart. I think for most of us in our class, with the adults in our life, it was the same.

CHAPTER NINE

This was a good time for teachers to be teachers. Our parents believed that better was possible, and the most certain way to be better was through education. They had a huge stake in our schools and in our teachers. These teachers were "educated"—a word our parents said almost with reverence. They had graduated from high school and gone to teachers' college, most to university, and were far better educated than our parents were, and our parents respected that. And now in those postwar years with more kids being born and more staying in school longer, and many more having the ambition and opportunity to go to university, teachers were becoming more important still. Better teachers were capable of helping our kids, our families, our communities, our country, our world to achieve these possibilities and aspirations.

The township of Etobicoke, as it was called then, had been this little place next to Toronto forever. In 1941, its population was just nineteen thousand, and it had only one high school, ECI, which had opened in 1928. Then its population tripled in only ten years and a second high school, New Toronto, opened. The township was having to play catch-up. In 1953 came Royal York Collegiate Institute, then Alderwood in 1955, Burnhamthorpe 1956, Thistletown 1957, Richview 1958, Kipling 1960, the year we started at ECI, then Vincent Massey 1961, North Albion 1962, Scarlett Heights and Kingsmill 1963,

Silverthorn 1964. Eleven new high schools in fourteen years—all this before we had graduated. Etobicoke needed teachers and lots of them. But so did Scarborough and North York, two other big, fast-growing Toronto suburbs, and so did lots of cities and towns in other parts of the province. Ralph Prentice, who as a young teacher had come to one of these new schools, Alderwood, in 1961, and later became a principal and superintendent in Etobicoke, recalls that every spring the *Globe and Mail* ran twenty pages of want ads (remember them?) from school boards all over Ontario looking for teachers. Prentice taught high school business. In his graduating class from teachers' college, there were thirteen business specialists like him; in Ontario's high schools, more than two hundred business-teaching positions were available. Teachers were in the driver's seat.

So why choose one school board and not another? Etobicoke was new, unknown to most, and though not exactly in the sticks it was *out there* somewhere, and not a leading choice for many. But Etobicoke needed teachers, so it was going to hire teachers. The question was whom? How could Etobicoke avoid being every teacher's, every highly qualified teacher's, last choice?

Members of Etobicoke's school board thought that if they played by the old rules they were just going to lose, so why not do new things? They couldn't change the rules themselves, of course, they could only pay what the province said they could pay—teacher to teacher, apple to apple—but what if they created a new kind of apple? There were already department heads in Ontario schools who were paid more. What if Etobicoke created a new category between teacher and department head for those with special qualifications who, these schools could see, were on the path to a headship, call them "master teachers," pay them a little more, and by doing so also demonstrate to them that with this special designation there was the very real prospect of advancement in the future? That's what Etobicoke did, and that's why Ralph Prentice and many of our younger teachers at ECI decided to come to Etobicoke. It was the only school board in the province that did this, Prentice recalls. He always wondered why.

The rest of the story, about us and our high school class, didn't just follow, it wasn't as easy as that, but it was this decision that gave the rest a chance to happen.

Part of what followed had to do with what is now called "giftedness." Because now that you have kids staying in school longer, growing up in better, more enriched circumstances, and have something special about them, what do you do with them? Kids who, when faced with challenges and opportunities, have shown they can handle more and thrive with more? Most of these kids would never work on a farm or in a factory, but would have more undefined futures ahead. Shouldn't there be something different for them? But then what about the rest? If a few get more, do the rest get less—less access to good teachers, to good schools, and if that's the case, with what results, for them, and for all of us? After all, isn't this a "raise *all* ships" time?

Prentice remembers the exhausting debates at school board meetings, debates that never really did end because the question of giftedness never became less important or easier to answer. Many different approaches made sense; many of them, once implemented, didn't work. Underlying every one of these approaches was an understanding: if a kid can do more, let them. One-room schoolhouses of the past had accommodated kids of all ages. The younger ones couldn't not hear what the older ones were learning, so if they could learn what the older kids did too, why hold them back? Sports leagues in most parts of the country were organized in two-year age categories—peewee, bantam, midget—so first-year kids played with older kids. And if they were good enough, why not? That's what my father always believed. That's why I played on hockey teams with kids two years older. It meant you had to learn the skills to do that, but it was a personal test as well. You had to be able to deal with getting thrown into the deep end and not drown, and if you weren't able to swim, at least to be able to tread water until you could. Sports and education were to build character, weren't they, so why not?

There wasn't much thought given to social development at the time. The debate over being with peers had to do more with being with your skill peers, not your chronological peers. So if you weren't as emotionally developed, or as able to deal with new people and new situations, suck it up. Learn. Educators didn't pay much attention to the potential consequences of doing this, to social learning—how bad experiences might lead to kids wanting to avoid new experiences, or new people in the future. How not learning certain things or developing in certain ways might colour the way you live for the rest of your life. Educators think about that a lot more now. When my brother, Dave, who is six years older, was identified as having certain special abilities and Lambton-Kingsway School wanted to reward him, it did what seemed like a good idea at the time. It allowed him to skip a grade entirely, to go from grade 5 one June to grade 7 the next September, along with two other students, putting the three of them into a class of thirty other kids all of whom had done their full grade 6 learning, and with a teacher who was responsible for all thirty-three of them but whose main focus had to be on the thirty who were at grade 7 level and not on the three who were trying to catch up. It was a disaster. My brother never felt the same about school or himself until he got to university.

By the time my classmates and I came along a few years later, Lambton-Kingsway and other Etobicoke elementary and middle schools had learned to take a different approach. It was called "acceleration." As Mr. Kidd, the principal at Islington, told Marilyn Cade's parents when Marilyn was selected for the program, it would be one that "suits the way Marilyn learns things." All thirty-five or so students would move through three years of curriculum, usually grades 4, 5, and 6, in two years, slowly, gradually, and together. That was our "gifted" experience in elementary school, and we could do it, as it turned out, and because we could, why not others? It was only in high school, when growth spurts happened and bodies began to mature, that social learning, not just academic learning, came increasingly to matter.

This was also a good time for teachers because they were paid enough to live the life they wanted to live. They weren't looking to be rich; rich wasn't in their minds. A good, solid, stable existence in the suburbs, a life they saw on their TV screens and in magazines, a life the parents of the kids they taught lived and aspired to, that was enough. A life that had purpose, that was respected, and had all the possibilities of better. A life they believed in.

Teachers of all kinds were prized at the time. Teachers who we called "coaches," or "leaders" of Brownie and Cub packs, teachers who were role models in sports and entertainment, politics and business. Teaching was about passing on knowledge, ways of behaving, ways of being, it was about others, and the future. Schoolteachers were sometimes our neighbours. Mr. Thom lived near Daryl, Ken, Diana, and Craig, Mr. Steels's house was almost next door to Judy Tibert's. Mr. Durrant, the principal, lived in the Kingsway, not far from about half our class. Pat recalls a routine he and Wilf had before school. "I'd go to Wilf's house and through a window at the back of his living room, we could see Mr. Durrant's garage, so we could see when he'd go out to start his car for the morning. And we'd get on our coats and start walking, and he'd invariably pick us up."

Teachers had the whole summer to themselves, and could afford the same rudimentary cottages our parents could afford, and be there more often than our fathers could. Their kids could live the life we lived. Women teachers, before they were married, could earn a solid income, and a good supplemental one if they came back to work after their kids were old enough. This at a time when not many families had more than one income. And because so few good jobs were available to women in other fields, the best and brightest of generations of women were there in our classrooms, and not being paid fortunes to teach us. It was the great societal bargain of the age, for Canada, Toronto, Etobicoke, our parents, us, and the future. But because women were seen by decision makers and commentators of the time—men—as natural carers and nurturers, this contribution wasn't much noticed or appreciated.

But as much as we remember our teachers, we remember more the struggles and feelings we had about fitting in—or trying to fit in.

We were thirteen years old when we arrived at this imposing place. Barely teenagers. "Who *am* I? What can I do? What am I good it? And what am I good at in *this* class, in *this* school?" We needed to know. Maybe you were the funny one in your old class, and everyone knew that. That's how you fitted in. Are you still the funny one here? The smart one? The one who knows everything there is to know about sports, or Elvis, or George Bernard Shaw? Or is there someone funnier or smarter? And if there is, how else do you fit in? And how do you *want* to fit in? Not many kids in this new class know you, and none of your teachers do, unless they taught an older brother or sister and think they do. You know you're growing, you think you're smarter, now you can be other, different things if you want to.

There are school teams now to try out for. For the boys that first fall there's the junior football team. Not many kids had played much football before, and wearing the garnet, green, and gold jersey of the ECI Golden Gophers would be a way to prove yourself, to you and everyone else. And football was a big deal at ECI. Once or twice each season the school let out at noon so everyone could travel to another school and watch our junior and senior teams play. Maybe to watch you.

There were also clubs you could join—science, photography, French, the UN. Choirs and bands. The school play—auditions started in the fall. Imagine standing up on that stage, singing in a way you've never heard yourself sing before, acting, really *acting*, all those eyes on you, a new you, the one that's inside you. How scary, how exciting. Just having the *feeling* of joining something, of being part of the wider school, not just the Brain Class. Being with kids from other classes, in other grades, who are older, who have interests more like your own. The chance to fit in with them, with the you that you might also be.

So Gord went out for football, and later in the year for basketball and track and field; Barbara, Margaret, Mary, Judy Tibert, and Peggy Clarke were in the junior girls' choir; Bruce and Peggy Sibbald in the UN Club; Penni in the school play; Judy Clarke and Cheryl in the

Drama Club, which, among other things, provided backstage support for the play. As younger kids, in Guides and Scouts, on teams, they had been encouraged, sometimes pushed, by their parents. Now in high school, these were their choices. Our choices.

Fitting in also had to do with *how* you wanted to fit in. To fit in to be noticed—to sit in the front row, your hand up all the time, helping out all the time, your eyes always making contact with teachers', with classmates', eager and always engaged. Or to fit in just enough so as *not* to be noticed—your hand up occasionally, helping out when asked, mostly attentive, sitting anywhere *but* the front row—like most of us. For some it meant to fit in but on your own terms. To keep a little of yourself, and what you think you might be and want to be, for yourself. Like Lisa, Pat, Penni, and Roger. Roger was a back-corner kid, funny, a bit of a smartass, and enough of a rebel that in a very non-rebel class like ours he came across as one. A few others seemed not to want to fit in at all—Kathy Vodden, Ted and Steve. Instead to fit into some image they had of themselves, maybe even wanting to be different more than they wanted to be anything in particular.

I wanted to fit in enough so that I didn't need to worry about not fitting in, so I had the freedom to be whatever else I wanted to be. I didn't know how others saw me. I never asked, and I didn't really want to know. I saw myself as someone good at doing *things*, especially sports, good at being around older kids because I liked to do what they were doing, and I was good at trying, and games made you try, and I wanted to be with these kids and that's why they'd let me. Outside of school, they also let me be with them because all the ball hockey games in our neighbourhood were played in our backyard, and my brother was the best player, so they couldn't tell me I couldn't play, which didn't occur to me at the time. I just thought I was good enough.

But as adventurous as I was at doing things, I wasn't adventurous with people. I didn't have long heart-to-heart talks with friends, I wasn't sure enough of myself to have them. I wasn't quite able to say what I'd have to say with older kids because I didn't know enough, and I didn't quite know what to say with younger kids because I didn't feel like one. I didn't go to Cubs or Scouts like the other boys did. I didn't go on sleepovers. I only went to camp one year, and that was a mess. At the big games day at the end of camp, I won most of the on-land competitions, but on water I was hopeless, and I wasn't used to being hopeless. We didn't have a cottage, we didn't go camping, I passed all my Red Cross swimming tests but I wasn't a good swimmer. I'm still not.

The disaster of the camp, and the main reason I didn't go on sleepovers, was that I was a bedwetter. I turned ten that summer at camp and I was still wetting the bed every night. As campers, we were housed in large canvas tents set on high wooden platforms, about ten of us in each one—and my fellow campers were . . . umm . . . a bit taken aback. It took a few mornings for them to notice. I don't know when I did stop bedwetting, but it wasn't much before high school.

In the end, I didn't spend much time just being with other kids, doing whatever, talking about whatever. I was busy. And I was good enough in school and in other things that I didn't need to be good in easy, breezy ways. But in high school, especially with girls, I did.

For most of us, as hard as it was to fit in academically, fitting in socially was harder by far. I was used to being around boys. Girls to me had just always been other kids, only a little different, until in high school they became GIRLS. And I had no idea what to do. I knew I was definitely not cool. At ECI, if you were cool and a boy you were called a duke, and I was so much not a duke that a friend of mine used to call me Duker. He still does. I knew that at least in terms of girls, I had to do better. I knew I had to try. I knew I had to learn to dance. I knew I had to be nice and polite to them, and in ways different than I was used to being nice and polite. Lorna and I were in the same class at Humber Valley. She had two much older brothers who were outstanding athletes. She was tall and big, and apparently I used to call her Moose. I thought I was being friendly and nice. This was now high school. I now had to remember to hold the door for girls, to talk to them about things other than last night's game, and say kind words to them. The rest I didn't know, and knew I'd have to learn at some point, but I would put that off as long as I could.

In that regard, the Brain Class was perfect for me. I could be around girls without ever really being with them, and feel like I was with them. I could get to know them without ever having to talk with them, by just listening to what they said and watching what they did in class. I could get to know what they were thinking without ever asking. I could come to grow comfortable around them and not have to do anything other than what I was already doing. And if being in that class meant I was around kids who were younger, well, except for a few, we were *all* younger, so I didn't feel younger. Two other important things in those years made me, and other boys, at least a little less uncomfortable: our class parties, and ECI's annual Sadie Hawkins Dance.

Class parties were genius. We probably had one each semester, though most of us now think we must have had more. They would be at somebody's house—not everybody had a finished basement or parents who were willing to host, but there were enough who did and were. The word would go out—"In two weeks at my place"— and they were always on a Friday. The host supplied potato chips and dip—dip was important, onion was the best—and a variety of pop. We all chipped in for the important stuff: donuts and pizza. A long time before there was Tim Hortons and a donut shop on every corner, there was Freddy's, on Dundas West not far from Cheryl's house. Its donuts were chocolate-covered pillows, doughy and squishy and fantastic. Wayne worked there later in high school, part-time, and never told us, and never shared. For pizza, there was only Vesuvio's. It was in a rundown area somewhere in the middle of the city near where many of our parents had grown up, and for class parties the host-parent would drive there to get some. I don't think many of us had had pizza before (I certainly never had), and it was becoming a sensation. Like burgers and fried chicken, pizza was something we were actually supposed to eat with our hands.

In the basement, there'd be a record player. Some kids would bring their favourite LPs to play and others their new 45s, hits from that week's "CHUM Chart," from Toronto's biggest rock station. And then the dance before the dance: girls on one side of the room, boys on the other. Who would make the first move, which boy to which girl? It was torture. And if he went where we didn't think he'd go, it was chaos. Our minds needing to recalibrate. Even when the dancing did begin, the dance didn't end: Is this a one-off dance or a dance-to-see-how-it-goes dance? A fast dance because I'm a good fast dancer or a slow dance because I might be more? And after that slow dance, do we just kind of stay around together and if the next song starts up quickly enough, then, oh well, let's just keep dancing? Or will it be an "Oh, I'm so hot. I think I'll go get a Coke"? Here, in this basement, in a social setting, the boys could be "sociable" without needing to be "social." We could hold a girl's hand and put our arms around her, and that would be acceptable, even encouraged, because it was dancing.

I loved class parties. As far as I was concerned, we couldn't have enough of them. There's a picture from one of our parties where Ken, who was not a small guy and was more awkward than I was, is being held up in the air in a chair somehow by Judy Tibert, Cheryl, and Joan Boody, the three of them laughing uproariously, Ken with a grin on his face. Later, seeing that photo, one of the women from the class commented that Ken must have been shocked to be "attacked" that way. Ken would have loved it.

For most of us, class parties were really important, until at least grade 11. Then the crunch. Because asking a girl to dance in a classmate's basement is altogether different from having to get on a phone and ask a girl *to* a dance. In one case, she can hardly say no—it's just one dance, after all. In the other, it's a whole evening's commitment and she could say no, crushingly so. That's where the Sadie Hawkins Dance came in. Thankfully, most high school administrators were men with long memories.

For the Sadie Hawkins—only once a year, unfortunately—the girls asked the boys. So I, we, waited and hoped. Someone, almost anyone, call. Please. For us boys, the Sadie Hawkins was our social report card. Being asked to the Sadie Hawkins meant that at least one girl knew you existed, thought of you in *another* way at least a little, and maybe might be just a little interested in you. The Sadie Hawkins took so many pressures off, *if* you were asked. If you were asked by sort of the right girl. Because then, after the night was over, if it hadn't been a complete mess, you had the right to talk to her again, even as early as the following Monday morning, and depending on how that went, maybe you'd even be willing to risk everything and ask *her* out on an actual date. At one year's Sadie Hawkins, Judy Tibert asked Doug, in other years she asked Wayne, Wayne was asked by Mary, Marilyn Cade asked me. If Labour Day was my least favourite time of the year, the Sadie Hawkins may have been my favourite.

Fitting in would get a lot more complicated in later grades. A friend, the same one who called me Duker, had a crush on a girl who was way, way out of his league. That didn't mean he couldn't dream, of course, yet to actually find a way to be with her was a problem. But he knew what time she left school at the end of the day, so he left then too, and he knew the route she took home, which was sort of his route too. So as she was walking north on Islington Avenue, he was walking north on Chestnut Hills Parkway, one street east, and for a stretch of about a hundred metres there was a park between Islington and Chestnut Hills—open space, no houses—and he could see her. So each day, he would walk with her, in stride, step by step. "'Oh, Patti, sweet Patti,'" I used to mock him, "'there's nothing between us . . . except grass and pavement and weeds. Oh, Patti.'"

Ahead for him, for us, was *actually* going out (not with Patti), then maybe going steady, then breaking up, and lots in between. The class for me, for a lot of us, I think, was a way of easing my way into, getting myself through, a very awkward time.

CHAPTER TEN

Things also began to change in the class itself. Lorna went into a different class after grade 9; she wanted to be with the older kids. A year later, Ted and Steve left too. They each had felt a little separate from the class when they were in it, but now, hanging around the same hallways, involved in many of the same activities, it seemed like they had never left. Joan Boody joined the class from Burnhamthorpe CI and moved into the house my soon-to-be sister-in-law, Sandra, had lived in. Joan was the oldest of seven kids. Though Burnhamthorpe was only next door to ECI, the Kingsway was considered a move up, something that worried Joan's mother. Before Joan's first day at ECI, her mother cautioned her that she would now be going to school with girls who wore cashmere sweaters, and that she wasn't going to have things like this, and that she couldn't feel any less of a person because of that. Joan arrived and saw no cashmere sweaters (except on Mrs. Botterell). After grade 10, Kathy McNab's family also moved away to a newer, bigger house not far from Richview. Wilf's family bought a farm in Mono Mills, about an hour north of the city, as a summer and weekend escape, but soon it became their permanent home. One of the other Joans, Wayne's vision and reality check, also moved away after grade 10 and no one heard from her again. It wasn't that she was unfriendly or unlikeable, but she had been so beyond us, the girls as well as the boys, that she really didn't know anybody in the class, and when she left no one kept in touch with her. She is the only one from the class I haven't been able to find.

Through our pre-ECI years, we had been what we'd always been, what our parents and teachers expected, what we thought we should be, but now we were growing up and spreading our wings. Until high school, none of us had ever been in a band or in a real play. None of us had ever taken algebra or dissected a frog. We'd never had an English teacher quite like Mrs. Coupe or an art teacher like Mrs. Alexander. We'd never had so many choices of our own, or been around so many others who had so many choices of their own. The boys, now beginning to shave, the girls to wear bras and girdles (whether any of us needed to or not), we were becoming something else.

Fewer of us were in the French Club, more in the Science Film Group and the UN Club. Only Penni was in the school play. Many of the girls were still in the girls' choir, some were on the GAA, the Girls Athletic Association, a few on school teams. Doug Little was on the United Way Campaign committee that raised $2,100 from raking leaves, washing cars, and anything else they could think to do, more than any other school in Canada, we were told. Wayne was our class rep on student council. The student council president was a boy, the vice-president a girl, the treasurer a boy, the secretary a girl. Every year. We were developing our *own* interests, making friends in other classes, getting busier. We had more homework. Our social life, never as fabulous as we dreamed, was slightly more than we feared.

In the classroom itself, we didn't change much, or didn't think we did, or our teachers or classmates didn't think we did. Our own expectations of ourselves and those of others had become largely settled. Those students at the top of the class remained largely at the top, those at the bottom stayed at the bottom, and the great majority of us were still somewhere in the vast middle, a bit higher or lower depending on the subject and on whether we aced or blew the last exam. Wayne had his downs and ups, the downs he anticipated, the ups were enough of a surprise to him that he didn't quite let himself notice them. Except, he did have one big down. One afternoon there was a crashing noise from the back of the room. We turned around and there was Wayne on the floor, spasming, vibrating, his eyes halfway up into his head. I'm sure the teacher must have sent somebody to the office for help; we could only watch, or not watch. We were scared. He was so exposed. Later, he told me it had happened to him one other time, in church. Eventually, his episode was diagnosed not as an epileptic seizure as we'd all assumed, but some much less serious condition. Yet to Wayne the greater damage had been done. He felt humiliated. Somehow things just seemed to happen to him, he thought.

But that same year he also discovered a very big up. He started running. For me, the worst single day of the phys ed year was when we had to run the cross-country course. It was probably not much more than a mile, around the track, then across the bridge over the creek, around the ball diamonds and through Central Park, but it felt like twenty. And in the fall, on cross-country day, it was always raining. Canadians and Americans didn't run distances then, East Africans and Europeans did. We ran to chase a ball or to rush to an end zone, something that had a purpose other than running in itself, or for a finish line but only if it was a hundred yards or so away. But for phys ed, all of us had to run, and finish, the cross-country course. It was agony.

Except it wasn't for Wayne. He ran, thought his thoughts, and kept on running. He wasn't fast, he was steady, but because none of the so-called athletes, the hockey and football players, wanted to run cross-country, he made the team. He ran races we never saw because they were in the city at High Park or in some conservation area miles beyond the suburbs. He won the TDIAA cross-country championship—the TDIAA, which included all of Toronto's suburban schools, was the largest high school sports district in Ontario—then the following spring in the school's track and field meet, when his classmates had a chance to jam the bleachers and cheer, he ran four times around the track in front of them and won the mile race. He did the same at the TDIAAs, and at OFSAA, the all-Ontario championship, and got his green leather jacket.

Other pieces in his life also began to fit together. He'd had a paper route as a kid, and when the other kids thought themselves too old and stopped doing theirs, he continued on, and made some more money, and made some more at his part-time job at Freddy's. Then, on October 8, 1962, he turned sixteen and did what every boy did when he turned sixteen—he got his sixty-day temporary driver's permit, and sixty days later took his test and got his licence to freedom. With the money he'd earned and saved, he bought his own car, a white Mini Cooper, which he drove into the ground, then with the money he still had left he bought a navy blue Volkswagen, like Mr. Miller's. He lived only a seven-minute walk—or four-minute run—from school, yet every day he drove. A car meant every possibility, and everybody, especially every girl, needed to know he had one. *Where have you gone, Joan?*

By the end of grade 12, we had been around each other more than two hundred days a year. We knew pretty much all there was to know about each other, or thought we did. Yet in a group of thirty-five, some people you spend time with and others you don't, and often for no particular reason. Margaret Silvester seemed very nice. She had the same sweet, timeless face as my mother, yet I don't think I ever talked with her for more than a few seconds at a time. It was the same with Judy Clarke, and Mary McIntyre, who seemed quiet and shy but who always laughed when things were funny, and when Mary was with the other girls and said something, they'd always laugh too. I didn't talk to Craig much, or to Marilyn Steels, though Marilyn and I had been in the same class at Humber Valley, or to Barbara until we became lab partners. Really, most of us were a little shy and awkward, and if there wasn't good reason to say something, we didn't.

There were also some I had no idea how to talk with. Diana, the way she spoke, slow and drawn out, as if she was thinking her way to things that were deeper than I'd ever know. Most of us knew answers to the questions we were asked, but needed our teachers to confirm what we knew. Not Diana. There was a knowingness in her—it didn't matter about what—*duh*, she already knew. Even those times I was sure I was right and she was wrong, I knew I must be wrong. What would

I ever say to her? Or to Peggy Sibbald. Her mind and tongue were so quick and certain of themselves that whatever I'd say she'd probably thought about it last week. And Kathy Vodden, who seemed always to be lying "in the weeds," watching, noticing everything, some private dialogue going on in her head. She certainly didn't need to know what was going on in mine. And Penni scared me. She was a year older and had matured early, and had the power and presence of the actress she was in every setting she inhabited. In *The Pajama Game* she played Mae, a feisty, boisterous, loud-mouthed character who, like Penni herself, was a force. I knew that Penni knew things I didn't know, and I knew she could cut me off at the knees any time she wanted. She never did, and was probably nice too, but I didn't want to risk finding out. And why would Kathy, Penni, or any of the others have reason to speak with me anyway?

A few others I thought I knew but I didn't. I thought I knew Lisa. I thought she was, as our grade 9 *Etobian* described her, "Five feet of heaven minus a ponytail." She had honey-blond hair, and giggled when she laughed but wasn't giggly. She smiled most of the time, but wasn't smiley; she was shy, but she wasn't coy. She was so cute she couldn't be anything *but* cute. So cute that I thought she couldn't be smart, and couldn't be serious. I was wrong.

She called her mother Adèle. Not the same way I called my mother Margaret, very rarely, and only when no one else was around. Lisa introduced her mother to her friends as Adèle. When Steve Whistance-Smith dropped by their house, which he did often through high school, it was to see Lisa *and* Adèle. "My friends were all very impressed with Adèle," Lisa remembers. She was Adèle with an accent, though she wasn't French or French Canadian. She was from Toronto, and her maiden name was Stillwaugh. She had gone to high school but no further, and while she loved to learn, university was never a big deal to her. She didn't talk about the value of university with Lisa or her siblings. When Lisa later became the first in her family to go to university, it wasn't the result of any family aspiration or dream. Adèle talked more often about IQ instead, the capacity to learn, and how important it was to realize all that was in us, not just through school but in everything we did. That Lisa was in the Brain Class mattered to Adèle because it would give Lisa the chance to be around lots of smart kids, to stretch herself.

Lisa's father, George—she called him that, though he didn't much like it—was also smart but not very curious, Lisa recalls. He had been a high school football star in Winnipeg, and as the family story goes, never got over being a football star. He had a good job in Toronto as the manager of a Household Finance office, but he was a weekend drinker, something that Lisa began to notice a year or two before high school. And while George was around in her life, he wasn't very present. Not like Adèle.

Adèle had grown up in a boarding house in Rosedale, an area of Toronto of old mansions and big trees not far from downtown, where the city's early generations of rich had lived. But by the 1920s some of these mansions had been converted, officially or otherwise, into rooming houses. My mother and grandmother lived in one of them after my grandfather died in 1920 in the flu pandemic. Adèle and her mother, Phyllis (Phyllis was divorced, something not common at the time), and Adèle's aunt Dot owned a series of mansions all over Rosedale, and moved from one to the next every few years, always with their big grand piano and their cats. They kept a basement unit for themselves and rented out the rest. Legally, these weren't rooming houses, and when building inspectors arrived Phyllis always had a hard time explaining that the five young guys the inspectors could see popping in and out, who looked about as much like brothers as Laurel and Hardy, really were her nephews. Phyllis had dyed red hair and liked to wear a cape and green stockings, Lisa recalls, and as the family story goes, she'd once dated Cab Calloway. Lisa has a photo of them sitting together in a nightclub.*

---

* Lisa's mother had a story of her own that she liked to tell. She loved backgammon. Once she played in a tournament in the Thousand Islands with "Barry Freed," FBI fugitive, and Yippies co-founder, Abbie Hoffman.

And every Christmas when you went to Phyllis's for dinner, Lisa says, there'd be twenty people around the table, multiple bottles of wine, and the meal would go on for five or six hours. It was great, she remembers.

Toronto was a very provincial place in the 1920s. Explosive immigration early in the century brought people from many different parts of the world to the city, but they didn't mix much with long-standing Torontonians. Their own histories, religions, jobs, and classes kept them apart. But the new evolving Toronto did come together and did mix in rooming houses. All kinds of people in the middle of all kinds of transitions—economic, family, age, lifestyle—lived in them. In Phyllis's rooming houses there were alcoholics, intellectuals, homosexuals, eastern and southern Europeans, western and eastern Canadians, some of them on their way up, some on their way down, some it was hard to know. This was Lisa's mother's childhood. By the time she arrived in Etobicoke in the 1950s, she had experienced many lives. Adèle was, with others at least, very tolerant.

She read Camus. Lisa thinks she had seen one of his books on a library bookshelf and picked it up. Adèle didn't know who Camus was. Even years later when she spoke of him, she always said "Ca-miss," not "Ca-moo." She had never heard anyone say his name. She just found what he wrote interesting. My mother never read Camus, neither did any other mother or father I knew. Adèle also read Nietzsche and Ginsberg. She went to foreign films. She liked Bergman and Fellini. Their movies were never on at the Kingsway Theatre. Penni's father never ran them on his projector at the Westwood. And when Adèle went downtown to see them, she often took Lisa. The movies were usually restricted. Lisa wasn't sixteen and looked twelve, so Adèle would dress her up in a trench coat to get her in. The rest of our parents wanted us *not* to look as old as we did, *not* to go to restricted movies.

Adèle was, by chronology and temperament, a beatnik not a flower child. She was also an atheist—no one else's parents I knew were. She didn't go to dentists or believe in chiropractors, and she wore black tights. She didn't watch *Dobie Gillis* on TV because the show's resident beatnik, Maynard G. Krebs, with all his "far outs," was sappy. Adèle was serious. She believed in ideas. Life was hard, it had an edge to it, she had seen that in her own mother's boarding houses. She smoked five or six cigarettes a day but no more. Drank wine, but not too much. She wanted to experience everything, but everything had to be in moderation, so she could deal with the next thing that came at her.

"I just thought everything she thought was correct," Lisa said later. "If there was any opinion to be offered, Adèle, to me, would be on the right side of it. I always thought she was the smartest person on the planet until I went to university. She could talk about anything. And until I was fifty, I thought smart was the most important thing. Then I realized it was being kind. I think I looked for that in men too, smart rather than kind."

When Adèle died, Lisa wrote her obituary. It begins, "Formidable matriarch and citizen of the world," and ends, "Alas and farewell, Adèle." She was ninety-two.

I didn't know this Lisa. I didn't know that in elementary school she had tried out being a goody-goody, as she puts it, but didn't find that interesting, and came to reject anyone who thought they were, who insisted they knew what was right and what wasn't for everyone. Almost always these were girls, and to them, she remembers, she wasn't very nice. I also didn't know that in high school, while all of us called her Lisa, she pronounced her name "Leeza." She never changed the spelling, just the sound. Why? "Lisa" was goody-goody enough, she explains. "Lisa" and "Sweeting" together made your teeth hurt.

Lots of other important things happened in our lives during high school that I didn't know about at the time. Maybe no one talked about them, or maybe in focusing so hard to make sense of my own life I didn't notice. In our grade 9 year, Penni's father died. He was much older than everyone else's father, older even than most of our grandparents, already sixty when Penni was born in 1946. Penni's mother was twenty-two at the time. A year after he died, her mother remarried, and a year after that, in 1963, Penni's half-sister was born—Penni

was seventeen—all the time that Penni was rehearsing and performing, and getting bigger and bigger roles, in *The Pajama Game* and
Caught in the Act. I didn't know that Daryl's father had lost his career
as an engineer when the Avro Arrow was taken from him, and that his
mother had to recreate herself as a cashier, then as a teacher. Or that
Margaret Silvester was at that very same time deciding that her church
would be her mother's church, the Christian Science church, rather
than her father's, the United Church, which she had attended until
then, a decision that would change her life.

I didn't know that Judy Clarke's father was in the early stages of a
lockout that would turn into much more. In Crawley, England, south
of London, he had been raised by a foster mother until, at fourteen,
just after the First World War, he came to Canada by himself and
began working at the *Toronto Star* as an apprentice linotype operator.
He had been there when Hemingway was filing stories for the *Star*
from Paris, and he may have set some of them himself. He was at the
Star through the twenties, through the Depression and the war years
and the boom years that followed. He had survived a hard childhood
in a class-ridden country, married, had two daughters, the younger of
whom, Judy, had been chosen for the accelerated class at Lambton-
Kingsway and the Brain Class at ECI. He had been able to provide for
his family a modest new house on the periphery of Kingsway Park. Yet
in his own mind, he remained a blue-collar guy with little education
surrounded by his betters as he had been all his life. He was a member of the Toronto Typographical Union, the oldest union in Canada.
In July 1964, after Judy had finished grade 12, without a contract for
more than a year and after months of negotiations, the *Star* locked out
more than one thousand workers. At the heart of the dispute was the
use of new printing processes that would allow the *Star* to do faster
and cheaper what Judy's father did. The lockout dragged on through
Judy's grade 13 year, then through university, her father receiving his
strike pay, until finally, in 1971, *seven* years after the lockout began, the
union announced that all benefits would cease. The union had been
broken. Judy's father was sixty-six years old. I had known about the

Star strike at the time, but I had no idea that Judy's father as a linotype operator, or Peggy Clarke's as a lawyer, worked there.

I didn't know much about Cheryl either. She was this bright-eyed, big-toothed sprite who was everywhere, all the time, doing every-thing. Not as much in grade 9, after she had come down with mono-nucleosis the previous spring and had spent the summer in bed. Her white blood count had been so low that her parents were afraid she had leukemia. Even after a few weeks, when it seemed she should be better, something wasn't right. Her sparkle was missing. When school began in the fall, her parents insisted that she come home right after classes each day to keep up her energy. She did manage to join the Drama Club, but it was in grade 10 that she really began to take off. In the years that followed she was in the French Club, the girls' choir, and the UN Club, she was on the junior and intermediate intramural girls' baseball champions, on student council, the GAA, the School Spirit Committee, she sang and danced in *Best Foot Forward*, she was the Posture Queen, and in grade 13 a cheerleader.

She loved languages especially. She thought of Miss McKinnon, our grade 9 French teacher, her chirpy voice and the way she puffed out her chest, as a robin. And Mr. Lover, in grade 10, he used to run up and down the aisles in class, he was so enthusiastic about everything. He even started the class's very own French-language newspaper, *Le Soleil*. That summer, Cheryl went to Montreal on a French exchange program organized by the Canadian Association of Christians and Jews. Six hundred English-speaking kids like Cheryl got on a train in Toronto, stayed with six hundred French-speaking kids' families in Montreal, and two weeks later six hundred English-speaking kids, now with a lot more confidence, a little more French, and a lifetime of stories to tell, got on another train back to Toronto along with their new six hundred French-speaking best friends. She was just turning fifteen. That one month, after her year with Mr. Lover, resulted two decades later in her own kids going to French-language schools, one of her daughters spending a university semester in Switzerland at the École Polytechnique de Lausanne, another working with the federal government in both official languages, her son earning a bilingual law degree from McGill, and a few decades after that four of her grandkids enrolled in French-language daycares and elementary schools. And, when Cheryl was looking for her first real teaching job after a few false starts, it was Mr. Lover, by then a vice-principal, who hired her. All these things that connected. She noticed things like that.

Cheryl remembers Mrs. Coupe, and who wouldn't. Her exuberant, high-pitched, Julia Child–like chortle, and the textbook she co-wrote that Cheryl still has, and the notations she made on almost every page, which are still visible nearly sixty years later. Mrs. Coupe's book was the first Cheryl had ever seen where there was enough space on each page to write something yourself, as if that space was there to make you a participant in your own reading, as if that's what Mrs. Coupe intended. In Dylan Thomas's "Fern Hill," Cheryl circled "as I was young and easy" and "as I was green and carefree" and drew a line between them, and between "Time let me hail and climb" and "Time let me play and be," so that later she could wonder why Thomas had used such repetitions and rhymes, why he had constructed his poem that way. Even more than she loved reading Thomas's words, she loved to hear herself say them. She found that she learned best and most deeply with her ear, not her eye. It's why she loves music so much, she thinks now, why she sang in choirs at ECI and at the church, why in Mr. Lover's French and Mrs. Coupe's English, it was music she heard. "If I had to categorize my approach to life," she said later, "it's about figuring things out. That's the driving force for me. I look for patterns, patterns make sense to me. They help me break things down into manageable bits. I connect it all to music."

But some patterns she found harder to understand. Her father was a cop, who worked just around the corner from their house, in the township hall on Dundas Street. Etobicoke was growing, it needed cops, and with his wartime background in the military, he got hired. A 1954 photo of the Etobicoke Police Department shows twenty-nine uniformed officers, and three in plain clothes, one of them her father. He is wearing a fedora, on the same slight rakish angle my father wore his. When Cheryl dropped by the station to visit him, the other officers called her Smiler.

The problem began a year later. She wonders now if it had something to do with the war. Her father had been in the tank corps, and among other battles, he had fought at Monte Cassino. Over fifty thousand Allied troops died or were wounded there during that five-month fight. He never talked about it to Cheryl, but years later one of Cheryl's daughters, to commemorate her grandfather, posted on her Facebook page a story he had once told her of how at Monte Cassino he'd had to crawl from under a burning tank and on his belly for more than a mile to find some measure of safety.

Or, Cheryl wonders, if it had to do with his drinking. It wasn't that he did it all the time, it was just at certain moments. His own father had had a car dealership in a small town about three hours north of Toronto, until the Depression came and wiped him out. It was about this time, as the Beagan family's stories go, that Cheryl's grandfather's drinking began. Her father wasn't yet a teenager. There were ten kids in the family, two others had died very young. Her father escaped this life only when he joined the army.

Or maybe the problem was money. He didn't make much as a cop and Cheryl's mother was at home caring for the kids. Or maybe it was the job itself. Her father was a "really brilliant man," Cheryl recalls, but he never felt recognized. He was great with numbers; like Cheryl, he could see patterns. He was the one in the department who could see through the knot of twenty-nine officers, twenty-four hours, seven days, time on and time off, to come up with a staff schedule. He was the one, later as an insurance salesman, who created the first term life group plan for Etobicoke teachers, and the one who later still, as a salesman at a metal coating company, could look at any object that might need galvanizing, figure out its surface area, the cost to galvanize it, the profit margin the company needed, and come up with a price—all in his head. But he could also be brusque and rude, Cheryl says. He seemed always frustrated, never getting the chance to do all the things he knew he could do.

But whatever the reasons, her father would fly into rages. Not all the time—things would just seem to build up until he couldn't stop himself. But the rages didn't need to be all the time. Cheryl knew they could come anytime.

One night in 1955, when she was eight, she witnessed a violent incident involving her father. The details of it don't matter. The impact it had does. After it happened, Cheryl had no idea what to do or how to feel. He was her father. But it happened, and might happen again.

Cheryl did what any kid would do. She tried to make sense of it, she never told anybody, she tried to stay clear of her father. "My release time", as Cheryl describes it, was from eight-thirty in the morning, when she went out her front door to school, until four in the afternoon, when she arrived back home again. She thinks of her childhood weeks now "almost as a pattern from Greek art," she says, "a line that goes across horizontally, then down, then horizontally again, then up again. The up-part was the week at school, ending with Friday night, then *boom*, Saturday morning things dropped," until she'd get to school again Monday morning.

Summer for her was the best. The family had a cottage about two hours northeast of Toronto, and she was there from the day after school ended in June until the day before it began again in September. Her father was there only on weekends. At ECI, things also got better for her. With all its amazing activities and clubs, she could be the Cheryl who she wanted to be, the Cheryl she was and had it in her to be, that nobody could stop her from being. So at ECI she pumped up that big smile to full, light-up-the-room brightness. And every year at school, she did more, and discovered she could do more, and loved it.

At home during those high school years, things also improved. Her father changed jobs, her mother went out to work and became a special ed teacher. There was more money. Her parents could live their lives, and she could live hers. He had never drunk much, but now he drank less. Still, every so often her father would get to a point where he just wanted out of whatever was going on, to take what he called his "piss on it" pills, and go to bed, and Cheryl and the rest of the family would have to walk around as if on egg shells just so they didn't wake him. Cheryl later told a therapist that in these years she felt as if for her there were two cliffs facing each other with a deep gully in between. One cliff was home-Cheryl, the other was ECI-Cheryl, and it was up to her always, always to keep them apart. And for the most part, she did.

At ECI, we didn't know any of this. To us, Cheryl was Cheryl.

CHAPTER ELEVEN

Gord remembers the moment vividly. It must have been the first day of grade 13, we were in algebra class, and Mr. Jackson was getting us ready for the year ahead. It was part speech, part pep talk, and most of all a cautionary tale. This would be a year like no other we had ever experienced, he told us. How we did would determine whether or not we went to university, and what that meant for our parents, and for our own lives. It would determine what school we got into, what field we'd have the chance to pursue, what path to the future we'd be able to take. He reminded us, too, very solemnly, that grade 13 was unforgiving. Every course we took would have the same content as the course that was taught to every student everywhere in Ontario, and that in June, we would write the same exam on the same date at the same time as every other student in the province. Whatever grade we got would be the grade every university admissions officer saw. And if anybody in this room, Mr. Jackson's tone suggested, even for a moment believed that his or her teachers, who had always had a professional obligation to grade our exams with absolute objectivity, but who in every other year if something went wrong on exam day and we blew the test, knowing this and knowing us, would give us some benefit of the doubt, well, for grade 13—forget it. As Mr. Orton, our English teacher, liked to remind us, it's some teacher in Coboconk who's going to grade our papers. Which meant, Mr. Jackson continued, all of us had to focus. Which meant, he said, looking at Gord and me, no sports. He had us right up until then.

No other province in Canada and no U.S. state had more than twelve grades. Whenever we asked why grade 13 existed, we got back an answer that suggested the questioner was offended by the question: "Grade 13 is harder, it makes you much more advanced and more mature coming out of high school . . . It is like everybody else's first year of university . . . Our system is better *period*." Except, after we graduated, we weren't put into second year in any university in any other province or state. The real answer is probably that grade 13 had been instituted at a time when almost no one went to university, to give students at least one more year of schooling. By our time it was an anomaly, but one that would cause more disruption to change than simply to maintain. Students saw through it. Those who had no intention of going to university simply dropped out after grade 12. The number of grade 9s pictured in class photos in the *Etobian* in our first year was 347; the number of grade 13s was 127.

By our grade 13 year, the number of grad photos had increased to 229, not because a higher percentage of students had stayed in school, but because the school had expanded a year earlier, becoming what was then called a "composite school," offering three different streams of instruction: traditional Arts and Science, the much smaller Business and Commerce, and the new and smaller still Science, Technology, and Trades. Most of the school's growth was in the early grades. In our grade 9 year, there were ten classes; five years later there were seventeen.

But Mr. Jackson was right, grade 13 did feel more serious to us. Serious enough that Marilyn Cade's father built her a door-desk in a room of her own in the basement, and Joan Boody, in a family of seven kids in a house that didn't have enough room even for them, was allowed a space of her own in the furnace room, with her own little card table, just to escape the commotion. Serious too in the courses we selected. This wasn't like picking music or art in grade 9, or German or Russian in grade 11. This had to do with deciding the fields we wanted to pursue in university and choosing the courses that were required to get us there. In grade 13, we all had to take English and French, but apart from that we had options. To a degree. If we took history or geography, that meant we'd have to take one fewer math or science course, which meant at university, engineering, medicine, or any of the sciences were out. Forever. And we didn't want to rule anything out forever. The course mix that left open the widest range of future options was three maths (algebra, geometry, trigonometry), two sciences (physics and chemistry), English and French (each of which counted as two courses). That's what I and most of us took, nine courses, which would get us into any field of study in any university in Canada. Except, now that we knew we could get into anything, what did we want to get into?

In every year's *Etobian* there's a photo of each grade 13 student and beneath it a short blurb, from information provided by the students themselves. The information might include school activities (S.A.), pet peeve (P.P.), favourite expression (F.E.), romantic interest (R.I.), and future plans (F.P.). In 1961, in our grade 9 *Etobian*, of the 127 grads pictured, 65 were boys, 62 girls, and of the 57 boys who answered as to their future plans, 21 said they were going into engineering, mostly mechanical, but also chemical, electrical, aeronautical, and geological, 9 into business, 8 into science, 4 each into teaching and medicine, and 3 into dentistry. Of the 57 girls who answered, 18 said nursing, 17 teaching. No other occupation was mentioned more than once except for home economics and physical and occupational therapy, which were each listed twice. Five years later, in 1965, in our own graduation year, of the 229 grad photos, 101 girls and 128 boys were pictured, and of the 92 boys who answered as to their future plans, 15 said business, 14 engineering, and 10 dentistry, the others listed most often being accounting 7, maths and sciences 6, leaving medicine, law, general arts, and maths, physics and chemistry each with 5. Of the 82 girls who responded, 18 said teaching, 15 nursing, and after that, way back, were general arts 6 and dental hygienist 5.

The grad photos were also intriguing. Some of us look our age—Marilyn Adamson, Joan Cliff, Joan Boody, Marilyn Steels, Judy Tibert, Kathy Vodden. Some of us look like kids trying to look older—Cheryl, Daryl, Ken. Some look almost sophisticated—Gord, Roger, Barbara, Penni, Lisa. Some look like kids because they can't help it—Marilyn Cade, Peggy Clarke, Doug, Bruce, Wayne. I still have my buzz cut, and still haven't grown into my ears.

The *Etobian*'s forms for our blurbs had to be filled out before Christmas to meet the yearbook's publication deadlines. By graduation, for many of us our future plans had changed. I say in my blurb that I'm going to Trent University in Peterborough, Ontario, but I was never going to Trent. I was always going to a U.S. school, but I hadn't yet visited Princeton and Cornell, my first two choices, and because the Montreal Canadiens, who held my draft rights, sponsored a junior team in Peterborough, Trent seemed a reasonable answer. But whether reliable or not, our blurbs tell something of the time. With all the amazing projects that were being developed across the country, for boys in both 1961 and 1965, engineering was a big favourite, as was business, even more so in 1965. Maybe we *had* been reading the articles and the ads, maybe by 1965 corporate and not just government projects had begun to look exciting. But dentistry? Trending?!

More remarkable were the girls' answers. These were girls who were living in a fast-rising middle-class suburb of the fastest-growing city in North America. Girls who had been raised on postwar dreams and possibilities, of "Canada Unlimited," who had worked hard, and learned well, who were not going to drop out or pack it in after high school, and whose grades were just as high and probably higher on average than those of the boys. Girls who were in the Brain Class whom Bruce, years later, would describe as "strong, intelligent women with strong, bright personalities," and Daryl as "the smart ones, the energetic ones, the intellectual giants, who'd be able to do anything they wanted." And yet girls knowing that they were about to go to university, with all of the possible areas of study it offered, when provided the opportunity to write in their own words what their own future plans ("F.P."s) were, five years later overwhelmingly still said nursing and teaching.

Marilyn Adamson and Marilyn Steels listed nursing; Sandie, Penni, and Lisa said English; Peggy Clarke and Judy Tibert science; Joan Boody medicine or science; Marilyn Cade math or science; Joan Cliff phys ed; Judy Clarke teaching; Margaret Silvester social work; and Cheryl said just "university." (As it would turn out, twelve of these thirteen spent all or some of their careers in teaching or nursing.)

Marilyn Cade remembers our guidance counsellor, Mr. Steels, who was also our German and French teacher, telling her that teaching or nursing was the right direction for girls. His reason? Something about girls not having the "stamina" for other jobs. Mr. Steels's own daughter, Marilyn, was at or near the top of our class in almost every subject. She did end up taking nursing at McMaster University in Hamilton and spent most of her career with the VON, the Victorian Order of Nurses. But if she had known then that she wanted to go into health care, why not into medicine? Why not become a doctor? Was it because of *everything* else—the many years it took to be a doctor, its cost, and was it even possible with marriage coming soon and kids on the horizon?

Was it because of the role models that the girls had around them— their teachers, their mothers, who had been gainfully employed only until family needs and social expectations had brought them home and kept them home? And who only years later, and only out of family necessity, and only in a very few cases, might go back into the workplace—Daryl's mother because Daryl's father had lost his job, Cheryl's mother for lots of reasons.

Was it because of the absence of role models for girls in the bigger world? Almost all the girls had read Nancy Drew. Many had read *Anne of Green Gables*, some *Little Women*. Nancy, Anne, and Jo were feisty, adventurous, intrepid characters who were up for anything and unwilling to take no from anyone. But all of them were childhood characters, no one ever saw them as adults, no one ever knew what they did later with all their great intelligence and energy. Most of the boys had read the Hardy Boys. They, too, were intrepid and adventurous. They, too, never grew up to be the Hardy Men. But the boys also read stories of swashbuckling heroes and real-life explorers. My all-time favourite book in school was *Pirates and Pathfinders* in grade 6 social studies. We followed along on voyages with Vasco da Gama, John Cabot, and Columbus. We went round the world with Magellan, Drake, and Cook. We went into "deepest Africa" with Burton, Speke, Dr. Livingstone, and Stanley. We could actually see how it was possible to be feisty, adventurous, and intrepid in real life. When we read the front pages of newspapers, stories about prime ministers and presidents, scientists and their life-changing discoveries, businessmen and their country-altering projects, war heroes, sports heroes, even crooks, all of them were about men.

For Mr. Steels, it was likely that "stamina" was a simple practical consideration. He knew, and every man and woman at the time knew, that whatever job the girls would go on to would be *in addition to* their job as wife and mother, family-maker and homemaker. It *was* a matter of stamina. Who, girl or boy, could manage all that?

The message to us as boys, without our knowing it, from newspapers, even from guidance counsellors, was that we could make the fullest of these postwar times and possibilities. For the girls, even for the best and brightest in this Brain Class, with many fewer imaginable destinations in their heads, the future would be a somewhat more expansive, exciting version of what the past had been.

The class wasn't together as much in grade 13. Mostly that was because of the courses we selected. The majority of us took three maths, two sciences, French and English, but some didn't, which scrambled our timetables and put us with different teachers and different kids even for the same courses. Sandie Barnard had come into the class the year before. Funny, smart, and edgy—"We don't *have* to get Mr. Hagerman a Christmas gift if we don't really like him"—she was what many of the girls had become but weren't yet quite sure

how to pull off. They would think what Sandie thought, but sometimes needed Sandie to say it. It's not easy to become part of a long-
settled group like ours, but with Sandie it was as if the group joined
her. She added spice. Her parents had divorced several years before,
her mother remarried, her father died, her stepfather managed the
Westwood Theatre. I knew none of this at the time, probably few
of us did. What we soon learned was that the school play, *Best Foot
Forward*, had been just waiting for her.

One person who wasn't there in grade 13 was Murray McKenzie.
Murray had a deep radio-rich voice and crackling laugh even as a
skinny kid in grade 9. He did well enough in all our courses, but not so
well as to draw much attention. Nor was he in the UN Club or French
Club, or in the band or school play, or on student council or on any of
the sports teams. He did play the violin, but he wasn't a prodigy. After
school, he and Ken sometimes went to his house and played chess.
He also loved golf. Every September he'd arrive back to school with
a right-handed golfer's tan—bronzed face and arms, bronzed glove-
less right hand, and a left hand white as a ghost's. I and maybe a few
others couldn't stop ourselves tormenting him about it. Murray would
crackle a semi-tolerant laugh back. But this September, this grade 13
year, no Murray, no white hand. He was at Neuchâtel Junior College, a
private school in Switzerland, most of whose students were Canadians
and which followed an Ontario grade 13 curriculum. Neuchâtel was
talked about at times at ECI and some kids may even have brought up
to their parents the idea of going there, but rarely as a serious possibility. It was so far away, and almost none of us had been to Europe. It
meant being away for ten months, and it was expensive at a time when,
for parents, school wasn't supposed to cost money. So when Ken also
brought up the idea of Neuchâtel with his parents, they gave him a
choice: he could go to Queen's University in Kingston the following
year as his father had, but with its additional high cost of room and
board that his parents would incur, or he could attend Neuchâtel for
his grade 13 year and attend U of T the year after. Ken, not without
great ambivalence, chose Queen's.

Neuchâtel changed Murray's life. For a full school year, the continent was his classroom. He and his classmates travelled everywhere—to Italy and France, to eastern Europe and North Africa. The paintings he saw now weren't just photos in books, turning-point battles not just words on a page, they were right there in front of him. He was doing what none of us had ever done—he had gone away, he was living on his own. He grew up five years in one, he remembers. He lived the independence of university a year before the rest of us.

For those of us he left behind, it was a pretty good year too. It wasn't just Gord and I who paid little attention to Mr. Jackson's wisdom, it seemed as if everyone took on things like there was no tomorrow. Pat and Daryl were in the Science Film Group, Penni and Judy Tibert on the United Way Campaign Committee. Cheryl was a cheerleader. Boris (Bruce), Katya (Kathy), Stepan (Daryl), and Peggy Sibbald were in the Russian Club, Joan Cliff and Cheryl on the GAA, Joan and Marilyn Adamson on the senior volleyball team. Gord was on the football team, and he and I were on the basketball and track and field teams. Penni and Sandie were in the school play, which ran four straight nights and filled the school's five-hundred-seat auditorium. After playing "loud-mouthed" Mae in *The Pajama Game* and "brassy" Gale in *Best Foot Forward*, in the final year's play, *Where's Charley?*, Penni played one half of a "charming middle-aged couple," an acting stretch, as the *Etobian* put it. The senior and junior football and basketball teams each got one page of coverage in the *Etobian*; *Where's Charley?* got four.

Marilyn Cade was everywhere: on the student council, on the formal committee, and, along with Gord and Peggy Clarke, in prefects, where she was head girl. The prefects were students in grades 11, 12, and 13, twenty-six of them, thirteen boys and thirteen girls, who had been nominated from among their classmates by the incumbent prefects and by teachers, on the basis of "scholarship, leadership, and maturity," and then elected by the student body. They were a presence around the school in their white cardigans with ECI's garnet, green, and gold stripes at their left elbows, entrusted with functions that

teachers might otherwise need to do: ushering at school events, helping out with hall duty during lunch, supervising a class when a teacher
was briefly absent.

But it was less what the prefects did, and more what they represented. In a time when all-roundedness was prized in academics,
sports, and everything else, prefects were ECI's all-rounders. They
exemplified what I wanted to be, and I was crushed never to be nominated. I was told later that when my name came up for consideration, a
teacher said that with all the other things I was doing in school, and out
of school in hockey and baseball, I wouldn't have time to give the role
its proper attention. Six years later, John Durnford, the dean of law at
McGill University, didn't say I couldn't be a law student because I was
playing for the Montreal Canadiens, and Sam Pollock, the general
manager of the Canadiens, didn't say I couldn't play for the Canadiens
because I was a law student. They left it to me to show that I could.

If not becoming a prefect was the lowest moment for me at ECI, winning the senior basketball championship against Burnhamthorpe
Collegiate was the highest. Each team had beaten the other during the
regular season and had dominated every other school in Etobicoke.
The championship game was held at ECI's gym. It was packed and
loud. With three seconds left, we were ahead 52–49 when we fouled
one of their players. He had two shots. If he sank them both, we'd still
be ahead by a point with almost no time remaining. He hit the first
shot and intentionally missed the second, the ball rebounding off the
rim, all of us leaping for it, the ball going off our hands, another shot,
missed, another, the ball still bouncing around, many more than three
seconds passing, it seemed to us, the ball finally going in at the buzzer.
A game that should've been won was now into overtime. We ended up
winning 54–52. As soon as the game was over, I knew I had a problem.

That year I was also playing Junior B hockey for the Etobicoke
Indians. We played about twice a week and practised once. In basketball, we played many fewer games but practised more often, our games
and practices always being after school. For the four years I played

at ECI, I had an understanding with the coach that if there was a conflict, I would have to play the hockey game. It had never happened.
Our hockey games were always at night, but now, in the playoffs, some
of our basketball games were too. By beating Burnhamthorpe we now
advanced to the TDIAA final-four beginning the following Friday
night. We would play Don Mills, whom we had beaten earlier in the
year 68–66. Besides Burnamthorpe, we were easily the two best teams
in the entire Toronto area, city or suburbs. Whoever won that semi-
final game would win the championship. I had a playoff hockey game
that night.

The Monday morning after our Friday-night win over Burnhamthorpe I went to see Mr. Thom. Before I could say anything, he said
that he knew I had a conflict and that it was too bad but that I'd have
to play the hockey game. He didn't try to persuade me otherwise.
He never made me feel more uncomfortable than I was. We lost to
Don Mills.

Many years later I was talking with Ken Church. We hadn't spoken for a long time, and when we had momentarily run out of things
to say, after an extended pause, as if this had been on his mind since
high school, he asked, "I know you had a hockey game, and I know
you had to play it, and after all that's where your future was, but
did you feel bad about not playing that night?" I told him my decision had nothing to do with my future, that I never thought I'd ever
play hockey as a career, but that I had started with the same hockey
team many years before I was at ECI, so my first obligation was to
them. I think Ken understood, but he had felt hurt—as a fan and as a
friend he had committed himself to that basketball team too—and he
couldn't not feel hurt even now. I was surprised he remembered, and
surprised at how embarrassed I still felt. The hockey team went on
to the Ontario finals, and lost too.

Eighteen years later, in my first book, *The Game*, I thanked six
coaches that I'd had in my life, three from hockey, two from baseball,
and Mr. Thom, saying, "To my early coaches—who understood the
game but never forgot the rest."

I've been asked a lot what it feels like to win a Stanley Cup. After trying for many years to explain, and from the confused looks I received, failing, I tried a different way. I asked the people, Have you ever won a championship before, in any sport, at any age? Really, have you won any big award, in any field? They would look at me a little puzzled and say, "Well, yeah, when I was ten we won the flag football title at school," as if that didn't count. And I'd say to them, "Well, that's what it feels like. You're on a team, you begin with hopes, you have good moments and bad, sometimes you think you'll never win another game, but you keep at it, and keep at it, and finally, if everything works just right, you win. And you're so completely excited. You don't step back at that moment and think, *Well, yeah, we won the championship, but it's not like we won the Super Bowl.* No!" I'd say to them, "You're a team, you had a goal, you worked for that goal, just like the New England Patriots or Montreal Canadiens did, and you achieved it. You won the biggest thing you could win that year." Then I'd tell them the story of how one year we won the Etobicoke high school senior basketball championship against Burnhamthorpe. "That's what winning the Stanley Cup feels like," I said.

Grade 13 was a busy, complicated social year. Most of the boys had begun grade 9 awkward and naive, if not petrified, around girls. We had come a long way in five years, or so we thought; many of the girls may not have agreed. Yet for the most part, in one way or another, into one group or another, we had managed to fit in. But some didn't. They weren't just being rebels, rejecting what is as all teenagers do— their parents, their teachers, their religion, their way of life. They were different.

It's hard to be different, to not just *not-be* something, but to actually be something of *your* choice, something *you* want to be. What is that *something*? How do you be it? Who are your role models and teachers, what are the structures and institutions that will help you pull it off? The path to sameness is well worn. To difference, it isn't. You've got to be really, really good at whatever it is that's different about you, to be it. You've got to want it, be strong enough to resist all the incentives to join the pack, to be one of "the herd." Those who pull off difference best, I think, start down the same path most people do, then little by little discover that this isn't quite theirs, that they aren't being them. And little by little discover what *is* theirs and them. And be different not because their parents are, or some character in some book is, but because *they* are. Then jump in with both feet, and just be.

Yet for some, it doesn't matter how hard they try. They have a different way of being. They don't understand others, and others don't understand them. They don't fit in, and never will. Not tomorrow, not ever. And the older they get, the more the gap between "normal" and different widens, the more different they seem. Until not fitting in becomes not belonging. Which makes life tough.

I don't think we were very nice to people who were different. I remember one kid who was smart and athletic, but who would get too emotional, too out of control, inappropriate. We'd shake our heads and say he's "touched," "a little off." As if it was his fault, as if somehow he was a burden to us. We didn't think often how it must have been for him. For someone to assert and embrace their difference—*I'm not you; I have a right to be me*—that was still many years ahead. I'm not sure we're much nicer now.

But whether we had journeyed from awkward to cool, well, that's another story. Cool requires an absence of self-focus, which mostly we could manage, and a worldliness and nonchalance, which we couldn't. Some boys in the other classes decided it would be cool to start a fraternity, but not many of us were invited to join. So, in a totally uncool move, some in our class created a fraternity of our own. It didn't work. At the time, smoking was also cool. Every serious thinker and doer in the Western world not only smoked, but in photos had themselves portrayed with a cigarette, cigar, or pipe in their mouth or hand, inhaling thoughts, exhaling truths. One year the school started an anti-smoking campaign, Wayne was its chair, Steve, a nine cigarette a day smoker, allowed himself to be its designated cautionary tale for a story in the *Toronto Star*. That didn't work either. Smart, we could manage. Cool, no.

Of the girls, Lisa was cool, so was Sandie. Of the boys, maybe just Ted. Ted was blond, smart, funny, adventurous enough to fit in with any group, but comfortable enough in himself to keep himself slightly apart. He read a lot, and played ball hockey, and did all kinds of things because he liked to do them, not because anyone said he should, and didn't do lots of other things others said he should. His independence of mind had probably started about as soon after birth as awareness sets in. Ted and Steve were twins, yet they looked nothing alike, and were nothing alike. They had no interest in dressing like twins, acting like twins, being treated like twins. Later, when someone would approach Ted, knowing that he and Steve were twins, and ask, "Now, which one are you?" he would think, if not say, "What do you mean, which one am I? Do you ask other kids who look totally different 'Which one are you?'" They were also different from the rest of the class. They were not perfect, were not going to be perfect, and had no interest in being perfect. In grade 13, at lunch, Ted would go to the pool hall on Bloor West, less than a ten-minute walk from the school, and skip the rest of the day's classes because they didn't interest him, and because he liked pool and mostly because he liked to hang around the guys there, many of them salesmen, in their late twenties or older, who'd already done enough for the day. Every boy had a crush on Lisa. Ted was so cool Lisa had a crush on him.

Cars were also cool, no matter the car's age or condition, especially if it was your own. High school is a time when big things can begin to go wrong, and sometimes stay wrong. We are just enough older by then, more able to do more things, more independent in fact and in mind, as teenagers more stubborn without being more confident, more aware of our power to say no, and much less willing to listen to anyone else. We're also much more aware of our own *invincibility*, and much more often with friends who think they are just as invincible as we are. And at sixteen, we have the perfect passport for the perfect instrument to live out this independence—a driver's licence,

and a car. Until the postwar years, most teenagers most of the time
had looked like and acted like mini versions of their parents. How
uncool was that?! They wore the same style of clothes, often even the
same clothes as hand-me-downs, they styled their hair the same way,
talked the same way, and listened to the same music. It was postwar
money that offered them the opportunity, and rock music the identity,
but it was the car that allowed the *teenager*, as a way of life and not just
as a time of life, to happen.

Roger, one of the few back-corner kids in our class, has a picture
from later in high school. The sun is shining, it looks like a weekend
in summer. Roger is standing in his family's driveway, in blue jeans,
his sleeves rolled up above his elbows, leaning on the hood of a car as
if he's leaning on a bar in a pub looking to chat someone up, a cool
"king of the world" look on his face. The car is a wreck, but it's his
wreck. Roger, clearly, has it made. The way Wayne had it made with
his Mini Cooper and VW Bug. The way the rest of us without a car
didn't. We'd always have to ask, "Hey, Dad, can I have the car Friday
night?"—few families at the time having more than one car—and asking led to uncool questions to answer: Where are you going? What
are you doing? Who else is going? What time will you be home?
If in our preteen years trains and swimming pools were our parents'
biggest fears, in high school they were cars, alcohol, and sex. Those
were the big things that were in *our* hands, that could go really wrong.
And despite lots of misadventures, because of our parents' vigilance,
our own eleventh-hour, fifty-ninth-minute, fifty-ninth-second good
sense, and lots of luck, no one in our class in those years got killed
or maimed, or became dysfunctional from drinking, and no girl got
pregnant, no boy became a father.

Most of us had our first girlfriends and boyfriends in high school.
Most of us had no idea what we were doing. We had these feelings
that we'd never had before. Exciting feelings, scary feelings, ones we
couldn't get enough of, didn't know what to do with, didn't understand, and had no idea how to handle. We seemed always, and only, a
heartbeat away from getting really big, "end of the world"-like things

wrong. Good first experiences in really caring for somebody mattered a lot. So did bad first experiences. They could set you on your way, or set you back, sometimes for a very long time. Sometimes for your whole life. It was really good, and really lucky, if you had a girlfriend or boyfriend who didn't really know what they were doing either, if you were both able to live with the things that you each got wrong together, and learned as you did, who had lots of other important things going on in their life and lots of exciting things ahead, and who through all the missteps was nice.

One thing was even harder. Some students at ECI, some in our class, were gay. I didn't know who was, I don't think many of us did. And probably some who were gay didn't yet know it themselves. We wouldn't have called them "gay," but "homos" or "fags," words that, in moments of indiscriminate anger, we might have called others too, insults that to us weren't any more abusive than other putdowns we used. Except it would not have seemed that way to someone who was gay. I didn't think a lot about homosexuality then. I didn't know much about it. It had something to do with boys liking boys. I don't remember it having to do with girls at all. It didn't seem part of the world I lived in. I thought about it a lot more in university and after.

In 2005, I was in Paul Martin's cabinet when the government brought forward its same-sex marriage legislation. It's hard to imagine now, less than twenty years later, how contentious and emotional the subject was at the time. There were wide divisions in all of the parties. The debate was political, but more than that it was personal, religious, and fundamental, for some deeply so. I thought at the time that, while the vote would express yes or no certainties, most Canadians had very mixed feelings, that they weren't 100 percent in favour of or opposed to same-sex marriage, but were divided even within themselves, and understood the other side even if they didn't support it, and that that was OK. I decided to write an op-ed for the *Toronto Star* with this in mind, and for those who hadn't yet decided, and to keep two people in my head as I wrote it: a person I was working with in Ottawa, and any student at ECI in the early 1960s who was gay.

I thought how awful it must have been for those students. How alone they must have felt. The rest of us thinking the world had come to an end because a girl had looked at us a certain way, and here's this kid trying to figure out feelings he or she doesn't understand and isn't supposed to have, which make them believe they're a bad person. I wrote about how wrong that is. How nobody should have to feel this way, but how a lot of people at ECI did. Must have. People we knew and people we didn't, and people we only thought we did. How rotten. The effect that must have had on them then, the effect that that time in their lives has had on them in the years and decades since. For those in our high school class, a story that came later.

Very few of us now think of our high school years together as a life-changing time. Some teachers remain vivid in our memories, but in the context of many decades of other teachers and mentors, there are few that we see as transforming. It's the same with the friends we made, with the experiences we had. If the Etobicoke Board of Education or our parents thought the Brain Class would be a life-altering experience for us, the experiment failed. It wasn't.

But maybe the Brain Class is seen most clearly another way. What we learned in class and learned from each other didn't turn out to be the making of us, but it offered solid and fertile ground for what was ahead. I arrived at ECI loving to learn, and I left loving to learn. I left wanting to learn more, open to learning more, and feeling ready and able to learn more. I didn't leave thinking I was a math or an English genius, but I did leave feeling that if I needed to face something that had to do with math or English, I wasn't hopeless and I'd be willing to try. I feel the same about the experiences I had with my classmates. None of them were my best friends then, and none are now. But they helped make me more comfortable with other people, more open to being around and learning from different people in the future. Once burned, twice shy. Sure. But as it turned out, I left ECI neither burned nor shy. To have good experiences is a good thing, and not to have bad ones is good too. As Pat put it later, "You get influenced by the people around you, even those you don't talk to. And I think that was true of that class. We were together for long enough that even people I didn't know, I knew."

For us, this was not a time defined by the Brain Class. It was a time of life. Out from under our parents' wings for the first time, at least slightly, out of their sight, beyond their control, even if it often didn't feel this way, able to do more things, believing we could, insistent that we try. We were changed in these years, but most of us not too much, I don't think. We got bruised and cut, and scars don't go away. Yet over time, in most instances, they become less noticeable. Still, while we like to think we can wipe the slate clean, have "closure," "put this behind us" and "go forward" as if nothing has occurred, we *will* never be the same again. It's not just about getting back up when we're knocked down and getting on with things. It's getting on with them as this slightly different you that will never be the old you again. It's great if these high school years inspire, excite, energize, and generate appetites for the future. It's sad if they deaden and demoralize. Both can happen, both can be story-shaping, identity-making, and life-affecting. For most of us, I think, our Brain Class years were neither great nor tragic, they were at least neutral, leaving open the possibilities of what can come next.

We arrived in grade 9 knowing what our parents wanted us to be. By grade 11, we were becoming what we thought we were. As we got to the end of grade 13, we were starting to be what we thought we could be, and would be.

In those five years of high school, Canada had begun to feel different too. "We are getting tired of Canadians who are getting tired of their country," a *Maclean's* editorial exclaimed on April 3, 1965, less than three months before we graduated. "We are weary of citizens who worry so much. We have become impatient with the panicky and the pessimistic, with Canadians who are so preoccupied with our problems, so overwhelmed by our crises, and so upset by our scandals that they want to give up, or run away, or join the United States." It was politics that triggered this change in mood. It was something else that triggered the politics.

These were the Diefenbaker and Pearson years. In 1957, after twenty-two years of Liberal governments, Canadians decided, at least politically, to go in a different direction. John Diefenbaker's Progressive Conservatives won a small minority, then won again a year later, this time with a massive majority, earning more than four times as many seats as the Liberals. Diefenbaker was from Saskatchewan, only the second prime minister in the country's history from west of Ontario. But whatever Canadians might have been hoping for with his government, they didn't get it, and in the election four years later the Liberals narrowed the gap, then a year after that, in 1963, won back power, winning again two years after. All three of these elections, 1962, 1963, and 1965, in which Murray's father campaigned for the PCs, Bruce's mother for the Liberals, and Marilyn Steels's father for the NDP, had resulted in minority governments, the first in more than thirty years.

The public and the media had no perspective on how such a government would function or what it would mean. Because the government could fall at any time, and there could be an election at any time, *everything* in Parliament, not just most things, became about politics. So, as the rest of the world focused on feeding the planet's exploding population, colonialism and the fate of newly independent states, the viability of the European Economic Community and the stability of Europe, and missiles in Cuba, issues worthy of governments and politics, in Canada, day after day, newscast after newscast, as Pierre Berton put it, politicians "gabbed incessantly" and "prattled on," pretending molehills were mountains. So politics and governments looked stupid, and political leaders, even Lester B. Pearson, the Liberal leader who had won a Nobel Peace Prize, even John Diefenbaker, a Prairie lawyer who had come from nowhere to sweep the country, even Tommy Douglas, who had brought first Saskatchewan and then his country health care for all, looked petty and ineffectual. Deep disappointment set in during our high school years, making the public and media commentators wonder what Canadians are never far from wondering, but which the postwar boom had distracted us from wondering: What is wrong with us? Why aren't we more than this?

The floodgates of gloom opened. "The plainest fact of our national life is that Canada suffers in 1962 from a profound sickness of the spirit," journalist Robert Fulford wrote in *Maclean's* in its October 6th issue. This has nothing to do with the problems of the day, he said, it's a "spiritual bankruptcy," an absence of "what most other nations of our time abundantly possess: a purpose that stretches beyond our own needs and reaches into the lives of other peoples and other generations." Other countries have had to overcome war and deprivation, we haven't, and as a result "we lack a genuine reason for working hard, for sacrificing, for paying taxes, and for being proud of ourselves."

There was more and more talk now about the "brain drain." Canada had always been a place of immigrants—particularly from Europe—and emigrants—particularly to the U.S. And Canadians understood why. In both cases, the reason was opportunity. But that continuing southward flow of emigrants to the U.S., even after all that Canada had become in the postwar years, was seen as a particular affront. That awful phrase—*brain drain*. The essence of all of us, our brains—our possibilities, our futures—sucked south. In *Maclean's*, Christina McCall-Newman catalogued the loss: Nobel Prize winner in chemistry Dr. William Giauque, Pulitzer Prize winner Leon Edel, the founder of Fuller Brush, the president of Sarah Lawrence College, the mayor of Seattle, more than fifty members of the medical faculty at Johns Hopkins, all gone, to say nothing of countless artists and entertainers—Saul Bellow, comedian Mort Sahl, musicians ranging in style from Guy Lombardo to Paul Anka. More profoundly, the thousands of engineers, doctors, professors, and other professionals and managers whose names we didn't know, who made their part of the world work in a thousand different ways. And, once gone, forever gone; as the article put it, the loss of their gene pool was a loss to the future of Canada. And because of our underlying feeling of disappointment, we noticed. Lots of articles were written, lots of hands were wrung.

Canada in the early 1960s was growing in virtually every measure, in population and wealth, but after two postwar decades when we had had it all our own way while so much of the rest of the world struggled to rebuild from the rubble of war, it was now clear we were never going to be truly big, never truly important. The reality of this was setting in.

This was the Canada into which we were about to graduate. We were seventeen, eighteen, nineteen years old. We had university and the rest of our lives ahead of us. We were excited, not disappointed. And we had our final exams to think about.

The grade 13 exams felt almost as traumatic as Mr. Jackson had warned. It didn't matter what we had achieved the rest of the year, these were exams created by someone we didn't know, and prepared in a style different from exams we'd ever taken. In the exam rooms, and especially in the hallways before and after, there was greater unease. Somehow we survived. In September 1960, when we arrived at ECI for the first time, there were 347 students in grade 9. Five years later, after all the exams were marked, 167 graduated—less than half. Of those who had remained in our class through all five years, everyone graduated; a few who had left the class but remained at ECI took another year and graduated then. Every one of us went to university.

On graduation night, Pat won the Science Award, Sandie the English, Daryl the award for languages. They and Marilyn Cade, Marilyn Adamson, Marilyn Steels, Judy Tibert, Ken, and Gord won other major awards as well. Of the top five grade 13 students at ECI, four were from our class: Gord, Ken, Marilyn Steels, and Peggy Sibbald. (The other? Yes, Russell Hann.) As for the teacher in Coboconk who marked our papers, apparently he didn't understand that someone on the football, basketball, and track and field teams could not also be a school's top student, and gave Gord the highest marks. He was also valedictorian.

I did fine. I was probably just inside the top half of our class, where I had been most years. I arrived at ECI knowing I was a good student for being a good athlete, and a good athlete for being a good student, and I left knowing the same. I didn't think about it then, because my parents wouldn't have allowed it, and always being up against those who were older it wasn't so evident to me, but in those years, for my age, in baseball, hockey, and basketball, I was probably one of the top five players in the city in each sport, maybe better. Still, if I was a good student as a student and a good athlete as an athlete, it would take me a few more years to know it.

Just days before exams began I made a decision. I'd had a buzz cut since I was four. Now, instead of applying Butch Wax to the front of my hair to hold it upright, I used it to create a part on one side. It looked kind of stupid, but I didn't care. No more buzz cut. High school was over. I was ready for what was next.

III

THE
UNIVERSITY
YEARS

CHAPTER TWELVE

To truly move on we needed to move out. Away from home. For some of us, that still took a year or two, or more.

Most of our parents didn't say anything, but we knew what they thought: "We have a perfectly good university in Toronto, the best in Ontario and one of the best in the country. It's only a bus and streetcar ride away, and the subway is expanding and soon will be out almost to our front door. Tuition is expensive, room and board costs a lot more, why not live at home? Besides, if something goes wrong—and we're not saying it will, and we're sure it won't—but if it does, we're right here. And you have so many other things to think about. It'll be so much easier."

More than half the class, directly, subliminally, or because we believed the same as our parents, got the message. Fifteen of our thirty-five students enrolled at the University of Toronto, three at York University, Penni went into nursing at St. Michael's Hospital, Lorna into training as a child and youth worker at Thistletown Regional Centre, all of them remaining in Toronto. Three more went to McMaster, less than an hour away, one each to Waterloo and Brock, which weren't much farther, three more to Western, two hours away, and four to Queen's, which was three hours. I was about four hours away, at Cornell, across the border in Ithaca, New York; Barbara was across the country at UBC. Within two years of graduating from ECI, almost all of those still in Toronto had left home.

Pat Gregory lived all four of his university years at home, but so absorbed in what he was doing, it didn't matter much where he was. Even in high school, he seemed always to know where he was going. As a kid, when other boys dreamed of being policemen or firemen, he wanted to be a zookeeper, then a veterinarian. "I wanted to work with animals," he says, but "it was my first encounter with a snake that changed things for me." He was about ten, with his family on a Sunday drive outside the city, they had stopped for something, and his brother, Dan, spotted a garter snake beside the road. "It was the first one I'd ever seen in the wild. I was immediately fascinated." For most kids, fascinations come and go. Pat's grew. They led to more of his meanderings along the Humber River, the Edgar Rice Burroughs Tarzan stories that he loved to read, the adventure of them, Africa, the animals, the wildness, the Science Film Club at ECI, and Mr. Walters, who took him to Royal Society lectures, the field trips to Mimico Creek, sampling water, collecting specimens. Then finally to U of T. "I found university liberating," he says. Not because, away from ECI and the Brain Class, he could be someone other than the kid who loved snakes, but because it gave him the chance to love snakes more. To be around others who loved snakes, or who loved, if not snakes, *something*, it almost didn't matter what. If they loved Chaucer, he could understand that, and they could understand him.

He found at U of T that he could go as deep as he wanted to go in whatever interested him. To find whatever he found, to learn more, which was exciting, but then to have new questions, which led him down new paths in search of answers, to find whatever more he found, which was even more exciting. He realized that this was more than a love of animals, it was a love of *science*, and that "I really did want to spend my life doing some aspect of it." And now, at U of T, he not only had time to observe, but also to think about what he saw, which took him in all kinds of new directions. What had fascinated him most about snakes, he says, "is how both like and unlike us they are. They're like us in sharing a skeleton and eyes and a mouth, and all those things that make us fellow vertebrates. But their sensory systems are very different. Their reliance on other senses, their way of getting around, their physiology." Most of this he already knew. The question was: Why did that matter to a snake? To a snake in being a snake? Snakes are also ectothermic, cold-blooded, humans are endothermic. "We generate our own body heat, we maintain a more or less constant body temperature in winter and summer, whereas a snake, if you cool it down, its body cools down. But warm it up and everything comes back. No harm done. I can put a snake in the fridge for a couple of weeks and it comes out just fine. But if I dropped my body temperature by that much I'd be dead in no time." Again, he already knew that. But how does that feel to a snake? That he didn't know. "I can't share the sensation of that," he says. But he knew he had to try. In a sense, to *be* a snake. To experience the snake-ness of a snake. Which would then lead him to other new fascinating questions, and other new fascinating answers, which had no end. Never to know. Just as he wanted and loved.

One big thing did change for him at U of T, and one big thing didn't. What didn't was his love of ball hockey. He had been born in England and his family didn't settle into Canada until he was eight, too late to learn to skate very well, but not to run around in his boots with a hockey stick in his hands in the parking lot at Lambton-Kingsway School, especially with Bruce and Wilf. Wilf moved away in grade 11, Bruce went off to Queen's, but at U of T after a hard day of labs or cramming for exams, Pat found that an hour or two of ball hockey with his friends was a way to reopen his mind. The one big thing that *did* change for him, what would have shocked his ECI classmates: "I became more of the life of the party," he said, "at least in the circles I hung out with. I'd always been introverted, but I found the diversity of people at university, with all sorts of different attitudes and ideas, really refreshing. I'd been a lousy dancer and was always embarrassed about dancing, but I took to the dance floor and just generally opened up a bit. I think I found myself there."

—

Marilyn Steels, Judy Tibert, and Marilyn Adamson were three of the four girls from our class who went into nursing, three of the fourteen students who went away. McMaster University in Hamilton wasn't much more than twice as distant from their homes in Etobicoke as the University of Toronto was, but it was far enough that in deciding to go there they knew, and their parents knew, they were leaving home. And after the first few months of the first semester commuting back on weekends, they came to know that their old friends had dispersed and were well and truly gone, and that any friends-to-be were now where they were. It's when they began living their new life.

Marilyn Steels had been one of the top five students at ECI in grade 13. She and I had been in the same grade 7 and 8 classes at Humber Valley. She was quiet, and always appropriate in the way she dressed and held herself. She never intruded on the class's time, or asked questions that were of no interest to anyone but herself; she never intruded on anyone. It was the same at ECI. And she seemed unfathomably smart. Without having to raise her hand, it was obvious to us that she knew every answer.

Her father was our German teacher. Mr. Steels was almost fifty years old and had been at ECI for more than two decades by the time Marilyn started grade 9. Born in 1910, he had grown up on a small, dirt-poor farm near London, Ontario, the third-youngest in a family of many children, several of whom died of childhood diseases. After the family's last child was born, his mother died and his father moved out, leaving him to be raised by his older siblings. He was the student in the family, the special one, the only one who stayed in school beyond quitting age. He skipped grades. In his spare time he worked in a garage and a grocery store to earn the money he needed, and entered the University of Western Ontario, graduating in modern languages in 1932, and with his master's degree a year later. He got married, he was fast creating a different life for himself, but then his wife died. He left London and took a teaching job at Pickering

College, a private school in Newmarket, just north of Aurora, where he met his future wife, Marilyn's mother. They married and moved to Etobicoke in the late 1930s.

When we entered ECI in 1960, he was head of the school's Languages Department. He was unlike our other language teachers— he had none of the chirpiness of Miss McKinnon, or the off-the-wall animation of Mr. Lover, or the charisma of Mr. Smith. Mr. Steels was a good, solid teacher. Older, with a distinguished salt-and-pepper moustache, he had presence, yet, curiously when he was teaching, and when the whispering from the back of the room got loud enough to be noticeable, and almost disrespectful, he carried right on. We would've stopped if he had said something, but he didn't. We knew nothing about him, nothing about his life. He just seemed slightly disengaged.

Marilyn liked music and played clarinet in the junior band; she liked science. At home, free of the classroom's constraints, she was less reserved. She loved nature, exploring, getting her hands dirty. She had a garter snake she named Pathfinder that she kept in a long wooden box her father had built, that had glass at one end and a screen at the other, just so she could watch it. She loved doing cowboy things, getting dressed up in her duds and going to Saturday-afternoon "dusters" at the Kingsway Theatre, watching after-school and Saturday-morning westerns on TV. And in a house where her father and mother loved listening to opera on the radio, and for whom Crosby and Sinatra were a stretch, she loved Elvis. At school, she played clarinet, at home, guitar. She did Elvis impersonations. This was no phase for Marilyn, no act of teenage rebellion. She *loved* Elvis. I hardly knew the in-school Marilyn that she allowed us to see. This one I couldn't have imagined.

Now she was off to McMaster. She had liked science enough that during high school she worked one summer at Queensway Hospital, where her interest grew. She decided nursing was her university destination. She would be an excellent nurse, but she could also be an excellent doctor. Her father had been the guidance counsellor who had advised Marilyn Cade to be a teacher or nurse. For boys *and* girls, this was a time of possibilities. But Mr. Steels was a realist. He had grown up poor and all his life never felt more than a step away from being poor. He read two newspapers every day, the *Globe and Mail* over breakfast, the *Star* over dinner, and he knew the difference between what might be and what was. In national elections he campaigned for his local CCF (now NDP) candidate, whose party's message of safety-net caution had no chance of winning in central Etobicoke against the sky's-the-limit enthusiasm of the Liberals and Conservatives. He was deeply involved in the teachers' federation. He knew how life worked.

In class, what I thought I'd seen in him as slight disengagement, or resignation, wasn't that. It was recognition. For years, he had seen girls like his own daughters do everything right in school and head out into the world with a degree next to their name, and into the same jobs as teacher or nurse. And soon married, and soon with kids, into the same life. That is the way it was. So why put in extra years and extra expense to become a doctor or lawyer? Mr. Steels wasn't a retrograde, stuck in decades-old ways. He had taught through generations of teenage change. He was capable of seeing change, accepting change, changing himself. When Marilyn's sister, Cathy, five years older, was in high school, rock and roll music had been for "the fast crowd," and every day in his classrooms and guidance office Mr. Steels saw what that fast crowd was like. They were the smartasses, they knew what they wanted to know and paid no attention to what the world said they had to know, dropped out of school, and dropped into nothing. So for Cathy, opera, and maybe operetta, were acceptable; rock was not.

Six years later, when Marilyn was in high school, rock wasn't just for the fast crowd. Really good students whom Mr. Steels saw every day in his classroom and guidance office, who he knew were going somewhere, also liked rock and roll. So rock may still have been incomprehensible to him, but Elvis and a guitar were OK for Marilyn. Music may have changed in those six years between

Cathy and Marilyn, but the job world, and the gender world, hadn't. So Mr. Steels didn't change his mind. Nursing, he believed, was a better choice for girls.

At McMaster, Marilyn did as well as she had done at ECI. Her class had twenty-eight students, not much different from high school, all of them girls, Judy Tibert and Marilyn Adamson among them. But in most every other way, for the two Marilyns and Judy, this would be a new experience—a new school, new city, new classmates, each of them living away from home for the first time. And for Marilyn Steels, one more thing she wasn't expecting. At Christmas that first year, she failed the chemistry exam. It was likely the first exam she had ever failed. She was shocked, and even more shocked were Judy and Marilyn Adamson. In those early months at McMaster, Marilyn Steels had established herself as "the one," as she always did and always would. She was the responsible one, the one who kept her head, the one who, when everything was new and confusing, somehow knew. And someone who has never failed often doesn't know what to do when they do at last fail. They have no experiences to draw on, no strategies, concrete or psychological, to apply. Failure can shake their sense of themselves, the confidence they have, and their willingness to take on unknowns in the future. They can feel lost. But Marilyn did what Marilyn always did: she worked harder, if that was even possible, righted her own ship, and sailed back to the top of the class. And in doing so, she showed the others that she was also the one to go to when things went wrong.

Marilyn Adamson had failed more frequently in her life, not often in school, but in sports, because in sports nobody wins all the time. She was an athlete at a time when not many girls were. She wasn't physically gifted enough to play at an elite level, but at the time in Etobicoke, and almost everywhere in Canada and the U.S., there was no path for girls to Olympic glory anyway, only happenstance. You're swimming at a local pool or running in a park and the right person spots you. Or you have parents who are bound and determined that you'll have the chance they never did. But this wasn't Marilyn's story.

She just loved to play—games of all sorts, in parks and playgrounds, on front lawns and back lawns, on the street with the other kids, after school, on weekends, mostly with and against the boys. But then the boys would go home, get changed, and head off to do the serious stuff, to play organized games in baseball, hockey, and football leagues, with referees, uniforms, and schedules. The girls had nowhere else to go.

Her elementary school didn't have girls' teams. ECI had girls' volleyball and basketball teams, but they didn't hold much prestige even among the girls, and nowhere near as much as the boys' teams, or the bands, or the school play did. It was the same at other schools. It was as if girls' sports couldn't be allowed to be fun. The girls were so constrained in what they could do, as if exertion and sweating were somehow wrong and contrary to nature. Girls' basketball was played six-on-six: three defensive players on each team were allowed to play only on the defensive two-thirds of the court, three offensive players only in the offensive end. A girl could dribble the ball twice and take two big steps, and hold on to the ball for three seconds before she had to pass it. OK, now go out and have fun. The boys' game was about what you *could* do, the girls' about what you *couldn't*. And when the girls' team played against other schools, they wore blue bloomers, the same ones they wore in gym class, that billowed out *attractively* at the bottom, with bibs around their necks, one team in one colour, the other in another, not even in their own school colours! Whereas the boys had *real* uniforms. It was so demeaning. Still, Marilyn played. She loved the pride she felt in playing, the sense of achievement, never more so than when, bloomers, bibs, and all, she was part of a team. Great training, it turned out, for nursing.

At McMaster, sports and nursing came together in one way she expected—she played all four years on the school's volleyball team—and in another she didn't. In high school, we had been in the same class but we worked mostly independently. The pass or fail, A or F, was ours, no one else's. In nursing, the two Marilyns and Judy and all the others worked on projects together, on hospital floors together, felt exhausted together, had the same patients together, experienced those patients get better together, and sometimes watched them die together. Not many people share experiences like that, ever. They went through all the ups and downs, the hopes and disappointments together, just as a team does. The first two years they all lived in residence with each other. They saw each other after class and on weekends, and the more they saw each other the more they wanted to know each other better. They knew each other's weaknesses and strengths, they knew when each needed help and didn't. They knew things were never perfect. Nobody wins every game. Not every patient lives. At times, you have to struggle, and Marilyn liked the struggle. The point is, with others, you get there. One year she heard a story about some of McMaster's medical students who, after being given an assignment to review certain articles that were on reserve at the library, read them, then tore out the pages so that their classmates/co-competitors couldn't read them themselves. Real athletes wouldn't do that, Marilyn thought. They want to win and they want to feel every microscopic pleasure of the victory they've earned. Nurses wouldn't do that either.

The closeness of the nursing class had a particular effect on Judy. She was an only child. She had decided to go to McMaster precisely because of the smallness of its class, thinking that that would make it a little like high school. But it was nothing like that. It was so much more. Our high school class was small; this was intimate. She had decided to become a nurse because she saw nursing as a "caring" profession. Medicine was too, and offered the drama of heroic cures, but it wasn't as personal, she thought. In high school, when Judy thought of the future, she had never been able to imagine herself as a neurosurgeon, even though academically she knew she could do the work. She wanted the caring, not just the curing, and at McMaster she was learning that in nursing the caring went so much deeper. She could see the effect it had on actual people and their families, and she could feel the caring among those she worked and trained and studied and lived with, and she loved that. So did Marilyn Adamson and Marilyn Steels. They had each thought nursing was right for them, and now they knew. They knew where they were going.

That wasn't the case for all of us. It wasn't the case going into university, or during, or right after.

Some set off in this direction, then that, to find their answer; others waited as if the future would reveal itself. The nurses and teachers seemed the lucky ones. They had a destination in front of them. For them and some others, it was as if they had a calling, and they knew how to get there, and they knew that they could. Most of us didn't have a destination in mind. Some wanted nothing to do with having one. We had never needed one before. Elementary school led to high school, high school led to university. Some other people wanted certainty, and still others craved discovery and surprise. Most of us, through university and for a few years after, didn't know which we were. But without a destination, some of us found ourselves lost.

Murray didn't know which of these camps he fell into, but Murray had an outlook. He had always seen life, and his life, with a rosy glow. It's not that he went around with a big "can't wait for today" grin on his face, that wasn't his personality, but it's pretty much how he approached things. Each day was a new day to do, to learn, and to experience who knows what, and what he had found was that nearly all of that doing, learning, and experiencing, he liked and found interesting. His father, a lawyer in a midsize downtown Toronto firm, was calm, measured, and thoughtful. His mother was a classically trained pianist, a graduate of the Royal Conservatory of Music. They had a Steinway grand piano, which she played after dinner as Murray's father read his newspaper and law journals, and Murray and his sister did their homework. Murray also liked to read, especially the Hornblower novels—he read all ten of them—which told of great naval adventures during the Napoleonic Wars, and of a modest hero who saw himself as anything but a hero, driven only by his sense of duty. Murray also liked stories of the real people he read about on the front pages of their newspaper, who did exciting things in exciting places and saw the world the way he was coming to see it himself. Also stories of people who couldn't possibly be real in places that couldn't possibly exist, except there they were, in photos and words, in *National Geographic*, right there in front of him.

He was a good student. He liked to do what was expected of him, and what he was asked, and then a little more. He found this made others happy, which he liked, and brought them to trust him, which gave him the chance to do lots of other things he wanted to do as well. He never could understand those who always needed to challenge and fight back. He noticed that this need to rebel, instead of getting them what they sought, only got them the attention of the people who could get in the way of their life, notably their parents and teachers, which only gave them less freedom, not more. Going along had its advantages, Murray learned early, especially because most things in his life were pretty good, most of the rest didn't matter much, and anything else he'd just do anyway, his parents and teachers never having to know and rarely noticing, because living under the radar as he chose to do, they never imagined he'd do the wrong thing. Going along gave him more freedom, not less.

Murray wasn't ready to be a star in high school. He was good at his subjects and the activities he did, but not special. Neuchâtel was his breakthrough. He never imagined it would be, he knew only that he wanted to go. He knew it would be different from anything he'd ever done, but he didn't know what those differences would make him feel, or whether he could handle them. He'd be gone ten months. A letter home would take a couple of weeks to arrive and two more to get a reply, and phone calls were too expensive so were reserved for Christmas. He was eighteen, he'd have to figure out so many things for himself. The year turned out to be so much less bad than it might have been, and so much better than he ever imagined. For Murray, it was about the discoveries, but this time discoveries that he made on his own.

At Neuchâtel he lived with a Swiss family. He *lived* in French. At ECI, he had been no French scholar. In Switzerland he had no parents around to encourage or push or match-make or soothe or fix things. He met his future wife, Marilyn, on the *Carinthia* on the trip over, on her seventeenth birthday. She was his first real girlfriend, he was her first real boyfriend. They had to manage that as well.

Because school filled school hours but also its after-hours, weekends, and holidays, his teachers were ever-present. Great teachers, he remembers, even better than those at ECI. They could be an incredible source of knowledge, guidance, advice, they could be friends and mentors if he allowed them to be, if he was up to it. They might be an immense opportunity, or an immense opportunity missed. Just as the whole Neuchâtel experience was. It was in his hands. "It was one intense experience after another," Murray says of that year. "The school's mission was to make us citizens of the world, and that's what it did."

Murray's ancestors had come from Scotland and settled in Manitoba and Saskatchewan, and his parents had moved east from Prince Albert to Toronto, for law school and the conservatory. And there they stayed. It had seemed then that Toronto and Etobicoke were some final destination, where the world stopped. But at Neuchâtel, Murray discovered other possible destinations, other worlds. And maybe most important for him, he not so much discovered as had reinforced in him an outlook he'd always had. Life is interesting, learning is fun, experiences are exciting, people are good to be around.

One more bonus. At Neuchâtel, he got a chance to play on the school's hockey team. At home, he hadn't been good enough to play on teams, but here it was different. And because Neuchâtel's students were mostly Canadians, the Swiss considered this a Canadian team. The kid who hadn't been good enough to play for Humber Valley was good enough to represent Canada.

He arrived at U of T in September 1965—ready.

He took the academic subjects he had to take, and found others he would come to love. He discovered research, and the joy of *not* knowing, of going beyond what his parents and teachers and books and newspapers told him and coming upon things that maybe nobody knew, that were truly, and felt truly, *his* discovery, *his* knowing. His major was economics. He had thought about being a lawyer like his father and uncle, but now he began to think about an academic life. Learning, teaching, teaching in order to learn more, all the time surrounded by people who are doing the same. What could be better? He began to think of getting his master's, his Ph.D.

At the same time, he was discovering other interests and abilities. He had never been in any of the school plays at ECI—they were all musicals, and he didn't have the voice for that. But U of T had productions of all sorts, some dramas and comedies, but also some that had only a little bit of singing, little enough that if he used his deep, rich voice the right way he could get by. After being in several productions, he met a director he couldn't fool. She knew him, and knew what was in him—Marilyn, whom he'd met on their way to Neuchâtel. She was now in nursing. They had seen each other occasionally in their first two years at U of T, mostly for lunch, remaining good enough friends that Murray would often burden her with stories of his romantic misadventures. She was directing the Faculty of Nursing's annual production, a variety show, they were short of guys, and she asked Murray if he'd be interested. It's not easy for a nineteen-year-old to direct a twenty-year-old, for a friend to direct a friend. But Marilyn had been president of her high school's student council, and by age twenty-one would be head nurse of the cancer unit at the Hospital for Sick Children, or SickKids, in Toronto. She could handle Murray. They started going out again.

Theatre, for Murray, was a revelation. He had never been in a band or choir, and had played mostly individual sports, golf and tennis, never having to depend on others or have others depend on him. (The exception was Neuchâtel's hockey team, but that was playing for *Canada*.) But "there's something about a standing ovation," he says, recalling the opening night of their show. And a feeling that comes with it that's bigger than anyone. "It was the first time I'd done something collectively where I felt really pleased with the result. When you work together to achieve a bigger goal, those lessons stay with you. That experience shaped me." And Murray, who believes in life lessons and big stories, made sure it did.

There was for him another happy accident ahead. He graduated with a degree in economics, got his master's in political science, and then, as he was beginning work on his doctorate, he took a job as a researcher and editor of a history of Canadian hospitals. But before the book could be completed, its author, Dr. Harvey Agnew, died. Agnew's widow asked Murray if he would finish it. It wasn't so much his work on the book that would change his life, or even seeing the product of Agnew's and his efforts physically *there*, between two covers, in other people's hands and minds, changing the way they thought and acted. It's what Murray learned in doing the research.

Until then he had known as much about health care in Canada as any other young, well-educated, publicly engaged person. For him, health care and hospitals were just there, a part of his life, to be used when he needed them and complained about at other times. The book was called *Canadian Hospitals, 1920 to 1970: A Dramatic Half Century*, and immersed in its research he heard stories about what it had been like not that many years earlier, when his grandmother was growing up in Dauphin, Manitoba, and his grandfather in Moose Jaw, Saskatchewan. And later in Prince Albert, where his grandfather owned a funeral home and was a prominent businessman and knew the local M.P., John Diefenbaker. Not once when Murray visited him did he ever wonder, *Who are these people my grandfather is burying? How did they die, and of what, and at what age, and did they have to die?* Murray was twenty-three years old when he worked on the Agnew book, born and raised in a solid, middle-class family in Etobicoke. To him, disease happened or it didn't, you died or you didn't. He did know that his father and uncle had survived TB, but he didn't think much about that then. Both were vigorous and strong when he knew them. Health was good luck or bad.

But now in his research he was learning what it had been like in all those years before he was born. With few hospitals or doctors nearby, Canadians did the best they could, and the rest was God's will. He heard stories of the immense public and political struggle over health care that had gone on for decades, and about the extraordinary people involved, not just Saskatchewan's premier, Tommy Douglas, but so many others too, some almost of Murray's own time. He could see how committed they were, how Canadians had died that didn't need to die, and how while times don't change by themselves, people can change times.

"I gained a profound appreciation of how important universal health care is," Murray says about his experience completing the book, "and decided that hospital management would be a pretty neat career. Because there were some just totally remarkable people doing it, and that saving lives and restoring people to health is a pretty good thing to do."

In the 1930s, the country's focus had been on roads and highways, at war's end on education, and now in the late 1960s it was on health care. Murray's university focus on economics and political science, then research and health care, had shown him how learning and doing could be connected. For Canada and for him, these fields and these lessons would come together in the 1970s.

As we were all trying to figure out where we were going, the country was too. Most of us were finishing our second year at university when Expo 67 opened in Montreal. At the time, world's fairs were a big deal. Before the world could go online and discover the latest and best in an instant, a world's fair offered a place to travel to every few years to see what a host city and country's idea of the future might be, and how important to that future they wanted us to believe they were. On display were the most advanced architecture, products, and designs, and the latest thinking each represented. Iconic structures were created, symbolizing the possibilities and excitement of the time and of times to come: London, 1851, the Crystal Palace; Paris, 1889, the Eiffel Tower. My father went to the world's fair in Brussels in 1958, its signature creation and main pavilion, the Atomium, nine giant balls of shimmering stainless steel and the tubes that connected them, in the shape of the atoms of an iron crystal magnified 165 billion times. Not a structure that was historically important but it is still an image I have clearly in my mind. This was the Atomic Age. I was ten.

As well as his stories, my father also brought back a fan, developed by Braun, a company I'd never heard of, German, made entirely of plastic and not much bigger than a closed fist, with a cylinder that rotated hundreds of times a second, it seemed to me, with louvres to catch the air and throw it back, and a small awning-like piece to direct the flow. It was my father's to use, then my brother's, then mine, and I still have it, and it still works. For years in the summer it was on my bedside table whirring almost soundlessly through the night, the air directed at my face as I slept. A miracle of technology I could understand.

The theme of Expo 67 was "Man and his World," a straight-forward enough concept that seemed to suggest one thing but really was about another. The phrase *Terre des hommes* in French had come at the suggestion of Quebec and Manitoba novelist Gabrielle Roy, from a work by the French writer and aviator Antoine de Saint-Exupéry. This was not "Man" in the sense of heroic master of the universe (at the time, it was always "man" and "he," except for countries and ships, which were "she"), but man as a remarkable, though vulner-able, being. Saint-Exupéry's inspiration had come from an experi-ence he'd had one night flying alone over a remote part of Argentina and seeing below him widely scattered lights in an immense black landscape, finding himself drawn not to the lights but to the black-ness, the space, the solitude between the lights. In that solitude, Saint-Exupéry discovered the need for man to connect. Our need for solidarity. For Roy, living in a later time of Cold War blocs and divi-sion, Expo would offer an opportunity to come together.

Maclean's, in its lead editorial to begin our Centennial Year, four months before the fair opened, described Expo as "a firm assertion of our late-blooming self-knowledge and self-confidence." We have come a long way in our one hundred years, it says. "Confederation did not magically erase the stubborn differences of language, culture, and clashing regional ambitions. But if we have not solved all our inherited problems we have learned to live with most of them." Expo's aim, the editorial states, "staggering in its scope, is nothing less than 'to tell the story of man's hopes, his fears, his aspirations, his ideas and his endeavors.'" "Four million Canadians and six million foreigners are expected to visit Expo," it says. "It is the greatest opportunity we have ever had to open our doors and windows and our minds and hearts to the world—a fitting birthday party for a nation come of age."

For Canada, what a success that would be. If only.

Then it opened. In 1967, Canada's population was 20 million. Between April 28 and October 29 of that year, almost 55 million people attended Expo, more than five times as many as *Maclean's* in its wildest dreams had hoped. It was the most widely attended world's fair since the Paris Exposition of 1900.

Expo had its showcase structures, most notably Buckminster Fuller's geodesic dome for the U.S. pavilion, and Moshe Safdie's Habitat, a construct of large concrete boxes perched atop each other, or side by side, Lego-like, each box a self-contained apartment, none of the boxes in line with the others next to them. But Expo's biggest achievement wasn't its buildings. Nor was it in being the centrepiece and inspiration for hundreds of mini Expos that were created across the country. Each community, faced with the same opportunity as Montreal, asking itself the same questions: Who are we? What do we need to be, what do we want to be? And everywhere centennial theatres, centennial libraries, centennial arenas, centennial museums of all kinds went up—these would be the bricks-and-mortar legacy of Canada's centenary. We were changed by this, our cities and towns became nicer places to live. But Expo and these other civic projects also changed us in a bigger way.

It's what creating those projects forced us to do, and what we had to do to pull them off. As it turned out, they offered a living demonstration of "man's" need for solidarity and of what solidarity can do. Until 1962, Moscow was to have been the host of the next world's fair, but then suddenly it pulled out. Montreal had less than five years to plan, to finance, to build islands in the middle of the St. Lawrence River, to construct a subway, to build the fair itself. But more than that, Expo *had* to be a huge success, a source of national pride. It *had* to thrill us and thrill the world, and with so little time available, lurking around every corner was the real possibility of local, national, and international humiliation. It was the same, on their own smaller scale, for all those cities and towns across the country. In all the decades before, all those theatres, libraries, and arenas hadn't gone up for a very good reason: they were too big, too expensive to take on. Now they had to be built, and fast.

For all those same decades, our politicians and thinkers had "prattled on" about Canadian identity. They had tried to write an inspiring and coherent story with their words, and couldn't. Maybe with Expo we could do it with our actions. This was our chance. We could not blow it. If we build it, we will be. But no matter how successful Expo was, this is a task, and a hope, too large. If this was to be Canada's "coming of age" moment, what age were we coming of? In reality, we were coming of an indefinite, indeterminate age, and Expo couldn't do it all. Less than a decade later, in 1976, the Parti Québécois, committed to taking Quebec out of Canada, was elected. In the two decades that followed, with sovereignty referendums in Quebec in 1980 and 1995 and the failed Meech Lake Accord in between, the question of what we are and what we will be would become a preoccupation. And the prattling intensified.

In 1967, as Canadians, we proved two things to ourselves. We showed we could pull off one big national thing and countless big local things. And we discovered what Saint-Exupéry and Roy had discovered: the need, and possibility, to do them together.

Expo would prove important in one other way. After an accumulation of arguments had failed over many years, Expo's highly visible success was probably the final reason that Major League Baseball came to Canada, and we got the Expos. Which made many of us very happy, and those of us in Toronto mostly happy. "Mostly" because *it*, Montreal, got the Expos, and we, in Toronto, didn't. Just as *it* had the Canadiens, and *it* would get the Olympics in 1976. (*It* would get me in the 1970s too—and for me, that was quite OK.)

No one from our high school class worked at Expo that summer, but almost everyone went. Many travelled with their parents, others with new university friends, some visited more than once. Judy Tibert remembers staying at a synagogue that, for that special summer, had been remade into a hostel. For Judy Clarke, except for camp, Expo was her first time away from home. Murray, having spent his grade 13 year living in French, took a French course at McGill and went to Expo often. For Lorna, Expo was on the way to Europe, and for Kathy McNab, it was on the way back; for Gord it was en route to Boston with his family to drop his brother off at Harvard Business School. Joan Boody travelled to Expo with the U of T Chorus and they performed, officially, several concerts and impromptu, in the spirit of that summer, endless renditions of "A Place to Stand, a Place to Grow, Ontari-ari-ari-o." Wayne ran his first marathon, in nearby Saint-Hyacinthe, on a Sunday, and the next day, sore, drained, and slightly euphoric, went to Expo. Nine years later, he would be back in Montreal to run another.

Only two of us, I think, never made it to Expo, Wilf and me. Wilf was in Europe for the whole summer. I was in Ithaca, New York, not even as far away from Montreal as Toronto, working construction, building a Woolworths. I'd been told Expo was really busy, and I'd been to fairs before, and I thought, well, if everyone's going, how interesting can it be. So, more influenced by Yogi Berra—"Nobody goes there anymore; it's too crowded"—than by Saint-Exupéry and Roy, I didn't go. The next summer, when most of Expo's buildings were still there, and it was a lot less crowded, I went. Sometimes it takes me a while to get the point.

CHAPTER THIRTEEN

Gord had graduated from ECI with some idea of what he wanted to do, and after two years studying engineering at U of T he was beginning to see how he might do it. He loved learning, but he wanted his learning to have direction, application, purpose. Mr. Thom's Tuesday practices needed Friday-night games against Burnhamthorpe.

For much of their history, universities had been academic institutions, their scholars looking for big timeless answers, not immediate, pragmatic ones. So university disciplines had focused on the academic and the theoretical, by their very intention keeping themselves many ivory towers away from the real worlds of agriculture, industry, and government which, scholars believed, bent and distorted learning to meet their own needs. What universities taught was pure, and because universities for centuries had only been for the few who were privileged or brilliant, academic and theoretical was all universities needed to be. For anything else, go to a steel mill, it's the kind of science you can learn on the job.

But by the 1960s, universities were no longer supposed to be only for the brilliant or privileged. Kids like Gord, like us from ECI, and thousands more like us were now in university, and we were just as smart, if not as privileged, as the university students before us, and we too had to make a life for ourselves. We had to solve different kinds of problems that the world now presented—population growth, vast numbers of newly independent countries, the bomb. Gord's older brother, Chuck, also an outstanding student and athlete at ECI, had started out taking maths, physics, and chemistry at U of T, but after a month found it too theoretical and switched into commerce. Their father had graduated from high school yet all his career he really had worked as an engineer without a degree. And, using the math and science that he'd learned in high school and on the job, having to calculate the amount of sheet metal that was needed to cost out big jobs, he had really been a businessman as well, also without a degree. So when Gord applied to U of T, learning from both his father and brother, he knew he didn't want maths, physics, and chemistry, but he did want more science than what his brother was getting in commerce, and so he chose industrial engineering (which until a few years earlier had been called "engineering and business").

"It was sort of an all-round, multidisciplinary engineering," Gord recalls. First-year students took courses in all of the engineering fields. "Even in second year, we took some electrical and mechanical, and chemical too. But then they added in some math courses—operations, research, statistics—and a business component—an accounting course, one in economics—and in third year we started to use computers."

The chair of the Department of Industrial Engineering was Arthur Porter, a Brit who had studied and worked in the early days of analog computers in England. Now in his mid-fifties, he'd already had many careers, and, as it turned out, fascinated by everything and living until he was ninety-nine, he had many more careers to go. His first interest had been quantum theory. When told by his advisor at the University of Manchester that no research opportunities were available at the school, Porter gave as his second choice "mathematical instruments," "things for solving," as he described them. Which led him to the office of Douglas Hartree, a professor of applied mathematics whose interest was in employing numerical analysis to deal with complex problems, and so to Hartree's famous Meccano set, which was sitting right there on his desk, pieces of it attached together at odd angles into some unrecognizable shape, which would become a differential analyzer, which would become a computer. Which, for Porter, would become a mathematical instrument to do numerical analysis and a lot more. It was this "lot more" that most interested him. A machine that could be used "for solving." But solving what? The Second World War offered him his first answer.

For Britain, this wasn't a time for the academic and theoretical. Porter was assigned to the army's anti-aircraft command, his task to bring together its big guns and their gunsights with radar, then early in its development, in order to pick up and track incoming aircraft earlier and bring them down with much greater frequency. London had been hit by the Blitz in 1940, and other big industrial centres, including Manchester, were next, but none of them had sufficient radar. Porter had to come up with a plan. Half of London's radar capacity would need to be moved to the other cities, leaving all the cities with less than what they needed. The radar equipment would have to be repositioned in such a way that it still provided the essential protection. It was a job for the differential analyzer.

Porter understood that the computer is a tool, most fundamentally an *educational* tool. It was a way to learn more things faster and better, something that could be used by anybody to take on anything. The war had presented a real-world problem and he had used the computer to take on that problem. Now that the war was over, there were new problems for computers to take on. Porter was hired by the Royal Military College, in Sandhurst, as professor of instrument technology. There he built his own differential analyzer and taught future military leaders how new technologies could yield new information, new ways of thinking, and new strategies to employ. After Sandhurst, he went to Ferranti, an electrical engineering and equipment firm in Toronto, to set up and head its research division. One of his projects involved installing sensors on every ship in a convoy to create an information network that would collect data and pass it to the convoy's commander to better inform decisions.

Porter went back to England as professor of electrical engineering at Imperial College, London, then returned to Canada, to the

University of Saskatchewan, where as dean of engineering he helped establish the first biomedical research program in Canada, its purpose to put more information in the hands of researchers and clinicians to help them analyze, diagnose, and sort through the puzzle of disease.

His interest was the practical, not the theoretical. He wasn't so much a conceiver—he didn't feel the need to think up problems to solve—as he was a perceiver—there were so many big problems already around him to answer. He believed, too, that while it was important to know more and more about every field and discipline, real-life problems don't respect boundaries or disciplines. Wars need weapons, weapons need to hit targets, so he had brought together science and engineering. He had done the same with science and medicine. And in 1961, at the University of Toronto, he brought science and business together. Four years later, Gord became one of his students.

At U of T, Porter also became a great friend of Marshall McLuhan. When they first met at a cocktail party, Porter initially thought McLuhan was crazy, he recalled later, but after a few more cocktail parties he thought him a genius. Later, when McLuhan went to Fordham University for an academic year, Porter was the acting director of McLuhan's Centre for Culture and Technology, and when McLuhan died in 1980, Porter gave the principal eulogy at his funeral. It might have seemed they had little in common. Porter, the mathematician and scientist; McLuhan, the philosopher, communications guru, and superstar. Porter, best known for his low-visibility, high-influence work as teacher and administrator. McLuhan, best known for the concepts he introduced, including "the medium is the message" and, presaging the interconnectedness of people through technology, "the global village," concepts that to many represented near-biblical insight, and to many others were incomprehensible nonsense.

But most fundamental about both McLuhan and Porter was their ability, and their willingness, to see the familiar in unfamiliar ways. For Porter, the computer wasn't only a machine, because using it affects what we experience and how we experience, and therefore what we learn, and therefore what we do and how we do it. Which affects other people, what they experience and learn and do. So whatever substantive information a computer produces and conveys, the fact that the information is produced and conveyed by a computer has more effect, and is therefore more the essence and the point, than the substance of the information itself. The computer—the medium—is really the message.

Whether Gord knew it or not at the time, this was the world he was entering.

He was one of about seventy students in his industrial engineering class. By Christmas he had the highest marks and had been elected class president, a position he'd hold throughout his four years. Porter couldn't help but notice him. "He seemed to like me," Gord recalls. "And somehow he knew I was on the track team." Gord was no longer a high jumper. He had injured his knee, and in any event by this time he was unable to jump much higher than six feet, and others had passed him. He was now too small for the shot put and discus, so the javelin became his event. Though undersized for it as well, his technique, as always, the importance of which he had learned from his father, saw him through. Porter, so far as Gord knew, had no background or interest in sports. It may have been that Porter was interested in someone who was interested in many things. But more than that, Gord thinks, it was because "I got very interested in computers."

After his first year, he got a summer job as a research assistant, working with a graduate student who was doing a paper on safety in the workplace. Porter had created a course called Human Factors Engineering that required students to think of tools, machines, and systems not just from the perspective of what they do, but, taking into account human capacity and behaviour, how safe they are from a user's perspective. To do his job, Gord recalls, "I was stuck up on the top floor of the engineering building at a desk right beside these guys who had welding machines and soldering machines and microscopes and drill presses trying to create devices that could be used in medicine. They were graduate students working with some medical people—this was Porter's first project in developing biomedicine."

This was Hartree and the Meccano set all over again. For Gord, the summer job meant more accidental learning.

"The first computer science course I took was probably in second year," he recalls, "and we were literally using punch cards. You'd work away with your cards, and then take them over to the computer science building and hand them in, and a day later you'd get a big pile of paper back with all the results. Then you'd have to go back and figure out why it all didn't work, then do all your cards again and repeat the process." By late in third year, "we were doing all this with teletype machines. We didn't have to use punch cards any longer." That summer, he got a job at IBM. They put him in a training course to learn how to program in a language they were using in their business, and after a few weeks sent him to one of their customers who had just installed a new computer and was short of staff. "So I just sat there, the lowly guy on the totem pole," he recalls, "writing programs to help them get their computer going as part of their business." The next summer, Honeywell was making inroads into IBM's market dominance—its programming language appeared to be better—so Gord's job was "to go through the Honeywell program and figure out how it works, how well it works, where it didn't work, and what problems it had. It was pretty interesting, and all pretty new."

Late that summer of 1968 Gord got a letter from the treasurer of Orenda, a large aircraft engine manufacturer that had also worked on the development of the Avro Arrow. At the end of the typewritten letter is a handwritten note that says, "I am particularly pleased to see one of our scholarships going to someone I know personally. Ken was very pleased to hear of your award too." It is signed by K.R. Church, Ken's father.

In September, Gord was back for his final year. Porter had been bringing in some new professors, some of whom were "top whizzes in mathematics," Gord says, "but who were more interested in applied math than theoretical math. Other departments at U of T were now using computers more and more as well." His summer jobs at IBM,

his experiences with Porter, the courses he was taking: the interconnectedness of computers with everything was becoming ever
more clear to him. The interconnectedness of his learning as well.
Computers were becoming the way things got done.

When he graduated, he followed his brother to Harvard Business
School. "When I went there I was still intent on going back into the
computer industry when I was finished," he says. "It was only when
I got to Harvard and took a finance course that I thought, *This is pretty
interesting.*"

Pat, Judy, Marilyn, and Marilyn knew, when they arrived at university,
where they were going. Murray had to discover his path, and Gord
the possibilities of the one he was on. Lisa thought she didn't know
where she was going, but in fact she may have known better than any
of us. She needed to, because first came a surprise.

Lisa had never been a planner. She was good at school, smart,
nice, cute, she could get along with anyone, and anyone would want
to get along with her. In grade 13, she knew only that she would go to
university, to U of T probably. She loved reading, so she would take
English literature, she would, as she puts it, "go with the flow." But
it was *her* flow, one she liked and was good at, that had been hers all
her life and would continue to be. Why not? Then she got pregnant.
Flowus interruptus.

"I was probably the first person in my neighbourhood to know
how not to get pregnant," she says. Adèle had made sure of that.
"Then I got pregnant the first time I had sex." She was twenty-one
when her daughter, Taia, was born in December 1967.

Lisa had met Taia's father, Henry Tarvainen, about a year earlier, in a class at U of T, on one of those days he showed up. For
the artsy types who were really cool, and for those in the class who
knew what was going on in the world, Henry was a star and his arrival
was an event. He was only twenty-two, but two years earlier he had
played one of two main characters in a movie, *Winter Kept Us Warm*,
a student production that cost only $8,000 to make but which was

reviewed by the *New York Times* and *New York Post*, which described it as having "more character perception, better plotting nuance and livelier dialogue than many Hollywood productions." It was also chosen as the opening film of the Commonwealth Film Festival, and, in a special category that highlighted the works of new filmmakers, was the first English-language Canadian film ever screened at Cannes. David Cronenberg, then a U of T science student, wrote later that the moment he saw up on the screen the backdrop of the U of T campus and people who looked just like him, he realized that film might be part of his world and that he might be part of it. "When I saw *Winter Kept Us Warm* that did it for me," he said.

And Henry Tarvainen, boyish, shy-appearing, serious, was in Lisa's English class. The "first book he gave me to read," Lisa laughs, "was *A Clockwork Orange*."

The arts were coming to matter more on university campuses in the 1960s, because politics was coming to matter more. Civil rights, the women's movement, questions of identity—Canada-U.S.; English-French—lots was in the air. There had been such energy in the postwar years, Canada on the Move, Canada Unlimited, there was so much to do, lives to make, no time to waste. Then the momentum slowed. Articles in magazines and newspapers offered doubts and asked questions: Who are we as a country? Where are we going? The jumble of federal elections in the late fifties and early sixties had demonstrated clearly that no significant new visions were forthcoming from politics. Where else might they come from? Theatre, TV, film, writing of all sorts, and from new, emerging voices. Margaret Atwood and Dennis Lee had graduated from U of T in the early 1960s, and also others who would have less well-known but still important careers. They all knew each other. They read each other's work, saw each other's plays, talked into many long nights. As a country, they insisted, we're a lot more and a lot different than what our politics and our media, and the suffocating bigness of the U.S., suggest we are, and we are going to say that, loudly, proudly, angrily to Canadians, in whatever way and every way we can.

TV was becoming hugely important, so CBC, the country's only
TV broadcaster, became a big focus. Peter Pearson, Larry Zolf, Beryl
Fox, and Patrick Watson, an earlier U of T grad, along with some
others—*les enfants terribles*—came together on a weekly news program
called *This Hour Has Seven Days*. It was provocative, angry, subversive,
and cocky. It looked at Canada in a different way. It was looking for
a Canada of a different sort. Reverence was out, *ir*reverence was in.
This Hour became the second-most watched program on CBC, after
Hockey Night in Canada. But to network bosses, the show sometimes
crossed *way* over the line. Both CBC and the show's producers, spoiling
for a fight, got what they wanted, and two years later *This Hour* was
off the air. But the genie was out of the bottle. No future journalist, playwright, filmmaker, or writer could even pretend to be serious
without adopting *This Hour*'s attitude. At U of T most particularly,
no student newspaper could. In the late 1960s, Bob Rae and Michael
Ignatieff, future politicians, writers, and commentators, both wrote
for *The Varsity*, the U of T's paper. And when he wasn't directing plays,
or popping into some of his classes, so did Henry Tarvainen.

This was also the time of Pierre Trudeau, in his pre–prime minister days. Trudeau too was provocative, angry, subversive, and cocky.
And smart. In Quebec, the connection between the arts, media, and
politics was very close. Its thinkers and commentators believed that
if someplace else—Ottawa—had the ultimate say, if that had to be,
then how Quebeckers live and think belonged to them only. When
This Hour was casting the show, Trudeau was even considered as one
of its hosts. But unlike *This Hour*, Trudeau wasn't only looking for a
different Canada; he already had one in mind. Quebeckers had been
addressing the question of identity for centuries. Up against English
Canada, and their own Roman Catholic Church, the question was:
As Quebeckers, what are we, and how do we fit in?

But if Quebec was always the little guy in the fight, Trudeau
refused to act like a little guy. "Little" didn't occur to him. Trudeau had
the talent, and on Quebec's small stage he had the chance to develop
and hone the qualities of a star. In these different times, it wasn't just

money and privilege that gave you power. Power was *attention*. And media, and especially TV, gave you that attention. And if you were more interesting than the next guy, you got it. You mattered more than he did. Trudeau wasn't Pearson or Diefenbaker or Mackenzie King. Or Eisenhower or Truman. Like John Kennedy, night after night in our living rooms, love him or hate him, he was interesting. He was different. *Alternative*. And in the 1960s, different and alternative were at least as important as what, in substance, different and alternative might actually produce. Trudeau could never have emerged from English Canada. Not then. English Canadian politics would never have offered him a stepping stone.

But developing out of sight to English Canadians in Quebec, now in his late forties, there he was, fully realized, on the centre stage of Canadian politics, with a multitude of messages, but one that hit home for us twenty-year-olds in the rest of the country: because he didn't act small, we, as Canadians, as Canada, must not be small. And we were ready to feel this way. Trudeaumania followed. As a nation we weren't big enough to do big things on an international stage. We had come to know that. But as individuals, as Trudeau, as McLuhan, as writers and musicians just beginning to find their way, we could. After three straight minority governments, in June 1968 Trudeau swept the country.

Lisa had finished her second year at U of T the previous May— living that year with Kathy McNab—and then with the baby due in December, she decided not to go back to school in the fall. She and Henry bought a house near campus—Adèle, a real estate agent by this time, found it for them. They rented out two of the rooms to help them manage their expenses. Late in the summer, six months pregnant, she went to Expo with Henry, wearing, she recalls, a pink chiffon dress.

Lisa hadn't pictured herself as a mother, certainly not at twenty-one, but soon she would be one. She hadn't pictured herself out of school, but now she was. This was her life now, and she would live it. But it wasn't necessarily Henry's. He was a director and writer, he did plays at Hart House, U of T's main theatre. He helped found the New Directors Group, some of whose members would be central to the growth of alternative theatre in Toronto in the 1970s. His friends, two of whom rented the rooms in their house, included Paul Ennis, who would become an influential music and film writer, and Joe Medjuck, who founded the Cinema Studies Program at Innis College at U of T and produced many of Ivan Reitman's films, *Ghostbusters*, *Twins*, *Kindergarten Cop*, *Stripes*, and *Dave*, among others. This was Henry's world. It wasn't entirely Lisa's.

She read a lot, and, when she was young, before the family had moved to Toronto, she had taken dance lessons at the Royal Winnipeg Ballet School, and continued her dancing in Toronto until well into high school. But she wasn't artsy and political the way Henry was. When Henry and his friends talked, Lisa's head hurt, she recalls. They went too fast, too deep, everything was so intense, she couldn't keep up. She was there, but wasn't there entirely. She had always been able to talk to anybody about anything, because she listened, because she liked immersing herself in other people's lives, because she was interested in what they said, and in them. And they could sense it. But Henry and his friends were so smart. Lisa had always thought Adèle was the smartest person in the world until Henry came along. And artsy types, even when they don't think they do, can come across as a little condescending, which didn't help. Lisa felt like a "bystander"— to Henry's theatre, his politics, his life. Like she didn't belong.

They decided to give up the house—it was too expensive—and moved into Rochdale, near campus. Named for the city in England, which, emerging out of the Industrial Revolution, was the birthplace of the modern Cooperative Movement, Rochdale was, as it described itself, "an experiment in student-run alternative education." Students and their instructors, more than eight hundred of them, lived together. It was a housing co-op, but also a "free university" that required no tuition or fees, offered no classes—only informal discussion groups— and awarded no degrees. In time, it had its own health clinic, library, newspaper, radio and TV station, and its own co-op nursery school, which Lisa helped to start. Rochdale reflected, and was looking to create, the spirit of the times. It questioned, it doubted. Are there no other ways to learn, to relate, to live? If not, why not? At its best, it was a learning community: lots of interesting people of different backgrounds and deep interests, in one place, bumping into each other, talking about who knows what, with who knows what result. It offered a trial (-and-error) run for the different lives they were about to live.

But Rochdale wasn't always at its best. The students and instructors moved in, but so did lots of unplanned-for others. Not everybody *remembered* to pay their rent. Then there were the drugs—the uncrossable line, not just for the *tut-tutters* but for mainstream Canadians at the time. Rochdale was a place easy for insiders to love and for outsiders to mock—student-run, government-paid, free *this*, free *that*. To outsiders, Rochdale was in the spirit of the times, and they didn't like it. The experiment lasted less than a decade. Lisa liked it there, the people, the learning, the pace, the life. She liked the other young mothers, she liked helping to create something that was changing lives, like the co-op nursery school. That didn't quite work as it was supposed to, like a lot of things at Rochdale. As a co-op, the parents were supposed to help out and give six to ten hours to the school every month, but many focused on their own children instead. Still, it was an experiment. It was something.

After Taia was born, Lisa returned to U of T and graduated in 1970, a year after the rest of her class. At twenty-four, she was the first in her family to have a university degree. But she and Henry were not getting any closer. Henry knew what he wanted. He would go where he was going. Theatre was first for him, and Lisa knew that. He was dedicated, driven, self-focused. Lisa wasn't. He had a plan. Lisa wasn't a planner. She had a daughter, she was a mother, that much she did know and want. Other than that, she recalls, "When I graduated all I knew was that I didn't want to be a teacher." She knew one thing more: she wanted to be Lisa.

CHAPTER FOURTEEN

For some of the students in the Brain Class, their university years were smooth sailing. For others, a bumpy ride. In university, we were in many different places, exposed to many different outlooks and possibilities, we were living thirty-five different lives. Each of our paths was more personal, and individual, than it had been in high school.

Bruce McLeod was the youngest in our class. After high school, he decided to take a year off, to "mature," as he put it. He got a job in a bank, learned he never wanted to work in a bank, and went to Queen's University as his father, mother, brother, and grandfather had, and became a teacher.

His friend Wilf Wallace, the second-youngest and the smallest in the class, who had moved with his family to a farm north of Toronto in grade 11, did well enough at his high school there that Brock University, in its first year and looking to enhance its enrolment, admitted him after grade 12. He was sixteen, looked eleven, and would be living away from home for the first time. For Wilf, the next few years were a blur. He became the cox on Brock's crew team in the rowing hotbed of St. Catharines, but otherwise, as he puts it, "I just fooled around and didn't do any work at all, as a result of which I didn't complete my first year." He got a job at Capitol Records in Toronto, hung around the clubs in Yorkville, the hub of Toronto's folk rock scene, met Marianne Faithfull, and his wife, and never went back to school.

Penni Harcourt went into nursing at St. Michael's Hospital in downtown Toronto, her strong, formidable side becoming ever more evident, her caring side ever harder to hide, then went to McGill and earned her degree. Lorna Casey trained as a child and youth worker in northern Etobicoke, working with kids whose lives were very different from her own, then, drawn to these kids, went to teachers' college, her interest becoming her instinct and life's work. Others in our class moved more directly towards teaching, if not always with teaching in mind. Mary McIntyre through political science, then history at U of T, Joan Cliff through phys ed, Judy Clarke through French, Sandie Barnard, as Sandie would, through medieval English and Chaucer. Cheryl Beagan took mostly English and psychology courses and thought about grad school, but with the extra years of study that would require, and not wanting to be "poor," as she puts it, and remembering the stress that money had put on her father and her childhood life, says she "fell into teaching as the only job I could see possible after an English degree." Wayne Yetman too ended up in English, at Western University, never to become a teacher but, as it turned out, to work in an office where, as in many offices, his ability to write, in the midst of co-workers who hated to write—letters, reports, presentations, speeches—made him an indispensable person. He kept on running as well.

Others started down one path at university, then changed direction. Ken Church and Daryl Browne chose math and physics, and math, physics, and chemistry, respectively, as their majors at Queen's, but unlike Gord and his brother took one long year to find out that the courses were way too theoretical and not for them. That first year, they didn't do well. They had never not done well in school; like Marilyn Steels at McMaster, they had no experience with failure and no strategies to deal with it. And in university, if things went wrong they could go so far wrong, so fast, it would be hard to make them right. Yet Ken and Daryl were almost unfazed. Their parents too. They had simply taken the wrong courses. So together they rode out that first year, Ken playing bridge a lot, Daryl rediscovering badminton, and found the right course the next year, Ken commerce, Daryl engineering, and became Ken and Daryl again.

For Marilyn Cade, it was much the same. She won a scholarship to Western and started in maths, physics, and chemistry, but then for the first time in her life, she didn't do well, and even more surprisingly didn't buckle down and work her way out of her problem as she always did. Instead she switched into French, chose not to beat herself up, and was on her way again.

Barbara Vaughan-Parks, who had been on intramural baseball and volleyball teams at ECI and loved to play tennis, had a healthy, robust British disposition. She had long known what she wanted. Although she won a scholarship to the University of Waterloo, instead she chose UBC, in physiotherapy. At first, so far from home, she felt alone. But soon her British and sporting instincts kicked in, and she would graduate second in her class.

Kathy Vodden had always marched to the beat of her own drum. As the rest of the orchestra played one song, she played another. Dissonant, acerbic, contrary. I was often afraid of what she was thinking. Kathy's target: those in the class who all their lives had been told what was right, knew what was right, always did right, and who insistently played in tune. Kathy thought there was something not entirely right in what's unquestionably right. Don't be one of "the herd," she'd remind/encourage/admonish her classmates. While she was at U of T studying sociology, she decided to volunteer at St. Christopher House, a neighbourhood centre in a neglected part of downtown. Suddenly, she had in front of her kids not much younger than she was but whose lives were unthinkably different. The food they ate or didn't have to eat, the clothes they wore, their traumas and tragedies, here they were, living less than half an hour away from where she had lived all her life. This was real-life sociology. Why hadn't she known? How could she not have? Whatever else her pre–St. Christopher House self had known was right, or wasn't, this definitely was not right. Years later, she still seemed embarrassed by that earlier self, who had always thought she knew so much.

Peggy Clarke was this fun, tidy little person who took up no more space than she needed. She wasn't much over five feet tall, probably weighed a hundred pounds. She had short hair. She liked to talk and laugh, but not too loud or too much. She was eager without being annoying, upbeat without being exhausting, nice but not teeth-achingly so, capable and competent without being anal. She was good at lots of things, yet she seemed always more focused on those who she thought were doing truly amazing things. She didn't put herself at the centre of any group, and she wasn't a storyteller, because that might suggest that she believed her life more interesting than others' when it's they, she thought, who should be talking about theirs. She went to Western, studied English, and four years later graduated in English. No fuss.

Ted Whistance-Smith was always going to do fine. He took two years to complete grade 13, not because he got sick, or there was a trauma in the family, or he couldn't do the work. He just wasn't in a hurry. The academic side of life was important, he knew, he didn't dismiss that, and he had always liked to read, but there was a lot more to life than just the halls of ECI. He knew you could learn a lot on playgrounds, in pool halls, from people, in everything you do. This is the world, this is how it works. So you go out into that world and experience it.

His twin brother, Steve, always wanted to look at everything from every side, then to think about it, then to talk about it, then to think and talk about it some more to know it even better, and, of course, never really to know it, because there was always a next thing to learn and think about. What Pound or Camus or any number of other writ-ers had said in books Steve read, he found all that so exciting. Books offered him a timeless world and timeless learning and meaning.

For Ted it was, yeah, well sure, but let's get on with it, let's do it. Ted could seem dangerous, he would do stuff most kids wouldn't even think about, but he wasn't stupid-dangerous. He was too sen-sible for that. Dared to walk a tightrope, he'd probably do it—but put a net underneath. That too was the real world. So to him, all this academic school stuff—sure, I'll do what I need to do, learn what I have to learn, and then head out to work, to an office like my father, to a business of some sort, and live that life. So eventually Ted went to Waterloo Lutheran University (now Wilfrid Laurier), graduated, and did just that.

Because Ted took two tries to get through grade 13, Steve was the first in their family to go to university. He arrived at Queen's in September 1965 with an interest in English that would become a whole lot more. For Steve, what an opportunity! A lot of our ECI classmates had been big readers as kids, the girls more than the boys, but in high school, we all read less. There was more homework, and too many other things to do. But Steve kept reading. And in high school he met Lisa, and through her, he met Adèle. In those years he was at their house almost as often as he was at his own, at the kitchen table, Adèle talking politics, philosophy, literature, about the books she'd read and films she'd seen, Lisa interested, tolerant, Steve fascinated. Now he was an English major, his *job* was to read!

He still needed a minor to fill up his course timetable, and though he had no real interest in theatre, and had never been in the play at ECI, he was even less interested in his other options. So theatre it was. The Drama Department at Queen's put on a few productions each year, and as it turned out auditions were being held for Tennessee Williams's *Suddenly Last Summer*, and a friend of Steve's suggested they both audition. Steve was cast in one of the main roles, as Dr. Cukrowicz, a brain surgeon whose specialty is lobotomies. The play's director was Fred Euringer, one of Steve's professors, later the head of the department.

They were a few weeks into rehearsal when Steve had a "come to Jesus" moment, as he puts it. He was asleep in his room late one morning. "I'd been at a party the night before and had been drinking too much, and yelling and carrying on, and the phone rings. I say 'hello,' and my voice is just a croak, and I hear the phone slam down in my ear. I think, *Ohmygawd*, rehearsal!" He got dressed, rushed to the theatre, and went to the green room, where all the cast hung out. No one was there. He climbed the spiral staircase that connected the green room to the stage. The stage was brightly lit, everything else was pitch-black. No one was there either. Out of nowhere a chair flew past him and smashed against the back wall—not close enough to hit him, but a shot across his bow. At the back of the theatre a door opened and banged quickly shut. Steve knew who it was. He went back down to the green room and waited. And waited. About ten minutes later, Euringer walked in and said, very calmly, "You do know that if we didn't open in a week you'd be gone." Steve nodded. "OK," Euringer said, "let's go up to the stage." When they got there, Euringer said, "OK, yell." Steve yelled, but not much came out. Euringer yelled. Steve yelled again. They went back and forth. "In about ten minutes my voice was back," Steve recalls, "and Euringer just said, 'OK let's go.'" And they rehearsed what Steve had missed.

"You don't often see grown-ups who are passionate about what they do," Steve says, "or at least I never did. This is someone who deeply cares, and cares enough to do what he did, to throw that chair and yell with me. It was an incredible experience. It was the absolute making of me, because it demonstrated that it matters what you do. If you don't want to do it, you don't dick around, and you don't do it. But if you do want to do it, you've got to be there, all-in, give yourself 110 percent to it. It's the only way you make anything of value."

Steve says Euringer was different in a lot of ways from Mr. Orton, our high school English teacher, but in one big way, they were the same. "A great teacher creates an equal ground for himself and the student, or makes you feel that way. All the time without losing their authority. It's what allows the student to accept what they're taught." And a great teacher also affects others, who affect others, and others. Steve's roommate at Queen's was Michael Mawson, who would later act and direct, and teach at the National Theatre School. In the early 1970s, "there was a little burst of theatre in Toronto," Steve recalls. "Five or six new theatres and new companies. I helped create one of them, and Fred Euringer had former students in at least three of them." One of them was Mawson, and one of Mawson's students was

Ted Dykstra, who through a long career as an actor, director, and playwright in TV and film but mostly on stage has played in almost every big and small theatre across the country, including co-writing and starring in the long-running show *Two Pianos Four Hands*. Dykstra would later write about Mawson, "If you think of six degrees of Kevin Bacon, it's one degree of Michael Mawson. You go to any show in Canada, and he's there in some capacity by one degree."

Euringer, Mawson—this was Steve's life at Queen's. "Kingston was a tough town in the late sixties," Steve says, "four prisons and an aluminum factory, and I had hair down to my shoulders." But Queen's was its own community, and the Drama Department its own community within it. Steve was coming to be hooked by theatre, but he wasn't sure he wanted to be hooked. He liked to be able to go in all sorts of directions, follow his fascinations wherever they took him. "I used to blow hot and cold about theatre," he says. It wasn't so much a love-hate as a love-fear. A fear of what that love, that 110 percent of himself, might mean for the rest of his life.

"So I still have a year to go at Queen's to get my B.A. in English," he says, "and all I really know is that I really don't want to be an English professor, and I don't know what the hell I'm going to do, and I'm getting desperate." A friend told him that a director was coming to town looking for actors for a show, and that they should audition for it. "And once again I'm doing my blowing hot and cold—but he pestered me and finally I went and met this guy. Bill Glassco." Glassco had gone to Princeton and Oxford and had taught at U of T, but was fed up with teaching. Theatre is what he wanted to do. "And we connected. All I remember is we were walking along the lake and talking and talking, and I can't even remember what we were talking about—he had taste and courage, a rare combination; he was always ready to do something—and sometime towards the end he said, 'I want to start a theatre in Toronto. Do you want to help me?' I said yes." Steve still had a year to go to get his degree. "But I just dumped that, and the real adventure began. I had an experience in the next three years that I don't think any university in the world could've given me." It wasn't what his parents expected. "It was a pretty horrible time for them," Steve says. "Neither of them had been to university and they were proud that Ted and I were going. But it didn't matter, this was more exciting, and I didn't know what I was going to do with an English degree anyway, so it made sense I do this. But I'm sure it was very difficult for them."

Glassco, Steve, and others spent the year preparing. They did summer stock at the Red Barn Theatre in Jackson's Point, on Lake Simcoe, about an hour north of Toronto, "to give ourselves more experience," Steve says. "I'd been in a few things, but God knows I had no training as an actor. And we began to look for a place we could turn into a theatre in Toronto, and a play to produce." That theatre would be the Tarragon, and its first play, *Creeps*.

Diana Boylen, as so many in the Brain Class did, loved the outdoors when she was young. Her interest came not from summer camps or a family cottage but from the suburban outdoors, wandering and exploring the still undeveloped land on the fringes of her neighbourhood in Etobicoke. At York University, her focus on science shifted slightly, but critically, to a focus on the environment, which was just beginning to become its own field of study, which led, after graduation, to the big open spaces, to a life in the West.

Roger Peacock didn't think he knew where he was going—he might even have rejected the idea for a time—but he ended up where it seemed he would always go. His grandfather was John Wellington Pickup, who had been a chief justice of Ontario. Roger had grown up with family stories where certain of his ancestors were talked about more often, with greater pride than others. Nothing too overt, but still, messages that, as a kid, he absorbed. So he got his law degree at Osgoode Hall, and law became his path.

Kathy McNab wanted to be a journalist. At the time, she probably would've said "reporter" or "writer"—but somebody involved in the news. There were maps all over the walls of her father's office, large-scale construction maps showing the roads her father, first as a surveyor, then as Ontario's deputy minister of transportation and communications, had helped to build. Her father needed to be aware of a larger world to do his job, so Kathy's interest came naturally. After grade 10, when she left ECI and went to Richview, she got involved in the school's yearbook. She liked the energy and buzz of the yearbook, how it connected to every aspect of the school's life, clubs, activities, teams. She liked its urgent, unforgiving, ball-on-the-four-yard-line, last-play-of-the-game deadlines, and also lots of other times where you just hung around the yearbook office trying to figure out what to do, getting to know people as you were doing it, letting them get to know you, so that when those big, urgent moments happened, you could pull them off together. In Kathy's grade 12 year the yearbook editor was Michael Kesterton, later a long-time columnist for the *Globe and Mail*. The year after it was David Black, a classmate of mine at Humber Valley elementary who later in life, after a stint at the *Toronto Star*, began accumulating small community newspapers, today more than 170 of them, including the Honolulu *Star-Advertiser* and the Juneau (Alaska) *Empire*. "I liked the people," Kathy says of her time with the yearbook. "I liked putting everything together. I liked being part of something."

She decided that when she graduated from Richview she would go to Ryerson Institute of Technology (now Toronto Metropolitan University) for radio and television arts. U of T was *the* university in Toronto, York University was just starting up, and Ryerson was where you went if you couldn't get in anywhere else. But only Ryerson offered the program Kathy was looking for. Her father arranged for her to talk with Betty Kennedy, then a prominent broadcaster at CFRB, Toronto's biggest radio station, and a panellist on *Front Page Challenge*, one of CBC TV's most popular programs. He wanted her to know that a woman could have the career that she aspired to. (More than a decade later, twice I sat beside Betty Kennedy as a guest panellist on the show. The panel's task was to identify a major news story. My job was to ask a few lame questions of an invited guest associated with the story, then turn her way and say, "Betty?" and then she, Gordon Sinclair, and Pierre Berton, the two other panellists, would take it from there.)

After grade 13, and after lots of askance looks—"Ryerson?!"—Kathy decided instead on social sciences at U of T, to learn *what* she needed to know before learning how to communicate it. She arrived on campus in September 1965, just as U of T's Radio Varsity (now CIUT-FM) was launching. She was part of the founding group.

The station became, as she puts it, her "home away from home." "The U of T was so big," she recalls. "When I got there, I needed something smaller, something where I could belong." She liked the station for all the reasons she'd liked working on the Richview yearbook—the common purpose, the deadlines—but now she was with other students from so many different places and backgrounds, with so many different interests, from the engineers and techies to the philosophers and political activists, all at a time when university students were finding their voice. Serious questions were being debated and lived: human rights, civil rights. Betty Friedan's book *The Feminine Mystique* had come out in 1963. Toronto was a prime destination for Vietnam War draft dodgers and for disaffected faculty from U.S. universities. Two Cornell professors, later in the decade, crossed the border to U of T, and one of them, political philosopher Allan Bloom, whose course I'd taken, would write the huge bestseller *The Closing of the American Mind*. Students, suddenly living in a grown-up world, were dealing with big-world questions. Questions that, as Kathy recalls, had been on the back burner when she arrived at U of T and which, just a few years later, were on the front burner and getting hotter.

Kathy lived downtown with Lisa during her second year, the same year that she and another female student started their own show on Radio Varsity. It was called *Twelve by Two*—twelve minutes long, two hosts—later *Every Other Thursday*, sometimes live, sometimes in studio, sometimes on location. The program might be about anything, because U of T students, they knew, were interested in more than what happened on campus. Kathy and her co-host went to Toronto's new city hall, and to the old one across the street, and reported from there. Kids playing with toy guns in a time of war, did this make them more militaristic? They wanted to know.

At first, the station's signal was confined to the U of T campus, its cables running through steam tunnels underground connecting to amplifiers and speakers. Then its reach expanded, and Kathy and her co-host began imagining their audience as all of Toronto. They were bringing the campus to the city and the city to the campus. In her last year, Paul Shaffer, later David Letterman's bandleader and sidekick, came south from Fort William (now Thunder Bay) and joined the station. It was all so exciting. Everything she did, everything around her, felt part of a bigger world. At her graduation she watched as one student crossed the stage, received his degree, then tore it up, to pro-test the university's involvement with armament makers. As students, they *mattered*. And they were going to matter. In grades 9 and 10, all I'd seen of Kathy was her Annie Hall flighty, spontaneous, outgoing exterior self. I had missed her serious, deliberate interior self.

After she graduated she became a teacher, but teaching offered her only one path to learn and to share what she would discover. She would find others.

At university, Doug Little would find a whole new interest. Or maybe he already had that interest, and nobody, not his parents or friends or brothers and sister, knew. With Doug, you never did quite know what was on his mind. He wasn't a contrarian, he was an "other." As everyone else took in the world straight on, Doug shifted his gaze a little to one side or another, to see it slightly askew, as if to catch it with its pants down. The only indication of this—Doug's crinkly eyes and crinkly grin. The world was his own private joke. So naturally, as everyone else in the class went into English, history, or engineering, Doug went into East Asian studies. Years later, his brother, Tom, would just laugh at the thought of it. Not that Doug didn't like East Asian studies, or take it seriously, because he did. But as the youngest kid in his family, who did whatever he wanted because no one had any energy left to fight his notions, this was also "Doug being Doug." Being "other," however, isn't easy.

—

Joan Boody was probably the only one in the class whose family size—
she was one of seven kids—and her placement among them—the oldest—was life-shaping. She had to grow up responsible. When she met
her second husband, Gus, and discovered that he was the oldest of six
kids, she said to him, "So you didn't have any fun growing up either,"
which wasn't actually true for Joan, but they both got the point: a big
family is complicated. As one of many kids, you grow up as an individual, but mostly you grow up as a family. "Family was paramount,"
Joan says, because it has to be. After Joan came a set of twins, a boy
and a girl, then a year later another girl. Joan's mother had four kids
under four to care for, her father, a young accountant trying to make
his way, four kids to provide for. After a pause of five years, three more
kids followed, the "top four" and "the other three," as Joan and her
next-oldest siblings off-handedly put it, not so off-handedly it seemed
to the others. But being the oldest was its own unique role. Again and
again Joan heard her mother say, and still hears in her head, "You have
to act your age." There are certain ways to behave that are a necessity,
because you have to set an example for the younger ones or the family
can't function. (The title Mr. Smith had given her in Russian class,
after all, was Exemplary Party Member.) And mostly Joan did, and
mostly the other kids did for each other. "I was, I had to be, an organizer from the very beginning," she recalls.

Her mother ran the house—she was "the strong one," Joan
remembers. Her father was around as often as most fathers of the time
were, and was "very, very quiet, and introspective." Later Joan wondered if there was more to his story. Her father had fought in North
Africa, then Sicily, then in the bloody campaign north, then in Ortona,
where in a single week, in house-to-house fighting, more than a thousand Canadians died, and where, nearly a year later, on September 28,
1944, as they were "crossing the Rubicon," as her father used to say, he
and his unit were captured. Joan remembers the date because thirty-
one years later her first child was born on that day. The Rubicon River
wasn't much more than a ditch in Ortona, they just jumped across
it, her father told her. But what had been good for Caesar wasn't

for them. This part of the story her father told with a laugh. The
rest of the war he didn't talk about, not what had happened before
Ortona or what came after. Joan would need to piece that information
together herself.

With shrapnel wounds in his head, her father and hundreds of
other POWs were marched—to where, they didn't know—then put
onto trains. Back home, for months, his family knew only that he was
missing in action. He ended up at Stalag VII-A, the Germans' largest
POW camp, not far from Munich. A German doctor, using only a local
anaesthetic, removed the shrapnel. It was winter, Germany was falling apart, conditions at the camp were worsening. On April 29, 1945,
only nine days before the war ended, Stalag VII-A was liberated. In
letters he and Joan's mother had exchanged before his capture, they
had made plans to get married as soon as he returned. A June date was
set, then postponed as he recovered in a hospital in England. They
had known each other for only two weeks before he was shipped out.
In August 1945, they were married. Joan never knew her father before
the war. She didn't know if he had always been so quiet, so introspective. That was just him.

Most of us didn't know our grandparents very well. But Joan's
mother's father would have a profound influence on her all her life.
As a baby, when Joan tried to say "Grampa," the word came out as
"Pampi," and that's what she would always call him.* Joan's grandfather was a doctor in Georgetown, now only a long commuter ride
from Toronto, but during his fifty years of practice it was deep countryside. In his early years, in winter, he'd hire a horse and cutter to get
through the snow to do his rounds, never knowing what accidents of
life or death were ahead of him. During the Depression, some patients
paid him in chickens and eggs. In the mornings he'd do his house calls,

---

* My story is similar. My brother couldn't say "Grandma" and said "Bama" instead,
  which eventually got shortened to "Bam." She lived with us all our growing-up
  years. When our daughter had kids and asked what I wanted them to call me,
  knowing how I felt about Bam, she made a suggestion. They call me Bampa.

and in the 1950s, when Joan was ten or so, she'd sometimes go with him. "I'd keep a little pad of paper and write on it the name of the patient he was seeing, what was wrong with them, and when we got back to the office he'd tell me what the patient's temperature was, and I would record it." Joan decided right then she wanted to be a doctor. But it was another experience with him that had an even greater impact on her.

Her grandfather and grandmother had a cottage on an island in Isabella Lake, not far from Parry Sound, a few hours north of Toronto. When Joan was old enough, she would spend whole summers with them. It gave her parents a little break, having one less kid around, and Joan, being the oldest, some summers went alone and had her grandfather to herself. "He wasn't someone who'd lie around," Joan recalls. He had fought at Vimy Ridge and a few months afterwards he'd been gassed at Hill 70, was invalided to England, and as plans were being made to send him back home he was plotting his return to the trenches.* He had this sense of purpose about him. Even later, Joan recalls, "He always had projects. One summer, I was about five, we scoured the island for every different wildflower we could find, and pressed them, and named them, and made a scrapbook. And by the end of the summer, I was supposed to know the names of all of the wildflowers on the island. What we did always involved learning of some sort, but he always made it exciting and interesting. It never seemed like a chore."

She has an image of her grandfather in her mind that lasts to this day. They're on the island together, just the two of them, and they're walking somewhere, her grandfather in motion, but not going too fast, Joan tagging along, able to keep up. And they're talking about something. She still has in her head some of his sayings, like when she'd ask him what he was doing and the answer to him seemed obvious:

---

* On the 100th anniversary of the 1917 battle, a small platoon of Joan and her family travelled to Vimy Ridge to celebrate him—four of his grandkids, seven great-grandkids, seven great-great grandkids, nine spouses and partners, twenty-seven in all.

"Just playing checkers on Grandpa's shirt." Or when he'd be teasing her about something, pulling her leg: "I'm just exerting pressure on your lower limb." And the sun is shining.

When she thinks of that memory, she thinks of a Japanese movie she and Gus watched called *After Life*. In the movie there's a way station between life and death where the recently deceased are given a few days to pick an event from their life, which others will then film and which the deceased will get to have played over and over for them for all of eternity. "When I watched that movie," Joan says, "what came to me was that island and my grandfather. I still have this vision: the smell of it, that warm pine smell; running along the path between the cabin and the boathouse where we slept. And that soft feel of pine needles under your feet, we were in bare feet all summer. And the warmth of the sun. After seeing the movie, I thought that's what I would like to live over and over and over again. Maybe overlaid with the smell of woodsmoke from the wood stove."

In grade 13, Joan applied for pre-med at U of T, to become a doctor like her grandfather. But her marks weren't high enough, so she took science instead, hoping to apply to medical school again after she got her degree. Inspired by the feeling of those summers with her grandfather, she took an ecology course in her second year. "Early in the semester," she recalls, "we went on a weekend field trip to Grand Bend"—on southern Lake Huron, about a four-hour drive west of Toronto. "I still remember it so vividly. We worked all weekend. We were digging pits in the sand dunes, looking at how they had evolved, and how several feet down there was a layer of black carbon." They had all dug in sand before and had seen those darker colours with their different textures, but it had never occurred to her that this might mean something. "But now we realized there'd been a forest there, and we could figure out when that had happened. It was like an epiphany to me. I'd read all these books, but until you experience it first-hand you really don't understand. And there it is, right there. It was just amazing. And the professor was really great. From that moment on I started to focus on environmental science, and that field trip became the foundation of my teaching. Certainly you do have to do the book learning, but if you actually did things in the out-of-doors, that's what made it come alive. It was the turning point for me."

That great professor was Bill Andrews, who wrote some of the textbooks that Joan later used when she taught environmental ed in high school, textbooks that, unlike the others, Joan says, read as if they were written by someone who had actually set foot outside the class-room. Andrews made science and research exciting, and he did one thing more. One day he overheard Joan explain something to another student in the class and he said to her, "You'd make a good teacher." That's all it took. "Another little light bulb went on," Joan says. Pieces that had always been there suddenly fit together. Her grandfather, her love of nature, at home with her sisters and brothers setting up desks, taking turns, pretending to be the teacher (Joan more often than the others). "I hadn't really thought of teaching as a career before. It was that, and the fact that I didn't have the marks to get into medicine." After she graduated from U of T in environmental science she did a year at the Faculty of Education and became a teacher.

For most in the Brain Class, going to university meant meeting new people, discovering new interests, finding new ways to live and discarding old ones. For Joan Cliff, not much changed after high school except that what had been her parents' choices and her own were now hers entirely. She had loved sports of all sorts at ECI and was vice-president of the Girls Athletic Association, and now at U of T, she studied phys ed and played on the volleyball team. When she was twelve, she had met Doug Milloy. He was two years older and two grades ahead at a neighbouring school. They started going out early in high school, and when he went to U of T to study medicine two years ahead of her, they remained together. They liked the same things and had many of the same interests and beliefs, but so do lots of high school boyfriends and girlfriends. What Joan and Doug didn't know yet was that what they believed together, religion included, went deeper, and would go deeper still.

In high school, almost everyone in our class went to church every Sunday. We were baptized as babies, were confirmed at twelve, and to most of us Sunday school felt the way regular school did when we hadn't done the homework. And on those Sundays when we had to sit with our parents in the sanctuary through the *whole* service, most of us drifted during the Bible readings and died during the sermons. But nevertheless we were there, and I think most of us thought we would always be there. Not all of us, and not always, with enthusiasm—Judy Clarke's parents, seeing her mope around before they left for church, used to refer to her "Sunday face." But church was part of life.

It was for Joan too. She went every week with her family, joined Brownies and Guides at the church, and went to Pioneer Camp, a religious-based facility, in the summers. A lot of her friends and, as it turned out, Doug's friends went to the same church and the same camp and lived nearby and spent so much time with each other that their parents got to know them, like and trust them, and encourage them to spend even more time together (or at least not discourage them). None of this was about sharing the same values or beliefs. You liked them, they liked you. "It was meeting Doug, and meeting his friends, and then his friends becoming my friends," Joan says, "that changed things. There was just something about them that intrigued me, and got me thinking a lot more about faith and God and the world, and all those big questions, and what are we here for? I remember a confirmation class I had done at Royal York United Church. We were asked to write a little essay on 'Who Is Jesus Christ?' And I came home and I really struggled with it. I knew all the Sunday school stories, but I had a feeling these friends of mine could answer this question a lot better than I could." Joan needed to know more.

University was our first real chance *not* to go to church. And most of us did stop going. As university students we were expected to be rational and logical. We were graded on being that in our courses, and proud to be. Proud too of confronting our parents with all the things they had done and said that now made no sense.

But Joan and Doug kept attending. They went to Little Trinity Church in the city, some distance from U of T. At the same time that Pierre Berton was shaking up the complacency of the church with his bestselling book, Little Trinity was anything but a "comfortable pew." University students were becoming more engaged in the world, and Little Trinity, an evangelical Anglican church, was a place of engagement. Its driving spirit was its rector, Harry Robinson, who, for his congregants, with energy and eloquence, and using his own broad intelligence, connected an understanding of the way we live to the Bible. "'Evangelical' has a lot of different connotations now," Joan says. "But it's Bible-based. Its belief is that salvation comes through faith in Jesus Christ alone, not by your own works." In the works tradition, she explains, "if I live a moral life, if I do all the right things, if I'm a good person, in essence, I *earn* my salvation. In the evangelical tradition, no one can earn salvation. Salvation is a gift to you from God, it comes through your faith, and your faith is in what Jesus did at the cross. So it's grace alone—'by the grace of God'—and faith alone, from which salvation comes."

Joan believes she continued in the church because of those friends from Little Trinity and Pioneer Camp. In them, she says, "I saw evidence of that faith, of what they believed, in their lives. In the way they lived. And I could see the difference in their lives from those of others' lives, and I realized it was out of this faith that that had come. I could see God working in their lives, which made me want to know more, and try to learn more, and to have that kind of life. And to me stepping out in faith more, and finding what I think is truth, so that it became real to me, not just theoretical." As most from our class at ECI were trying to understand life and our place in it, Joan already knew. Later, after she became a teacher and Doug a doctor, that faith was tested.

Margaret Silvester's experience with religion was different. Her father was a member of the United Church, her mother was a Christian Scientist, but families of the time went to church together, so on

Sundays the family attended Kingsway-Lambton United Church not far from their house. Margaret had gone to a Christian Science church once, to its Sunday school, when she was five, something she recalled in a speech she gave later when she was in university. She remembered the "friendliness and love which the [Sunday school] teacher expressed towards me," the "greater knowledge of Bible stories" the kids had compared with those at Kingsway-Lambton, and the letter she received from the church a short time after—five-year-olds don't often get letters—inviting her to attend in the future.

Her memories of that Sunday became significant when she was twelve and had reached confirmation age. For most of us, moving from baptism to confirmation was like going from elementary school to high school. It was something you just did. For Margaret, it was an important moment. Religion mattered to her in a way that was supposed to matter to all of us. Confirmation wasn't about deciding whether to become a teacher or a nurse; this was about how you lived your *life*, all of your life. As a family, the Silvesters said grace before every meal, they said their prayers before they went to bed. At her school, just as it was at all of our elementary schools, every kid and every teacher said the Lord's Prayer. Margaret thought about big questions in a way I never did: "What is God?" "What is my purpose?" But at Sunday school at Kingsway-Lambton, all she got were "hazy answers," which at this moment of confirmation, as she put it, were not sufficient "for responsible church membership." So Margaret did what none of the rest of us did: she "rejected church confirmation." Instead, she enrolled in the Sunday school at a Christian Science church, "as a regular pupil," she said, "for a trial period of one year." She needed answers.

There, they read *Science and Health with Key to the Scriptures* by Mary Baker Eddy, the Christian Science church's founder. They also read the Bible, and in these two books, and through the guidance of her teachers and Christian Science practitioners, Margaret found, as she said in her speech, a "practical religion," one "that can be used every day and in every situation," one that "wasn't just a Sunday religion which is forgotten during the week," one that "helped me to see every-one as a child of God, in reality, regardless of race, religion, or social background." A religion in which she felt a deep peace, in which she found a God of love and the "complete and satisfactory answer" she was seeking.

It was almost five years after her trial year was up, while study-ing social work at U of T, that she gave that speech at the Christian Science church. Another speaker that day was George Cooke, whom she would later marry.

CHAPTER FIFTEEN

As for me, by the time I graduated from ECI, I was ready to move on. I wasn't entirely ready for what was next, but that's a different story. What I did know is that I wanted to go to Cornell University. I wanted something new. The University of Toronto, to me, wasn't new, nor were McMaster or Western or Queen's. I wanted an adventure, and the U.S. was an adventure.

I think that feeling began for me with baseball. The Dodgers, the Yankees, the big leagues, the World Series, the big ball parks, the big cities, the big stories in newspapers and magazines—everything big, everything exciting, I loved it all. I also loved TV, and in Toronto, TV at the time meant mostly American stations. I loved TV when it arrived in our house in the mid-1950s and we were all supposed to love it. And I loved it when I was told it was trashy and "a vast waste-land" and I was supposed to hate it. We had two bedrooms upstairs in our house, one for my brother, Dave, and me, the other for my grand-mother, Bam, and she had a TV in her room. When Dave decided to move into a closet-sized room in the basement to get away from me and have a space of his own, it was just Bam and me and her TV on the second floor. After dinner on nights I didn't have games or practices and after my homework was mostly done, I'd go into Bam's room and we'd watch TV together. She was sixty-six years older, but we were TV buddies, and when my mother would call up from downstairs,

"Ken, it's time for bed," and, buying time, I'd yell back "It's almost over" even if a show had barely begun, I knew that Bam knew she should take her daughter's side, but I knew she'd take mine.

Bam loved comedies—Jack Benny, *I Love Lucy*, *Our Miss Brooks*, Jackie Gleason, Red Skelton, later Danny Thomas, Andy Griffith, and Dick Van Dyke. She liked quiz shows—*I've Got a Secret*, *What's My Line?*, *To Tell the Truth*, *The $64,000 Question*. And variety shows— Ed Sullivan, Perry Como, Lawrence Welk—Bam loved Lawrence Welk, except when he danced with women who were much too young for him—and Myron Floren, and especially the Lennon Sisters. On the downstairs TV we all watched the family shows together— Walt Disney, *Lassie*, *Father Knows Best*, *Ozzie and Harriet*, Donna Reed. Bam didn't like dramas much, and I didn't either. They had nothing to do with worlds I'd ever seen. Not like baseball. They didn't seem real. Except *Dragnet*—hard-bitten, tough-talking cop catching bad guys on the unglamorous streets of L.A.—that I could at least imagine. And *Perry Mason*—what could be more real than a courtroom? And the show's star, Raymond Burr, was Canadian, and so was *Bonanza's* Lorne Greene, so I watched *Bonanza* too.

And also political conventions. I remember the Democratic con-vention in 1956. I got hooked on Adlai Stevenson, and even more on the vice-presidential showdown between Tennessee senator Estes Kefauver and a thirty-nine-year-old Massachusetts senator, John Kennedy. I didn't know who they were. I didn't know anything about them. It was the cheering, the big-voiced speeches, the campaign signs, the state names held high on poles that delegates carried, bob-bing up and down, and the climactic proclamations: "And the great state of ___ is proud to cast its ___ votes for the next vice-president of the United States!" It went to three ballots, Kefauver leading after the first, Kennedy after the second, Kefauver winning in the third.

I had just turned nine. What all this had in common—the com-edies, the variety shows, baseball, and politics—was the U.S., American people, American settings, American messages. All the shows were on the Buffalo stations. The only programs I watched on CBC—and

CBC was the only Canadian network at the time—were *Hockey Night in Canada*, *Wayne and Shuster*, and *Front Page Challenge*. I knew the names of the streets of Los Angeles and New York better than I did those of Toronto, east of Yonge Street, the city's main street (Etobicoke was on the west). And all those TV names also connected to the names I read on the front pages of newspapers and in the sports pages, to the news stories I heard on our radio, to all that was important in the world.

I loved watching college football too. I could've guessed there was a University of British Columbia and a University of Alberta, Saskatchewan, and Manitoba, but I *knew* there was a University of Oklahoma because I saw the Sooners play, and I watched the day Notre Dame ended their forty-seven-game winning streak. I knew about TCU, Texas Christian University, because of Jimmy Swink, and LSU, Louisiana State University, because of Billy Cannon and the Chinese Bandits. I watched Jimmy Brown score twenty-one points by himself— three touchdowns and three extra points—and almost singlehandedly beat Swink's Horned Frogs in the 1957 Cotton Bowl. TCU won 28–27. Every year I watched the Army–Navy Game. Navy was my team, Army was Dave's. Joe Bellino for Navy, Pete Dawkins and Bill Carpenter, the "lonesome end," for Army. The goat and the mule. The stadiums that were jammed. *This* was drama, not made-up stuff.

I loved Etobicoke and Toronto, and I loved Canada, but while my high school classmates, with their cottages and the camps they attended, had a northern instinct, I looked south.

When I arrived in Ithaca, New York, in September 1965, I knew I would major in government, and I knew I was headed for law school or for my master's or Ph.D. By Christmas, I wasn't so sure.

In those first few months, I wasn't yet able to sort out what was in front of me. I had never lived away from home before. I could go to bed when I wanted, get up when I wanted, go to class or not go to class, do my homework or not, eat ice cream every night of the week or for breakfast if I wanted. My call, my life. No one else had to know.

Some things I did have to do, like open my own bank account and do my own wash (occasionally). If things went a little wrong I was used to that, and I handled them as I always had. But if they went really wrong, now my parents were 250 miles away. I had to find my way, settle in. With trial and a lot of error, for most things it didn't take long. Some other things surprised me.

I knew that at the time, in the NCAA, or National Collegiate Athletic Association, the greatest stars in the biggest sports—Jimmy Brown in football, Bill Russell and Lew Alcindor (later Kareem Abdul-Jabbar) in basketball—had to play on freshman teams their first year. They couldn't play on the varsity, on the big team, on the teams we'd see on TV. I knew it was the same at Cornell. But I didn't really know what that would mean until after our first game, an exhibition game against the varsity team. The varsity were good—they would go to the Eastern finals that season—and after two periods, we, the lowly freshman team, was ahead. But it was only a little bit the score that was so amazing. It was the atmosphere—Lynah Rink, capacity four thousand; inside, four thousand students who had been waiting eight months, since March the year before, to watch a winning Cornell team. (The football team was never very good.) I had played Junior B hockey in Central Arena in Etobicoke and in rinks like it, capacity five hundred to a thousand, in front of some parents and a few girlfriends of the players on both teams, about forty in all. This was unbelievable!

We lost, then instantly it was as if the season was over. The varsity team went on their way, winning many more games at jammed-full Lynah and at sold-out Boston Garden for the Eastern championships, in front of fourteen thousand screaming college kids—and we went ours, playing in front of girlfriends (if we had one), our parents hundreds of miles away, against crappy freshman teams and a few just as crappy small college varsity teams. We beat Ithaca College 19–1; I played the third period as a forward, in my goalie skates, and scored a goal. We practised every day, which I'd never done before, and that was good, but that hockey year seemed a loss.

In class, I had to read more than I'd ever read and write more than I'd ever written. The reading I found hard. I'd start yawning. There was all this new material to learn, much of which I didn't understand, so I'd slow myself down and read every word, understanding less and getting more tired. In an introductory economics course, the textbook had been written by our professor, and his lectures were drier than dust. I noticed other students using a yellow highlighter when they read, to note the important ideas on a page, something I'd never seen before. So I bought one, and I highlighted, and highlighted. I understood so little, I was afraid *everything* was important. My pages looked like the side of a school bus.

I found I didn't like the government courses as much as I thought; they seemed too practical, too immediate and specific. Too American. History, on the other hand, was so much different than I had understood. Suddenly it wasn't just about names and dates and big events, it was about all the stuff in between. It was about what people do, individuals, groups, when faced with this situation or that, and why they do it. It was a story, of human nature and human behaviour through time. It wasn't about the past, it was about what those experiences and what that learning might mean for the present and the future. That if history does repeat itself, it's because faced with similar circumstances, people do. I'd liked Mr. Watson and Mrs. Botterell in high school. They were good teachers, but I hadn't understood that before. Maybe they had taught us that too, maybe I wasn't ready to learn it until later. I don't know. The first semester, overall, I had average marks, marks I wasn't used to. The second semester, I began to find my way.

Maybe the best thing about my first year at Cornell was Sigma Phi. There were more than fifty fraternities and sororities at Cornell, almost all of them in big old mansion-like houses. Freshmen (first-year students) lived in the dorms, while in their subsequent years many sophomores, some juniors, and a few seniors lived in these houses. Sigma Phi was one of the smaller fraternities, and about twenty-five or thirty students lived in the house. I was their breakfast waiter, and their breakfast and lunch dishwasher, and for doing this

I earned my room and board. I was the only freshman, and the only non-member living there. I had two roommates—Brad Perkins from Evanston, Illinois, who, having changed his major from architecture to history, was in his fifth and final year, and John Potter, from a dairy farm in Washington, Connecticut, who was in his third year in the agriculture school. Age and nationality aside, they seemed no different than me. But to them, I was very different. I was *the Canadian*. To their ears I said "oot" and "aboot." To mine I said just what they said, "owwt" and "abowwt." They never did stop hearing what they knew they'd hear, I never stopped hearing what I did. They were also really good to me.

They had no reason to be interested in a freshman—they had left that part of their life behind. And I was at least one or two degrees short of cool. I wore the same grey wool pants every day, dressing like the "duke" I'd been in high school, and hung them up every night on my closet door. I wore them so often they turned shiny, like Mr. Jackson's suits. Later, after threatening to do it for many months, my wonderful roommates conducted a year-end cleansing, Brad holding one leg of my pants, John the other, ripping them apart. I wasn't in them. To this day when I talk to Brad, almost every time he asks if I still have my "Rio Rialini" tie, not exactly Giorgio Armani, which I never unknotted—right fashion ancestry, not so great design.

The "house" was filled with achievers. In the room next to ours, one guy was the captain of the baseball team and also a guard on the football team. He was from Camp Hill, Pennsylvania. His roommate, from Davenport, Iowa—one of the Quad Cities, he never tired of telling me, Rock Island, Bettendorf, Moline, and Davenport—was a member of the Sherwoods, the university's top a cappella singing group. Harry Chapin had been a member of the Sherwoods a few years earlier. In the rest of the house, two others were on the basketball team, one was the team's best player. Two were on the diving team, three on the NCAA champion indoor polo team; John Potter was one of them. Another was an actor, another the All-American lacrosse goalie. Several were members of Cornell's top honorary societies, Red Key and Quill and Dagger. There were engineering, architecture, government, history, and English majors. There was an army vet. They were from Boston, Pittsburgh, Philadelphia, Detroit, Cleveland, St. Louis, Baltimore, Bethesda, and Washington, D.C., from Buffalo, Rochester, Johnstown, Pleasantville, Upper Darby, L.A., Honolulu, São Paulo, Hamburg, and Bermuda. And lots from New York City, Long Island, and the posh towns of coastal Connecticut.

Everybody was involved in something, and everyone seemed interesting. Brad's father was an important Chicago architect in a city with a history of important architects. Among other buildings, he and his firm had worked with Finnish architects Eliel and Eero Saarinen to create the Crow Island Elementary School in Winnetka, Illinois. Flat-roofed, a single storey high, with no classical columns in front like those of traditional schools, it was built with little kids in mind. It would be the inspiration for thousands of schools, for the new suburban school. Sunnylea, in Etobicoke, just beyond ECI's boundaries, was one of them. Humber Valley, where Judy Tibert, Marilyn Steels, Roger, Lorna, and I went, had much the same look.

Sigma Phi had also created a speakers series, endowed by one of its alumni. Influential people were invited to give a lecture on campus, had dinner with all of us beforehand, and stayed overnight at the house. The first speaker was Walt Kelly, the creator of the long-running and, during the Vietnam War, increasingly political and controversial comic strip *Pogo*—"We have met the enemy and he is us." Ted Sorensen, JFK's speechwriter and confidant, was another. He played touch football with us on the front lawn of the house. Muhammad Ali was another. I lived freshman year in the midst of this.

All of the guys at Sigma Phi also had to live with me. And if they weren't going to let me be the American I almost was from knowing almost as much about things American as they did, I was going to continue to let them know that Raymond Burr, Lorne Greene, *Star Trek*'s William Shatner, *Dr. Kildare*'s Raymond Massey, *Your Hit Parade*'s Gisele MacKenzie, as well as Paul Anka, Joni Mitchell, Neil Young, Robert Goulet, and Ian and Sylvia were Canadian, and that Saul Bellow was born in Lachine and Art Linkletter in Moose Jaw. And if all that wasn't enough, Minnesota, the "Land of 10,000 Lakes"? Big deal. Ontario has more than *two hundred thousand*. At Cornell, I became more Canadian than I had ever been. Insistently Canadian.

Maybe the best thing about Sigma Phi for me at that time wasn't being surrounded by good, accomplished guys—I'd feel the importance of that later. It was being surrounded by older guys who were more settled into their university years, who were beyond the angst of the freshman dorms and were getting on to things.

After Christmas that first year, I started to do better.

I spent the following summer, 1966, in Toronto, working construction, building a library not far from home. I worked construction most summers, because my parents liked the idea of me being outside, in the fresh air and sunshine. When I arrived back in Ithaca for my sophomore year, I didn't know it, but I was ready to fly.

I was taking more history courses, fewer government courses, and no economics courses at all. I wasn't living in Sigma Phi any longer— I had a room in a house with a family in Cayuga Heights, a residential area near campus. And just ahead were the "Lynah Faithful," as they were called, the fans that filled Lynah Rink.

We started our hockey off-ice workouts when the NCAA's rules allowed, then moved onto the rink. A goalie from the previous year's team, Dave Quarrie, was returning, and he was good. I thought it was likely that we would divide the games, but before the season began, he injured his ankle, so I played. We won our first few games, then beat Clarkson, the defending Eastern champions, in their home rink, and kept on winning, finishing the regular season with only one loss and one tie. Then came the ECACs, the Eastern championships, in Boston Garden, and it seemed like all of Lynah Rink had found their way there, except now, in the midst of ten thousand non-Cornell fans, they were even louder. We won, and a week later at the Frozen Four, the national championships, in Syracuse we beat North Dakota and Boston University and were NCAA champions.

Everything that year just elevated somehow. Came together. The better I was on the ice, the better I was in the classroom. My grades went up.

I discovered the library. After class and before our late-afternoon practices, there was time and no place to go, so I went to Uris Library. I worked, and talked with friends, then after practice and dinner, I went back, worked and talked, went to the student centre for a break, then went back and worked and talked until 11, when the library closed. And sometimes, just before 11, if somebody who had a car was interested, we'd make a "Purity run" to Ithaca's legendary ice cream parlour for a pint of hand-packed chocolate ice cream, which I ate right out of the container, every bit of it. It was that year I discovered that time didn't matter, that day was night and night was day, that work was play and play was work. Lynah Rink, the library, and Purity—it was a pretty good year. So good I didn't want to leave Ithaca, and I spent the summer of 1967 there working construction, and missed Expo.

One other thing. The week after we'd won the NCAAs in Syracuse, the baseball team was leaving for its spring training games in North Carolina. I had played on the freshman team the year before and had done well enough that the varsity coach expected me to be his first baseman that season. I wanted to go south. Spring training, when I'd read about it as a kid, sounded magical. Sunshine after all the winter grey, a ballpark, game after game, day after day. I loved baseball as much as I loved hockey. But going south, now, was too soon—hockey had just ended, but more than that, it would mean that for the rest of that year and for the two years until I graduated, I would go from one sport to the next, almost from the first day of school until the final exams in May. I would love it, but it would define my whole experience at Cornell. I'd have no time for anything else, and I was beginning to enjoy, more and more, lots of other things, things I'd never experienced, that I hadn't even known about, and who knew what other things might be ahead. So I didn't go. Baseball, which had been part of the pattern of my every year, like hockey and school, suddenly wasn't.

—

Years three and four at Cornell were much the same as year two, except for three things: I met Lynda Curran, I took Walter LaFeber's American foreign policy course, and I took a course in art history.

I met Lynda on a blind date. Her roommate, Julia, and my Sigma Phi roommate, Brad, were siblings, and they decided we should meet. Lynda was from Ithaca; she too was a history major. We started dating in September 1967 and within a few weeks nothing seemed like a date any longer, we were just always together. (She tells me that early on I gave her a quiz on Canada, a *written* quiz, the names of provinces, capital cities, notable people—all the things that Americans don't know. I gave her time to study for it beforehand. I think I may have wanted her to pass.)

Also that September, I signed up for Walter LaFeber's course. What I had begun to learn about history, LaFeber suddenly made clear. This was in the midst of the Vietnam War, of civil rights marches, murders, assassinations, riots, and burning cities. There were doubts about everything. I had become old enough, I had seen enough, to doubt. There was more to the story than what governments told, than what corporations told. We were all trying to understand where things stood, how we'd got here, where we'd go next.

Every Tuesday, Thursday, and Saturday morning for fifty-five minutes, LaFeber told us a story. He spoke without notes, with only the barest outline on the board. He began with the sentence he wanted, spoke in paragraphs, and ended with the sentence he wanted. It wasn't as if he spoke from memory, he just knew where he was going. He was from rural Indiana, not far from Chicago, and spoke in a softly resonant Midwestern voice, with authority and without drama, moving from moment to moment and place to place, as life moves, as if he didn't know the answers but his stories did. There were good guys and bad guys—this was a time of David Halberstam's "the best and the brightest," who were and who weren't—but mostly there were good decisions and bad decisions. And mostly there were circumstances.

Washington and Lincoln weren't born great. America didn't need an accident of birth to determine its destiny. Good things and bad things can happen. Here's why they did. Here's what you, we, can do. The answer is in the story. Steve Hadley was in the same class that year. He would become President George W. Bush's national security advisor. For the rest of us, LaFeber's class was training of a different sort. Things are as they are for reasons—human reasons, out of human circumstances, that require human decisions. It is up to us to get at those reasons, understand them, and make better decisions.

Even more unlikely than meeting Lynda and learning from Walter LaFeber was me taking an art history course. I had never liked art. In grade 9, when we were given the option of music or art, pick your poison, I took music because art, for me, was no choice at all. I couldn't *do* art, I couldn't draw, and I knew it. As a family, we did lots of things together, but we never went to an art gallery. As I saw it, there were kids who liked sports and there were kids who liked art. That's the way it was. Art was making things up, writing was the same. It was putting lines or words on a page. It was Jane Anderson's poem, "Spanish Moss," in grade eight at Humber Valley. "Ghostly rags," she called it. "Witches webs." Whose mind worked that way? Who could find such words? It was fanciful. It took imagination. I wasn't fanciful. I had no imagination.

My class schedule was filled with history, government, and sociology courses, so I thought why not take one in art history? Lynda took it too. I don't remember the professor's name. In the lecture hall, she projected works of art onto a giant screen. The first semester, she began with the French Impressionists—Monet, Manet, Renoir, Cézanne. She talked about each work, about what she saw on the screen. Van Gogh, Gaugin, Matisse, Seurat, Toulouse-Lautrec, the Cubists, Braque, Picasso, Léger, Duchamp, Chagall, de Chirico, Miró, Dali, and more Picasso. Most names I'd never heard before. Gradually, I began to see what I was seeing. The second semester was mostly American art from the end of the Second World War to the present, to 1968—the Expressionists, Pollock, de Kooning, Rothko,

Johns, Rauschenberg, Oldenburg, Lichtenstein, Warhol; Jim Dine, and Louise Nevelson, she mentioned a lot.

Somewhere along the way I came to understand that art wasn't just fanciful. Nor did it have to be an exact replication of a real object, scene, or person. Art was different ways of seeing things, and different ways of expressing and conveying what you saw. As Impressionists knew, not all information in a scene, in a moment, matters. You take in some things, others you don't notice. As Expressionists knew, with colour and line you can depict and convey a feeling. As both knew, there can be meaning behind the literal and the evident. I didn't understand that until I took this course. Just a random course, a subject that always had nothing to do with me—except maybe it had to do with me a little after all.

We went to the Frozen Four my junior year and lost in the semi-finals to North Dakota, then again in my last year, 1969, losing in the finals to Denver. By this time, as it had been in grade 13, mostly on my mind was what I'd do next.

One year had always just turned into another. I went to school, I played hockey and baseball, and so long as my marks were fine, so long as no coach ever said to me, "Sorry, son, not this year," there was no reason any next year needed to be any different. But this year, my graduating year, *was* different. I'd been drafted by the Boston Bruins five years earlier while I was at ECI, my rights had been traded to the Canadiens, things had gone well at Cornell, I had the chance to continue to play hockey. I'd also been accepted at Harvard Law School. I had a choice to make. School or hockey? And now it was a choice I *had* to make. Law school meant there would be no time for hockey. Professional hockey meant there would be no time for school. I talked with the Canadiens, I visited Harvard, I was told I could be a dorm counsellor there to help me pay my way. I talked with the Framingham Pics of the Massachusetts Senior League about playing some games with them. Fourteen years after I began playing hockey, seventeen years after I started in school, finally it came down to one *or* the other.

Or maybe not. After the NCAA championships in Colorado Springs I'd flown to Stockholm to join the Canadian National Team for the World Championships. It was March 1969. The team wanted me to play with them the following year. They were based in Winnipeg, where I could go to the University of Manitoba Law School and graduate in 1972, a few months after my teammates and I would play for Canada at the Olympics in Sapporo, Japan. Maybe I could still do both. I wasn't ready to give up law school. And I wasn't ready to give up hockey. I went with the National Team.

The late 1960s was a serious time. I was so much more aware of the world, I was at a serious age, and university was a serious place to be. I loved those years. Before that time, I was a good athlete, and a better one, it seemed, because I was a good student. And I was a good student, and a better one, it seemed, because I played sports. But at Cornell a coach took me seriously as a player, and we played and won serious championships. And at Cornell some professors took me seriously as a student—I was on the dean's list almost every semester—and I realized I could be a serious person and maybe do serious things.

And big, important stuff was going on. The students at Cornell, my classmates and friends, might get drafted. To them the Vietnam War was *their* war. To Black students I knew, civil rights was their fight. I didn't march in any protests, but what hadn't previously been part of my life now was. I thought about these things now, political and social stuff, I talked about them, I watched, I listened, I learned. I felt. The day after Martin Luther King's assassination, Joan Baez gave a concert at Cornell. I was there. Her final song: "We Shall Overcome." We knew what that night was about. Then that summer I worked in Alaska. As I was hitchhiking up the Alaska Highway, at Mile 300, Fort Nelson, after spending the night on the side of the road in the all-night sunshine and dusk of a Yukon June and not getting a ride, I went into a coffee shop and heard on the radio that Robert Kennedy had been shot, and later, when I reached Watson Lake, learned he was dead. When the summer was over, and after I'd hitchhiked to L.A. and flown on student standby to Chicago, arriving too late to catch the last flight to Toronto, I spent the night in the airport, while downtown, outside the Democratic National Convention, the city rioted. I knew about the convention, I didn't know about the protests. A year later, just after I'd driven from Toronto to Winnipeg to start my new life as a law student, Woodstock happened. A year after that, in May 1970, five days before Lynda and I were married, four students, protesting the Vietnam War, were gunned down at Kent State University by the Ohio National Guard, and on our wedding day in Ithaca, New York, a hundred thousand people, many of them students, marched on Washington. By this time and stage in my life, during and just after my years at Cornell, I would've loved to have been at Woodstock. I wished I'd been in downtown Chicago, and, under other circumstances, I would have been in Washington. I don't know how, but I would've been changed.

Academically and athletically, at Cornell I realized how important it is to do what you do where it matters. I was ready for more.

Everyone in our high school class—all thirty-five of us—went to university, and all but three of us graduated. We were twenty-one, twenty-two, twenty-three years old. From promise and possibility, from all those years in Etobicoke, at ECI, in the Brain Class, now we were immersed in a world of our own making. Big job decisions, big personal decisions were right in front of us that would set the course of the next big directions of our lives—marriage, or not, kids, or not, when, how many, living where, doing what. For some the next steps were not much more than a formality, one thing had led to another almost since birth. For others it would take some time. For all, there were twists.

IV

FIGURING
IT OUT

CHAPTER SIXTEEN

Joan Cliff was married in May 1968. She was the first in our class. She was twenty-one. Then Joan Boody that Christmas, then Wilf Wallace, then Marilyn Adamson the following August, Judy Tibert, Doug Little a few months later, Murray McKenzie in January, and Lynda and I in May 1970. Then Cheryl and Pat. Then Penni, Bruce, Kathy McNab, and Mary soon after. None of us were more than twenty-five.

The progression—from elementary school to high school, to university, to a job, to getting married—was to us the natural, normal course of things. We no longer needed to live at home, we had some money, if we did find somebody we loved we could be with them every night as well as every day, with no voice inside our heads to tell us we had to be home. We had time, many had the pill. We could take a love we were feeling further than we'd ever had the chance to take love before, to feel what we'd never felt and never had the chance to feel, to believe, to *know*, this one was *the One*. And if he or she was the one, why not get married? Marriage was going to happen someday, and so were kids. And if he or she made us feel this way, who's to say someone else might come along at a more opportune time, to you, to him or her? Don't lose her. Don't lose him.

We needed anyway to figure out how to live on our own, to discover who we were, what we wanted to do and where we wanted to be, to grow up, find new interests, make new friends, explore. Why not do it *with* someone? For those of us who, during our university years, might at some moment have felt the lure of a forever academic life, that feeling had passed. That seemed a life too much on hold, too long waiting to be lived. Gord had two years of business school ahead, Roger and I three years of law, Ken and Peggy Clarke a year to become accountants, and lots of others a year to be teachers. But nothing so long that if we did find "the One," our plans, our lives, would suddenly have to change. It was a life we could live married every bit as well as not. Having kids, that was a different story. Kids might get in the way of plans and dreams that we might not even be aware we had, or keep them from ever coming to mind, for the women especially. Kids weren't a game. They made you think differently about yourself. *Me, a parent?! That's my mom and dad.* In our jobs, those that moved on the most seamlessly were the nurses and teachers. Four nurses and eleven teachers.

The late 1960s and early '70s were still a good time to be a teacher. There were jobs. Only a year or two later, it was harder. When Joan Boody graduated from the Faculty of Education, she recalls, "they had this big, like a cattle call, at the Park Plaza Hotel [in downtown Toronto], where all the principals and school boards in the province set up their tables and their displays in this big ballroom. Every school that had an opening, and that meant most schools at the time, was there. I still remember walking in the door, and this principal had been waiting for me, and he rushed up and said, 'Come to my table,' and he had me signed up within five minutes. My salary was sixty-four hundred dollars." The principal was from Winston Churchill Collegiate in Scarborough. Joan had spent a few weeks there as a practice teacher. He had said to her before she left, "Look out for us at the Park Plaza." "I had been approached during the year by a couple of other principals too," Joan remembers. "One was at Royal York"—near ECI—"and a couple were at out-of-town schools. But I knew I wanted Toronto. I never even got to the second table. I remember calling my mom about ten minutes after I'd arrived and saying, 'I got a job.'"

For Judy Clarke, same cattle call, same pre-arranged set-up—she had practice-taught at New Toronto Secondary School in southern Etobicoke and was asked back to teach French. "Because I knew I had the job, that day I just sauntered in, and at the Etobicoke desk I said I'm here to sign up for the New Toronto job. And they said, 'When you didn't get here right when we opened, we gave it to someone else.'" She ended up in Brantford, a mid-sized town an hour and a half west of the city, for what she describes as a "year from hell. The worst year of my life. I had a couple of grade 9 classes that had me in tears every night." She had thought she had to keep everything in her class strictly controlled, but the kids would have none of it. Then she tried to get them to like her. "The respect has to come first," she would come to learn, the hard way. When the year was over, Brantford was cutting back on its teaching positions. "It was last in, first out and I was let go." Grateful, relieved, she applied to the Etobicoke board, and the superintendent who interviewed her, Mr. Evanson, had been our principal at ECI. She would teach in Etobicoke for twenty-six years, almost all of her career.

For Cheryl Beagan, things didn't begin well either. Her life was unsettled. She had created a life of her own at ECI, but she found York University too big to connect into, to get immersed in, to feel herself part of everything. She lived at home her first year, then moved into residence the second, commuting to Western every weekend she could to visit her boyfriend, Tom LaFrance, whom she had met the year before at ECI. When Tom got a scholarship to do a student exchange at UBC for a year, Cheryl applied as well, got the same scholarship, and followed him there, which wasn't what Tom had in mind. Their relationship had been moving fast, faster than Tom was ready for. He was looking for a pause to sort some things out. Then, in Vancouver, Cheryl had a breakdown.

She'd had a few other setbacks in the previous years, triggered by nothing in particular, it seemed. But this time at UBC was different. "Tom and I had a quarrel," Cheryl relates. "I remember standing beside this enormous boulder that was outside the residence where

I lived, and it was like the sky was just swallowing me up. I just felt so literally ungrounded." She checked herself in at the university hospital.

She was there for about a week. She and Tom had broken up before, but that was earlier, closer to the beginning, when any future for them was still far ahead. This was closer to an end, when something very big might be lost. Now he might be gone. Now she was in Vancouver, and might be alone. Until that moment Cheryl hadn't realized how central Tom was to her. "I was ready for commitment way sooner in life than he was. I truly felt in my twenties that if he hadn't married me, my life would have just blown apart." Cheryl also loved Tom's family. They got along, they laughed, they were the family she wanted.

The next year, Cheryl was back at York, Tom at Western, and they were very much together. They both graduated and both went to teachers' college, but Cheryl's first two years of teaching weren't what she imagined. At Howard Public School in Toronto she didn't have a class of her own, but rather, she says, taught everyone and everything and no one and nothing, doing joe jobs, filling in, taking students on twelve different field trips to the Ontario Science Centre, or so it felt to her. Then at Winchester Street School the next year, after only a month of classes, when the school's enrolment wasn't high enough to sustain the number of teachers they had, she was sent to Ryerson Public School, where there were 1,500 students. In an elementary school! The school had become so much bigger than intended that her classroom was Portable 22. She wanted to be a teacher, but this wasn't teaching. Yet it also wasn't the end of the world. In December 1971, she and Tom were married.

Bruce McLeod had taken a three-year B.A. at Queen's, but hadn't gone on to teachers' college. Still, schools in small, more out-of-the-way places couldn't be choosy, and he was hired to teach math in Orillia, about an hour and a half north of Toronto. There he experienced small-town life for the first time, and small-town teaching. At a city school, even at a suburban one like ECI, when four o'clock on a weekday hit, and every weekend, and every summer, teachers could mostly disappear into the busyness and multiplicity of life options around them. They never need bump into any of the kids they teach, or their parents. In a small town, though, you know the kids you teach, and their brothers and sisters, and their parents, you go to the same church and are a member of the same clubs. And so they know you. And your kids. You live together 24/7. You see all that you achieve and all that you don't year after year. For some teachers, maybe most, it's too much. For others, it's wonderful. After a year in Orillia, Bruce began teaching in Gananoque, population five thousand, less than an hour from Queen's and about an hour and a half from Glengarry County, where his ancestors had farmed for more than a century.

Marilyn Cade got a job teaching French and phys ed at Lorne Park Secondary School in Mississauga, a new suburb about to explode in size, just west of Etobicoke. Joan Cliff took a job teaching phys ed at Blakelock High School in Oakville. They both liked teaching, were both good at it, and within a few years found that teaching was also good training for other fields, and they both moved on to other jobs they liked more. Lorna Casey and Kathy McNab discovered that teaching is transportable. For Lorna, that meant moving north to live a cottage-country life twelve months a year in Muskoka, in the heart of the Canadian Shield, about two hours from Toronto. Kathy McNab went even farther, to Sudbury—to what her high school classmates and many in southern Ontario thought of as the cold, why-would-anyone-ever-want-to-live-there *north*—where she would first teach, then move into other community-focused jobs.

As for the nurses, Penni Harcourt, after doing her training at St. Michael's Hospital, had stayed on, met her future husband, who was a lab technician there, realized that to do what she wanted to do in nursing she needed a degree, studied at McGill University for two years, returned to St. Mike's, and got married. After graduation, Marilyn Adamson followed her new husband first to Oshawa, where he began his career as an accountant and she taught public health nursing, then to London, Ontario, where he got his M.B.A. and she continued nursing. Marilyn Steels joined the Victorian Order of Nurses in Hamilton, and Judy Tibert worked as a public health nurse in a part of Etobicoke that was very different from where she'd grown up.

Judy's father was a successful insurance salesman and executive, her mother a homemaker. Both her parents were involved in the church and in the Etobicoke community. Growing up, her world was nice, it made sense, it was fair, it worked. For many of the people she was now helping as a public health nurse in northeast Etobicoke, it was none of these things. "You're a new grad," Judy recalls, "you're so innocent. You have no clue about the kinds of things that people experience, whether it's chronic disease or mental health issues or poverty or abuse. You have some basic knowledge that you learned from school, but not the personal experiences from your own life." Part of her public health learning at McMaster, she said, was "to accept that we're all different. That you don't have the power to say to someone you have to do it this way. You don't have that control, and you don't have all the answers." She remembers one family she worked with where both parents were cognitively impaired and their child was developmentally disabled. "There the problem," Judy says, "becomes about everything: how to shop, how to buy food with the limited money you have, how to look after your child, how to provide stimulation, how to take your child out to the park and not just sit in front of the TV. The kinds of things we assume people know." She remembers one elderly woman who'd had her larynx removed because of throat cancer and could no longer speak. "When I was there we communicated by writing back and forth. But when I wasn't, we had this thing worked out where she'd call me and I'd answer, and she'd tap on her phone. Then I knew it was her. And I'd ask her a question, and she'd tap to say yes or no." This wasn't Kansas anymore, or central Etobicoke.

Judy worked at three schools in her area. She was at each of them at least half a day a week, the larger ones twice or three times. She'd

do hearing and vision checks for the students, offered immunization
clinics, and provided first aid. She also had some nursery schools to
assist, a seniors' building, and a public housing development. The
area included a large Italian community, whose population had come
to Canada a decade or so earlier, the men working construction, the
women working in factories or in homes as domestics. They spoke little
English. Judy wasn't a doctor, teacher, or minister, she wasn't a family
member or friend. But if any doctor, teacher, or any of the others saw
something, or sensed something wasn't quite right, she was the one
they called. She often couldn't provide the answer herself, not directly,
but, she says, "I worked with so many different agencies, I knew who
did what, and who might be able to help." She came to know which
schools' principals and vice-principals "were fully engaged with their
students [as people], who could see problems that were health-related
and would make use of you, and [to know] those who never thought
about that, or didn't care." She got to know the churches. She used
every tool she had. And oftentimes, she had no answer because the
federal, provincial, and city governments, the churches, schools, and
community agencies had no answers. Then her job was to listen,
maybe to help someone sort out their problem themselves, at least a
little, or if there was still no answer, to help them focus on other parts
of their lives that were satisfying and good and away from what wasn't.
Or to just plain listen, nothing more, when they had no one else to
talk to, to make them feel a little better about their lives than they did
the day before.

    In 1971, two years into her job, Judy got married. Her husband,
Chris, worked for Citibank in international real estate. Three years
later, their first child was born. A month after that, in September
1974, Chris was transferred to Panama, where the three of them
lived for a year and a half, then to Paris for six months, before returning to Toronto, where in 1977 their second child was born. When
Judy returned to work, it was part-time in Mississauga. Toronto and
Etobicoke had changed a lot in the more than a decade since she had
graduated from high school, and Judy had seen it all up close. In the

decade ahead, she would see Toronto change even more, from a very white, provincial city to one of the most multicultural and multiracial cities in the world.

Murray also worked in health care, but he experienced these changes through a very different lens. He had graduated with a B.A. in economics, then he and Marilyn got married while he was working on his M.A. in political science. Both of them had plans to work with CUSO, the Canadian University Service Overseas, in Sarawak, a Malaysian state on the island of Borneo, when he was finished. But political unrest in the area scuttled their intentions, and in the fall of 1970, Murray began his doctorate in political economy while Marilyn worked as a nurse at SickKids. Three years later, after he'd helped complete Harvey Agnew's book on the history of Canadian hospitals, he took a job as an administrative resident at Mount Sinai Hospital.

In 1923, the Hebrew Maternity and Convalescent Hospital opened in the Yorkville neighbourhood of Toronto. The Jewish population of the city had grown since the beginning of the century, from a few thousand, most of whose ancestors had arrived from English-speaking countries decades earlier, to more than thirty thousand, most of the recent arrivals having escaped the pogroms and persecutions of eastern Europe. Arriving into a not very receptive Toronto, but big enough in number and having no better place to go, they would need to put down roots. Yiddish-speaking and kosher-eating, they would need to create a community of their own. Jewish doctors and Jewish patients, having been barred, discouraged, or limited by quotas from existing public hospitals, needed a Jewish hospital. A year after it opened, in honour of a well-established Jewish hospital in New York, it changed its name to Mount Sinai.

For the next fifty years, the hospital grew and developed as Toronto and its Jewish community grew and developed, largely in parallel to each other, gradually together. Mount Sinai's mission—to offer a place for Jewish doctors, under Jewish leadership, to give the best possible care to Jewish patients—never changed during this time, but as medical knowledge advanced everywhere in the world, Jewish doctors would need to escape their parallel world, be allowed into the larger one, engage with its best doctors and researchers, Jewish or not, and bring that knowledge, and some of those doctors and researchers, to Mount Sinai, or else fail in the mandate to provide the best possible care for the Jewish community. Mount Sinai, in short, would need to be respectful of its Jewish traditions but be less Jewish in order to fulfill its Jewish purpose.

For Murray, as it turned out, Mount Sinai was the right job at the right time. It was the right time because Toronto was growing fast enough and was big enough and rich enough to begin to see this and to know this about itself, and for others, especially in the U.S. and Europe, to see it and know it too. There was a confidence developing, a belief, and an excitement, that whatever Toronto had been, in the future it would be a lot more. In earlier decades, much of Canada's growth had been government-driven, its focus on country-building—railroads, highways, waterways, giant mining and hydroelectric projects to open up our vast, remote interior and north—its focus on individual and national survival. But the focus shifted from the mid-1950s onwards, away from survival and towards prosperity, so the government shifted its infrastructure priorities to universities, hospitals, and the health care system. As this was happening, and with all this infrastructure as its solid base, Toronto's burgeoning private sector was growing more confident and assertive, and richer.

Toronto was beginning to see itself as a world-class city, and others outside Canada were coming to see the same. A world-class city has world-class universities, hospitals, cultural institutions, and neighbourhoods, and a world-class ambition, energy, pride, and standard of living to support them, all of which encourage world-class talent to come here, thrive here, and stay here. The driving forces for the next decades of the twentieth century, *our* decades in the workforce—cities, governments, big corporations, universities, hospitals, private wealth, philanthropy—were all coming together in the 1970s. When Murray walked through the doors of Mount Sinai for the first time in 1974, he knew he was entering a place of importance and learning, but *really* he had no idea.

A new Toronto was being born. The suburbs would continue to grow, and Toronto would become Metropolitan Toronto, which would become the Greater Toronto Area. But unlike in most U.S. cities, as many people moved out of the core, many others stayed, and Toronto didn't diminish and die. The city remained a place not only to work and play but to live.

All this might have been different if the Spadina Expressway had been built. The city needed access to the suburbs, and the suburbs needed access to the city. In the west, connecting north and south, was Highway 427, in the east, the Don Valley Parkway. In the middle would be the Spadina Expressway. Highway 427 had been built over the market gardens and open fields of western Etobicoke, the Don Valley Parkway over the trees and scrub of the ravines along the Don River. The Spadina Expressway would cut through long-established neighbourhoods and communities. Because growth and development in the 1960s and '70s had been possible—money and ambition being present in abundance—these highway routes seemed inevitable, irresistible. It's how the future, and modernity, worked. The first few miles of the Spadina Expressway were built, making its construction even more certain.

Then, in 1971, it was stopped. Sometimes big decisions get made that are even bigger than we know. This one changed the future of Toronto. For is the purpose of a city its downtown or its neighbourhoods? Is a city a place to hang around in non-work hours and on weekends or a place to escape? A place of work or life? And if it's both, in what balance? And it doesn't take much to shift that balance. Toronto, beginning in the 1970s, without necessarily knowing it, was casting its lot to be a place to work, play, *and* live. A decision that, in spite of ups and downs since, and not without missteps, is reflected in the city today. Its most obvious downside—it being a downtown city whose outer suburbs keep growing, which without commensurate expansion of public transit, means more people looking to travel between the suburbs and downtown on more congested roads.

Toronto became, as an article in *Harper's* in 1974 put it, "A City That Works," a designation that if not entirely true was true enough, and true by comparison. Big U.S. cities were coming apart. Divisions that had always been present had turned violent. For many who had a choice, cities were becoming uninhabitable, and countless "What's wrong with America?" articles followed. Looking for scolding life lessons and counter-examples, these articles had no further to look than Toronto. Not Canada so much—for U.S. readers Canada was too cold, too different—but Toronto looked like them, except it was clean, polite, civil, and safe.

Big stories like those in *Harper's* come and then are gone. Of more pervasive effect are the many small asides that follow, offered as little inarguable certainties, each building on the others, that shift the angle and become the story. It was of no small importance that in 1977 Toronto got the Blue Jays. A major league team was concrete evidence that Toronto was a major league city. But more important, all the American teams in Major League Baseball now came to Canada to play, and to see for themselves, for three or four days a few times each season. Baseball writers, sportscasters, and players talked about how this foreign city was nice. And because this surprised them, they may have exaggerated slightly the stories they told. Opening every broadcast with skyline or waterfront beauty shots, they spoke about Toronto routinely, almost ritually, as "a great town." Years later, and during all the years he hosted the *Late Show*, David Letterman, whenever one of his guests mentioned Toronto, would say, "A great town." *Every time.* All these words mattered because they allowed people in Toronto to feel what they were wanting to feel, to make what they were already feeling seem right, because they made them feel proud. Important, too, because all this attention made them feel they had to live up to this story that was being told about them, making them do more and try harder, in time helping to turn aspiration into reality. Making Toronto a "better town."

This random buzz mattered to Murray because over time, as a vice-president (then called assistant executive director) of many different departments, in selling Mount Sinai to doctors and researchers all over the world, but especially in the U.S., to people who were so good they could live and work anywhere, he was selling Toronto. And it also mattered to him in selling Mount Sinai to Toronto's rich, who could live anywhere, move their wealth anywhere and give it to anyone they wanted, because this excitement about Toronto, and pride in Toronto, made them want even more to be a part of what was happening, and made them want to give and help to make it happen. And the more good people Mount Sinai was able to attract, the more good people they in turn would attract, because good people want to work with other good people.

Murray was selling the chance for prospective donors to have their name associated with this big, important story. Having one's name on something—a street, a school, a bridge—was once recognition for having done good deeds, but that had all changed. It no longer had to do with past deeds but with present ones—you give the money, *that's* your good deed. Signs became the monuments, rather than statues and bridges. And signs went up on buildings, on wings of buildings, on "institutes" and "chairs"—on things concrete and inconcrete that said to the world: important work is being done here. These were working, learning, achieving monuments-in-action that were more valuable to the legacy of the donor than a statue or an ice rink. This is what Murray, and Mount Sinai, had to offer.

The manifestation of this formidable Toronto was especially visible on University Avenue, where Mount Sinai was located, six lanes across, the widest, most ceremonial and imposing route in the city. At the top, on a rise facing south towards Lake Ontario, Queen's Park, Ontario's Legislative Building. To its west, the University of Toronto; to its east, a large cluster of government buildings. Then to the south,

on both sides of the street, Toronto's powerhouse of hospitals—
Toronto General, Mount Sinai, SickKids, Princess Margaret Hospital
moving to this location later; then the American consulate and the
stolid edifice of the Canada Life Insurance company with its weather
beacon on its roof; then Osgoode Hall courthouse, once home to the
oldest law school in the province; and just in behind it, the new city hall
and Old City Hall with its law courts. All these monuments to government, university, medicine, law, business, and the future. Running
down the avenue's middle, a boulevard of trees, flowers, commemo-
rations of people and events of the past that few notice. Then finally
at the bottom of University Avenue are Toronto's downtown office
skyscrapers, the Royal York Hotel, and the city's train and subway hub,
Union Station.

This was the environment in which Murray, age twenty-seven,
had his first real job.

One more thing was turning Toronto's fortunes in the 1970s. On
November 15, 1976, Quebec was electing its next government. Central
to René Lévesque's Parti Québécois platform was a promise to hold a
referendum for Quebeckers to decide the future of Quebec in Canada.
There had always been tension and disquiet between the province's
French-speaking majority and its English-speaking minority, but the
divide had widened during the previous decade, the debate growing
angrier, less patient. Finally, this was an election campaign where this
question was *the* question. Finally, there would be a referendum where
its answer would be *the* answer.

Election night, I was on the ice at the Montreal Forum in the midst
of a game between the Canadiens and the St. Louis Blues when the words
flashed across the message board—"Un Nouveau Gouvernement." The
PQ had won in a landslide. Thousands and thousands of people rose
from their seats and cheered. And thousands and thousands of others
stayed in their seats—silent. People who for decades had sat side by side
loving their Canadiens together at that one moment discovered something about each other they hadn't known, and now couldn't un-know.

The result of the referendum, which would be held on May 20, 1980, was unknowable. But the deep uncertainty the election vote caused was enough to get English-speaking Quebeckers, many of whose ancestors had come to the province as immigrants even before Canada was born, and who had never lived anywhere else, to think hard, really hard. And to get senior executives of big companies, many of whom were anglophone, whose companies had been founded in Montreal and had grown to nationwide and worldwide dimensions out of Montreal, to think hard, really hard. To think about moving. Out of Quebec, particularly to Ontario, and most particularly to Toronto, to where their futures, and the futures of their companies and their children, felt more certain. The same people who had grown up and lived their lives hating Toronto, certain of the superiority of Montreal—its history, its food, its *je ne sais quoi*—were suddenly feeling the need to go. And having moved out of Montreal, over time, coming to feel the need, if not to embrace Toronto, at least to tolerate it, and, so long as they publicly didn't have to say so, maybe even like it a bit. (So long, of course, as they didn't have to give up their beloved Canadiens, which, given the ineptitude of the Leafs most seasons, made even Leafs fans understand their allegiance.) This evacuation out of Montreal meant new talent, new learning, and new wealth for Toronto. It was a bonanza. Already on its way to becoming a more cosmopolitan place, Toronto's transformation happened even faster and became more complete.

"Every day I went to work," Murray recalls, of his sixteen years at Mount Sinai, "no matter how big the problems, it was exciting. Intellectually, it was terrific, because every day was different. And complex. And really important. We developed so many new programs. We'd begin with an idea and develop a priority list: What are the greatest needs? Where is the community in greatest need of expertise? And are we positioned to fulfill those needs? Then, just from that idea, we'd take it and run with it. We got the University of Toronto onside. We'd go to the board of Mount Sinai and they'd say, 'How much do you need?' and right away try to figure out how to get it. And then they just raised it. Then we'd go out and get these giants of medical research on the world scene, people who had won huge awards, and get them to the hospital. Then they would attract a whole cadre of the most promising young researchers coming out of medical school. There was a synergy that was built. We were able to create something that the best people wanted to be part of. One after another, these people came, and we knew the fantastic legacy they were going to leave."

CHAPTER SEVENTEEN

Wayne Yetman graduated from Western along with Marilyn Cade and Peggy Clarke, majoring in English literature. He had always enjoyed reading, though no more, and probably less, than most of his high school classmates, but he enjoyed thinking, questioning. In his second year, he had an "amazing teacher," as Wayne describes him, Ross Woodman, who taught a course on Romanticism. "There were only about ten of us in the class," he remembers, "sitting around a table, and he'd come in and just lecture for fifty minutes or so, and you were enthralled by every word he dropped. He was able to weave his way through the various poets and prose writers of the Romantic era and create a marvellous story of achievement and creativity, and I fell for it hook, line, and sinker, in the best sense. Somehow his ideas gelled in me, of doing something heroic and special with my life, rising above the ordinary and daring to risk failure in order to achieve something glorious. And of course, this is my fantasy world, my dream world, and in none of the things that I'd done in my life had I been truly heroic or truly great."

Wayne had always had a romantic streak in him. When he ran, even when he was just starting out and wasn't very good, on those dark, drizzly late afternoons in fall and spring, alone, he'd see in front of him the home stretch of a race, the finish line, the tape, and him, arms in the air, triumphantly breaking it first. When he had worked downtown as a "hopper" for the *Toronto Star* in grade 13, "I just loved jumping off the back of a truck and rushing across the street, delivering the newspapers to, as they say, the captains of industry. People waiting—just like in the movies: 'Extra! Extra! Read all about it!'" The *Star* had its five o'clock "All-Star" edition with the late stock market results, and "I was the one who was going to save the day. I had this fantasy about the heroism of what I was doing. It was drama. I loved it. Then driving my Mini Cooper home at night."

It was this part of him that his parents couldn't grasp. "I'm a dreamer," he says. "They were not." Wayne's parents didn't pretend. They were working-class people, and from Newfoundland, something they never wanted to tell anyone. In their world, everything was tough, hard, and uncertain and always would be. The fish that fill our nets today might be gone tomorrow. But his parents loved it when their son did well in school, and loved it when he made the Brain Class. "My apparent brain power and my apparent future success really brought great happiness to them," Wayne says. They were also proud when he started winning a few races, then fearful when he won more and began to train more, when his running stole time and focus from the real world of his future. But Wayne wanted nothing to do with the dreamless world of his parents. He knew why they felt the way they did. He thinks it started on the day he was born. His parents were older, and their first child had been stillborn. Wayne was, literally, as his parents said to him and as he knew, "the one and only." "They didn't want me to come to any harm. They were very determined that I was going to avoid any pitfalls, which was their attitude in life. They were trying to do their best, but I didn't want to be 'the one and only.' They wanted to protect me from the world, but success involves going out and facing the world and dealing with its strange and unknown things. They were very steeped in getting a job, holding that job for life, and being secure." It was the life his father had made work for him, and them. "And I had no aspiration for that."

Wayne recalls a poem we had studied in high school. It was his favourite, and it's one I also remember best: Robert Browning's

"Andrea del Sarto." In it is a line that is still stuck in both our heads: "Ah, but a man's reach should exceed his grasp, / Or what's a heaven for?" "Those words have always been an inspiration to me," Wayne says, "to try to do more and more and more, and, if I fail to a certain extent, that's all right. Man's reach must exceed his grasp." Wayne believed those words, and tried to live them. But when his reach did exceed his grasp, it could also feel like hell.

After taking Woodman's course, against his nature and contrary to what he wanted to believe, Wayne had a realization. "I was in love with English literature, and I wanted to be a university professor and spend my life working with great literature and hopefully writing great literature. But I wasn't up to it. I didn't have the intellectual strength, or the articulation, or the conceptual breadth to embrace the broadness of the subject. I decided—and this is something I'm proud of—that that was not going to be me, and that I'd have to focus on what I am more talented at in my life. And that was running. I said to myself, that's what my destiny is going to be, and I'm going to pursue it as far as I can."

Wayne was a good runner, but he wasn't better than that. He was a good runner in a country that didn't produce, and didn't believe it could produce, long-distance runners. Distance runners at the time were eastern European, Scandinavian, or East African. Bruce Kidd, a teenager from across the city, had caused a sensation in Toronto and Canada by winning gold in the six-mile run and bronze in the three-mile at the British Empire and Commonwealth Games in 1962, when Wayne was still in high school. But two years later, at the Olympics in Tokyo, Kidd finished twenty-sixth and ninth. At the time, North Americans preferred team sports. Distance running, especially for newcomers, was agonizing to do—stride after stride, in training and in races, with nothing in your head but your pain—and boring to watch. It made for bad TV.

In 1967, when Wayne ran his first marathon in Saint-Hyacinthe, the winning time at the Boston Marathon was 2:15:45. Wayne's time in Quebec, 2:51:56. He had an impossible 36 minutes and 11 seconds, and 6.95 miles, to make up. A year later, he won the Motor City (now Detroit) Marathon in 2:32:19. The next year, 1969, running in Boston for the first time, he finished nineteenth, in 2:30:23, then a year after was tenth, running eight minutes faster. Little by little, he was getting there. But Boston's winner that year, the legendary Ron Hill, setting a race record, was still more than twelve minutes, and two miles, faster. Wayne had gotten to this stage without having a lot of speed, just churning out the miles in his races, one mile every five and a half minutes. But to catch Hill, he needed to go almost thirty seconds faster *every* mile. Good enough to see the top of the mountain, he could now see how far he had to go.

After Western, he was accepted into a master's in museology program at U of T. No one he knew had any idea what museology was. Most assumed that he'd mispronounced "musicology." He tried explaining that it had to do with museums, then, growing tired of that, when asked what instrument he played, he said the oboe. To those who didn't know him, the oboe seemed interesting, and curious, which was kind of the way Wayne seemed to them anyway. So that was the end of it. To those who did know him, especially those who'd gone to ECI with him, a few of whom might have remembered that he'd dropped music after grade 10, they might have wondered a bit, but if they did, they didn't say anything. They maybe thought that somehow at Western, in all those moments he disappeared from view, when other guys were, if anything, learning to play the guitar, Wayne must've been learning the oboe. Not exactly a chick magnet, but *Amazing. Good for him. That's Wayne for you.* So, in all the decades since, whenever he's asked to say something about his master's in museology, he adds the oboe part. He's never played the oboe in his life.

He did go to work in a museum, located in a small former manor house that belonged to one of the early settlers on Lake Simcoe's south shore, about an hour and a half north of Toronto. Wayne had no interest in the outdoors—as he puts it, "I don't like to get dirty, and

I'm terrified in the water"—but he loved telling stories, and that area and that house had a story to tell about rural life in Ontario in the mid-1800s. And in telling that story, and doing it well, Wayne advanced rapidly to other positions in the Ministry of Natural Resources in the Ontario government, as parks people were coming to understand that it really wasn't "If you build it, they will come"—they had created these beautiful parks and not many were coming—but was instead "If you create it, *and* if you tell people about it, they *might* come." These parks needed selling, selling was storytelling, and Wayne was a storyteller. This was about communications. Marketing. About strategy and planning. And Wayne was trained for that too. That's what a marathon runner's life is. You can't run many races. It's about preparing for the races you *can* run. About strategizing, planning out your schedule, so that you arrive on race day at your absolute maximum. The ministry used to send Wayne to other parks, to create "interpretive programs"—stories for them to tell, and ways to tell them better. "I gave speeches all over the place. I was seconded to the Northwest Territories for six weeks to assess their marketing opportunities."

All this time, he told everyone he hated his job, and said that to himself as well. But he knows now he didn't. More than that, he knows the job was right for him. It gave him an income. It gave him independence. "I learned the methodology that planners bring to their tasks: first, assessing the resources, and the opportunities and downsides available from the resources; then establishing a general goal; then measurable objectives; then general strategies, and more actionable tactics. They call this master planning. The magic moment was realizing that I could apply these same master-planning methods to my own life. With one fell swoop," he recalls, "I turned from a fellow adrift in his fate to someone who recognized that he had the power to change everything." Plus—and this wasn't unimportant—his parents were "pleased as punch" when they heard about his government job: solid, white-collar, a steady paycheque for now, a nice pension in the future.

But for Wayne, it was a job that held no dreams. His dreams were as a runner, and all that was left for him were two big dreams—Boston and the Olympics—and try as he did, even with all those goals and objectives and strategies and tactics, he just couldn't see himself on that victory podium. Those last few minutes and miles seemed beyond him. Then, at a weekend retreat in 1975 at the Abbey of Gethsemani, a Trappist monastery south of Louisville, Kentucky, he had another magic moment. He looked into his own figurative mirror and saw again that if there was something special about him, it was running. Once again, he decided to commit himself. He was a year away from the Olympics in Montreal. He was twenty-nine. It was now or never.

At first, things didn't go well. "I had resolved to make the Olympic team and I was training my head off, and I was exhausted, I wasn't getting anywhere. Then Peter Pimm became my coach." Pimm had been a runner at the Toronto Olympic Club where Wayne trained—though they didn't really know each other—and had recently graduated with a degree in kinesiology. Wayne was the first runner he coached.

"He said to me, 'I've got some ideas. Why don't you try them?' And we started. He'd call me and give me my program for the week, then check in on how I was doing. His main thing, he cut back on my work. I'm a workaholic by nature, just like my father, always working at something, and he told me I was doing too much. I was killing myself. So instead of having me do fewer miles and all sorts of fast work, which I wasn't good at—I'm a slow-twitch athlete, I've got tremendous endurance, but I can't do anything fast—he concentrated on having me do things at a moderate pace, doing, say, half-miles in two minutes and twenty seconds, which is under a five-minute-mile pace—very close to what you do in a marathon—with a forty-five second rest between them. I'd do a whole series of those." Between slow-twitch and fast-twitch, "somehow that fitted my body and mind perfectly."

Wayne did his reps so often that the pace he ran them became almost automatic. "I had this feel. If you told me to run seventy-four"—a seventy-four-second lap—"I'd run seventy-four. I'd always be pretty well dead on. My body was learning to do this over and over and over and over again. My endurance was building." He thinks now that he'd been building this endurance since he was a kid, when always on his bike, pedalling for miles and hours, doing his paper route, wandering. The next day, doing it again.

"Peter Pimm's strategy was to have me under-train, to work well within myself. He had me doing seventy miles a week. Derek Clayton [of Australia], when he set the world record in Belgium, was doing 140 miles a week. I tried that once and broke down completely. Pimm wanted me to do a dull thing endlessly rather than something spectacular once or twice." Yet to Wayne this wasn't dull at all. "It was a tremendous challenge. I love the feeling of success, of being halfway through a workout and realizing, *Hey, I'm doing this.* And at the end of the workout saying, *Wow, I put in a really great effort. This is going to lead to good things, Wayne. Wow, this feels good.*" And as he ran, because the stride-after-stride pain he'd once felt was now well behind him, his head could fill with other things. "I remember many, many training sessions where my main thought was how much I hated my boss at work, how much I hated my staff, how much I hated the work we were doing. I had a real thing about the government, that I was ashamed to be there, that I didn't want to be there, that it was the wrong place for me. So I'd be running around the track fantasizing about telling my boss off, and the intervals would drift by."

Pimm knew what Wayne needed to do in Montreal. "I was very dependent on keeping a moderately fast, steady pace throughout the race. I had very little sprinting ability. The fastest I had ever done a quarter-mile lap was fifty-nine seconds, and that was in high school. The fastest mile I ever ran in my life was 4:26. He knew that if I wasn't ahead in the last two miles or so, someone would out-sprint me for sure. Peter Pimm was a genius."

Wayne had always been a "marathon runner" in everything he did. Running or not, he was steady and relentless. This was Wayne at his best, Pimm knew. "I think I'm a slow-twitch person," Wayne says.

"I'm sort of a dogged workaholic who keeps persevering endlessly at whatever he's doing until it finally results in something. I remember my boss at the ministry, he said to someone one time, 'Wayne Yetman can do anything. Just give it to him and he'll make it happen.' And I sort of prided myself on that."

The Olympic trials were in Ottawa on May 2, 1976—two and a half months before the Montreal Games began. On race day, Wayne felt good. He started well and just kept going, mile after mile, just as Peter Pimm had imagined, just as he had executed day after day. And he won. His time, 2:16:32. Six minutes faster than he'd ever run before. He was going to the Olympics.

In Boston two weeks earlier, the winning time had been 2:20. Sure, it had been an excruciatingly hot day in Boston—they would call that year's marathon "the race for the hoses"—and sure, Bill Rodgers had won the year before in 2:09. But Wayne was now in the big game. Close enough to think, *What if?* Also Wayne enough to shut down the thought whenever it invaded his mind. "I had no illusions about winning that Olympic race," he says. "I knew someone much better than me would probably run 2:11 or 2:12. I was in superb shape, so I thought I could do 2:13 or so, which would probably put me in about the top six, and that would make me very satisfied." But, he adds, "I guess I also had in the back of my mind, based on my experience in racing, that anything could happen, and with a little luck I might even slip in closer to the leader." In Montreal, if he had a good day, if some of the others had bad ones, well, who knows?

He went right back to training. "It was such a great year," he remembers. "It was the magic of Peter Pimm. I did my training and whatnot, and turned all the thinking over to him. It was a tremendous relief. He ran everything. All I had to do is run." The Olympics couldn't arrive fast enough.

When the Olympic Village opened to the athletes about three weeks before the Games began, Wayne was right there. The Village was brand new, all the stadiums and arenas and facilities were big and brand new. It was all exciting. Wayne did his work. He had twenty-four hours a day to focus on his running, to run, to get himself ready. Everything was right. The Olympics people couldn't do enough for him and the other athletes. The restaurants in the Village were always open, the food was great. He ate to keep himself strong, and because the food tasted so good, and because it was there.

The Games began. They seemed to take over not only his world but the *whole* world. All the athletes, the flags, the anthems, the ceremony and pageantry. The medals the athletes won that they brought back to the Village that Wayne couldn't not see. He kept doing his work. He soaked everything in.

He has this photo. It shows the Olympic Village sometime during the two weeks of the Games. He's sitting outside, on a patio, with five others, a centrepiece of flowers in the middle of their table. Wayne has on his red-and-white warm-up suit, "CANADA" across the back. To his right are two other athletes, then a middle-aged woman in a floral dress and summer hat. She is looking down to her left, as if she is reading something. Wayne is looking in the opposite direction, up, and into the distance. It is the Queen. There is no obvious chemistry between them.

About a week before the race, Wayne recalls, "I went out for my regular twenty-mile run, which I did once a week. A number of others went with me, some of the Canadian guys. And the military came along, part of the way, because there'd been some threats—but I ran the most spectacular twenty-mile training run of my life. I ran away from those guys. I was flying. I was like a machine. I was possessed. It was just so fast and so easy and so controlled. It was wonderful." Then, when he got back to the Village that night, "I felt the beginnings of a cold. And that cold settled in. And it disrupted my whole week." Now with something other than running to think about, he started thinking about everything. He got nervous. "I started walking around the Olympic complex. I was eating an awful lot. Nervous eating. By the time I got to the race, my cold was still there, I'd put on some weight, and I was down." And Peter Pimm was in Toronto.

"I lost track of him that last week before the race," Wayne recalls. Faced with a problem, Wayne turned inward to solve it. "The morning of the race I tried to phone him but something went wrong, and I couldn't connect with him."

Finally, the race. Sixty-seven runners from thirty-six countries, the best in the world. "My usual pattern when a race started, I'd go out with the leaders. But this was the Olympics, I knew I couldn't go out with the absolute Bill Rodgers–type guys, but I wanted to be up near the front, then to watch for an opportunity to pick off some of these guys as they fell back, as the going got rougher and rougher at the end." That was the plan. "But I didn't run that way at all," he recalls. "As we lined up, and as we started off, I remember thinking to myself, *This doesn't feel good today*. When we left the stadium, I was the last person out." Almost twenty-six miles, more than two hours, to go.

"From start to finish it was no fun at all. It was awful. This is the peak event of my life and it's not going to work out at all. And I'm going to come out of this feeling I've buggered this up." In a 100-metre race, the agony of awfulness lasts ten seconds. In a marathon, it goes on and on. You feel everything slipping, slipping, slipping away, and there's nothing you can do to stop it, and nothing you can do to stop the feeling. Mile after mile. You can't get out of your own head. Any thoughts about how bad your job is, how terrible your boss is, don't work. Feeling losing as you're losing sucks.

"At some point early on I said to myself, *Oh no, I'd better start trying to move up on people*, and I tried, but I had none of the energy and fluidity and dynamism and joyousness that I'd had in the twenty-mile run. Then near the end, I decided I wasn't going to finish. That I would not go into that stadium and run around the track in front of all of Canada and be humiliated. I was going to stop when I got to the stadium. But then I passed Bill Rodgers, this great American runner, and I thought, *At least I've beaten Bill Rodgers. He must've had a terrible day*. And I continued into the stadium, and I finished." Wayne was thirty-sixth. His time, 2:24:17. The winner, Waldemar Cierpinski of East Germany, ran 2:09:55. If Wayne had matched his time in the Ottawa

trials, he would have finished twelfth. If he'd run 2:13 as he had imagined, he'd have been fifth, just ahead of Lasse Virén of Finland, who
had already won the 5,000- and 10,000-metre races.

Maybe it was seeing Bill Rodgers that kept him going, maybe
it was what his boss at the ministry had said about him: "Wayne
Yetman can do anything. Just give it to him and he'll make it happen."
Maybe his pride at that moment was stronger than the humiliation
he feared.

On July 31, 1976, he was the thirty-sixth best marathon runner
in the world. Nobody else in our high school class ever made an
Olympic team. His reach had exceeded his grasp, and now he made
sure he'd make himself live with that.

CHAPTER EIGHTEEN

Three months after his race in Montreal, eight days after René Lévesque and the PQ were elected, Wayne met Ken Church in Paris. Ken was working in Price Waterhouse's office there, having transferred from their office in Toronto. Wayne had decided he needed to get away. As his journals make clear, he wasn't in a good frame of mind. He was sad, and because he was sad, he saw sadness everywhere. Being with Ken brought back thoughts of his high school years, how he hated them and hated the Brain Class, and also a sudden deep, overwhelming affection for his classmates, more than he ever imagined. All of us now were eleven years older, all those things that might have been, that we might have been and seemed would be—great jobs, great loves—that weren't. Nothing at that moment seemed good enough to Wayne. Ken was still doing *audits*! "I don't like it," he wrote. "Why can the most intelligent and best-educated students to come out of ECI turn out to be ordinary human beings? They were superhuman before—why must they be made level with everyone else? Why can't the strength and discipline which got them high marks get them what they need now?"

Now in our twenties, most of us were feeling our way along in our lives, doing what we expected, or were expected, to do, each chapter following on from the ones before, with few big twists or turns to our stories. If anything, in those years it wasn't the academic or work setbacks that affected us most, it was the personal ones. The ones that made us wonder if the person we thought we were was really us.

Craig MacGregor was the first in our class to die. We heard it was suicide, when he was a student at U of T or slightly after. But we didn't really know what happened. I don't think any of us knew Craig very well. Not even Ken or Daryl or Diana, who lived nearby and had gone to elementary school with him. Not Wayne, who was his locker mate in grade 9. What most of us probably would have said in high school was that he was nice and a little quiet. After the news of his passing brought us to think harder, we'd probably say that he always seemed a little awkward, uncomfortable, withdrawn, and very nervous. And despite spending five years together, day after day, more than ten years if you were Ken, Daryl, and Diana, none of us felt close enough to keep in contact with him after high school, to follow up later with his parents, his brothers or sisters, if he had any. The truth is, we don't know much.

Doug Little was one of the first of us to get married and have kids, and the first to get divorced. He and his wife had been raised in nice houses in Etobicoke. With their young daughter they found an apartment only a few minutes away from where they'd grown up. It was small, not much different from what any university student might live in. But they weren't students any longer, they were a family with a child, and this didn't seem like a place a family should live, in a part of Etobicoke that didn't feel like Etobicoke. For them, at an already challenging time—new marriage, new family, new jobs—this was demoralizing. At some moment, not many years after, their marriage ended and their daughter continued to live with her mother.

Marilyn Adamson was the next to divorce. Then Joan Boody. For each of them, looking back on what went wrong, the answer was the same: they had been too young. Too young for the responsibility, too young to see their lives moving down what seemed to them a narrow, never-ending path into the wrong future. More than that, too young to know a lot of things we can know only later—what we love to do, not just like, what we're really good at, what we really want to be, not just what we seem to be, whom we really need to be with and can't live without and maybe whom we can. Young enough that after each day's experiences and learning, we aren't the same as we were the day before, and our new young husband or wife isn't either. In the end, ultimately and actually, both spouses "growing" not in the same directions or at the same pace, but growing apart.

Divorce, where we came from, was failure. Marilyn and Joan did come to understand, and accept, that for them divorce was the right thing to do. Without a doubt. But emotionally, never entirely. They both moved on, Joan sooner and more completely than Marilyn. With Marilyn, there seemed a lingering melancholy. It's not clear that Doug ever did. A sadness came into his eyes that never left.

Lorna Casey's husband's death might have upended her life. They had been married less than three years, their son was five months old. Suddenly, instantly, she was a twenty-seven-year-old widow. And as much as that felt at that moment the end, of hope, of joy, of what life might be, she couldn't let it be. Her son wouldn't let it be.

Joan Cliff's life too might have broken into pieces. She had married her childhood sweetheart. She was a teacher, he was a doctor, they began to have kids. They had their friends, they had their church. Then in 1978, their youngest, Rebecca, age three, was diagnosed with leukemia. It was an excruciating test for their family, for their beliefs.

By 1978, the prognosis for survival for kids with cancer was about fifty-fifty. A few years earlier, when Murray's wife, Marilyn, was working on the cancer floor at SickKids, every one of her patients died. *Every one.* No exceptions, no flukes, no miracles. All that Marilyn and the other nurses, and the doctors, had to keep them going was their compassion and a scientific act of faith. Every one of those kids was a life, and every one of them allowed those doctors and nurses to learn a little bit more, and a little bit more about leukemia and cancer, and to believe that someday all of those little bits were going to add up to something. They had to. By the time Rebecca was diagnosed, though Joan was told the odds were no better than even, they did add up to something.

"First, Rebecca had intensive chemotherapy to get her into remission," Joan recalls. "This went on for ten or twelve weeks. Then radiation." One critical thing researchers had learned in the years since Murray's wife had been at SickKids was that kids often initially went into remission, then about eighteen months later saw their cancer flare up again. "The leukemic cells would get into the spinal fluid and hide out in the brain," Joan explains. So they gave Rebecca cranial radiation. After that, she'd go to the hospital about three times a week for various treatments, later once a month, taking her pills at home. This went on for about a year.

Then, just before March break, Joan remembers, as they were planning to go to Florida, "she didn't look very well. She started throwing up. I took her to the hospital, she had some blood work done, and her counts weren't too bad, then they did them a day later and her count had dropped. I could see she was getting sicker and sicker. My immediate fear was that she was going out of remission. Then you're starting all over. Then your chances go way down." What does a parent do? "I remember praying," Joan says, "and I remember a part of me being frightened, and also a part of me, deep, deep inside me, that was completely calm. I felt this incredible peace, this sense that it is going to be all right. And still this other part of me was saying, *Joan, you should be really upset. Why aren't you crying? Everyone else around you is.* But if I had, it would've been almost like an act, because deep down I thought everything *was* going to be fine." The immediate problem, it turned out, was Rebecca's medications. They were changed, and Rebecca's health started to improve. They went back to focusing on the leukemia.

Joan hadn't known that she would feel this way. She hadn't known how she would feel, or how she was supposed to feel. She remembers a day not long after Rebecca was diagnosed. Joan had come to visit her in the hospital. "I remember getting off the elevator and just standing there, because in front of me there were kids everywhere, and they were in all different stages of therapy. There were kids with IVs, there were kids who had lost their hair because they'd already had their radiation. And I remember looking at all these kids and not thinking, not asking, *Why me? Why my daughter?* but thinking, *Why* not *me? Why* not *my daughter?* All these other kids right here were having to deal with this too, and I had such a good support system, and Rebecca did, and I knew that not all of them had." Seeing those kids, Joan recalls, "changed everything in me."

A big part of that support system was Joan's faith. If there ever was a time not to believe, this was it. How could God do this? Surely, if there is a God, God wouldn't inflict such pain on a little kid. Yet that's not how Joan responded. "For me, this was trying to live out what I said I believed. To see if I could trust my belief." This was the test. "Faith, for me, over my life, has been very important. And I fall back on faith. It's sort of my go-to position, and it's grown over the years. I believe in God, I believe in prayer. A lot of my strength and peace, and being able to cope with situations, comes back to a trust, and a God, and relying on prayer." Rebecca is now forty-eight years old.

Most of us in our twenties were moving along some sort of path, gradually, slowly, figuring things out. It was "ready, aim, fire." For Steve Whistance-Smith and me, it was "fire," maybe "aim," and certainly not "ready"—not that we knew of.

Tarragon Theatre. Opening night. October 6, 1971. Steve was twenty-three. The production: *Creeps*, written by David Freeman. Bill Glassco, the driving force behind the Tarragon's creation, thought he knew what they had with *Creeps*, but he and Steve had no idea. The play took off. In theatres like theirs, plays ran for about a month, and if they became hits they were held over for an additional week or two. *Creeps* ran two and a half months, until, with another production already scheduled, it couldn't run any longer. It was, as Steve described it, "theatrical lightning."

The play was about four men with physical disabilities who worked for seventy-five cents an hour in what was then called a "sheltered workshop," folding boxes, weaving rugs, sanding blocks of wood, to keep these "unfortunates" busy, to help make them feel they were "productive" members of society. The entire one-act play takes place in a disgusting washroom where these "poor blunders of God" find their own shelter hiding out from their supervisor, offering a whip-lash of angry, bitter, frustrated, savage, sardonic comments about their lives, about how they are treated by the world of non-creeps around them, and about the charities who wallow in their own patronizing good deeds. David Freeman, who had cerebral palsy, had written the play on a typewriter using a mouth-held stylus.

Steve played Sam, a wooden-block sander, who also has cerebral palsy. He is on stage the whole time, is maybe the most cynical of all the four main characters, and the audience takes in the indignity of his life as he manages his way into toilet stalls, onto toilet seats, from his wheelchair. Allowed to laugh—these guys, these situations, are cringe-worthingly funny—the audience laughs, and cringes. Nathan Cohen, in the *Toronto Star*, wrote that "Freeman treats his people as people, showing how in their world there is humour in abundance." Audiences loved it.

In a small theatre with big ambitions and just beginning, Steve says, "everybody did everything." Besides acting in *Creeps* and being one of Tarragon's co-artistic directors, Steve slapped up notices on telephone poles, hung lights, ran sound, and did his turn at the box office, and the more he did, the more exciting it all was. There just weren't enough hours in the day to do what needed to be done, and to feel all he wanted to feel. But *Creeps* would need to end at some point, and there was the rest of the season to think about. Next in Tarragon's pipeline was *Cabbagetown Plays*, a trilogy of one-act plays. Steve was in two of them, rehearsing during the day and performing *Creeps* at night. He had no role in the theatre's next production, then directed *Surd Sandwich*, and while that was running, he was rehearsing, as an actor, *The Wonderful World of William Bends*. At the same time he was also Tarragon's dramaturge, his job to read every script that Canada's playwrights submitted, and in every way he could, to get the word out that he wanted to see even more and better of them. When you're on a roll, Steve discovered, more and more of *everything* is better and better. And the roll goes faster, gets bigger.

Canadian theatre, like many aspects of life in the country, had begun to find its energy and purpose in the 1950s. Tom Patterson, a *Maclean's* journalist from Stratford, Ontario, a town whose only apparent connection to Stratford, England, was its name, had the ridiculous thought that Shakespeare might also connect the two, and with a little bit of money and a lot of guts made a ridiculous approach to famed director Tyrone Guthrie, who in turn did the same to famed actor Alec Guinness, to get their help in creating this illusion in the form of the Stratford Festival. Because England was still living in postwar privation, the pair, happy for the extra income, accepted. By this time, there were also more rich people in Canada who were interested in supporting theatre. By the 1960s, Broadway shows were playing in Toronto's new mega-sized O'Keefe Centre, mostly touring productions, but some had their tryouts at the O'Keefe ahead of their New York runs. My parents watched Julie Andrews, Richard Burton, and Canadian Robert Goulet in *Camelot*; I saw Tommy Steele (and John Cleese) in *Half a Sixpence* and Diahann Carroll in *No Strings*.

But in postwar years, as Canada was beginning to discover itself, more of Canada's novelists and playwrights wanted to tell Canadian stories. By the early 1970s, there were the big five alternative theatres and their big five artistic directors in Toronto—George Luscombe at Toronto Workshop Productions, Ken Gass at Factory Theatre, Martin Kinch and John Palmer and others at Theatre Passe Muraille and Toronto Free Theatre, and Glassco at Tarragon. All of them knew there was more to Canadian theatre than Shakespeare and Stratford, Broadway, the West End, O'Keefe, and the Royal Alex. These productions, as good as they were, did not capture our stories. Not even close.

For Steve, *Creeps* wasn't just theatrical lightning, it was his own personal lightning. The experience was beyond exciting. Tarragon's next four plays, however, were "more or less disasters," as he puts it.

One of them, *Surd Sandwich*, which he directed, and "which I really liked, about three weeks into rehearsals, about four days from opening, I knew that I didn't have another idea in my head, and it wasn't working." There was talk that there might not be a second Tarragon season. Then along came David French's *Leaving Home*. It was a story of immigration, about a family that had left Newfoundland for Toronto before Newfoundland became a province. It was about torn, complicated lives, of the children, of the mother and father, of leaving and staying. Universal, timeless, *Leaving Home* was a big hit. As Steve said, "It saved our bacon." A Canadian setting, a Canadian story—it was what this new Canadian theatre was meant to be about.

It had been an almost perfect first year for Steve. Even the bad had been good. He and Glassco learned what everyone in the big alternative theatres was learning: that there was a Canadian audience for Canadian stories, who would come back again and again *if* the productions were good. Otherwise, a bad Canadian play, like a bad British or American play, is a bad play. They knew they had only to stick to their mission and do their jobs. "We were really an ensemble," Steve says. "All of us, audiences, writers, actors, directors, we were all learning our stories together."

After a few more years at Tarragon, Steve moved with Glassco to CentreStage, a bigger downtown theatre with a bigger budget. There were more successes, and more flops, and he had learned by this time that you never know which production will be which. So long as it was just him he was responsible for, these big ups and downs and big uncertainties were fine, even exciting. Then in the late 1970s, between gigs, working as a bellboy and all-round gofer at a lodge north of Toronto, he met Heather, got married, and they had a child. Now the itinerant theatre life, living paycheque to paycheque, room rental to room rental, didn't work. He got a job at Grolier's selling books to schools and libraries, was promoted to sales manager and liked the job well enough, until after three or four years he began to hate it and hate himself for doing it. He had continued doing small roles in movies—a day on a movie paid more than a week in the theatre—and after leaving Grolier's he did more still, and found other jobs to support himself and his son, he and Heather having split up.

Steve had never thought of theatre as a career, not even at Tarragon or CentreStage—he doesn't think in terms of careers. "The value is in the experience," he says, what you discover, what you learn, what sense you make of it, what bigger truth you find. Theatre is a way to explore life, as reading books, even as selling books is. Great plays are not about careers, they are about testing, life-revealing moments, of learning and insight. Life isn't something you plan, then live. Life is what happens. Great writers know that. "The unexpected is not always your enemy," he says. "It's OK to live with mystery." He hates it when a movie director doesn't trust his story or his audience and pumps up the music to tell them how they're supposed to feel. He wants to feel the way he feels. How this moment, in this play, movie, or book, makes him feel. Nor does he believe in things that take him out of this moment of his life, into the past or into the future. "I don't believe in hope," he says. "There's something false and sentimental about it. And despair is a blunder."

Imagined life, good or bad, is a waste of time, he thinks. He lives his own life as both a performer in it and an audience to it. "My life has been a life of improvisation," he says. "I keep finding myself being astonished."

In many ways, he thinks, he has lived his life in reverse order. "I know actors who spent a year touring schools in Canada when they started out. There'd be four or five of them in a van, they'd sleep in crummy motels and hotels and put on performances before grade 6s and 7s, and that was their work. I didn't do that. I had this early success. And I wasn't just somebody in the show, I helped create a theatre." Along the way he had skipped some steps, and in the 1980s and '90s, older and with a son, when it was harder, he had to take them for the first time. He has thought a lot about that. "I read this a long, long time ago about how some people have amazing things happen at the beginning of their life, and some have amazing things happen near the end of life. The experience I had with the theatre was so startling and unexpected and unplanned and turned out so well in so many ways, I think in a way it warped my understanding of life." He says this as observation, not regret. It's how life is.

Forty years after that opening night at Tarragon, when Steve was sixty-three, he was asked to be part of a panel for a class of students in the acting program at George Brown Theatre School in Toronto, to discuss Tarragon's first season. The panel was videotaped. I watched it years later. The panel included two actors, a sound technician, someone who would later become Tarragon's manager, and Steve, and they were there to get across to the students what a year in the life of a theatre is like. At first Steve didn't want to do it. He had done events like this before. A theatre life is full of stories, theatre people are storytellers, this would be just another sit-around-a-bar-swapping-war-stories occasion. But he said yes.

In the video, the other four panellists are smiling and laughing—it's like old-home week. Steve looks serious, and talks seriously. To him, this is a serious moment. The theatre students have stars in their eyes. They love everything that they know about theatre—the mission-like togetherness of it, the risk, the fear, the panic, the applause, its tingle and buzz. And they love the stories: all the impossible situations that ambush you, that are made that much more impossible by the urgency of the curtain—"the show must go on"—the certainty of embarrassment in front of an audience, the humiliations, then a year later, ten years, a lifetime of years later, all of it hysterical. The students can't get enough of it. But Steve knows that they already know this side of the story, and they are about to head out into this theatre world and make their lives. This is an important time. It's up to him to tell them, to make sure they know, the rest. And that's what he does.

He has thought about this question about the theatre life for decades. He talks to the students as if he were a teacher, like his favourite professors at Queen's had talked to him. He talks more than everyone else on the panel. He offers observations that after forty years of thinking about them had become wisdoms to him. How success is more dangerous than failure because success only confirms. Because success tells you that everything that you did was right. How failure tells you that what you thought was a certainty was only an assumption, and probably the wrong one. How, as he puts it, with quiet authority in his voice, there's "an enormous amount of frustration in theatre, it can wear you out, exhaust you, finish you."

At the end of the class, when the moderator asks if anyone on the panel has any final words, Steve says, "I guess I do." He says he had been asked by a lot of parents what they should tell their kids who say they want to go into the theatre. "I've never known what to say," Steve admits, "but I did end up saying to them, and what I do want to say to you is: Don't go into theatre unless you can't bear not to. Because it will take everything you have to offer, it will give you enormous amounts also, but it is a profoundly demanding profession. And you don't survive in that profession unless you have that kind of fascination with it, and are ready to offer your love." He pauses, and with an actor's and director's timing, concludes, "And other than that, good luck."

It brings the house down.

"My compliment," Steve says of the panel discussion, "came a year or two later when I'm in the subway and a guy comes up to me, an actor I knew, and we got to talking. And he said, 'I liked very much what you did that night.' He said it was a realistic description of what the profession is like. Because basically I was telling those students— less than one percent are going to get rich doing this. Maybe five percent are going to make a living. The others do what they can."

Two days before Steve opened in *Creeps*, I opened my first full season with the Montreal Canadiens. My own personal lightning had begun seven months earlier, when I'd been brought up to the team from the Montreal Voyageurs of the American Hockey League. But for me the surprises hadn't yet begun.

Canada had withdrawn from international ice hockey after a dispute with the International Ice Hockey Federation, the National Team had folded, and I was left without a place to play. I came to an agreement with the Canadiens to play a limited schedule with their minor league team, the Montreal Voyageurs, while attending McGill Law School. Lynda and I got married. We arrived in Montreal in early September 1970. Lynda was about to start teaching grade 5 at Holy Family School, my classes at McGill were beginning, the Canadiens' training camp was only a few days away. The team had missed the playoffs the year before—the Canadiens never missed the playoffs—and in their first few exhibition games played poorly. I was at the Voyageurs' camp, and in our dressing room, our coach, the *opto optare* Ron Caron, told me I was to fly to Halifax to play an exhibition game the next night against the Chicago Black Hawks. That meant playing against Bobby Hull, who as I knew from my TV screen shot the puck a thousand miles an hour, and Stan Mikita, the NHL's four-time scoring champion. I thought I'd get killed. We won, 3–1. I played two more exhibition games, the last one in Boston Garden against the Boston Bruins, the defending Stanley Cup champions, who had two players who at the time were even greater than Hull and Mikita, Bobby Orr and Phil Esposito. We won again.

Suddenly I seemed on a new path, and moving faster than I knew how to move. I was supposed to be a law student for two years until I graduated and play with the Voyageurs eight or nine games a season until then. I had been able to avoid making the choice I thought I'd never have to make—hockey or school—when I went with the National Team. And I avoided it again when I signed with Montreal as a part-time player and full-time law student. Now, it seemed the Canadiens would ask me to stay. But this wasn't the me I thought I was and thought I was going to be. What should I do? The Canadiens took the choice out of my hands. When the regular season began, they sent me back to the Voyageurs.

But things weren't the same anymore. Maybe now I *could* play, maybe I *was* good enough. And what *had* always been me was to do whatever I did at the highest level I could. That's what my parents had believed in, that's what the Brain Class was. And playing only every so often, even at this high AHL level, wasn't interesting. I was a goalie. A goalie has to feel responsible for his team, responsible for the outcome of every game. You can't do that playing once every two weeks, and not playing on the road where the team needs you most. During the first few months of the season, the Voyageurs weren't doing well, and I was asked to play more. I'd finished my mid-term exams and written some term papers, and I was doing OK. I thought maybe I could do more. So I went to the Canadiens' general manager, Sam Pollock, and before Christmas I signed a new contract. I was now, to them, the same as every other player. I would be available to play every game and attend every practice. Law school, I would need to do on my own time. Neither McGill's dean of law, John Durnford, nor Sam Pollock told me they could make it easier for me, allow me to delay certain assignments or miss certain games or practices, but neither of them told me I couldn't try to make the arrangement work. Constitutional law and potentially the Bruins were each their own test. The Bruins and constitutional law together, that was an interesting new one.

So I played almost every Voyageurs game and went to school, and McGill went well enough and the Voyageurs went better. In early March, on the final day that players could be brought up from the minor leagues (except because of injury), I joined the Canadiens. From then on, for me, life was like what it would be for Steve. His opening night of Tarragon was like my first playoff game in Boston Garden against the Bruins. He had no idea if he could do what he was asked to do, nor did I. What he had going for him, as I did, was that he didn't know he couldn't do it. He just sat in that wheelchair and spoke his lines, and I just stood in my crease and played the game. For him, as it turned out, after all those classes with Mr. Orton, the kitchen table talks with Adèle, the lessons he learned from Professor Euringer, all the Queen's and summer stock productions, often flying by the seat of his pants: he was ready. For me, after all those ball hockey games in our driveway and backyard, the shots I had blown and saves I had made, the games we should've won but lost, the games we should've lost but won, our overtime victory over Burnhamthorpe, all the situations my parents and teachers and others had put me in that I'd never been in before, and had no idea I could handle, where humiliation was a breath away: I was ready. *Creeps* was a sensation; we won the Cup.*

Now I was paraded around at the Calgary Stampede. Now, having read his books, I was working with Ralph Nader in Washington. Now I was on the way to something, to becoming something, and had no idea where I was going or what I was becoming.

It was the same for Lynda. She was a teacher. This had been the first year of our marriage. She thought she'd married a law student who also played hockey. We were on this rocket together, and while it seemed like our own, it certainly didn't feel like we were driving it. That rocket was going where *it* was going. It had happened so fast, and kept happening so fast. May turned into September, one season, one school year turned into the next. And we were off again. And I loved it.

This next year, Lynda didn't teach. We were trying to figure out how to live this life. I'd always had choices—school *and* sports together—and I was still doing both, but now it felt like *I* had no choice at all. Life was choosing. These years were going to change my life, Lynda's life, our life.

The Canada–Soviet Union Summit Series in 1972 was an even more impossible ride, from losing the first game in Montreal that we couldn't lose, to winning the last game in Moscow that we couldn't win. And I played in both. Then another Cup a year later, winning it in Chicago a week before I graduated from law school.

Now, for the first time since kindergarten, I no longer needed to do both hockey and school. I could do what I wanted—all those non-playing hours between games and practices were mine. It was fantastic. And almost right away, I felt lost. Now that I had a real choice, not just between hockey and school, but between hockey and *everything* else, what would I do? What was I if not a player-student?

---

*   On the eve of the first game against Boston, I received a telegram from my father. It read: "Ruin the Bruins. Love, Dad." After we'd beaten them in game seven, I telegrammed back: "Bruins ruined. Love, Ken."

Every season, the players were issued special visas so that we could easily travel to the U.S., and each year filling out its application form, we had to state our occupation. And every year, I wrote "law student." I wasn't a lawyer, but also I never felt "hockey player" was my occupation. Now, having graduated, what would I write? Before I needed to answer, before the next season began, I got into a contract dispute with the Canadiens, and knowing that someday I'd need to article, or intern, for a year before I could practise law, we went back to Toronto and I started work at a law firm. We rented an apartment in Etobicoke, in a new high-rise at 25 Mabelle Avenue. The high-rise, and one other like it, had gone up in place of some small houses that had been torn down. One of them was Wayne's old house.

I learned two things that year in Toronto. I liked law OK, but I didn't love it, and I learned where I wanted to play, and why. The World Hockey Association had just been formed as a rival league to the NHL. The Toronto Toros, one of its teams, offered me a contract to play with them the following year. We negotiated the terms, the Toros offering to pay me much more than I would ever have been paid in Montreal. But because there was no need to sign then—I couldn't play until the next season in any event—I didn't, and instead spent the season watching the Toros and the league, to see if that's where I wanted to play. Before Christmas I knew: half-filled arenas, game stories on page 2 (or 3) of the Sports section, no kids on the streets with Toros jerseys on their backs, announcing Toros games in their heads. The Leafs mattered to Toronto, the Toros never would. I had been around the best—the best coach, GM, arena, fans, and players (who were on their way to getting even better). Once you've been surrounded by people who know what they're doing, you don't want anything less. I knew I'd hate being with the Toros. And because I didn't love it, I knew I'd hate practising law.

When the year was over, with a new contract, we went back to Montreal, bought our first house, and moved in just over a month before our first child, our daughter, Sarah, was born. I now had all

my law school time free to do something else. I discovered reading—
I had read a lot more at Cornell, but that was different, that was for
assignments. I found out what my ECI classmates had learned decades
earlier. When I was young, I had all the adventures and fantasies I
needed in the games I played, all the heroes and role models in the
players I watched. Then, I'd had no time to read. I had always wanted
to go everywhere and do everything. In Montreal, with money and
hockey-free summers, we travelled—to Moscow and Leningrad the
year after the series was over, to Czechoslovakia, dark and depressed
after the failure of the Prague Uprising had sunk in, to Corsica to learn
French and wander, to London and the Cotswolds riding on mopeds
we rented. But I realized that until I actually could go everywhere and
do everything, books could put me there. During the season, on road
trips, on planes, and in hotel rooms especially, sleepless after games,
there was time to read. At home, everything about Montreal that had
been interesting seemed more interesting.

Soon the people of Quebec would have a chance to decide their
province's future, something that never happened in our part of the
world. The talk, in newspapers, on the streets, became more urgent.
There was *meaning* in the air. Consequence. Growing up in Etobicoke,
my classmates and I didn't really know Quebec's backstory. Nor did
many others in the rest of English-speaking Canada. We knew about
Jacques Cartier and the European "discovery" of Canada in 1534,
and what he, a Frenchman, had claimed for France. In *Pirates and
Pathfinders* in grade 6, we read about John Cabot and his discoveries
and claims more than thirty years before Cartier. I remember at the
time wondering whether his last name was pronounced "Cabot" or
"Cabo," and whether, though he'd been sent by the British Crown,
he was actually French, not English. (It turned out he was Giovanni
Caboto, an Italian.) We knew about Wolfe and Montcalm and the
Plains of Abraham, and the Treaty of Paris that followed in 1763, and
the end of French rule and the rise of British dominance in our part
of North America. We learned about the tensions and conflicts in the
centuries that followed, which, though ostensibly about something

else, seemed to us about French Canadians being, as we called them, "sore losers."

In more recent times, in our newspapers and magazines, we knew about bombs going off in mailboxes in Montreal's privileged Anglo neighbourhood of Westmount. Yet then there had been Expo, all of us—French, English, and the world—*together*. How could anyone want anything other than that? But then in 1970, less than a month after Lynda and I arrived in the city, we saw tanks on the streets, after British trade commissioner James Cross and Quebec labour minister Pierre Laporte were kidnapped, and Laporte was murdered. We were living this. We could feel all around us the need of Quebeckers to be *maîtres chez nous*, whether as part of Canada or in an independent Quebec. Fundamental, visceral stuff. The pride. Wondering how I would feel if I had grown up as a French-speaking Quebecker, what would *I* do? And in 1976, that election night at the Forum, the bifurcated response of the fans. So clear. So honest. I used to say to people, inside and outside the province, that to me during the 1970s, there was no more interesting city to live in than Montreal, no more interesting place to be than Quebec.

In the late 1970s, our son, Michael, was born, and our very good Canadiens team became a great one and won four more Stanley Cups. Also, as if out of nowhere, I felt old for the first time. Feeling old happens young to musicians and actors, but even sooner with athletes. Physically, we can't do it anymore. Only a few years earlier I had been a kid from nowhere, then overnight an emerging star, then a core member of the team, then, I remember the day, in a newspaper story I was referred to as a "veteran." I wasn't even thirty! The life that I'd never imagined, and that had taken over as my life, was now closer enough to the end than to the beginning, and I began thinking about what would be next.

I had a very good idea of lots of things I knew I didn't want to do— practising law and staying in hockey in some non-playing role being two of them—but I had no idea what I *did* want to do. I was thirty-one when I retired. And while it might not seem so, this retirement was as real as those that happen when people are decades older. One Friday morning you arrive at work and are good at something, where others count on you and you count on them, where you have a purpose, where you matter. And the following Monday morning, you have nowhere to go, don't know what to do, and have no one around you to talk to and complain with, succeed and fail with, and you don't know why you matter. It's not the paycheque you miss, it's the sense of purpose. When you're a player, you retire twice: once when everyone else does, and once thirty years earlier. And you retire the first time when all your ECI classmates, when everyone you grew up with, are just finding their stride and moving into the core work years of their lives. And you know what they're going through, and what's next, because you went through it a few years before.

Now I had the chance to start up again. I had money others my age didn't have, and a public reputation to get me inside any door. I had learned a lot in my lifetime in sports. I'd had responsibility put on me that would've buckled the most senior CEO, even one twice my age—how about that eighth game in Moscow in 1972; how about those Stanley Cup finals, the Bruins, the Flyers, surviving Boston Garden, and the Montreal Forum on a bad night. I had learned how to succeed and fail with millions watching. I had learned to be a public person. But I wasn't going on in hockey, or in politics, so that training was of little use. And I had already worked my way up before. I had expectations now. I liked to be good. I liked how people treated me because I was good. I liked how being good made me feel.

I also liked to feel that I mattered. The Montreal Canadiens mattered to a lot of people. But I learned then, and came to learn much better, that if I mattered it wasn't for the Stanley Cups and other trophies I'd won. I wasn't like Bobby Orr or Wayne Gretzky. I didn't change the way a game was played. Not even close. Which may sound modest, but isn't. If I had an impact at all, it's that I played and did this *while* I went to law school. It was because one or ten or a hundred or a thousand kids who loved hockey but also kind of liked math or music or something, or who liked math or music but also kind of liked hockey, could see it was possible, and their parents could, and their coaches could, and that those kids themselves might come to believe, might feel, they had the right to try to do more than one thing and learn lots of things as they did that would take them in lots of different directions, which would change them, which would change their kids, which would change their grandkids. Which may sound immodest, but I don't think it is.

OK, so now what? I had never asked myself that before. I'd never had to. I started the 1980s where my classmates had started the '70s.

V

———

BECOMING WHO WE ARE

CHAPTER NINETEEN

"Give me a child until he is seven, and I will give you the man."

The phrase is attributed to Aristotle, as well as to St. Ignatius of Loyola, founder of the Jesuit order. These are also the words expressed as the ongoing maxim in Michael Apted's *Up* series of films. In 1964, the documentary *Seven Up!* appeared on TV in Britain. It followed fourteen seven-year-olds from different parts of the country, at home, at school, on playgrounds, and allowed us to hear their voices, to get a glimpse into how their minds worked, and how their lives were. Apted, a young researcher for the show, in choosing the fourteen subjects, had social class very much in mind. In the highly privileged and deeply underprivileged kids he selected—the child "until he is seven"—he wanted his audience to see the U.K.'s CEOs and cabinet ministers, taxi drivers, teachers, and housewives of 2000—giving them "the man." Ten boys and four girls were chosen. It was many more boys than girls because Apted and his audience knew it was boys who would go on to varied and dramatic futures—the girls would be mothers and housewives, teachers and nurses. Apted came to regret his decision. The film was done as a one-off. The audience would need to fill in the decades of the kids' futures themselves. But in 1971, with Apted now in charge, 7 *Plus Seven* followed. The series became unstoppable.

28 Up was the first of the films I saw. I remember being excited to see it. I'd had a different enough public life that I'd often been asked: How did it happen? How could it have turned out this way? During those years in Montreal, I wondered a lot about what Apted was wondering: How did I get from there to here?

I had missed the first three instalments of the series, but Apted began each film with clips of the kids at their earlier ages. At seven, they looked mostly like every seven-year-old looks, except the privileged ones, the boys in private schools who wore their proper school uniforms, jackets and ties, and talked with plummy accents. The underprivileged ones sounded like Eliza Doolittle's father in *My Fair Lady*. At fourteen, some of Apted's kids still looked like kids, but most had begun to fill out, becoming bigger and fleshier teenagers. Seven years later, at twenty-one, they all looked different. The boys had long hair—this was the seventies. But mostly it was the way they talked. Until then, they spoke as if they were trying to sound like what their parents thought they were supposed to sound like. Now they were more assertive. They seemed to be trying out potential new versions of themselves, sounding like what they thought they were, or should be, and were on the way to becoming.

At twenty-eight, they were different again. They'd had a few more years of life experiences and, after having told everyone, and themselves, at twenty-one who and what they were, now they seemed unsure. It was the way Wayne sounded in his journal after he'd met up with Ken in Paris, the way most of us were at that age. When I was with the Canadiens and playing in cities where Cornell friends had moved to take their first jobs, I'd get in touch with them or they would with me. The first few years it was fun, until into our mid-twenties it wasn't. It seemed to them that I knew where I was going, and it was just as clear to them—though they hoped not to me—that they had no idea themselves. They tried to sound excited. Everything felt awkward. In *28 Up*, this is what those seven-year-olds had become.

By *35 Up* there was little pretending, and little need to. They had not become whatever they were supposed to be and instead were whatever they had been for enough years that most seemed OK with that. Apted's subjects were ten years younger than us. They were thirty-five or so in the 1990s; we were that age a decade earlier.

By the 1980s, most of us who were going to get married were married, most of us who would have kids had kids. Most of us would remain in jobs in the fields we were in, would continue to live in the cities or towns where we were living. For most of us, life had figured itself out if we hadn't figured it out for ourselves. We were thirty-three or thirty-four when the decade began. It was a time of settling in, mostly with acceptance, often with pleasure, rarely with resignation. And even as we advanced in our jobs, it was a time of the family.

We were different from our parents. Not as much as we wanted to be, but we were living in different times, and those times helped to shape our perspectives. To shape us. Our parents' backdrop was the Depression and war. For them, change had meant bad news, and an unchanging world was good. Our backdrop was prosperity and peace. It was a middle-class life in Etobicoke, filled with possibility, where change was exciting. Our parents never entirely shed their working-class instincts even in their new middle-class world, but we, their children, raised middle class, were thoroughly middle class. While they heard footsteps from the past, we saw footprints to the future. While they had told us cautionary tales, we told our kids aspirational ones.

For the girls in our ECI class, the years after we left university were especially different. Our mothers were "gainfully employed" only until they got married. Unless she became widowed or her husband was unable to work, a woman knew she would never go back to the workforce after getting married. But the girls in our ECI class did keep working once they got married and continued to work until they had kids. And when they left the workforce, most had in their minds that they would return when their kids were in school and solidly into their childhood lives. By this time, these young mothers also had come to know that it was a lot harder with an extra body or more in the family to feed, clothe, and raise, and harder still if there was only one income to do it with.

By this time too, the postwar consumer society that had offered us more was offering us more still—bigger, nicer houses, more cars, more distant places to travel—more for us to want and more for us to miss out on. The possible had become a need, the need an expectation, and the standard of what it was to be middle class, and what it takes to live it, rose. It would be harder now for us as young parents to "keep up with the Joneses," not to live fabulously but how the Joneses now lived, which gave young mothers a further reason to return to work after their kids were born.

And there was another motivation. These young mothers, our classmates, had had four years of training at university in a field of their choosing. Many of them had been excited by what they had learned and wanted to pursue those interests to fulfill who they had become. The pointed question that society asks women was flipped. It was no longer "*Why* are you working?" but "Why *aren't* you working?"

When our female classmates did return to work, it was not single-mindedly. They weren't looking to rule the world, few even to rule their part of it. Maybe if they thought they could, some would have wanted to, some would have tried, but Canada wasn't ready to make that easy for them. There were assumptions to overcome—a mountain of them. You may now have a university education, their prospective employers, almost always men, said, you may be as well educated as those who become CEOs and prime ministers, but if you're a woman, and even if you're serious about your job, at some point you're going to want to have kids, you're going to leave, and if you leave you may not come back, and if you do come back you'll be four or five years behind those men who stayed on. And we can't afford to hang back with you to help you make up that ground, and you can't expect us to. We're in a race too, our competitors are not standing still. You think you're serious, and maybe you are, but you made a choice, you decided to have kids, and to leave, and you're not serious like men, like we, are serious.

Twenty years after Betty Friedan had published *The Feminine Mystique* in 1963, the state of women was different, but a lot less

different than it might have been. Mary McIntyre taught elementary
school through most of the seventies, had her kids, and returned to
teaching. Cheryl Beagan also went back to teaching after she became
a mother, as did Lorna Casey and Joan Boody, as Penni and Marilyn
Adamson returned to nursing, Judy Tibert to public health, Barbara
Vaughan-Parks to physiotherapy, and Peggy Clarke to accounting. A
few went into different fields after their kids were born: Kathy McNab
into editing books, Joan Cliff into managing her husband's medical
office. Lisa had her kids early, worked a few jobs, then decided to do
what she'd thought she would never do—she went into teaching and
never left. Judy Clarke, Kathy Vodden, Sandie Barnard, and Marilyn
Steels never married, never had kids, and never stopped working.

Only Margaret Silvester mostly lived as her mother had lived.
Margaret left social work to have her kids and didn't go back to a
paying job until well into her fifties. She and her husband, George,
decided they would live off one salary—his. He was a photographer
for Ontario's Ministry of Transportation and Communications. Soon
after he started, one of his assignments was to go with the deputy
minister to take pictures of him opening this or reviewing that, photos
that ended up in the *Toronto Star* or in trade association or internal
publications so people could see their government in action, their tax
dollars at work. That deputy minister, it turned out, was Cam McNab,
Kathy's father.

As a government job, George's was solid and secure, and paid
well but not a lot. He and Margaret wanted nice things for their kids,
not more than they needed but enough to give them a good life now
and a chance to make a good life of their own in the future. They
wanted them to go to a good school, live in a safe community, and
have around them families who wanted the same for their kids, even
if the parents of those kids almost certainly both had paid jobs to provide that. Margaret and her husband had to know their limits and be
creative. Margaret had to approach being a mother and wife much
as a commercial entrepreneur seeking out their next buck might: be
vigilant to everything, see the gaps, identify the needs, and work to

fill them. If her three daughters needed something new to begin the school year, or a dress for the prom, she made them. For birthday parties, no Chuck E. Cheese for her daughters and their friends, let's make some fun of our own. Summer weekends and holidays, rather than rent or buy a cottage, they went camping. If the school or church needed a hand, Margaret was the first in line to help because schools and churches were part of her family's life, and if something was good for them it was good for her family. Margaret needed always to put herself into the mind of her kids and her husband to see what was required often even before they did, and to provide it often without them ever realizing they needed it at all. Practical needs, spiritual needs, emotional needs—whatever was required, Margaret was always just there.

One of our classmates who never left the workplace was Sandie Barnard. She had arrived in our class at ECI in grade 12, not so much immediately barging her way into the middle of everything as knowing where the middle was and going straight there, as if that's where she belonged. She had a glint in her eyes—a knowingness, a suspicion, a mirth—as if she not only saw things that I couldn't, but was already scheming up ways to do something about anything and everything. She majored in medieval English at U of T, got her master's at Carleton University, in Ottawa, and started teaching at Centennial College, in the Toronto suburb of Scarborough. Centennial was the first of Ontario's colleges of applied arts and technology, opening in 1966, about ten years before Sandie arrived. Post-secondary education in postwar years had become an aspiration, and a need for Canada's and Ontario's future, but a university's traditional academic curriculum was not for everybody. The colleges offered two- or three-year training in the trades and in technology and awarded diplomas, not degrees.

Sandie's students at Centennial didn't come from rich families, in high school they hadn't been the best students. In other words, they didn't exactly sign up for her courses with either aptitude or delight. But Sandie knew they were looking to make a future too, and in the trades, English was going to matter to them. So she taught them that way. Seriously, and with ambition. She didn't dumb down the curriculum or mock them or, among her friends, mock what she was doing.

As the colleges found their place, tensions grew between their administrations and professors. Universities were the fair-haired children of the post-secondary system, colleges the poor cousins. Universities were respected, colleges much less so. College professors were given workloads much more like high school teachers' than university professors'. They went on strike in 1984 and again in 1989, to help right that imbalance. Sandie was one of the union's leaders. She spoke at protest marches and rallies, with a power that comes only when you know you are right. Those involved with her in the union might have thought of her as a union activist. Those involved with her on women's rights and gay rights might have thought of her as a feminist and human rights campaigner. And she was all of those, but not just all of those. She knew that people who have power insist on holding on to that power, using it, and disempowering everyone else. Sandie believed that was wrong.

As a kid, she had been in Brownies and Girl Guides, but as other girls moved on to other activities, Sandie stayed and became a Guide leader. She believed that every girl needed strong women in their lives. Women who may not be in history books but who are also doing important things, women that girls should come to know, and realize they can be like, and one day be.

During her years at Centennial, some of those she worked with knew, or didn't entirely know, that Sandie is gay. Her sexual identity was part of her, just as being a labour organizer, feminist, and human rights activist were parts of her. She was herself. And she was going to be herself. Her feelings, her beliefs, her actions—they didn't have to do with women or the workplace, not entirely. They had to do with injustice, experienced by anyone, anywhere.

In her house, in her dining room so everyone could see it, she hung a photo of Nellie McClung. From the late 1800s until her death in 1951, McClung fought for a woman's right to vote and for other issues of women's equality. Underneath the photo are McClung's words: "Never apologize. Never retreat. Never explain. Get the thing done and let them howl."

Marilyn Cade had been one of the top students in our class every year of high school. She had been the head girl prefect. The question: What do you do when it seems you can do anything? She went to Western on a scholarship but found maths, physics, and chemistry wasn't her answer (a 58 in calculus helped her decide), and chose to major in French instead, knowing what that would lead to. After a year at teachers' college, she was hired to teach grade 9 French at Lorne Park Secondary School, in an affluent area of big 1960s ranch-style homes on large treed lots in southern Mississauga. Like Miss McKinnon, she spoke to her students in irrepressible French, looking for, hoping for, by mid-year getting, at least some glimmers of understanding. She also taught phys ed and helped coach the girls' field hockey team, which for many years had been provincial championship contenders. Lorne Park was a good school, on its way to becoming Mississauga's ECI or Richview. It had a good staff, with only a few "coasters," as Marilyn called them, and good students, many of whose parents were professionals or in business and believed in education. And Marilyn liked the courses she was teaching. In other words, as a teacher, things were not going to get much better than this. But only a few months into her first year, she began to wonder. Her parents sensed her disquiet. "They'd ask me, 'Is there something else that interests you?'"

She taught for two more years. The summer after her third year, her mother suggested that they go antiquing for a few days in the Eastern Townships, about two hours southeast of Montreal. On their way back, Marilyn recalls, "Somewhere between Kingston and Toronto she asked me, 'Have you ever thought of being a CA?' Just like that, out of the blue. I almost drove off the road." It was July. Marilyn was due back teaching at Lorne Park in September. The next week, her father set up a meeting with an accountant who showed her around his firm's offices. Marilyn called Peggy Clarke, who had been her roommate at Western and who had just finished her first year of business school at McMaster. Marilyn drove to Hamilton, met with the director of admissions at the business school, bought a book to prepare herself for the GMATs, took them, was accepted, moved to Hamilton, and roomed with Peggy again.

Most of her new classmates had majored in business-related courses as undergraduates, almost all of them were men, one professor smoked a cigar all class, every class. But Marilyn liked the straightforward way of the school, and of her classmates. It offered four main paths: accounting, marketing, industrial relations, and human resources. Marilyn chose accounting. Most important to her, she says, "The business school gave me the credentials for the next step, whatever that would be." She also got to know Larry Schreiner, who was in the same year and had grown up in Weston, just across the Humber River from northern Etobicoke. It was only after they both had graduated and taken jobs in Toronto at Deloitte, one of Canada's big five accounting firms, that they began to go out.

On her first day at Deloitte, Marilyn looked around: in her group of thirty-one, there were twenty-nine guys and one other woman. Her job much of that first year was doing audits and being "the low person on the totem pole," which meant "standing eight hours a day at the photocopy machine." At the end of the year, she was asked to move into the small business unit. For big accounting firms, small business is that forever area of great promise that is never quite realized. Small businesses employ vastly more people than big ones. They are an immense source of innovation, growth, possibility. The problem for large accounting firms in dealing with them is that while collectively they are big, individually they are small, widely separated, and inefficient to reach. More than that: small businesses don't have much money, and certainly not enough to collectively pay the overhead of big accounting firms in high-rise buildings on high-price real estate in city centres. And they're not prestige enough. Tell your friends you're working on the Acme Butchers account or the INCO account, and it's the difference between *ho-hum*, and *oh wow!* But small businesses need accountants, and Marilyn knew something about small business. Her father had one—Don Cade Insurance. He dealt with people, with families, with small businesses like his own. And to do that, he had to know them: what they did, what they needed, how they understood their businesses and themselves. Just as there are family doctors and family lawyers, he was a family insurance guy. Marilyn, working with these small businesses, would be a family accountant.

She and Larry were married in 1977. They moved into a small house on Robin Hood Road, only a few streets from where she grew up, then into a slightly larger one on Nottingham Drive, a few houses away from her childhood home. Larry left Deloitte to work at Touche Ross, another of the big firms. In September 1981, their son, Robert, was born.

Five months and one week later, about a month after she had returned to work after maternity leave, Marilyn was at one of her clients' offices, working on their audit, and got a phone call. It was from her babysitter. Robert had died.

He had been totally fine, totally healthy, just a few hours earlier. Even as she searched and searched her mind in the days that followed, she could come up with nothing, no indications, no signals of any kind, of *anything* that had been wrong, or even not quite right. He had been a big, healthy baby, over nine pounds when he was born, happy, he loved being around people. He was just fine. Besides feeling numb and sadder than she ever thought sad could be, inside, Marilyn was a whole screaming muddle of feelings and thoughts that didn't add up to what had just happened. She had been the one who could always handle anything, with calm and with competence. Because a baby had died, the police came to the house. And the fire department. There had to be an autopsy. She understood. But this is their son. She talked to the firemen and to the police. In the evening, she went to her parents' house. They had asked the minister at Islington United, Bob Trimble, to be there. Marilyn wasn't going to church much any more, but her parents liked Reverend Trimble and knew Marilyn did too. He said to her, "C'mon outside," and she and Larry went outside with him. "We had our arms around each other's shoulders," she remembers. "He said, 'Look up at the stars,'" and they did. "He wasn't preachy, he wasn't anything." He wanted them to feel something else, in the silence and bigness, though they wouldn't know what, or what he meant, until a few weeks later.

The head pediatric forensic pathologist at SickKids performed the autopsy and called them in later that day. Robert had died of sudden infant death syndrome. "[The pathologist] was absolutely amazing," Marilyn recalls. "He spent about forty-five minutes with us. He went through all the indicators, how they don't know the causes, but that dopamine levels seem somehow involved, how perhaps there might have been a buildup of indicators over time that in the end resulted in a shortage of oxygen. He wanted us to know everything there was to know, because he wanted to assure us that this was nobody's fault."

Some days later a partner at Deloitte offered Marilyn his condo in Florida, and she and Larry went away for a few days. When they got back, Reverend Trimble called and asked if he could drop by. They talked about their trip, and then he got to what he needed them to hear. "He said, 'I'd like to give you just one piece of advice: give yourselves a time limit, and don't do too much navel gazing. Maybe it's two weeks. In some countries people dress in black, sometimes people wear a band for two weeks or a month, whatever. It doesn't matter. But set a time limit that works for you, and then get back to what your life is.' And that's what we did."

This wasn't about getting back to normal. This was getting back to life. It was wanting to get back to life. It was feeling that they had a right to get back to life. And that meant feeling their way back, and others feeling their way back with them. Robert had died on February 17. On Mother's Day that year, Marilyn recalls, she and Larry "decided to go up to the cottage by ourselves. And everybody accepted that." By Thanksgiving, and Christmas, gradually, they were doing some family things. Some of their friends knew absolutely what to do, and others, who felt just as sad, didn't. A friend called her up and said simply, "Let's go for a walk in High Park." Another, a week before the anniversary of Robert's death, phoned her and said, "I have tickets to the symphony on the seventeenth. Would you like to use them?" There was also the day Marilyn walked into Deloitte's offices and two or three of the women were talking about pregnancy, so Marilyn said something. "It was like just everything stopped. I knew something about being pregnant, so why can't I talk about that?" There were also people who, the instant after having said something, couldn't believe what had just come out of their mouths: "You can have another one." "I can imagine how you feel," they said.

She went to a parents' support group for a few years. Being around people who *did* know how she felt, and were living a life, the life they had, helped a lot. "A big part of that group was the laughter. Hilarious laughter," she says. "If you laughed at work, they'd think you're unfeeling. Or unhinged." But Reverend Trimble had understood that you cannot allow yourself to wallow. He had Marilyn and Larry look up at the stars the night of Robert's death to show them that there was *also* a bigger world. You will always be a woman and a man who lost their child, he was saying, but don't allow that to be the definition of who you are. You are lots of things. You are you. And yes, you are a *mother*, and you are a *father*.

Her own mother was amazing, Marilyn recalls. Her father was the dreamer in the family, he was a salesman; her mother was the practical one. She had moved from the academic stream to the commercial stream in high school to learn to become a secretary. Then she became a wife and a mother. She had three kids. She made Marilyn and her sister Darlene's clothes, and taught them to make their own. Marilyn had been a star student, but, she says, "I don't remember her having any specific expectation of me and my future. She wanted us to find things that we wanted to do, and that would sustain us, and have us never depending on someone else." Sometime after Robert died, her mother did something that Marilyn and Darlene never expected. "She gave us both a brand-new sewing machine and some lessons on it. She bought us each a Cuisinart food processor and some lessons on it too."

This was her mother again "dropping things in my way," as Marilyn puts it, just as she had done between Kingston and Toronto about becoming a CA. Her mother knew. If you have a sewing machine, you sew. You do things. If you have a Cuisinart you make things, and you make things for other people too. Nottingham had block parties, and Boxing Day was coming up. Make some hors d'oeuvres, and when you do, you deliver a message to your neighbours that you're ready to be a neighbour again. You'll have fun. You won't be able to stop yourself having fun. You'll laugh, they'll laugh. Allow them to have a good time. With you. Allow yourself to have a good time.

Some months later, Marilyn was back at Deloitte working part-time, and she told her mother she was starting to enjoy not being at work so much. She thought her mother would be happy at the news. Instead her mother said, "very matter-of-factly, 'I don't think you should get too far away from your work. It's probably good for you.'" "No sitting on the couch hand-wringing," Marilyn says. "Life goes on. You still have responsibilities, you still have things you can do."

Marilyn did gradually go back to work full-time. In 1985, their second child, Laura, was born, and Marilyn and her family moved to the house they still live in today, a little north of the neighbourhood where she grew up. She did leave Deloitte, but when she did they asked her to take some of their small business clients with her. She opened her own office down the hall from her father's office, where her sister had come to work, not much more than a stone's throw in one direction from her childhood home on Nottingham and from the home, five houses away, where she and Larry were living when Robert was born. In 1989, their third child, Sarah, was born.

CHAPTER TWENTY

During the 1980s, the Brain Class took in Canada from many different perspectives. Bruce was still teaching in small-town eastern Ontario, Kathy in Sudbury, and Lorna in Gravenhurst. Peggy Clarke and Marilyn Steels were in Ottawa, Peggy with the Department of Defence and Marilyn in the head office of the Victorian Order of Nurses. Diana was in Alberta, having lived through oil's incredible ups in the late 1970s, as its price surged globally and everybody in the oil patch got rich, and now its incredible downs in the early 1980s. She was also living through the feelings that Albertans have for people like her from Central Canada, especially Ottawa and Toronto, which fluctuated, depending on the decade, between angry and angrier. But Diana's life in Alberta focused on what was *on* the land, not deep under it, on ecology and the environment, and if she didn't antagonize Albertans with her Central Canadian background, which she didn't, they didn't antagonize her.

By the 1980s, Pat Gregory was very much established a little farther west, in B.C., as a biology professor at the University of Victoria. While there might seem a very straight line from there to the snakes and salamanders by the Humber River behind his house, it was learning's and academia's meandering path that got him there. First, a summer job researching ducks in Manitoba while he was a student at U of T. Then, as he was deciding where to go for his graduate work and realizing that the cost of U.S. schools was beyond his reach, he came to know two prominent ichthyologists at the Royal Ontario Museum, W.B. Scott and Edwin Crossman, co-authors of the seminal reference book *Freshwater Fishes of Canada*, who put him in touch with an ichthyologist at the University of Manitoba who also had an interest in herpetology. If Pat's time at U of T had been formative, his four years at the University of Manitoba earning his master's and Ph.D. were his launch pad. "Every year was better than the last," he recalls. "I was developing my skills and knowledge, and for me it all seemed like a flower that was just opening up."

In Manitoba, he also met Linda, who was working as a lab technician and would later become a grad student in physiology. They were married in 1971. They rented a farm in Saint Adolphe, south of Winnipeg, an easy drive from the university. The farm offered Pat prairie space, solitude, a place to walk and discover and think, just as the Humber River had done. "I like my own company quite a bit," he says. "It doesn't mean I don't like other people's, but I enjoy walking for itself, and for what I might find when I'm doing it. And even if I don't see anything interesting, I do a lot of my best thinking when I'm walking." When he moved to UVic in the mid-1970s, they bought four acres of land in a rural area about fifty kilometres from campus.

His early years at UVic were a scramble, as they are for any beginning professor. He had lectures to think through and write and grant applications to write to support his research. Snakes are not everybody's fascination or priority, but each grant he received allowed him to discover a little more, to write papers on what he learned, to be invited to give presentations, to meet other interesting people who loved snakes. He went from lecturer to assistant professor to tenured assistant professor in 1979, at age thirty-three, to associate professor to full professor, and after forty-four years, to professor emeritus in 2018, when he was seventy-two. At different times, he was acting chair, interim chair, and chair of the Department of Biology. He received more than one hundred grants, from many different sources, often in small amounts, to research something that mattered to him, that might

matter to snakes. His most frequent and largest funder was NSERC, the
Natural Sciences and Engineering Research Council of Canada. His
grants were for research on Okanagan snakes, garter snakes, rattle-
snakes, rubber boas, oviparous snakes, gopher snakes, and sharptail
snakes, as well as painted turtles and lizard, salamander, and toad ecology. He authored or co-authored nearly one hundred peer-reviewed
articles in scientific journals. In Victoria, to this day, whenever there is
a local snake story, media outlets know whom to contact.

During this time, his two daughters were growing up, and his four
acres of property needed to be tended to. He and his wife had left
most of it wooded, they liked having wildlife around them, the deer,
raccoons, and birds, even the occasional bear, and as evidenced by two
goats they had lost, likely cougars as well. They also had their own animals, always a few dogs and cats, but some chickens, ducks, geese, and
rabbits, as well as the goats, from which, from one or the other, they
got much of their milk, meat, and eggs to go with the vegetables
they grew in their garden. They also had a donkey. Linda had given it
to Pat one year at Christmas. They named him Fred, and Fred and the
goats kept each other company. Later, when Pat's field work expanded
to other places and countries and took over more of his time, they sold
off all but a few chickens and goats, and Fred. "I could never have
sold him," Pat said. Victoria expanded, its suburbs gradually spread
out towards him, but Pat's four acres, which over time they allowed to
become more and more wooded, might as well have been forty. They
were his place to walk, and think, and not think.

In 2022, the Herpetologists' League, an international organization "devoted to studying herpetology—the biology of amphibians
and reptiles," as it describes itself, honoured Pat with its Award for
Distinguished Service to Herpetology. Given for lifetime contribu-
tions, it is the organization's highest honour. An article published on
the league's website includes a photo of Pat from 2018, the year he
retired, holding a barred grass snake, about five feet long, at his "long-
term field site in Kent, England." The photo was taken by his wife,
Linda. Pat is lean and angular, with receding white hair and a white

beard. More than its details, the impression left by the article is that this is someone who loves what he's doing.

Pat's CV is twenty-seven single-spaced pages long. His bio, in contrast, in which he tells his own story, is two pages. In point form he lists his job title, employer, place of birth, and schools he attended (including Lambton-Kingsway and ECI), and after giving a synopsis of his current research and noting a few of his recent publications, he concludes this way:

"My career choice was based on two factors: (1) deep interest in animals (especially snakes, as it turned out), particularly in their natural setting; (2) interest in science and solving problems. The best way to marry these interests was to go to graduate school and then become a university professor. This job also exposed me to teaching, which I like very much as well."

We were raised to be all-rounders. Sometimes the way to learn a lot of different things is to do a lot of different things. Sometimes if you know one thing really well, you know lots of things really well. And know them even better.

Wilf Wallace came to know the small towns and mid-sized cities of Canada. It wasn't his plan, but his jobs took him there. He had moved with his family to a hundred-acre farm in Mono Mills, north of Toronto, in the middle of grade 11. It was a bit of a shock at first—the move from city suburb to country. There they had an old wooden crank phone, and their phone number was 31. They grew some vegetables, raised some chickens, and had some cows, all of whom had names. He could drive a tractor at fifteen, so on the morning of his sixteenth birthday he got his beginner's driver's licence, in the afternoon took his test, and by night was out on the roads. Eat your heart out, Wayne and Roger. He finished high school, then had his unsuccessful year at Brock University, before finding himself back in the city, working near the airport for Capitol Records, living downtown just a few blocks from Toronto's folk and rock music scene in Yorkville. He met his future wife, Doreen, at Capitol when he was twenty and she was eighteen. She had come to Canada three years earlier, her family having split their time between Scotland and Nigeria in the previous six years while Doreen's father helped to set up Nigeria's telephone-telegraph system after the country's independence in 1960. Two years after they met, Wilf and Doreen were married, and not long after, their first child was born. They were twenty-three and twenty-one. Suddenly they weren't kids, and Capitol Records and Yorkville weren't going to be enough to build a future on.

One night, Doreen saw a commercial on TV: the Bank of Nova Scotia was advertising for bank manager trainees. Wilf had always been good at numbers. His first job after Brock was with an accounting firm, and at Capitol Records he worked in the accounting office. He always thought of himself as a "math guy." So he cut his hair and applied for the job. It paid $5,000 a year, he remembers. He also remembers saying to them that he'd always wanted make $100 a week, so if they paid him the extra $200 a year, "I'm in." Big smile, great story. The job pays five thousand, they repeated. He took it.

Wilf and Doreen moved to Kitchener, a city of about a hundred thousand an hour west of Toronto. The bank was on a corner in the heart of downtown, built both as an edifice and as a symbol in classic bank style. As a trainee, Wilf was moved from one department to another, learning varied functions and little by little learning how a bank fit into the life of a city, a business, a family, and how deposits and loans and "being good with numbers" was only the beginning of what he needed to know. He also learned one more thing he never expected he'd need to. Right after he started, he had to go to the police for a criminal background check because he needed a semiautomatic revolver licence, because, as he knew from *Dragnet*, *Mannix*, and *Bonnie and Clyde*, but hadn't put two and two together, crooks rob banks. From there he went to a police firing range to practise—this wasn't his family's farm anymore, shooting groundhogs with his .22. The bank's gun was placed in a special drawer, the drawer was locked, and maybe more happily for him than for any would-be robber—Wilf still looked twelve—he never had to use it.

When his year's training was up, the bank moved him to St. Catharines, a city of similar size an hour and a half southwest of Toronto, then a year after that to Niagara Falls, then back to St. Catharines for a year, and finally in 1979 to Jarvis, a small town of three thousand, his first posting as a branch manager. With five moves in five years and the birth of their second son, with one thing just leading to another, as Wilf put it, "I never got around to going back to university."

In smaller cities, a bank manager matters. You are a part of the community, and you have to think of yourself that way and operate that way. So you join the Board of Trade or Chamber of Commerce, or both, you join Kiwanis, Rotary, Lions, or Optimists, depending on whether you're in a "Kiwanis town," "Rotary town," or other. You join because your fellow club members include the mayor, some town councillors, the high school and elementary school principals, the owners of car dealerships, insurance brokerages, funeral homes, and other small businesses, the presidents and senior executives of the town's biggest employers, and also its most prominent lawyers, doctors, and accountants, because, together, they are the lifeblood of the town, and you need to know them and they need to know you. You might also join the golf club even if you're not a golfer. As a branch manager, you sponsor hockey teams and baseball teams, help fund school and church projects, and help build parks, playgrounds, rinks, and swimming pools. More than networking, this is being a good neighbour. You learn that for anything of any significance to get done, everybody needs to pitch in. Several years later, as a member of Parliament, I represented a riding in the big suburb of North York, in the big city of Toronto, and in the riding I could walk down any street and no one would know me. In Jarvis, as manager of the Bank of Nova Scotia, everyone knew Wilf.

Two years later, the bank sent him to Hamilton, first to a suburban branch, then to a much bigger one near downtown. Hamilton's population was about half a million; it wasn't Toronto, but it wasn't Jarvis. His focus was now less community-wide and more business-centred, and at the centre of that business was real estate. Real estate would also soon become the centre of his career world. He recalls a "cute blond lady" coming into the branch one day. She wanted to transfer her business from another bank and she needed a chequing account for her line of credit. Wilf asked to see her T4 slip. "She plunked it down in front of me, and it said two hundred thousand dollars!" This was the 1980s. Wilf was making $40,000 at the bank. The woman was a real estate agent.

Wilf signed up for some real estate courses and got his licence. He was hired by Royal LePage, the top real estate brokerage in Hamilton and in Canada. He remembers his first day. The manager took him to a desk and said, "Here's the phone, here's the phone book, start calling people." Before Wilf figured out what that meant, his phone rang. It was a friend who said that at church the day before a couple he knew mentioned that they were moving, and he had told them Wilf would give them a call. Wilf called them, met with them that evening, listed their house, found them a house where they were moving, did both sales, and along the way learned that while at an open house there might be only one buyer, there were lots of others there who were in the market. From that one Monday morning phone call on his first day at work, Wilf estimates he made twenty to thirty sales.

He also very quickly learned something about himself: he was more assertive than he thought. He had taken a public speaking course a few years earlier and was more confident now, in more situations. And if his ECI classmates would be shocked at how much taller he was, they'd be gobsmacked that little Wilf Wallace now had a big radio voice, and that the kid who played ball hockey with Pat and Bruce but was too small to play real hockey was in fact a bulldog when he went after a sale. "I call it 'the Thrill of the Deal,'" Wilf says, almost reliving the feeling of those moments as he talks about them. "When you put a sale together, particularly if it's a tough one and you have to do a lot of negotiating, and in slow real estate times, and when mortgage rates are high, you've got to find some way, some incentives, some answer."

A big part of that answer, as Marilyn Cade's, Judy Tibert's, and my father had learned, was that you've got to know your client. You're not selling insurance, bricks, blocks, or real estate, you're selling yourself, and to a real person. The best doctors treat people, not diseases, the best teachers teach kids, not subjects, the best real estate agents sell to people's needs and dreams. Just as there are family doctors, family lawyers, and family accountants, Wilf was a family real estate guy.

There would be bad years—1989 was particularly bad all across the country. In Hamilton that year, out of thirty-five thousand listings, there were seven thousand sales; in a normal good year, thirty thousand listings, twenty-five thousand sales. But in bad years or good, do things right, Wilf learned, and those clients, those people, will come back. A few times, at Royal LePage's urging, he went back into management, twice the market turned down, twice Wilf was given his severance. Both times, he went back to selling, and both times the market turned. He kept on well into one's normal retirement years. He and Doreen live not far from the house that was his first-ever sale. "I drive by it often," he says. He remembers the feeling that day, when the deal was done. Some real estate agents lose the thrill of the deal; Wilf never has.

CHAPTER TWENTY-ONE

When change comes to a country, it is most obvious first in the cities, and in the cities, it is most obvious in the schools. The first to see big changes are always the teachers, who see them in their students, right there in front of them in their classrooms. At ECI, Mr. Jackson and Mrs. Coupe saw what their predecessors, and their predecessors' predecessors, had seen—row after row of white faces. In Huron Street Junior Public School in downtown Toronto, Mary McIntyre was seeing kids of all ethnicities with all sorts of life histories. The school was in the Annex, a neighbourhood near the U of T, that was filled with professors and people in the arts, some who worked at the CBC—all people who valued education. But as Mary describes it, these parents' kids represented only about half of the school's population. The other half were the children of immigrant families.

There were fifty-seven nationalities at the school, many from Asia and the Caribbean, and their parents had a real mix of education and income levels. As Mary's students were learning how to learn, she and the other teachers were learning how to teach them. "We used to stress to the parents, because we were told this and because it made sense to us, that they had to speak to their kids at home in English. Which is the absolute wrong thing to do, because you want kids to hear stories and hear things in the language their parents are fluent in, because kids have to get the concept"—and the logic of things connecting to other objects and actions. "They can fill in the language later." What couldn't come later, but what was already present in these kids, because it was already present in their homes, was a willingness to work hard, an ambition to make something of themselves, a respect for the institutions and for the elders around them, and an understanding of the importance of learning. If these habits and structures of learning were in place, the rest would follow. Just how much Mary's world had changed became evident to her a few years later when she was visiting a school near to where she had grown up in central Etobicoke. "I just got this shock" she says. "There were so many blond heads."

In northern Etobicoke, Judy Clarke taught kids from a range of backgrounds at North Albion Collegiate. When she arrived at the school in the early 1970s, her students were mostly the kids of Italian immigrants. Over the next decade, change was gradual at first, then came in a rush. Older immigrants moved out of the area, replaced by new immigrants from different places. Many of the Italians moved north and west to what had been small towns and villages but were now part of Toronto's explosive sprawl, into newer homes, with more grass to care for and enjoy, and more space for fruits and vegetables to grow, harvest, and preserve. In their place, first, those we called "boat people" fleeing the turmoil in Southeast Asia following the Vietnam War. Then families from the Caribbean, many of them moving west from public housing in the Jane-Finch neighbourhood of North York. Later in Judy's sixteen years of teaching at the school, many South Asian families moved into the area, from India, Pakistan, Sri Lanka, and Bangladesh, until North Albion's yearbooks looked almost the obverse of ECI's during her years there—about three-quarters Black and one-quarter brown, and very few white students. Hardest for Judy was the marking. In her early years, she'd been able to read about six essays an hour, then it was three, then two. Many of her students struggled to learn a new language, and Judy struggled to comprehend what they wrote.

Public health nurses also see societal changes early. After Judy Tibert had her two kids, she went back to work part-time in the 1980s.

Etobicoke had been largely built out, while Mississauga, where Judy now lived and worked, was one of Toronto's new big-growth suburbs. Its expansion was coming from those now able to move up from tired mid-rise apartments in the city to something that was their own, to the affordable suburbs beyond the unaffordable ones like much of Etobicoke. Beside these new homeowners, making their own new beginnings, moving up in a different way, were the immigrants of the time. In the late 1970s and '80s, as in northern Etobicoke, families from Vietnam, the Caribbean, Africa, India, and Sri Lanka were moving to Mississauga.

Judy worked two days a week as a public health nurse, mostly doing phone counselling from an office. Her job was to hear in strangers' voices, in their tone and through the limited English they knew, accounts of their lives and life practices that she had never experienced and could hardly comprehend, then to offer these strangers what might be life-changing counsel. And the more voices she heard, but especially when she began to make home visits, the more the picture became clear. She had learned—it was practically a mantra for anyone in public health at McMaster—that we are all different, that "there are things we don't have control over and don't have all the answers for. That we only have some knowledge, which we can share, but it's up to the person we're dealing with to decide whether they want to accept that or not. We don't have the power to say 'You have to do it this way.'" When she was a kid, she had been surrounded by white faces in her neighbourhood, by children and families who shared the same religion and culture, where there *was* a right way, which she knew and which she did have control over. Now, as a public health nurse, she had to un-learn, learn anew, and adapt. "I didn't find it difficult going into that kind of an environment," she says. "I just had to meet people where they were, to provide information to them about how we do things, in an accepting way."

The big questions, new ones at the time, and thus challenging: For those who came from other countries, who grew up with different understandings, ways, and laws, once they are in Canada, what right do they have to continue to live the way they once lived? And what right do longer-standing Canadians have to expect that these new Canadians change the way they live? The legal answer is easy: we all live under the same laws. But what if no law is broken? What if the differences are moral or ethical or religious or cultural? That's complicated, not just for a white-skinned Canadian public health nurse, but for many long-standing Canadians. Now that we're all side by side together, how do we live together? It's in this world that Judy worked.

Her work had mostly to do with babies and their well-being, and babies meant families, and some families, particularly in the South Asian community near the airport, were the product of arranged marriages, the young wives having no relatives in Canada other than their husband's family, with whom they would be living. "Sometimes the wives were abused by the men in the family. And they had babies, and that would be very, very difficult." Judy had to find answers. That was her job. She had to make sure the child was doing fine, cultural differences or not.

It wasn't just a matter of going into the child's home and offering the wife a way out for her and her child, Judy says, "because generally one of the male relatives would be sitting in on your visit." Instead, she would try to get the couples to agree to contact one of the countless local agencies that had sprung up, funded by the government, that was language-specific and culturally appropriate to them.

"We'd alert the agency that we had concerns, and they'd have to work with that and find the right answer. But it wasn't easy for the agencies either. This was a male-dominated culture. There were situations where these agencies would have to support a wife in leaving her husband because it wasn't healthy for her to be there."

At ECI, all but three kids had been white. At her own kids' high school graduations in the late 1980s, Judy remembers that "when the teachers announced the names of the kids as they walked across the stage, sitting there, looking at the program, maybe one in twenty of the kids had a name I could easily pronounce."

All this in one generation.

—

Toronto and Canada were becoming more global. Judy Tibert, Judy Clarke, and Mary McIntyre had seen it in neighbourhoods and classrooms, Murray McKenzie in hospitals and universities, and through most of the 1970s and '80s Gord Homer would see globalization as a senior executive at Wood Gundy, then one of the largest investment companies in the country.

After his experiences at U of T with Arthur Porter and later with IBM, Gord had followed his brother to Harvard Business School. It was September 1969, just after Woodstock, and the Vietnam War was on the minds of everyone around him. Some of his classmates had majored in business-related fields as undergraduates, but most had come out of math, science, psychology, political science, and English, because Harvard Business School was looking to prepare its students for business in all its forms and applications. Some graduates would make stuff and sell stuff, some would manage big companies that affected the lives of thousands of employees and tens of thousands of others in the communities around them. They would make big decisions and set important directions locally, nationally, globally. And if they were to run the world, they had better know something about the world and the people who lived in it, for their sake and the world's sake.

Harvard Business School was a serious, important, and often self-important place. Students wore jackets and ties to class. Student protests typically happened on the *other* side of the Charles River, the undergraduate side. Business school students weren't natural out-on-the-streets protestors. They didn't have to be. In their lives, they had mostly been able to generate the changes they wanted through their own status and talent, but Vietnam was different. And they had skin in this game. They might get drafted. So some stopped wearing jackets and ties as their protest until things "settled down," as Gord put it. Some never put them back on. But for all of them now, things wouldn't be the same. From Vietnam, through Watergate and on, there would be less respect for authority, for government and business, and for those who, like Gord and his fellow students, one day would run them.

For Gord, the business school's case-study approach to learning was something new to get used to. Every night, the students were given three cases, detailed descriptions of three different companies and problems they faced, fifty or sixty pages long. And the next day in class, the students analyzed these cases and proposed solutions to the challenges, the professor prodding the students, provoking them, and, as they answered, the professor looking around the room for the unsuspecting student, cold-calling anyone he chose—"Give me your analysis of the case. What's the problem? What's the solution?" Each student had a name plate in front of them on their desk, had to be in class every day, and had to be ready. Then after all this "thrashing around," as Gord puts it, just as the students thought the discussion was resolved, the professor would test them some more—"You assumed *this*, but what if you assumed something different? How would that affect your analysis?" And they were off again. This was performance, not only learning, and in front of a tough-minded audience of their peers. Grades, reputations, and pecking orders were on the line. It was full-contact sport. Gord had never been a hand-up kind of person, and his fellow students weren't slow-twitch, ponder-and-puzzle engineers. They were highly verbal people—political scientists, philosophers, arts types, power guys who had an opinion about everything and couldn't stop themselves from giving it. Which could be intimidating, until you realized that while they *knew* more than everyone else, they weren't right any more often. The competitive part of these classes, Gord could handle. The hardest part was the reading. The sheer volume of it, and every night.

"After the first two months, I was just floundering," he recalls, "because I couldn't get through the cases." Then he realized he had been reading them like an engineering text, where every precise word matters. "I said to myself, this isn't going to work. I've got to learn to speed-read. They also threw in a lot of text and background that wasn't essential to the issue. They wanted you to learn to sort through the crud and figure out what the important issues were."

In his second term he began to find his footing. He also found a
course, and a professor, that became important to him. The course
was in finance, and the professor was John MacArthur, who was also
Gord's section advisor, later the dean of the business school, and
also a Canadian. One of many professors who says to students that his
office door is always open and not to be shy, and one of the few who
meant it. And while many other students intended to walk through
MacArthur's door, Gord did.

MacArthur had been an undergraduate at UBC. One summer,
working at a sawmill, he was spotted by the owner, who suggested
he think about going to business school, and apply to Harvard.
MacArthur told him he couldn't afford Harvard. As Gord relates,
"The guy said, you apply, and if you get in I'll pay for it. And he did."
The lesson stayed with MacArthur. Later, as dean in the 1990s, when
the Canadian dollar dropped to sixty-three cents against the American
dollar and the barrier for Canadian students became higher, he created a program to provide fellowships and scholarships for Canadians.
Today, every Canadian who goes to Harvard Business School gets
$10,000 a year from the scholarship fund. Gord helped MacArthur
raise the initial money. "He was a role model type," Gord says. "He
had a real touch with people. It was fortuitous I connected with him."
("Fortuitous" is a word Gord often uses. But while a door may be
open, it's "fortuitous" only if you walk through it.)

The finance course proved a good fit. "It wasn't a mathematics
course but it involved math concepts. It involved numbers *and* applications, and I found intriguing how so much of it applied to companies and businesses. Not so much with the stock market, but how to
analyze a company in terms of results, of performance, why it would
borrow money versus equity. How it would set dividend policy." In his
second year, he took more finance courses, but he still wasn't certain
this was the right path. And for the first time in his academic life he
wasn't one of the top students in his class. Yet, not much distracted
by success when he was in high school and at U of T—his focus on

the doing—he was not much bothered by this either. There were still cases to read, problems to solve.

For Gord, in his second year with graduation only a few months away, the question was: What would he do next? In what field, with what company, and in which country? "I was still thinking about going back to IBM to continue in the computer world," he recalls, "but I had three different résumés, one for marketing, one for finance, one for computers." He interviewed with some companies in New York, Boston, and the Midwest and with several investment banks in Toronto. "But the military draft was still in place and even if you were Canadian, if you were working in the U.S. and did get drafted, if you went back to Canada you were considered by the U.S. to be a draft dodger for life." He decided that unless there was something special about any U.S. job, he was going back. But a recession had just ended, and there weren't many offers. "The offer I got in Toronto from Wood Gundy was sort of fortuitous."

Wood Gundy was the number one investment firm in Canada, but it had a budget to hire only three people that year, and by the time Gord contacted them they'd already hired four. Still, he flew back to Toronto and went to their offices. "I really wanted to see the guy who ran the corporate finance department, Ross LeMesurier. He was like the dean of corporate finance on Bay Street"—Toronto's Wall Street—and a Harvard Business School grad. "He spent about an hour with me, he was very intrigued with my computer background even though I told him I didn't want to be a computer guy per se and wanted to be in the mainstream part of the business. By five that afternoon I had a job." From Douglas Hartree and his differential analyzer, to Arthur Porter, to IBM, to here, it wasn't computers that interested Gord so much as what computers could do. At the time, only Wood Gundy's chief economist was using a computer, to do analytical work. "I would be the first guy on the corporate finance side to use one." It was the summer of 1971.

A few years later, Gord asked LeMesurier how he could have hired him if he only had a budget for three and Gord was the fifth?

LeMesurier told him that the real assets of a company are the people. "If I see somebody I like, I hire them, I never pay attention to budgets," he said. "Don't ever forget that in your career."

After Gord had been in Toronto for a year and a half, Wood Gundy asked him to move to its office in Montreal. He had been working on a financing project for a mining company in Port-Cartier, Quebec. He and a few others from the Toronto office had flown there for a meeting. Gord was the junior person. The next morning they went down for breakfast and none of the waitresses spoke any English. So Gord ordered for everybody in French. "A week later," he recalls, "LeMesurier calls me and says we've decided to beef up Montreal. We're bringing in the head of the Vancouver office and we want you to work with him. All the other firms are leaving the city. Dominion Securities and A.E. Ames have moved their people to Toronto because of the political unrest, and we've decided to do the opposite. Give me two years," he asked of Gord, "and if you don't like it and want to come back, that's fine. No hard feelings." Gord said OK. "I arrived the next weekend with a suitcase and a pair of skis." *Merci*, Miss McKinnon.

It was February 1973, not even three years after the October Crisis, an election was ahead, René Lévesque and the PQ were in the air. Any future Quebec government, even that of the ruling Liberals of Robert Bourassa, would become more nationalist in its view, whether as a pathway to an independent Quebec or not, and Montreal would become more and more French. Big non-French companies were moving, or planning to move, and it only made sense that the big investment houses would follow them, their clients, to Toronto. But LeMesurier was from Montreal. His father had been dean of McGill Law School in the 1930s and '40s. He knew that the Wood Gundy clients who had stayed would not accept, would *resent*, being served from Toronto and would soon go somewhere else, but if Wood Gundy stayed they would actually *win* business. "We just ate up our competitors," Gord recalls. By moving, the other investment houses also reinforced the PQ's message: it's only Quebec independence or the threat of it that will allow us to be *maîtres chez nous*.

There were other big issues at the time. A year after Gord arrived in Montreal, the oil crisis hit. OPEC cut production, the price of oil almost quadrupled, the stock market crashed. "There was a period for nine months to a year where we had virtually no business," Gord recalls. "'There's only so many times you can call a client and try and dig up some business, and he'd say, no, nothing." But overriding every-thing, the one question that wouldn't go away, and couldn't go away: Quebec independence. The year 1976 was going to see a showdown election—and once it was over, there would be a referendum, and then *everything* would be about *it*.

In this atmosphere, every fibre is on alert, long-held ways of think-ing and doing that had gone unnoticed are now unmissable. Gord remembers a Monday morning at the office talking to some people about his weekend, about having dinner at a restaurant on Rue Saint-Denis and how much fun it was. Saint-Denis was on the *other* side, the French side, of Montreal's historic French-English boundary of Boulevard Saint-Laurent. "This one fellow looked at me," Gord says, "he'd lived all his life in Montreal, and said, 'Saint-Denis? We don't go past Saint-Laurent.'" Another time he found himself at the end of a day, having worked on an acquisition, all the negotiations being in French, with a gigantic headache—"And I realized, boy, it must have been tough for a lot of francophones, all those other negotiations, all those other years, in English."

And another moment: "Sun Life had just announced they were moving to Toronto, and the Quebec government went crazy. A lot of people were saying that things were getting so bad Quebec wouldn't be able to borrow. So the Quebec government decided it wanted to show the world, particularly English Canada, particularly Toronto, that they *could* borrow. That they were still a viable credit risk. In the midst of all this, we got hired to do a bond issue for Quebec." Gord and some others went to Quebec City to negotiate with the govern-ment's finance people, and after a day of meetings they all went out to a restaurant. "This one fellow," Gord says, "an ardent PQ guy, leaned across the table and said to my boss something like, 'This isn't going to change, you know. I'm going to have your house in Westmount.' And my boss just looked across the table at him and reached into his pocket and said, 'Here's my keys. You can have my house in Westmount. So long as you pay my property taxes.' And he asked the guy, 'What're yours?' The guy said a thousand bucks or something like that, and my boss said, 'Mine are twelve thousand.'" Both of them delivered the message they wanted to deliver; neither of them understood the other. "You could see the tide turning," Gord says.

After the election, the changes came fast, then slowed to a drip. "I lost three or four clients very quickly," Gord recalls. "But some others were so entrenched you knew they weren't going to leave for a while. RBC didn't leave. Bell didn't leave for a long time, and the CPR and CNR weren't going to leave. But you could see the start of the erosion." What he found tough to handle was the media. "Everything had to do with Quebec and independence. Pick up the newspaper, it was constant, turn on the radio and TV, it was constant. And all of a sudden I had this feeling that there's a whole world out there other than Quebec, but everything *in* Quebec was looking inward. That's when I thought, and it wasn't all of a sudden, but this is going to continue."

For anglophones, there was the first wave of leavers after the election, and then a second wave a few years later. Those who had stayed were initially defiant and proud: *We're Quebeckers. We believe in Quebec and believe in what Quebec will be. We know it will be more and more a francophone province, but we're bilingual, or we can speak French well enough, and we want to be a part of building this future Quebec. So we're committed to staying.* The message back to them from francophone Quebeckers: *You can stay if you want, but you have to understand that this will be a real francophone Quebec, and that you, as anglophones, are irrelevant. You think you can play a role, and maybe you can play a* secondary *role, but understand, really understand, that you aren't necessary, you don't matter, and we'll hardly notice you're here.* It was at this point in Quebec, not long before the 1980 referendum, that the second wave began leaving Montreal.

Gord was now well past fulfilling the two-year promise he had made to LeMesurier. He had also met Carolyn, at a Grey Cup party in late 1977. She was working at IBM, in the same office complex, and a few weeks later, on a Friday after work, they were both in a bar with friends and bumped into each other again. She was from Cornwall, a city of about fifty thousand an hour west of Montreal just across the border in Ontario, and had graduated from Western University in one of its first computer science classes to which women were admitted. Cornwall was predominantly English-speaking, but with it being so close to Montreal she had grown up learning school French and neighbourhood French, and most of her work at IBM was in French, with some of Quebec's big francophone insurance companies among her accounts. But for both her and Gord, it was becoming time to think about the future. Gord was thirty-three, Carolyn twenty-seven.

"We decided we were going to get married and to have a family," Gord says, "and I'd always assumed I would be coming back to Toronto." In late 1980, they were married. They moved to Toronto.

It was a hard first year. Newly married, now in a new/old city, but more than that, in his new job as acting vice-president of finance, Gord says, "I went completely away from dealing with clients to being in charge of the accounting department, the computer department, the back office operations, the admin department. I went from having two or three people working for me in Montreal to eight hundred." In many cases, he says, until that time "I had never really understood what all those other people actually did." He had always been on the exciting problem-solving, deal-making front lines, working with CFOs or treasurers or presidents of companies. The people who got things done, it seemed to him then. Now, he was dealing with volumes of people, with volumes of different backgrounds and ambitions, with volumes of problems. Why didn't he understand that earlier?

On top of that, they were in the midst of dealing with a recession even deeper than that of the mid-1970s, and the inflation that resulted from it. "At the end of '79, '80," Gord recalls, "interest rates went through the roof. I did a bond deal at one point at 17½ percent!

Then, in the middle of '81, all of a sudden it crashed. The central banks decided to really tighten up on their policies to quash inflation, leaving the question: What was going to turn this around?" No one knew, or could know, how long it would take. Gord had seen a big downturn during the oil crisis, but then he had been on the client side. In a central role like the one he had now, it was front and centre every day in terms of the results, the issues, and the people.

"In those days," Gord says, "Gundy didn't lay anybody off." It was part of their corporate pride, part of their reputation. Everyone who worked there, everyone in the whole industry, knew it. But now, for the first time in its history, Wood Gundy let people go. On Gord's watch. The same company that, when LeMesurier had only the budget for three, took on four, and then five. But this recession was deeper, it was going longer, and there was no end in sight.

Meanwhile, Carolyn continued to work at IBM. Then, in 1983, their first child was born. Not long after, Gord was moved back to the client side at Wood Gundy as head of investment banking. The finance industry was about to change.

Until then, banks had been banks and investment houses had been investment houses. This had been the law in the U.S. since the 1930s, and while in Canada there was no formal law, the practice had been much the same. But in the 1980s, investment firms started doing interest rate and currency swaps and derivatives, which took away some of the banks' loan business. "The banks then started to get very antsy," Gord says, "and put a lot of pressure on Ottawa to change the rules. And ultimately Ottawa did. But the banks could also buy brokers, and about 1986 that began to happen." The first question was: Which bank would end up with which brokerage house? The next question: What would happen then?

"There was a huge debate within Wood Gundy about whether we should try and stay independent," Gord recalls. "I chaired their Strategic Planning Committee. We concluded that we should join up with a bank. It could provide more resources and backing, and if a bank didn't buy a broker, it would build its own brokerage division so the competition would only increase." The banks and dealers had long working histories with each other, Wood Gundy aligned with Royal Bank, Dominion Securities with CIBC. TD was the only bank determined to build their own brokerage. "So we started negotiations with the Royal, but those talks stalled and we ended up doing a deal with an American bank, First Chicago." Then Dominion Securities ended up doing a deal not with CIBC but with RBC, then Nesbitt with Bank of Montreal, and McLeod with Bank of Nova Scotia.

"But our deal faced all kinds of regulatory approvals and hadn't closed when the crash in October '87 came along, and First Chicago cancelled on the deal. We went through a period where it was very possible that if we couldn't find a new investor, we were going under." A meeting was scheduled with the Inspector General of Banks and Financial Institutions and "they might have closed our doors." But that day, Wood Gundy did a deal with the Brascan-Edper group, who provided the financing to keep them going.* "It wasn't a long-term solution, it only gave us time." In the end, Wood Gundy ended up with CIBC.

"CIBC bought 65 percent of us, and we retained 35." They would become CIBC Wood Gundy. "Then we had to figure out how to work together." A bank is bedrock, safe, solid, here today, tomorrow, and always. It is thought of this way, it thinks of itself this way, governments pass laws to ensure that it acts this way. Investment houses seek opportunity, take greater risks, experience bigger ups, suffer bigger downs. Bankers and dealers, at least until not many years ago, were very different people with very different personalities. The companies they worked for had very different cultures. Now they were coming together. One a big guy—a dealer—and one massively bigger—a bank. In good times, one that's profitable—a bank—the other massively more profitable—a dealer. The farmers and the cowpokes had to be friends, but how could they? And who would run the show?

---

* The principals of Edper were Edward and Peter Bronfman, who during most of my years in Montreal owned the Canadiens.

Wood Gundy, the little guy in the merger, had one big thing going for it. "Because we were still shareholders," Gord explains, "the bank couldn't just say, we'll do whatever we want." At Wood Gundy, Gord had been in charge of investment banking. In CIBC Wood Gundy, he became vice-chairman as well as chair of the audit committee. But for him, the match wasn't right. It was never going to work out. Finally, things came to a head. "We were having a rough year. The bank had lost close to a hundred million dollars, and I wasn't happy with the way some of the decisions were being made. I was doing basically client work, and I was looking to do more than that."

He had been at Wood Gundy, then CIBC Wood Gundy, for nineteen years. In 1990, he left. He was forty-three.

Two years earlier, Marilyn Steels died. She was the second of us. She had moved from her job with the VON in the Niagara area to a senior position at its national headquarters in Ottawa. She had been as successful in her work as she was as a student at Humber Valley, ECI, and McMaster, and at Case Western Reserve in Cleveland, where she had earned her master's. She had remained as grounded and responsible as the poster on her office wall suggested: "Bloom where you are planted." She had a house in the country. She had maintained her love of horses and music, and especially of Elvis. She was in her backyard, and suddenly she felt something. She was a nurse, and knew immediately what it was—a carotid aneurysm—and called 911. She had felt no symptoms beforehand. She was forty-one.

CHAPTER TWENTY-TWO

In the 1970s a few of us left Toronto and Ontario, to study, work, or live. By the 1980s, all but four of us had returned—Pat remained in Victoria, Diana near Edmonton, Ken in Paris, and Daryl was back in California.

Daryl's path was a surprise, probably for him, certainly for us. He was the fourth boy in a family of five kids, his brothers already twelve, nine, and six when he was born, so in his growing-up years they were always a stage ahead of him. His sister was two years younger. He would need to be the kid who grew up faster, who was twelve going on thirty. He did stats for the high school basketball coach while he was in elementary school, and pretty much ran the Rosethorn softball league when the adults couldn't get around to doing it. He wore a blue blazer and tie to school. He saw the harshness of adulthood when his father lost his job when the Avro Arrow was cancelled and his mother had to go to work as a supermarket cashier. Hearing his brothers testing their parents, he became aware early on that there were other ways of thinking, other thoughts to have. At twelve, in confirmation classes, he was one of the few who questioned what he was learning. "I had started to learn of the excesses and abuses of the church through history," he explains later. "And intellectually, religion didn't make sense to me." He didn't reject his confirmation like Margaret Silvester, but after he was confirmed, he stopped going to church altogether and never returned.

His three older brothers not only introduced him to new ideas but gave him the cover to think about them. The family was busy, so if Daryl didn't cause trouble, did his homework, and got good grades, he could drift out of sight, his absence unnoticed. He could wander off on his bike, see his own sights. He could disappear into books, immerse himself in the books his brothers had moved on to. Our librarian at ECI was Miss McKillop. We had library class once a week in the early grades of high school, then afterwards most of us didn't darken her door again. But she was "one of my best pals," Daryl says. He would wander into the library, they would talk, and when he arrived the next time Miss McKillop would have a stack of books set aside for him. He'd already read much of George Bernard Shaw in elementary school. He remembers one day picking up one of Shaw's books in Miss McKillop's library and finding that the most recent name on the borrowing card was from five or six years earlier. It was his brother Bevis.

Daryl was a deep learner when most of the rest of us were all-rounders. This was because he had developed the ability to be, liked to be, and because he knew he had few other options. He was, as he describes himself, "a total shrimp" in high school. In elementary school, size hadn't mattered much. Only a few kids were that much bigger, and tomorrow he would grow—that's what his parents told him, and that's what they sort of believed. But he says in high school his small size meant, "generally, I had no status at all." So, if sports were to be "large- and tall-centric," as he puts it, and girls paid him no attention, he would focus where he could succeed. "Academics were my compensation for not being a superior athlete," he says. As the other boys spent countless hours on sports and girls, "I had time to delve into things others didn't."

He joined the French Club, but finding it more clubby than French, spent more time in the language lab after school, where he could explore languages at his own pace, in directions of his own choosing, to the range of his own ambition. He did the same with Russian, a language he found not only intriguing but dangerous, which appealed to him, its strange-looking alphabet like a code only he, Mr. Smith, and a small subversive cadre of others knew. One day he wrote his siblings' names in Russian, in permanent ink, on their lunch pails, which even they found fun, except later, when his brother Derek, crossing the border on a motorcycle trip to the U.S., had a customs guard pull him over and ask him to explain the lunch pail. Daryl approached math and science the same way he did languages, always seeking more from his teachers, and more challenging problems to solve. They were all a game to him. Every Friday, in grade 13, Mr. Relf, our chemistry teacher, gave out a problem for those who were interested in extra work over the weekend. And every Friday night, Daryl and Pat would talk on the phone. "Daryl was the only other person I knew who would do it right away," Pat recalls. The two of them didn't do anything else together outside school. They never went to each other's house. But they played with science together, as Daryl did with math and languages as well, as I did with hockey and baseball. It didn't matter that none of this had any apparent application in our future lives. To Daryl, it was "intellectually stimulating." So by the time he got to Queen's, where his father, mother, and brother Bevis had gone, he was ready to leap into a diabolically difficult triple major of math, physics, and chemistry. That's when his predictable path to the future went astray.

That decision was, as he puts it, his "fatal mistake." He discovered in his first year that while he liked thinking deep theoretical thoughts, he liked thinking deep practical ones, ones he could apply, even more. So he transferred into engineering, losing a year's worth of credits, which didn't bother him as much as he thought, because he liked engineering better, until later he discovered he didn't like it much either. At Queen's he found that he didn't really love anything he was studying. He didn't have teachers he could approach who would challenge him with extra problems to solve and new things to think about. And he had so many required courses that he didn't have time to play around with any of them, or take on other subjects that might not lead him anywhere in making his career, but might lead to some unknowable somewhere in making his life.

But at Queen's, he did rediscover something he loved, and got a chance he never expected, because finally he had grown. He was now big enough to play on sports teams. He could play intramural, and at Queen's there were intramural teams and competitions in almost everything. And if some kids were good in the popular sports, almost nobody was any good in water polo or horseshoes (yes, horseshoes). So in intramurals he could start where others started, but also with an organizers' understanding they didn't have, which had come from his years on the sidelines at Rosethorn. Intramural competitions have schedules. At university, with no adult coaches or parents around to remind you, get on you, and stay on you, a few forget to show up. And if showing up is half the battle in life, in intramural sports it's the whole enchilada, because the team that fields the most players almost always wins. And Daryl, who became the engineers' unofficial team organizer, because no one else wanted the trouble, wouldn't let them forget. "My teams never forfeit and never default," he liked to say. For the first time, the engineers won the overall intramural team championship.

He also started playing badminton again. He had played intramurally at ECI—there was no school team. (Daryl and I faced each other in the school's intramural championship final in grade 13. I won because I was bigger.) At university, he joined a Kingston club, then tried out for the Queen's varsity team. He didn't make it, but he liked badminton enough that he volunteered to be the team's manager, doing all the stuff no one wants to do—picking up this, arranging that. But also, just by being there, before practice and after, and when a player was injured or sick and someone was needed to fill in on the other side of the net, he got the chance to play. And just by being there, when the coach did his coaching and the players did their practising, he watched, he listened, he learned, and with stolen moments of court time, got better. Ultimately, he got his break. Two of the team's better players decided they wanted to play doubles not singles. A spot opened up.

In the team's season-ending tournament, his brother Bevis drove from Toronto to be there. Daryl played. He also won his varsity letter.

Then he graduated in engineering and knew he didn't want to be an engineer. "I discovered at Queen's that I wasn't going to be a theoretical physicist or theoretical mathematician, that I wanted to do things more practical, more applied. I came to a realization that I wasn't necessarily cut out for everything."

His classmates from ECI were moving on in their careers, and he was still learning what he didn't want to do. But he was also continuing to learn that he loved learning. He was curious, he had energy, he was willing to take on the most mundane task as if it might be interesting and make it interesting: keeping stats for Mr. Thom, marking papers for Mr. Smith. At Queen's one summer he worked at Atomic Energy of Canada doing mostly typical summer joe-job stuff, but because he knew something about numbers and words, he helped senior people draft multi-million-dollar contracts for the sale of CANDU nuclear reactors, reactors which, after the demise of the Arrow, had become Canada's next great international engineering adventure. Another summer he took water samples on small rivers in southern Quebec, working in rural old-world Quebec French, not Miss McKinnon's Parisian French, also discovering that what he had always assumed were the pristine waters of Georgian Bay near his family's cottage, or even those of Mimico Creek, probably weren't.

At this stage in his life, he didn't need anything to be interesting for any future life path. He was having good experiences learning, and wanted more. Even more important, he was beginning to understand that whatever was ahead, whatever his great life interest might be, he could learn to do it. He didn't need to know everything at the beginning, and not knowing didn't frighten him. Learning was like an algebraic equation. Some numbers you know, and you use them to discover the ones you don't. Maybe that's why we learn algebra in the first place.

And for him, that future didn't need to be tomorrow. He wasn't married, he didn't have kids, there was no one he feared losing if he didn't marry, no job of a lifetime he couldn't turn down. His family had lived a modest life, he had lived a student's life since. He didn't

need wads of money. Still, *something* needed to be next. He had graduated from Queen's in the middle of a year; January didn't seem the
right time to look for a job. Maybe it would be better to wait until
September, he thought. Except when September came, he says, "I felt
I needed some world experience." So he bought a round-the-world
ticket on Air Canada for $200 and flew to London. The ticket was
good for a year.

He wandered around England for a while, then went to Amsterdam,
where he bought an old vw van, which, he soon found out, didn't
always start but which, if he parked it on a hill and turned the key,
with enough forward momentum, its engine would work. Not quite
Mr. Thom's physics, more like trial and error, and desperate hope.
Maybe like research. He stayed in hostels and parks, slept one night
on a haystack in a barn in the Italian Alps, skied in Austria, witnessed
totalitarian Europe in Franco-led Spain—"There were Guardia
everywhere"—escaped the winter by going to Morocco, and in the
medina, in its colours and smells, "experienced a world totally different
from anything I'd ever seen." In between, he worked for Siemens in
Nuremberg for three months, living with a German family, speaking
only German, even though in high school he (Stepan Semionovich)
had taken Russian, not German.

In Greece, he attended a performance of *Aida* at an ancient outdoor theatre near Athens, the music, the setting taking him back into
Mrs. Coupe's English class as she lived out the readings in her textbook. Then on to Santorini. He was bodysurfing. He was waiting
for the right wave, found it, felt the surge of it, felt himself thrown out
of the water with only air around him, then smashing into the sand.
So out of it as to be aware only of feeling himself being sucked out
to sea, believing what he did next would determine whether he lived
or died. Then, somehow, making it far enough up onto the sand. His
shoulder dislocated. His trip over.

He arrived home in the midst of the oil boycott and the stock
market crash. Again, it didn't seem the right time to find the right job.
He filled his six months of rehab time after his shoulder operation

working as a postie, which he liked, starting early so he could finish early and have the rest of the day to himself. He went to Montreal and got a job as a teaching assistant at McGill, tutoring some students in math and French as well. He worked with a small computer company, his first experience in business. He recalls little about what he did there, but remembers vividly that every afternoon they took their clients out drinking, and afterwards, after their clients went home, he and his co-workers stayed on and spent the rest of the night making fun of them. "It opened my eyes to this world of business that I didn't like at all."

Daryl was starting to feel he was running short of time. He was twenty-six. He didn't know it but he was also about to demonstrate the truth of Edison's statement "I have not failed ten thousand times—I've successfully found ten thousand ways that will not work." He had an uncle who was a professor of nuclear engineering at the University of California, Berkeley. Daryl decided to visit him. He imagined he'd be away for about two weeks. Three months later, he returned to Montreal, but only to pack up his apartment and go back again.

In those three months, he mostly spent his time on campus, auditing courses in astronomy, the humanities, it didn't matter what, listening to Nobel Prize–winning professors, being in the same room, breathing the same air as them. He wandered up into the hills above campus to the Berkeley Lab, where Ernest Lawrence had invented the cyclotron, where Robert Oppenheimer was teaching before he had been recruited to head the Manhattan Project and build the bomb, where fourteen elements of the periodic table had been discovered. "It was an amazingly exciting place to be around," Daryl recalls, "and to realize that so much history had been created there, and was still going on." He applied to graduate school in biophysics, and was accepted.

He had never taken biophysics before. "I hadn't really allowed myself to delve into living things," Daryl says, "unless you think of electrons and quarks as living things. But suddenly, oh my goodness, it seemed there was a whole world out there." And those living things included people. "I discovered I really liked working directly with people. It became more and more clear to me that that's what had been lacking. That's what I was yearning for. And more and more I was thinking about medicine." He hadn't taken the prerequisite courses he needed to apply directly to medical school. He would need to get a master's and go from there. He had just turned twenty-seven.

"I remember my first New Year's Day in San Francisco." He had just finished his fall semester. "I remember riding my bike across the Golden Gate Bridge. The sun was shining. It's January first! And I said, *This is unbelievable. I can't believe I'm here.* And then I thought, *Oh my goodness, I can play tennis all year round.*" Maybe even more exciting were his courses. "They just grabbed me, in ways I hadn't experienced in a long time." And the way they were set up, they allowed him time to be grabbed. "At Queen's, I had forty-five hours of engineering classes, which was absolute craziness. Here, it was fifteen to twenty hours. I had time to learn. In depth. To really delve into things, and to feel that I'm not just on top of it, I'm all over it."

He faced one big obstacle, however. Biology was at the centre of what he was studying, yet he knew little about it. But instead of taking Biology 101 with all the first-year undergraduates, and being always behind his grad school classmates, he took two graduate biology courses, trusting himself that he could learn fast enough what he needed to know. One moment brought together what he'd been learning and thinking and not quite grasping for many years, and gave sense to where he wanted to go. It had to do with a Brazil nut. A simple Brazil nut.

Daryl recalls, "I found that by using partial differential equations, which I had learned to do, I could calculate how many potassium-40 positrons the Brazil nut was emitting. It turns out you get a positron about every three seconds, every 3.13 seconds in my calculation. And to me that was amazing. I've got this nut, and it's sending out into me and out into the atmosphere a positron every 3.13 seconds, and I'm holding it in my hand, and I can calculate what it's doing, and it's interacting with my matter and with other people's matter. I just thought that was so much fun. It was challenging to figure it out mathematically, but it had this real-world, real-life application. I mean, this is what's really happening right now, all around me. And I can understand it. And I can calculate it." *This* was the actual world, not just the one where he could see, taste, and feel the texture of a Brazil nut, but one where he could also "see" and "taste" and "feel" it through his numbers. "I just thought, and I still feel, *Like, wow, there's a whole other world there that is waiting to be discovered, that I've not been aware of, and not experienced. And now I can.*"

Daryl began to think of some possible applications: "In various medical procedures. In radioactive isotopic interactions with matter. With human bodies," he says. "The fact that we live in a world of radiation, where cosmic rays are cutting right through us all the time and we're not even aware of it. Where a lot of these things are possibly the cause of mutations that have changed the course of evolution. So this has really profound implications for our existence, our past existence, our current existence, and our future existence." He talks about a play he saw some years later in New York, *Peter and the Starcatcher*. "It was one of the greatest things I ever saw," he says. The play was written as a prequel to *Peter Pan*, in which a young orphan and his friends are shipped to a distant island, and on the ship, in the captain's cabin, is a mysterious trunk containing the "greatest treasure on Earth"—not gold or diamonds but a greenish powder from the stars called "starstuff," which can turn horses into centaurs, fish into mermaids, birds into pixies, and which can allow people to fly. "The play is about how we're all made of starstuff," Daryl says. "And it's true. It's stuff from the stars that formed us, and is still forming us." Stuff that was created from the Big Bang, that through time had taken one form, and another, and another, and at this particular moment, now, has become us. "I found some of these concepts very humbling. It made me feel a very small cog in the universe, and at the same time a part of something. Which I felt I could celebrate too."

Daryl's years at Berkeley transformed him. "I was getting comfortable with finding myself, and feeling confident, and able to take on anything. The world was my oyster, and this was all just fun, and stimulating, and wonderful." And he learned something else at Berkeley. All his missteps and side steps, and putting-things-off steps through high school and university and after? "I learned why it mattered that it had taken me so long to get to this. I had to learn how to learn properly and study properly, and Berkeley provided me a reason why it mattered that I did. I would go to lectures actually having prepared for them. Then after, I could go over them for a couple of hours. I had never done that before. I had time now to think about things, and about their application."

Always a deep learner, finally he had a chance to go deep. And something to go deep for. As much as he liked learning about radiation and matter and the interaction between them, he says, "I really wanted to know a lot more about human physiology and the human body and how radiation interacted with it. And more than that, how that all worked. What it meant. I was getting more and more excited about the possibility of learning that in medicine. So I started planning my courses with that in mind, and what it would take to get me there."

It was far from certain he could get there. All around him were really smart people learning things nobody had ever been able to figure out before. He had started behind in badminton, he had worked his way onto the school team at Queen's and played a little, but he had never really caught up. He might now finally have reached the point where "next" was beyond him no matter how he had tried. But he never thought that. Instead, he remembers a professor he had. "Her father was suffering from dementia, and she decided that what was really needed in medicine was to figure out what was going on with dementia and to do something about it. This wasn't even her field, but she made it her mission. And I just thought, here is somebody who wouldn't stop reaching for things. I didn't know everything she was talking about, but I didn't think it was way beyond me." Nor, he thought, would whatever he'd make his.

He was off to Yale medical school. To New Haven, which wasn't Berkeley—more biking, less hiking; less Frisbee, more theatre. Beyond its academic schools, Yale had its drama school, and on campus and in

New Haven, Daryl remembers ambitious, exciting drama and musical productions it seemed almost every night of the year, and often going to them. Meryl Streep had graduated the year before he arrived, Sigourney Weaver the year before that, Wendy Wasserstein, Tony Award and Pulitzer Prize–winning author of *The Heidi Chronicles*, a few months earlier. It was September 1976. Daryl was twenty-nine years old. By this time, most of us were married and many of us had kids.

Medical schools put students through a series of rotations, a chance to practise on real patients, each rotation lasting up to a few months, giving students the opportunity to learn a little about a wide range of fields and a lot about themselves. Daryl hadn't thought much before about obstetrics and gynecology, and he discovered that he loved delivering babies. Pathology, less surprisingly, he found an "intriguing intellectual exercise." On another rotation, he got the chance to assist on several major surgeries, "doing things, frankly, that I shouldn't have been doing." And if earlier he had discovered that he didn't want to be a theoretical physicist or a businessman, in this rotation, he really discovered that he didn't want to do hip replacements. To anyone not hardened to it, this wasn't medicine, it was carpentry. "It was almost terrifying to see how brutal it was. In one operation, we actually snapped someone's femur—I heard the crack. *That* wasn't planned."

Internal medicine was another eye-opener. It seemed perfect for him. Many diseases and conditions aren't able to be conveniently isolated to a single organ, a single explanation, or any known cause at all. You have to uncover, and discover, and it's complicated. Daryl realized early on, "I can do this. I'm actually pretty good at it." But, he says, "it was the most miserable year of my life." What he found so hard was that "you were making life-and-death decisions on people, with scarcely enough knowledge, and with very little sleep. It was absolutely terrifying and exhausting." In internal medicine, he discovered, specialists "have to find a way to push that reality into the recesses of their minds, and certainly in my internship, I couldn't." He was up all night every third night, and every first and second night he'd still be at the hospital at ten. "You were living this essentially every waking second and minute. Those who do it get jazzed up by having that much excitement and pressure, and thrive on that sort of stimulation. Any doubts they have pass very quickly because they're so busy." At the end of your shift, "you're still high from working so hard and thinking so hard, and making decisions, that it's hard to sleep. I could do it, but I didn't want to do it all my life."

Instead, his rotations reinforced what he'd been learning all along, which was that really he wanted contact with people. "It was my psychiatry rotation that opened my eyes to what a fascinating world that would be. What I hadn't actually realized was that every individual patient was different. Everybody has a slightly different background, and while each may have similar conditions, diseases, disorders, each brings to them their own individual background, family background, genetic background, personality. So everyone is a new story. Everyone is a new challenge, a different challenge." And yes, he can use what he's learned from his other patients, but he has to find a way to help *this* individual, not seven or eight others who have similar conditions.

He remembers a patient he had during his psychiatry rotation at a hospital near New Haven. "He didn't talk. He was a total mystery to everyone, and I had no idea what to do. I spent fifteen sessions with him, fifteen hours, and he was totally silent." Daryl couldn't even tell whether the patient didn't want to talk or didn't understand what Daryl was saying. Almost nothing was known about him, except that he'd been silent for many years. Daryl read academic journals and studies, trying to understand the problem, searching for ideas about how to reach him. But what do you say when you're the only one talking? It's only so often you can bring up last night's baseball scores or the weather. "It seemed like I wouldn't be able to do anything," Daryl recalls. "Then I noticed that maybe he was following what I was saying a little better, and then suddenly he started talking. He told me about himself, about his life. I think he started to talk because I had tolerated his silence, and engaged in his discomfort with life, and never gave up." It was the personal interaction that made the difference. "Just my being there, and bearing with him, and showing total interest in him for so long finally made him feel I was trustworthy."

Daryl's learning had led him here. Psychiatry was where he was going. For his residency he decided on St. Mary's Medical Center in San Francisco. It was 1981. He was thirty-four years old.

The rest of the decade was about making a life of the life he had chosen. Now he was surrounded by intriguing, fascinating people, everyone different, everyone in some kind of pain. People with "anxiety and depression, increasingly those with bipolar disorder, many with psychotic symptoms," he recalls. Not like the people he had grown up with in the accelerated class at Rosethorn and in the Brain Class at ECI, or the people he had studied with at Queen's, Berkeley, and Yale. In those worlds, if something wasn't quite right, you thought about it, made a plan, and did something about it. You made it right. This wasn't so easy. He now had to deal in long, slow, rarely dramatic answers—when there were even answers at all—with people who were troubled, not easy to be around, and often not easy to like. He had to set all this aside. He had to think about his patients differently. He had to see them through their own eyes, not his. "I wanted to know how this person is processing their thoughts and emotions and experiences. I wanted to get into their mind and body."

He says, "I had always to remember, it wasn't their fault. It was their poor health. It was bad luck. It was bad genes—the apple doesn't fall far from the tree." His focus became adolescent psychiatry. "These kids had ended up with a genetic predisposition to their mental conditions, or had been horribly mistreated in their early childhood by their parents or others in their life. I felt with kids there was still a chance we could make a difference. Often with adults it seemed close to too late. They were often a product of their own parents. I was hoping we could interrupt that." He had to resist the sense of inevitability contained in the very words and phrases that he and the profession used: "genetic predisposition"; "the apple doesn't fall far from the tree." "It's a humbling experience," Daryl says, "when you often don't have a whole lot of ability to change things. I'm not sure when I came to realize both my impotence and also my competence. In medicine, we sell cures, and if you're a surgeon, maybe you can cure people. I'm not sure I can say I ever cured anybody. Most of the time amelioration is our goal. To help people function better and survive better in the world. And that's a laudable goal from my perspective."

Amelioration also offers time. To come up with *something*. Murray McKenzie's wife, Marilyn, couldn't offer that. Every one of the kids on her cancer wing at SickKids died. But six years later, Joan Cliff's daughter didn't die. The motto at ECI: *Semper ad meliora.* "Always towards the better."

One more thing was part of Daryl's life because he wouldn't let it not be. "After a difficult day," he says, "I'd go for a walk in the park or get some exercise." He rediscovered squash—he had played a little at Queen's—but not only as recreation this time. "It was such a wonderful release. In three-quarters of an hour I could get in a really good workout and forget everything that was bothering me. At one point I was playing every day." He also rediscovered baseball.

He had been too small to play as a kid. He'd played occasionally at Queen's, a little more at Yale, and now after many years, baseball discovered him. It had evolved. In the 1980s, slo-pitch baseball became popular. It is a game everybody can play and enjoy. It can be competitive or recreational. "I decided that if I was to play, I'd have to start a team, and manage it as well."

He started with a coed team, once a week, on Sundays. Then, because some other teams would always be short of players, he'd hang around the park after his own game and play for them too, sometimes getting in three or four games on a Sunday. Then he started a men's team that played on Saturdays. And the team got so much better that he could see that if they practised a little, they might become good enough to compete for the league title. So they practised some more, and won not only their Saturday league but the city championship too. His team was called Sang-Freud and the Jungbloods. He played third base, but his most important position was as manager.

As he had learned, if you get the right players and make sure they're there, you win. "My teams never forfeit, and never default." And on a coed team, he quickly learned, the most important players were the women. Half of slo-pitch's ten players on the field at a time needed to be women. Because so many fewer women had played baseball as kids, the disparity between the best women players and the average was much wider than it was for men. Get the right women, and you've got a chance.

One year, Daryl remembers, "we needed another woman desperately. I had made that known, and I guess this woman had called up and left her name on my answering machine months earlier, but I hadn't gotten back to her. But I really needed players, so I called her and asked if she could come and play that day. And I see this really short Asian woman walk down the slope to the diamond carrying her glove. I said, well, let's warm up. And oh my gosh, she had an arm, she could throw, you know, not like a woman." Daryl had thought, at first glance, she was too small to play. Just as others had been wrong about him, he was wrong about her. She played second base and catcher. Five years later, in 1990, he and Laura were married.

VI

BIG
CHANGES

CHAPTER TWENTY-THREE

Sometime in the 1980s, the mood in Canada and the U.S., especially in big cities, was beginning to change. By the nineties, the shift was obvious.

Government had been at the centre of nation-building for decades. After the Second World War, it was at the centre of the world's reconstruction, and of new aspirations and possibilities for the future. No longer focusing only on physical infrastructure—roads, bridges, rail lines—governments concentrated more and more on social infrastructure—schools, hospitals, investments in human development— and for everybody, because a nation's progress needed everybody, and "a rising tide raises all ships," yachts and rowboats alike. As citizens, we had no reason and right to think otherwise. Our own ancestors hadn't been much different than anyone else's—a generation earlier we'd all been working class. Whatever our achievements, they had more to do with "the grace of God" than our own wonderfulness. A welfare state was seen as a good thing at the time, and a safety net meant just what the metaphor implied: something that allowed the trapeze artist to risk doing dangerous things they'd otherwise never try, to achieve what they otherwise never would. Just as health care, education, and income support systems do. The welfare state wasn't just good for the ambitionless and lazy; it was good for everyone.

But attitudes were changing. We were changing. We were adults now, making our own money, living our own lives. We worked with and knew people who had bigger houses and nicer cars and lived in better neighbourhoods than we did, who went on once-in-a-lifetime trips every year, whose cottages were "country homes." What we didn't see in person, we read about or saw on TV, on shows like Robin Leach's *Lifestyles of the Rich and Famous*, his signature catch-phrase "champagne wishes and caviar dreams" generating envy in some, disgust in others, aspiration in many, amazement in all. And the more we knew, the more evident it was that there were two worlds: theirs, and everyone else's. Economically, politically, socially, maybe we weren't all in this together.

We were now into our core earning years. Some could see them-selves managing the giant leap to that other world, but teachers were never going to get there. Neither were nurses, museum curators, community development advisors, nobody in a government job. And working in the private sector, you certainly couldn't get there with government getting in your way, taxing you to death, taking your hard-earned money that you could have put to your own bigger purposes and frittering it away. All those things that government touched—our schools, our hospitals—they just weren't good enough. Our competi-tion was global. Our reference points were global. This wasn't about ECI and Richview anymore. We now knew about schools in New York and Boston, in the U.K., we could *see* better wherever it was. So, we thought, if Toronto is supposed to be a world-class city and Canada a world-class country, why isn't my kid's school as good as my friend's kid's school in the U.S.? By the 1980s it was clear—more and better was possible. And when more and better becomes possible, more and better becomes the expectation, and it sure as hell better become the norm. So why *them* and not us?

What's wrong with our government?!

These were the first cracks. But more and better costs money. A higher tide may raise all ships, but it takes a whole lot of very expen-sive tide to raise them as high as we want them to go. We put more money into schools and hospitals, and they got better, but not better like Harvard and the Cleveland Clinic.

The problem is the party in power, we say. It's time for a change. And a different party takes over in government. After this happens a few times and our schools and hospitals still aren't what they should be, we decide the problem isn't this party or that one, it's *government*. The whole thing. It's too big, too slow, too bloated and complacent. Useless. Hopeless. Which makes us mad. Our money, what we worked so hard for, out of our pockets, into theirs, and down the drain. Which makes us even madder.

To win elections, political parties came to campaign more and more against *government*. Even the parties in power. The more they trashed the system they were part of, or operated, they realized, the better their chances to win. The fair-haired child that had built Kathy McNab's father's highways, Mary's, Cheryl's, Bruce's, Lisa's, Lorna's, Joan Boody's, and Judy Clarke's schools, and Murray's and Penni's hospitals was no longer so fair-haired.

But we do need better schools. This is a tough, competitive world that will just get tougher and the only way our kids will make it is to be smarter than the billions of other people around them. If government can't be trusted to do the job, we're going to have to do it ourselves. So in Ontario, after decades of Conservative (mostly soft conservative) rule, after David Peterson's Liberals in the mid-eighties and Bob Rae's NDP in the early nineties, came Mike Harris. In 1995, Harris campaigned to cut taxes and cut back government. What was needed wasn't political or economic revolution but, as he called it, a "common sense revolution." The two biggest spenders in Ontario's budget were education and health care. Harris's Conservatives won. It's tough to take on the doctors. Bring on the teachers.

"It was absolutely horrible," Mary McIntyre remembers.

At ECI, Mary was shy and soft-spoken, except with those she knew best, and with them she could be wickedly funny. She was a good student in a class with several better ones. When teachers described our class as "special," she cringed. She didn't see herself as special at all. She graduated from the University of Toronto in history. She taught elementary school downtown, where she had in her class more kids from immigrant families than she'd ever seen in Etobicoke, got married to Jim Smyth, a lawyer, whom she had met at ECI, started her family, and stopped teaching to raise their kids. By 1990, she was back in the classroom.

She hadn't *become* a teacher the way some do, with their "teacher talk"—talking *slowwly*, enunciating *clearrly*, as if everyone around them is ten years old, driving non-teacher family and friends to distraction. When school let out she had another life, a good, less than perfect life, with her family, her friends, her summers, her trips, her cottage. But she also knew how important learning was. She had known that from her own life, from elementary school and ECI, from the teachers she'd had. And she was a good teacher, although always a self-deprecator, her way in everything to see imperfections, funny, stupid little things to laugh at, her own first and most of all. But she knew teaching was a serious, important job. And as much as she'd ever let herself say this, she was proud of being a teacher.

To win the fight against the teachers, Premier Harris had to take on the teachers' unions. To win that fight, he had to break them, to put in the public mind that unionism, like government, was a big, self-interested, sclerotic anachronism of the past that holds back the future. To make teachers, in and out of the classroom, the problem. To make the fight political, ideological, and personal. Harris's message, between every line: *Look at these teachers, they work five days a week, go home every day at three thirty, have the whole summer off, THE WHOLE SUMMER, they can't be fired, they can quit at fifty-five on pensions only God deserves, they're crucial to our children and their futures and they aren't doing the job, and they want more money, more prep time, smaller classes, and who knows what else.*

"I would get so mad," Mary says. "One night I'd been at a parent-teacher thing at the school, and I'm driving home, and I see this billboard saying all this stuff about us, denigrating teachers. Paid for by *my* tax dollars. I could've just driven off the road. Another time I was out golfing, and my husband, Jim, was in another group. And all of a sudden I see him running down this hill towards me. It turns out Mike Harris was also playing that day, with a client of Jim's, and Jim was afraid I'd do something in front of his client. You just felt demeaned," she says. Harris was telling Mary that what she had done all her career, what she loved and believed in, didn't matter. That *she* didn't matter.

"And so we marched," she said. She had been a teacher for sixteen years and had never marched before. "We marched at Queen's Park," in front of the Legislative Building. "We had this one march, I think it was in Hamilton, there were teachers from all over, and it was really cold. The wind was just howling. It was one of the most exciting things I'd ever taken part in. It was just this wave of people. This wave, it was almost physical, being caught up in it, this motion. This feeling of solidarity, because at some point you feel like nobody likes you. You're this low-life teacher. It was just amazing. We marched and marched. It turned me into a union man."

The aftermath of the strike wasn't nice. "A lot of my friends, literally some of the best teachers, who I'd taught with at Huron, retired early. They took a smaller pension, they just had to get out." Around schools, the environment changed. The parents of kids they taught now saw them a different way. "I remember one teacher telling me about a kid she'd been helping, who was really difficult, and she was working hard with him, and during the strike this kid's parent drove by the school while she was picketing and yelled at her, insulted her. She'd just been helping her kid."

Bruce McLeod, who was teaching in Elgin, a village north of Kingston, was used to picket lines. He had been a chief negotiator for his district for OSSTF, the Ontario Secondary School Teachers' Federation, since the mid-1980s, and later its chief negotiator. That he was a teacher and living in a small place might have surprised anyone who knew him in high school. That he was involved in argument and advocacy would not. He had been a member of the UN Club in all five of his years at ECI, a fervid participant in Model UN General Assemblies, someone in class who would say to a teacher "I disagree, sir," out of contrariness and habit, it seemed, as much as conviction. In his one year in the school play, he was cast as a professor, his big scene to stand on a chair and lecture everybody about something or other.

Yet we probably misunderstood Bruce. He was the youngest kid in the class. The youngest in the grade. We didn't know that his father was the chief economist of the Toronto-Dominion Bank or that his mother had run for moderator of the United Church of Canada, its top position. But we did know that his older brother had made himself a verbal force at the school. There seemed to be something that was pushing Bruce. It turned out there wasn't. What we saw as pushiness was just a kid acting out.

He graduated with a B.A. from Queen's and went straight into the classroom. He taught in a series of small communities before ending up at Rideau District High School in Elgin, less than an hour's drive away from where his grandfather had grown up and from the schools where he would teach throughout the rest of his career. It was the reality of living this small-town life, and his love of debate, that brought him to the negotiator's table.

In a small town, you don't have everything. For a small town to even exist, its founders have to fight, and their ancestors, to survive, have to fight even harder. Most often in Ontario, settlements began with a mill—grain or lumber—and with fast-moving water to turn its wheels. Then came a church, then another, and another, big, timeless brick or clapboard structures that would remain and define long after most of their congregants had gone. Then a store or two, and tradesmen's shops to support the mill, and a school. Eventually, the mill shut down, leaving the town with no reason to exist except to continue as the community it had become. Its last thing to fight for, its school. And for Rideau District High School, that was always a fight.

Schools work on a numbers formula aggressively negotiated. The province gives school boards a certain amount of money for each student, students are assigned to classes of a certain agreed-upon size, and the boards use the money to hire teachers to teach those classes. In elementary schools, the process works fairly easily. Every grade in every elementary school in the province has basically the same curriculum, and every teacher is trained to teach it. High school is more complicated. High school teachers teach courses, not classes. Every kid has to take English, math, and science, but not every kid takes French, history, or music, and through most of Bruce's years as a teacher, only a minority took the more advanced courses that are required for university. In a big city, there are lots of kids, enough to fill close to the average mandated size for at least one classroom's worth of students for almost any subject. The debate in a city is over whether the mandated size results in *too many* kids in a classroom. In a really small school like Rideau, you had to get creative, and you fight.

"It's all about staffing," Bruce says, "and staffing is about pupil–teacher ratios. Some courses you'd like to offer, you can't. There aren't enough kids. Some others, like a senior math course that you need for university, you've got to find some way to offer it. The class might only be for ten or fifteen kids, then you have to compensate by having a class somewhere else in your school, or in one of the bigger schools in the board, with thirty-five." And somebody has to make these decisions. The bigger schools, in bigger centres, have more political clout even in a rural area like Bruce's. Bruce learned early that if he was going to have some control over his teaching life, and therefore over where he lived and how he lived, he had to join the fight.

And he relished it, just as he had in high school. "I was never shy about expressing myself," he says. He'd had to learn the hard way. Making vague arguments at a kitchen table in front of his father, mother, and older brother hadn't worked too well, and although he had advanced the case of Sweden at a Model UN Assembly like a latter-day Dag Hammarskjöld, now, with the teachers, the stakes were real. He knew he had something to offer the district OSSTF executive. He knew small schools, and since most of the other members of the executive were from bigger ones, he would need to educate them. He would need them to know how one year, to teach a calculus *and* a linear algebra class to senior students who needed to take both, he'd had to put the two classes together and teach them lecture-style one day, and with the help of other teachers, seminar-style the next. He'd also need to remind them that small-town teachers are small-town citizens. They are volunteer firefighters and volunteer ambulance drivers, and if there's an alarm during the school day they have to leave, and other staff need to scramble to fill in for them. So he joined the OSSTF's staffing committee and, later, its bargaining committee. One big difference in Bruce from when he was in high school: he was no less assertive, but more confident, he now listened first.

By the time Harris had won election in 1995, Bruce had learned to listen well. He knew he was representing the teachers—that was his job and he never forgot that—but now he understood better that to do it he had to know what the person across the table was thinking, and why, and that person needed to know the same about him. Bruce was no hard-bitten unionist who all his life had been trampled on by his bosses and betters, and he couldn't pretend to be. He had lived a privileged life and knew it. He was forty-eight years old, he had been teaching for twenty-five years, he had lived around many very different families living in very different circumstances, and he realized now how almost embarrassingly easy it had been for him. His family had been financially secure. He'd lived in a good neighbourhood, gone to a good school and to a good university. Born at the beginning of the baby boom, "I had everything available to me. I had no problem getting any job I wanted. My job was secure. My income went up every year."

His parents had never felt, and never acted, as if things were easy or ever would be. His father was an economist who had grown up during the Depression. He knew nothing was certain, nothing was forever. He was a dyed-in-the-wool evangelical Keynesian. He believed that everybody deserved a fair shake, and that the market didn't always provide that, so governments and other entities of power and influence were needed to ensure that fairness. He opposed just as vehemently the Milton Friedman school of supply-side, trickle-down economics, which he believed was far more faith-based than numbers- and reality-based, its adherents those who *had*, not those who hadn't, which had led to increasing disparities, a wider income gap, increased poverty, and had distorted the world economy. After his father died, asked what he thought his father would want done with his ashes, Bruce said he'd want them thrown in Milton Friedman's face.

At the bargaining table, this was one part of Bruce. Another part was that he knew that his good income, good pension, and good life hadn't come from nowhere, that the province, its premiers, ministers of education, and finance ministers hadn't handed over this bounty to teachers out of the goodness of their hearts. It had happened because the teachers had fought for it, because after the steelworkers', mine workers', and teamsters' unions had had their day because their industries were no longer so essential, the teachers were represented by the biggest and strongest unions in the country because their industry still was. When Bruce, in the midst of a strike, invariably heard political leaders claim that the teachers, like sheep, were only following their union leadership and didn't believe in the strike themselves, he'd just laugh. "You've never met a more independent-minded, bloody-minded bunch of people than teachers," he says. "They love to argue more than anything else." But about one thing they didn't argue. "We believed in what we were doing," as teachers, as a union, "and understood that we were one of the few organizations with the strength to fight back."

Bruce, like his father, also believed that these hundreds of thousands of teachers, who made up the largest single work category in Ontario and Canada, made the economy better by not only helping to educate the young people who would direct and drive the economy in the future, but, by winning these fights with governments, put into their own hands enough money to help make the economy work at every given moment. So, at the bargaining table, Bruce believed that what he advocated for was good not only for teachers but for the economy, for the villages of Morton where he lived and Elgin where he taught, and that Keynes and his father would approve. So if you are on the other side of the table, know that this is what you're facing. And good luck.

"We all understood that the whole profession was under attack," Bruce recalls, "and we were the ones who were going to stand up for it." For Mary, this was a political fight. For Bruce, an economic fight. For both of them, an educational fight. And both knew they were right.

In the end, in the give-and-take of bargaining, the government won *this*, the teachers won *that*, which to them and to the media is what seemed most critical at the time. But what each lost, and what we all lost, was a little trust. Teachers in politicians, politicians in teachers, the public in both, both in the public. That, and a little less good feeling about the future. Life went on.

While most of us by the 1990s were living lives well set in motion, for a few life changed a lot. It was at about this time Cheryl stopped teaching and went on medical leave.

She had spent the previous twenty years trying to make her career, to make her family, to make her present and future, her past out of sight for long stretches, then in flashes that gave her no warning, suddenly taking over, consuming her life. Her father had helped her get to university. He had matched every dollar she saved just so she could afford to go. When she changed her mind about going into nursing at McMaster with the two Marilyns and Judy and it was too late to apply to U of T, it was her father, with a guidance counsellor he knew at ECI, who had helped her get into York. Yet she couldn't not remember that childhood moment. She had always gone a mile a minute in everything she did, in part because that was Cheryl, always wanting to do more; in part now, because it seemed she *needed* to go faster and faster. Doing, doing, crashing, trying to make sense, searching for patterns, finding sense, doing, doing. Every next thing the might-be answer. After she and Tom were married, she got a job teaching at a new high school, helping with its school's musical productions, and in creating its first yearbook, finding an outlet for her "creative and leadership sides," as she put it. But then she began to experience migraines, and the principal came to question her "frequent absences." She came to realize too that teaching kids to write wasn't what she wanted, that she wasn't and was never going to be her beloved Mrs. Coupe. "I wanted to do my own writing," she says. "I wanted to research and challenge my brain. I wanted recognition of my talents." After three years, Cheryl left the school and joined a consulting firm. There she could write, she could present, but as one of only two women in an office of ten, she found it hard. Her boss told her that she seemed "starved for approval." More than that, she thinks, she was "starved for recognition." For what she believed she could do. Cheryl needed more.

The migraines and nightmares came back. The this-way, that-way challenges of the present, the challenges of keeping the past at bay, were wearing her out. She cut back to part-time at the consulting firm and began working from home. "My focus became seeking the fulfillment that I thought parenthood would bring," she says. "I wanted to create my own version of what I envisioned a family could be."

She and Tom tried to have children, and unable to, they decided to adopt. A year later, she got pregnant, and by 1979, by age thirty-two, they had two kids, and moved into their first house. She'd had therapy after her breakdown at UBC, stopped for a few years, then resumed it after her struggles at the consulting firm, going once a week, as her migraines, nightmares, and feeling of exhaustion returned. The kids were getting older, they started in school, she took DanceFit classes at the Y, rediscovered her joy in movement and creation, and began teaching some classes herself. Their third child was born. Tom was still teaching. Things seemed fine, to everyone other than to her and Tom.

It was August, 1987. Wayne was (finally) going to be married and Tom was to be his best man. As a final bachelor's fling, Wayne bought himself a non-refundable ticket on a schooner that sailed in and around the Galapagos Islands, but at the last minute couldn't go because his father had become gravely ill. He offered Tom his ticket. Knowing Cheryl's interest in zoology, Tom suggested that she go instead, which she did, Cheryl knowing that when she returned she would need to go back into the classroom to pay for her flight. The trip was great, the resulting teaching was too much. Years passed. Other things piled up. Cheryl was asked to give a toast at her parents' fiftieth anniversary celebration dinner and, she remembers, "I broke into tears as I spoke, but no one really understood why." Then Tom's mother was diagnosed with Alzheimer's and Tom had to take on extra duties to help her out. Then one of Cheryl's sisters died.

When you go a mile a minute, and eventually hit a wall, you have nothing in reserve.

In 1993, she asked her doctor to request a sick leave for her from the board. "I felt close to breaking down in my classes. [I] could barely hold myself together." The doctor was surprised, telling her that she "presented as being so well." Months passed. As her sick days were running out, she needed to be further assessed, and decided to bring to her meeting with a psychiatrist poems she had written about her childhood. She was diagnosed with PTSD, and put on medical leave.

With the help of a psychologist, she wrote a letter to her parents telling them that what she had experienced as a child "was making it impossible for me to have a relationship with them and I did not want to see them for the foreseeable future." That foreseeable future would turn into nineteen years.

She returned to the classroom on a reduced schedule a year later, then moved to another school full-time. And still the migraines, still the nightmares, and the images within them—"running through willow trees and jumping down a manhole to escape a powerful witch," "flapping my arms vigorously and getting off the ground, and then crashing." And still the therapy, still going too fast, still the exhaustion—a teaching colleague had once said to her that she had a "Cadillac brain and a Volkswagen body"—still trying to work things out. When she tried to explain how she felt to herself and to her therapists, she found images worked much better than a literal description. In her childhood, the image had been of two cliff edges and a black hole between. At UBC, it was "the sky swallowing her up." Now in the mid-1990s, "I felt like I was in a garbage bag. I couldn't see. Everything was black. There was just no perspective. But I found if I could look up, and if I could just see a frame, an opening, a square of light, if I could just get some perspective on what was happening to me, then I could pull myself out. When I said this to a psychologist, she told me that once my brain gets working, I'm OK. But when I'm over-whelmed by the emotion, I can't think. I think the advantage for me was my brains."

As this was going on, life was going on. All their married life, Cheryl and Tom had lived teachers' lives. They had *some* money, they could afford a nice house, in a nice neighbourhood, but they couldn't afford extravagance. What they did have that most others didn't was time. One summer before they had kids, they worked for six weeks on a kibbutz in Israel. Another year, they drove to P.E.I., turning off the main roads, visiting historic sites whenever they came upon them. There were camping trips with the kids to northern Ontario, a full school year on a farm near Bridgewater, Nova Scotia, where Tom did a teachers' exchange. And because getting a department head-ship meant he had to improve his French, the family spent six weeks another summer in La Pocatière, east of Quebec City on the south shore of the St. Lawrence River, as he took his classes. When the kids got older, comfortable with travel and other languages, they went on their own exchanges, to Spain, to Germany, to Brazil, to Switzerland and France, and Cheryl and Tom and the other kids took trips to visit them. And for a quick get-away-from-it-all day or weekend in Toronto, they had a small sailboat which they moored at the foot of downtown near the Island Airport. Yet it was not enough.

Joan Boody met Gus Medina in 1989. Both were in their early forties. Both were established in their careers. Both had been divorced. Both had teenage kids. Neither was looking for something or someone.

They were attending an environmental education conference in Colorado. Gus, based in Washington, D.C., was representing the North American Association for Environmental Education, and Joan, at that time an environmental education consultant for the East York Board of Education, the Council of Outdoor Educators of Ontario.

A further conference, called ECO-ED, was being planned for Toronto in 1992. The conference's chair lived in Toronto, and every six weeks for planning meetings Gus flew in from Washington and stayed at the chair's house. Until one Friday the chair's daughter was having her twenty-first birthday party and the chair asked Joan if she could pick Gus up at the airport and billet him at her condo for the weekend. The rest was (excruciatingly slow-moving) history.

"I was enjoying my independence, and being on my own and planning my own life, and being in control of things," Joan explains, "and I think Gus was the same." But they came to enjoy each other's company, and when you do, when you're looking for something in common, you find it. "We both liked Glenn Gould, we both liked Gordon Lightfoot, and Moe Koffman," not exactly three musicians who might appeal to the same tastes (except if you're Canadian). And when you find difference, you find it *fascinating*. Gus's parents were from Puerto Rico, he was born in the Bronx, the family had lived in Queens, Brooklyn, and Manhattan, his father was an alcoholic, and as Gus explained, "every time he couldn't pay the rent, we moved." Gus was the oldest of six kids. Because his parents had never gone to high school, and because he was Latino, he was placed in a technical school.

The Manhattan High School of Aviation Trades, in Queens, had grown rapidly after the Second World War as the aviation industry boomed; Yankees pitcher Whitey Ford had gone there, as had singer Tony Orlando. Gus graduated, then worked for two years as an airline mechanic. But like Ford and Orlando, he had other things in mind. His had to do with nature, the outdoors, the environment, not obvious or easy destinations out of aviation and the streets of New York. But he found his way, and eventually earned his Ph.D. His interest was environmental education. After a year teaching in Boston and discovering that a college professor's life wasn't what he wanted, he joined the World Wildlife Fund in Washington.

For Joan, nature, the outdoors, the environment had been part of her life since her childhood summers at the cottage on Isabella Lake with her beloved Pampi. She and her first husband had lived in an apartment in Scarborough, and when their two children were born, they decided to build a house in a rural area a little over an hour north of the city, where, as Joan recalls, "I settled into my Earth Mother years, gardening, baking bread, preserving, foraging in the forest," eventually also discovering a nearby outdoor education centre, run by the East York Board of Education. It was "my dream job," Joan recalls. The centre had a small working farm on a two-hundred-acre site, and the students, from elementary schools, put up in a dorm for a week, for the most part were happy to be there. Joan could teach them *anything*, so long as it was done out of doors.

There was a little pioneer cemetery about a half-hour walk from the centre. "It had about seventy-five headstones, and the students' job was to go around and write down the names on the stones, when the people were born and when they died. None of the stones told the cause of death, but when we got back to the centre, first the students had to figure out how old each person was when they died." They made a bar graph—those who died between the ages of zero and ten, ten and twenty, and so on. "Almost every time, somebody would look up and say, 'Hey, we're doing math!' And they were. They were collecting data and analyzing it. Then there'd be questions. A number of women died in their early twenties. We would talk about why. One of the women had a little gravestone beside her, and you'd look and see the date she died, and then the date on the other stone, and they died at the same time. So the kids had to figure out why. These were grade six kids. And they figured out it was probably in childbirth."

Because the centre was also a farm, the kids had farm chores to do. They had to collect the eggs in the morning, then weigh them, classify them, and graph them. They had to mix feed for the animals, weighing out a certain amount of oats and barley. "We kept bees, we made maple syrup. We had a trout stream through the property. We did stream studies." It was, Joan says, "my kind of teaching."

She began working towards a master's degree in environmental science, taking one course each semester. Professors from a U.S.

university came to Toronto on four different weekends to give the classes, the rest was independent work. But to graduate Joan had to complete at least two of the courses at the school's campus. The school was Northern Illinois University, where Gus had earned his master's a few years earlier; one more thing they would have in common. Joan's kids were young, but her husband was there, and in the summer, with camp and a posse of cousins who mostly could care for each other, it would be fine. That's what she said to herself. And once again, she faced what she called "the growth choice and the fear choice." She hadn't gone away for university, and during her year at teachers' college, she got married. She had never lived on her own. She was thirty-six, and the other students were years younger. She shamed herself into the growth choice. While her new classmates were going back to where they never wanted to be again—a college dorm—Joan was going to experience what she had missed. When she arrived, "I was so excited," she recalls. "There were four women to a room, I was running around saying, 'Oh, look, we even have our own bathroom.' One of the girls said to me, 'Uh, Joan, you didn't go away to university, did you?'"

"It was a magical place," Joan says of that summer, "I know that's a silly word, but it was. Everything was so new and different. It was the first time I'd ever been in the United States. And you know how in *Oklahoma!* they talk about the corn being as high as an elephant's eye? It was like that there. You'd drive for miles through the countryside. I have pictures of us reaching up and the corn is still higher than our hands. And the fireflies at night were huge. Everything there was big." The outdoor education school, more than an hour from the main campus, had been an old artists' colony. "It was in just this gorgeous, beautiful location, with forests and fields and the river"—the Rock River, a tributary of the Mississippi. "And being with people who thought the same, and had the same interests, it was"—she pauses, searching for a less silly word and, not finding it—"magical."

In 1985, she graduated with her master's, and a few years later split with her husband—another growth-over-fear moment—moved back to Toronto with the kids, and started work as an environmental education consultant for the East York Board. She was forty-two.

Years passed. She was managing life as a single mother. The international conference in Toronto was a follow-up to the UN's Earth Summit in Rio de Janeiro a few months earlier. In Rio, 172 nations, a few thousand NGOs, and more than ten thousand journalists had gathered. The environment was now on more people's minds, and deeper in their minds, than it had ever been. The problem was no longer unseemly eyesores and despoiled nature. This was bigger, timeless, and existential. Rio was literally an Earth summit: it was about everything and everywhere. During its twelve days, there were lots of headlines, lots of studies released, declarations and agreements made, one of which would lead to the signing of the UN Framework Convention on Climate Change. The challenge, the delegates and media all knew, would come the Monday morning after the conference ended, in the capitals of those 172 nations around the world. What would these governments do now? What actions would they take? The ongoing challenge was to find a way to extend those headlines in time and reach and to make more people and more organizations in more places aware of what Rio had said. As its preliminary program read, the conference was "to build and expand partnerships and networks needed between education, business, science, government and other sectors in order to move from awareness to informed action." As Joan said almost thirty years later, "It makes you wonder."

Three thousand people attended. Joan and Gus were on the planning committee. Joan also helped organize the sessions and was in charge of the conference's signature concert. It was "my baby," she says. It was also "the biggest thing I ever did in my life." There would be lots of choirs, and at the centre of it would be Paul Winter, and the Paul Winter Consort. They would perform "Missa Gaia/Earth Mass," an ecumenical and ecological work Winter had co-written that brought together the sounds and voices of the Earth—human, instrumental, animal, land, water, air. The concert would be in St. Paul's, Bloor Street, the largest Anglican church in the city. Joan became so absorbed in its organizing that even today, when she refers to the conference, the word "concert" comes out.

She learned a few other things as well. The conference that began with Gus's group and Joan's group came to include Environment Canada, the U.S. Environmental Protection Agency, the United Nations Environment Programme, and ultimately their leaders and staff, both bureaucratic and political. "It became quite a monster," Joan says. "I remember sitting in a very heated meeting late one night where the person from Environment Canada was really, really angry. It had to do with a sort of turf war between Environment Canada and one of the other organizations. I remember thinking, *Aren't we all in on this together? If we can't agree in a committee room on things like this, how will the world ever get anything done?*" She found that the closer she got to what she had thought was the answer, the more distant from it she felt. "I thought that if these are the people who have influence on the decision makers, we're doomed."

The conference now over, what about her and Gus?

It had been three years since they met. They had gotten to know each other by working with each other, by seeing each other in moments of stress and joy. They could see how each other's mind worked. But now their only excuse to keep seeing each other would have to be each other, not the conference. They went for a long weekend to Joan's sister's cottage in northern Quebec. "We sort of thought, *OK, now what?*" Joan remembers. They had been meeting up every six weeks for most of three years, why not continue? So every six weeks, Gus flew to Toronto, or Joan to Washington. Her kids were in university, she couldn't move; he had a great job in Washington, he couldn't move. After a year, they decided to stop seeing each other. After a year and a week, Gus had another idea. There was a job opening at World Wildlife Fund Canada because of a maternity leave. It involved a project in Cuba. Gus spoke Spanish. He could work mostly from home. He moved to Canada. The maternity leave at the WWF ended, other projects with other organizations opened up, and in 1997, eight years after they met, Joan and Gus were married.

She was fifty, he was forty-nine. Marriage worked for them this time, Joan thinks, because they were older. "I think maybe when you marry so young," she says, "you're looking for somebody to complete you. And looking back, I hadn't even lived before I got married. I didn't know anything about anything." For her marriage ceremony, Joan found a reading by Rumi, a Persian poet. "I can't remember the exact words, but it was to the effect that a good marriage is like two trees standing side by side, not in each other's shade, close, but not too close. It seemed to sum up our relationship."

CHAPTER TWENTY-FOUR

When Lisa graduated from U of T, she knew one thing for sure: she would never be a teacher. Six years later, she was a teacher. In those six years, she and Henry, on his way to untold possibilities as a director, never did settle and went down different paths. Then Lisa met John Mills-Cockell. He was three years older and, like Henry, already highly accomplished. John created music, in all kinds of forms using all kinds of sounds, electronic, experimental music that defied classification, that many didn't consider music at all, putting together what had never been put together before, what a few liked, lots could not abide, and some worshipped. At fourteen, he had his own jazz duo. At fifteen, with his parents' blessing, he left Canada and worked in the music section at Harrods in London.

One night, after a BBC Proms concert at the Royal Albert Hall, he heard a piece of music being played as he was leaving the building. It was titled "Dripsody," and it was by Canadian composer Hugh Le Caine, who had recorded the sound of drops of water falling into a pail, then had manipulated the sounds by speeding them up, slowing them down, reversing them, turning them into their own sound, their own music. Into "Dripsody." *Musique concrète*. John knew this was the music he wanted to make.

But first he had to go home and finish high school. After that, at the U of T's Royal Conservatory of Music, he took seminars in electronic music and discovered the Moog synthesizer. In 1969, a year after he graduated, at the Art Gallery of Ontario in Toronto, with his multimedia, multi-sensory group Intersystems, in a one-hour work of sounds, lights, projected images, and spoken poetry, he gave what's been called the world's first live music performance with a synthesizer. He was twenty-five. Decades later, *Musicworks* magazine described his music as "astral excursions," his imagination as "exist[ing] in a liminal space." By the time he met Lisa, he had married, had a child, divorced, recorded five albums with two different groups, and was not yet thirty.

Lisa soon was pregnant. In 1973, she, John, Taia, and newborn daughter Juno headed to London, where John had a commission to write the music for Malcolm Muggeridge's six-part TV series, *A Third Testament*. They lived in Hendon for one year, then in a big house with lots of other people in Dulwich, a picture-perfect village, at the centre of which was an ancient cluster of schools, a church, and a gallery. All this in the middle of a countryside thick with green and shade only half an hour by bus from London Bridge. Lisa loved their two years in England. Taia was in a good school, learning, discovering, taking on the local accent as her own. London, so nearby, offering the incredible transforming, redefining arts scene of the sixties and seventies, all at the cost of living of the fifties. And the museums, endless numbers of them, free. For Lisa, it was like living in a candy store. She could walk, take the tube to almost anywhere and the bus to everywhere else. Later, she would describe these years as the best in her life.

Back in Toronto after John's work on the Muggeridge series was done, today's new always threatening to be tomorrow's rut, John discovered more different directions. Occasionally he worked with Henry. (One project was a two-hour CBC drama, another a CBC Radio production of *The Tempest*, and also four plays, one titled *The Legend of the Avro Arrow*.) But it didn't matter to John whether what he did was TV, radio, theatre, or music of his own. He needed to create, to *express*, a feeling, a thought, an idea. For him, absorbed, immersed, time didn't exist. For those who lived around him, it did.

"It didn't bother me that I wasn't first, that music was first on their minds, or theatre was," Lisa says of John and Henry. She had never felt that way about anything herself. "In school, I didn't have a subject I was really good in," she says. "I always tried to get reasonable marks, but I was never dedicated to one thing. I didn't really think ahead. I didn't have a five-year or ten-year plan. I just sort of floated along, floated here, floated there. I never got really good at something. I never felt I ever got really good." If Henry or John didn't have a plan either, they had a direction, and a need to get there. "And they were making money," Lisa said. "I wasn't, except as a waitress, and that wasn't much." The kids needed to be parented. So by instinct, and desire, but also by default, "I was looking after the kids. That was my job."

She loved that job. She was "Lisa" to the kids, as her mother had been "Adèle" to her. Looking back on those years, she says, "Maybe it was the pregnancies that drove me. I don't know. It certainly wasn't me. Then when we came back to Toronto I thought, *God, I've got to do something to make some money.*"

She did various jobs at Theatre Passe Muraille for two years, while Steve Whistance-Smith was making his way at another of Toronto's new alternative theatres, the Tarragon. She waitressed. By the late seventies, the kids both in school, she decided to become a teacher. As she put it, John and Henry "didn't mind."

She was at the Faculty of Education at U of T one day signing up for her courses. She needed two subjects to specialize in. One would be English, the other she thought might be kindergarten, but she wasn't sure. "Then I met an interesting woman in the line and she said, 'Why don't we take this one?'" Well, Lisa *was* looking for something different, and besides a little cooking, she had never really done much with her hands, and she *had* just read *Zen and the Art of Motorcycle Maintenance*—so they signed up for industrial arts. That was a good year to be a new teacher, but a year later, when she graduated, it was not. This was 1976. There were very few jobs. There was no cattle call for teachers at the Park Plaza, no pages of want ads in the newspapers. She signed up as a supply teacher, which meant every day waiting for an early-morning phone call that often didn't come, and then a day here, three days there in front of a class of kids that knew you weren't going to be around long and treated you that way. For most supply teachers, the only thing worse than not getting a call is getting a call. Yet mostly Lisa enjoyed the banter and game of dealing with students trying their best to be on their worst behaviour. These short-term placements went on for four years, followed by a series of six-month contracts. It was five more years of contracts like this before she got her first permanent job, at Donview Middle School in Toronto. It was 1985. She was thirty-nine.

As a supply teacher, she had been teaching not English, as she had expected to do, but industrial arts. Yet she liked it. At ECI, the boys took industrial arts, the girls home economics, but by the time Lisa was teaching, the courses and classes were mixed, the boys learning what boys had never had to learn, the girls the same. It was fun for the girls to see at the front of the room someone who looked like them doing stuff girls didn't do, and for the boys to see someone just as willing as they were to get her hands dirty. Lisa didn't think of herself as a role model, that was too much, too "goody-goody," but she could see the effect she had on the girls, *and* on the boys, and she knew that mattered. "It wasn't that hard to impress them," she says. "Just stand at the front and say, 'That's the drill press. That's the lathe. This is how you do it.' I taught woodworking and welding, we had a forge. We did drafting, first with T-squares and then on a computer. I liked working on a lathe, designing things and creating them. It was fun. We did electrical too."

She took on her own projects at home. "I was a master of nothing but I knew a little bit about everything. I redid my bathroom with tongue and groove, I created a pass-through window from my pantry to my kitchen. I made lots of bowls, and a lot of Adirondack chairs. I was good at it," she says, then corrects herself. "I wasn't that good, but I wasn't afraid to try anything. I figured you just had to do it a couple of times before you knew what you were doing." Her signature piece, a sculpture, stands in her backyard. "It's a bull's head on a music stand made with various thicknesses of metal and other stuff that I welded together." What surprised her most, perhaps, was that while she'd always liked to read, "on weekends I found I spent a lot of time reading catalogues." That and "going to Canadian Tire and Rona."

Her daughters were the same age as the kids she had been teaching. One thing she saw in the middle-school classroom bothered her. At ECI, she had noticed how different girls were when they were around boys, but it hadn't bothered her much. Now it did. How they talked to each other, behaved with each other. The effect they had on each other. The sexual tension that was never not there, that overwhelmed everything, that took over their brains, took over lives. It was just so easy for a girl to be what society says a girl is supposed to be, and for a boy to treat a girl the way a boy is supposed to treat one. Not ever to imagine anything else. In high school, bodies and hormones are *the* fact of life, so what can you do? But in middle school, at age eleven, twelve, thirteen, how sad. How wrong.

At Islington and ECI, she'd liked being with boys more than girls. They did stuff, maybe it was because they could, maybe because society told them they could. And she loved flirting with boys, but it wasn't like they were *everything* to her. She read, she went to movies. She had her own mind. And even if boys back then had meant a lot more to her than they should have, that didn't mean it had to be the same for her daughters. They have a right to take the lead, to be at the centre, but if they don't know that, or have a chance to do that and be that now, it'll never happen. So many things that they might do in their lives and think and try will be taken over by history, culture, expectation, before they even have a chance to be what they are and what they might be. "This just seemed like craziness to me. I wanted something different for my girls." So for middle school, Lisa put her daughters into an all-girls private school. Later, for high school, they went back to the public system.

After teaching for five years at Donview, Lisa was hired by St. Andrew's Middle School. Some of the kids there had been to private schools before, and many of them went on to the private Community Hebrew Academy of Toronto (CHAT) for high school. "They were the kinds of kids that have three nannies, one that drives, one that makes lunches, and one that puts them to bed at night. They were really well behaved, there were never any issues. I was the head of the department. I had a huge budget. It was fun being there." She had always thought that a teacher should change schools every five years, "to share the world you know." She was there twelve, until she retired.

For some of those years, it was less fun outside class. She and John were breaking up. What made it particularly hard, Lisa says, was that "it took two or three years before we managed to do it." They had been together for seventeen years. Smart had always mattered to her. She had learned that from her mother. Smart still mattered a lot to her, but not as much.

Lisa was the first of us to turn fifty.

In 1996, twenty years after the Montreal Olympics, and a few months before he turned fifty, Wayne retired. He was the first of us.

Maybe more than anyone in the class, Wayne knew exactly who he was, where he was going, and with what outcome, and had known almost all his life. We knew this because he told us. And what he knew was that he was smart but not that smart, funny but not that funny, athletic but not that athletic. He knew he was good at English but not good enough. He knew that to his parents he was "the one and only," but that he wasn't a one and only of anything. He knew he liked girls *a lot*, but worried that if somehow they managed to like him, eventually they'd see through him. He knew he loved money—his paper route, his part-time job at Freddy's—but that people like him never got rich. He knew he was totally risk-averse—he worked for the Ontario government, for god's sake—and that the only people on Earth more conservative than him were his parents, who loved that he worked for the government because that meant a steady job, a pension, and stability. And as much as he knew anything—he had said so even in high school, proclaiming in a Scarlett O'Hara–like moment, "As Sandie Barnard is my witness"—he was never going to get married. Ever. Which was a good thing because he was never ever ever going to have kids.

And one more big thing he knew, and had known all his life, even before the fundamental truth of it had been revealed to him in grade 13, in Browning's "Andrea del Sarto"—"a man's reach should exceed his grasp, / Or what's a heaven for?"—that life was a noble quest, it was Don Quixote, it was Sisyphus pushing a rock of hope up the mountain, that there was rightness and goodness in heroic failure. He had known that because he had lived it, time and time again, and he lived it again in his disaster at the Olympics. He had known he wasn't fast enough or strong enough. Still he had allowed himself that glimmer: if *this*, then maybe *that*. Serves him right! He *knew*.

But maybe Wayne didn't know as much as he thought he knew. After his post-Olympics escape to Europe and his full-wallow lunch with Ken Church in Paris, he went home and went back to being as good at his job as he'd always been. He knew how to write. He knew how to sell. He knew he had the product to sell—the fantastic parks and lakes and forests and wilderness of Ontario—and that even in the stodgy confines of the bureaucracy, he could do it. Because with the growth of cities and a life that was moving faster and faster, more and more people wanted a taste of the outdoors. More and more were going to his parks. (He wasn't, of course. He didn't like to get dirty.) But he was asked to make more presentations, give more speeches, tell their story, tell *his* story.

And surprise of surprises, people seemed to like him. His irrepressible smile, his cackly laugh, the weirdness and mischief of his mind, even that bit of *Seinfeld*'s George Costanza in him, where, when everything finally finally was right and nothing, *this time*, could possibly go wrong, and sure enough he'd push things just a little too far. When others could see the crocodiles and he couldn't: "Wayne, no, no . . . Wayne! No!! . . . Oh Wayne." You just couldn't not hope for him. And now something more, an even greater surprise. All these girls and women, who had been way out of his league, weren't treating him as if they were. Especially when he had a drink or two in him, when he got funnier, it seemed to him, more interesting, more gregarious, and came out of his shell and became who he knew he wasn't—a guy even *he* liked. In the office, or even in a bar, he had always worked to distance himself. Purposely, he'd take control of a conversation. *He* would ask the questions and get the women talking about themselves so they wouldn't ask him about himself. But now they were interested in him. Interested in the Olympics, in what he had done, not what he hadn't.

One woman in particular, Joanne Wright, also worked in the government and also liked to run. She was nice, sociable, smart, pretty, and nine years younger. She had, Wayne thought, every reason not to give him the time of day. But weeks and months passed and she was still there. Still there to the point, Wayne thought, where it's a good thing I'm never going to get married, something he'd told Joanne just as he'd told everyone, because if I were the sort who might, Joanne might be someone I'd marry. It was a good thing too he wasn't going to have kids, which again he told everyone, because if he were, Joanne might be someone he'd like to have them with. But just to make sure this new attractiveness of his didn't somehow bite him in the butt, he got a vasectomy, and told everyone that too. (Which, to his surprise, seemed only to make him more attractive to women. "It was a kind of feminist thing, I guess," he says.) He had done what *he* could do to not have kids. In terms of the Joanne thing and marriage, that would take care of itself. She'd get tired of him.

But she didn't. Years passed, and still she didn't. In 1987, a decade after he and Joanne met, with Tom as his best man, the guy who was never ever going to get married got married. He was forty. He had been so sure it would never happen.

And something else that he thought could never happen because he was so risk-averse: he started investing. He hadn't come from money, far from it, but he made a good salary, by government standards. And investing was just a little crazy. Risky. So many things beyond his control. It appealed to that part of him that loved clowning around in class, pushing things, even sometimes too far. And if he did make money, great, and if he didn't, that only proved what he'd always known about himself. A win either way. In his job with the government he had learned about master planning, the need to understand the resources you have, their limits and possibilities, then to set goals and objectives, to develop strategies and tactics. He came to employ this approach in his own life, beginning with Olympic year, 1976, keeping a journal in which, he says, "I wrote out what my ideal life would look like," updating his goals and objectives every New Year "to reflect changing realities." He was focused, analytical, competitive. Among his unchanging realities, both he and Joanne had secure jobs, Joanne wasn't going to leave hers to have kids, so their two incomes would continue, and they weren't big spenders. They knew they had enough money in the present and the near future, and in the far future they would have their government pensions, and Wayne, being an only child, would someday inherit whatever modest nest egg his parents had managed to accumulate.

So he invested, had some downs, but had more ups. Then, he says, "when Premier Mike Harris (God bless him) came along wanting to get rid of middle managers like me" and the government offered early retirement programs, "I had a plan and was first in line waving my hand." He would continue to invest, receive his pension, travel, and do what he had always dreamed of doing, what he had written in his journal as part of his "ideal life." He would write.

One more piece of unfinished business. He had never stopped running, but he hadn't run competitively in years. In 1996, he decided to run the California International Marathon in Sacramento, reconnected with Peter Pimm, and, at fifty, won his age class with a time of 2:54:11, only two minutes and sixteen seconds slower than his first marathon in Saint-Hyacinthe during Expo, twenty-nine years earlier. "I tell myself the California performance partially made up for the Olympic fiasco," Wayne says. Then he retired from competition.

In the late 1990s, Ken Church was still in France. He was the only one of us who went away to live and work on another continent, in another

language, and stayed away. He transferred from Price Waterhouse's
office in Toronto in 1972 to its office in Paris, for what was to be three
years, and now, nearing the end of the century, more than twenty-
five years later, he had just moved from Limoges and he was living
in Versailles.

It didn't seem like he'd be the one. At ECI, he had seemed too
shy to be adventurous. Adventurous guys talked loud, bragged, and
played sports, and that wasn't Ken. But there had been clues. He
was an excellent student, yet he liked to sit with Roger and Lisa in
the commotion of the back corner of the classroom. He had wanted
to spend his grade 13 year at Neuchâtel with Murray. At one class
party, when three of the girls carried him around in a chair, the Ken
we thought we knew would be frozen by the attention. The little
smile on his face said otherwise. Later, when he did go to France,
it was by cargo ship, not by plane. In PW's office in Paris, his co-
workers were mostly Anglos, their job to service clients of affiliates of
British companies, but unlike them he didn't use the weekends and
every excuse to hop the Channel to London. Nor did he haunt the
Canadian Embassy in Paris seeking out expats and travellers and news
from home. And when he did get the chance to escape the mistake
of his first apartment, in a modern, soulless international high-rise
ghetto, for a flat on the sixth floor of an old elevator-less building in a
real Parisian neighbourhood near the Place de la Bastille, he took it.
He was in Paris to be in Paris.

When his three years at PW were up, in 1975, he was looking not
for a reason to go home but for a reason to stay. And he'd already
found it, with a small group of eight or ten friends who were French,
and spoke French, and who, on the weekends and holidays they spent
together, excused his "atrocious" accent, found funny his language
lapses and jargony accountant-speak, and found in him not the life
of the party, never the life of the party, but someone they liked being
with. One of those friends was Sabine Adam. Ken knew that the
French, and the French business community in particular, was not
at all forgiving of someone who was so plainly *un étranger* and would

impose on him a life- and a job-ceiling that he'd never break through. But maybe that ceiling didn't have to matter so much. Maybe he'd find another life to live. His three-year adventure of coming to France had come to an end. The next, much less dramatic, more challenging adventure was in making a life.

Sabine had grown up in Morocco, in Rabat, her father a prominent professor at the university. She worked as a French-German translator, as did another in their group of friends. Two others worked at Renault, another was a farmer. Sabine invited all of them one weekend to her parents' summer house in Normandy. They all went to Indonesia the next year—all except Sabine travelled to Peru and Bolivia not long after. Ken was now reading more French books, watching French TV, talking in French to people in shops and restaurants, arguing French politics, while during the day, doing audits, he was working in French with people who were French. He still went back to Canada each summer to go to the cottage, but his parents, now with more time to travel, preferred to visit him instead. Phone calls to Canada in the seventies cost an arm and a leg, letters took forever, and while every Sunday his father got out his cassette player and recorded forty minutes of the week's news of home and mailed it to him, gradually Ken was losing touch.

In August 1976, just after the Montreal Olympics, he brought Sabine to Canada, to the family cottage, to meet his parents. One night, he took her out in a canoe, brought out a ring, didn't tip, and proposed. That much he had planned, the full moon he hadn't. Nor the voice they heard from the shore. They were on Lake of Bays in Muskoka, about two hours north of Toronto. There would be an election in Quebec in three months, and there was talk of how a win for René Lévesque might mean taking Quebec out of Canada. Ken and Sabine were speaking in French. In the darkness, unseen, the voice on the shore told them to speak English.

In December, they got married. Sometime in the weeks before, Sabine's grandmother had asked Sabine's mother, "Is she going to marry her Huron?"

Ken and Sabine moved into Ken's apartment. It had been small
for one, and it was just right for two. At work, he was getting bigger audits to do, moving up PW's accountant hierarchy from senior
to supervisor to manager. He was also learning that Paris is much
nearer to the rest of the world than Toronto or even New York. One
of his auditing jobs took him to Abidjan, Ivory Coast. PW's client, a
bank, was looking for a statement from him that their accounts were
clean. He found instead that their accounts didn't live up to "generally accepted accounting principles." Ken and the bank reached an
impasse. They weren't happy with him, he wasn't prepared to adapt
to them. His will stiffened even further after he spent a weekend at
a resort in the north of the country. He went for a walk outside its
walls into the nearby village. The people lived in huts, cooked in
big pots on open fires, and the kids seemed to have only one toy, a
wheel connected to a long pole, which they played with endlessly.
On his way back to Abidjan, he went through Ivory Coast's capital,
Yamoussoukro. He saw grand avenues, almost no people, and wall-
to-wall Mercedes.

By this time, he had had enough of auditing. As an auditor, you're
an outsider, hired to pore over endless numbers most of which are
intended to clarify, some of which may be intended to obscure, your
job to spot the difference. He knew what he was doing was essential, but often he felt like a snitch. He wanted to move from being an
outsider to being an insider, like his father had done. His father too
had started at PW, but had left to join the aircraft company Hawker
Siddeley, and Orenda, one of its subsidiaries, where he worked all
the rest of his career, not only doing its numbers but knowing that
Orenda was creating something, engines for airplanes to fly faster and
safer, including engines for the Avro Arrow, which might transform
Canada's aviation and technology futures. Ken also knew that for him
the next step up at PW was partner, and that truly he wasn't partner
material. He couldn't go out and sell and schmooze and get business,
as partners have to do. He was an accountant, not a businessman.
He did what others brought in. And if somehow he ever forgot that,

he never could, never would, forget he wasn't French, and to be a real higher-up in France, that's what you had to be.

A few years later, while still retaining his Canadian passport, he took out French citizenship. But he knew that didn't make him French. Instead, he called what he had done "adopting a French nationality." He read *Le Monde*, voted in every election, thought in French, dreamed in French, rarely spoke English—it would never matter. But that was OK. He was living a French life, with a French wife. He wasn't going anywhere, and he knew it.

He began looking for another job. It didn't matter to him in what field. Accounting skills, he believed, could be applied anywhere. In his job searches, he did fine until the interview stage, where, never being able to sell himself, he'd get passed over. Sabine was now pregnant, six flights of stairs had become a worse idea by the day, and they had moved to a bigger apartment. Finally, after two years of searching, while still at PW, Ken was hired as the head accountant of a building company. He was thirty-two, their son, Timothée, less than a year old. It was 1979.

The building company had begun as one man's vision, had grown, and was now looking to take on bigger projects in the Middle East. It would need to operate more corporately and less as a family business, as more international and less French. Ken seemed the right fit. He wasn't. He took two trips to Saudi Arabia and another to Iraq. In Baghdad, where the company was building a warehouse at the airport, he was asked by a co-worker to help him get "black cash" out of the country. Ken learned in his two years with the company, very clearly, that there is a line, and that you have to decide on which side of the line you want to be. Some can deal comfortably on the other side of it, and some can't. Ken couldn't. During these years, their second child, Amélie, was born.

Ken's next job was with a French subsidiary of an American company, Franklin Mint. It had only five senior people in its French office and only fifty employees in France in all. The company manufactured

and sold collectibles, sets of medals of historic figures made primarily of silver plate or gold plate; later it also sold porcelain plates and
other objects. In North America, Franklin Mint was known for its
full-page ads in major magazines. And while the names "Franklin"
and "Mint" suggested objects of substance, any buyer later trying
to sell their collections at a profit was usually disappointed. Every
company decision was made in the U.S., and the ads it ran in French
magazines were direct translations from the English. Occasionally it
did locally themed promotions—it had a special Napoleon collection
for France—but otherwise what it sold in Peoria was what it sold
in Paris.

There was nothing wrong with the job, Ken says, but there wasn't
much right about it either. The products the company sold, in his
words, had "no social utility." Yet it hadn't been easy to leave. Grégoire
was born in 1981, and Agnès in 1985. The family was settled. They
lived in a community of about five thousand in a far northern suburb of Paris that had in it, as Ken describes, "three hundred identical
houses," a school, a park, a forest a short walk away, and on the other
side of the forest, farmers' fields that extended into the distance. Not
much different than Rosethorn had been when he and his family had
moved in.

Then in 1991, after he had been with the company for ten years,
Franklin Mint made his decision easier. It decided to centralize its
European operations. Marketing, finance, and controlling were
moved to England, and only customer service remained in France.
The president was the first to go. Ken was named to replace him, but
as president his only real function was to manage the layoffs. Then
it was his turn to go. He got a comfortable package—he would have
money coming in regularly for the next several months—but he and
Sabine felt the urgency of the moment. The kids were 15, 13, 12,
and 8. Ken was almost forty-six. He had lived nearly half his life in
France. The French economy wasn't good, and, as Ken put it, he had
a "poor profile for the labour market." But instead of taunting himself

with existential questions—What am I doing here? Where do I really belong?—having already answered those questions for himself fifteen years earlier, he focused on the bigger question: How do I get a job? He answered ads in newspapers, got a few interviews, and finally was hired by a subsidiary of a big American paper company that was to open a new mill near Limoges, about four hundred kilometres away. The mill would be the largest private employer in the region.

It was a big move. Limoges was not the suburbs of Paris. It was old, and for more than two centuries had been the home of some of the world's great porcelain makers. The city's personality had been defined by its artists and artisans. It was insular, private, and not very open to a native-born Canadian with an accent who worked at the paper mill. The city had in it several large factories, and with them had come a history of fractious politics and angry strikes. Nicknamed "the red city," Limoges had been the first municipality in France to elect a communist town council. Ken's father had been an executive in a big aviation company. Ken had grown up in a world where unions did bad things and communists were bad people. Still, he liked the area, and the job. He especially liked walking through the mill itself on his way to the canteen for lunch, all around him the enormous machines, countless numbers of them, pumping out copy paper twenty-four hours a day, 350 days a year. This wasn't medals and decorative plates they were making. This was stuff people needed.

But things were changing. Ken's father, most of our fathers, had stayed with the same employers almost always for decades. If our families moved, it was to a bigger house within the same city or suburb. But during our own working lifetimes, the private sector had become much more the driving force, and government much less so. If a lot more was possible in our work and our personal lives, a little more wasn't good enough anymore. So in the private sector there were mergers, takeovers, and reorganizations, for companies to become more competitive, and more profitable. To the unforgiving eyes of the market, to anyone watching, if a company wasn't making big changes, it wasn't trying hard enough. And in the early 2000s, in a global world, with global competitors, with global risks and global opportunities, you had to try harder than you'd ever had to try before.

An accountant in a big firm in a big city doesn't move, their clients do. But Ken hadn't chosen this life. Now he faced disruptions. Hard choices. He had initiated the early moves of his career, now they were less and less his to call. After being in Limoges for four years, the company asked him to move to their Paris office. Ken and Sabine bought a small house in Versailles not far from the palace and its monumental grounds. Four years later, the company's head office in the U.S. decided to run things more centrally. Ken now had to report to an American controller who didn't understand the business and didn't know he didn't. The company then divided its operations, moving some to Poland, and others to Brussels. It was 2004.

Ken and Sabine decided not to go. Ken was fifty-seven. Versailles had many beautiful old buildings, a huge market, and a real town centre. Their younger kids were still in high school. Their oldest, Timothée, had taken two years of preparatory school in Paris and was now in business school. As well now for Ken, at his age, if he were to be out of work he would receive generous unemployment insurance until his pensions kicked in. He stayed off work almost a year, then took a short-term contract with the French subsidiary of a Dutch real estate company, and after that another. He liked the work he did, and in a time of reorganizations and mergers, controllers and accountants were always needed. Only gradually did he move into retirement.

Ken adventured further than all of us. He made a life in a different language and different culture. And even if his accent still betrays him, France is home. He is now more passionate about the French national rugby team than he ever was about the Toronto Maple Leafs. Three of his kids live in and around Paris, one is in Luxembourg. All four of them are thoroughly French.

In the early 2000s, something happened that Ken still thinks about. It has to do with the family cottage on Lake Muskoka. It had been getting harder to maintain, his parents were getting older, neither Ken nor his brother had much attachment to it any longer. So his parents sold it. That bothered Ken, he says, because they did it without telling him. The cottage was his last real connection to Canada.

CHAPTER TWENTY-FIVE

At ECI, Penni Harcourt had been a presence in class as well as onstage in the school's productions. Just before Wayne had won his final race in Sacramento in 1996 and Ken had moved to Versailles, Penni had a stroke. She was fifty. It came two years after she had been diagnosed with breast cancer.

As a kid, her life had been different from everyone else's in our class. Her parents married in 1946, the year she was born. Her father was Lutheran, his ancestors from England, and he had been married before. He was sixty, the only one of our parents born in the nineteenth century. Her mother, a Catholic, was from a francophone area on Georgian Bay, near Midland. She was twenty-two. They both worked at one of the local movie theatres, the Westwood, at night, from six until eleven during the week, on Saturday afternoons and evenings as well, and were at home all day. Penni's father was seventy-four when she started high school, seventy-five when he died. Her mother was a widow at thirty-seven. A year later, in grade 10, her mother remarried; Penni's new stepfather had been married before. A year after that, when Penni was seventeen, her half-sister was born. Her family rarely went to church. She didn't go on church getaways on weekends or to church camps in the summer. She never went to Brownies or Girl Guides. She was a year older than most of us, and more "knowing." Her love at ECI was theatre. And while in our earlier high school years, the other kids in our class who liked theatre got to do only backstage stuff, Penni inhabited centre stage.

After ECI, she was in a hurry. And while Judy Tibert, Marilyn Steels, and Marilyn Adamson went to McMaster for their nursing degrees, Penni took her nursing diploma at St. Michael's Hospital in downtown Toronto. Hospital programs were shorter and cheaper, and she could begin earning money of her own, and begin living her life, sooner.

One day in 1969, she was drawing some blood from a patient and, needing help from a lab technician, she met John Mansour. When they were done, he asked her to go for a coffee. He was, as he describes himself, the "darkest person" at St. Mike's. He is Palestinian. He was born in Jerusalem in 1942 in the same house where his father was born in 1915 and his grandfather in 1876, in what at different times was Palestine, then Transjordan, then Jordan, and then, after the Six Day War in 1967, Israel. John was Greek Orthodox. He worked in a hospital and clinic in Jerusalem and soon began to see the possibilities of "automation," as he puts it, of technology and of a machine that could analyze blood, which cost only $7,000 and which could make him lots of money, he believed. So he took a job in Kuwait to earn that money, and when that didn't pan out, he decided to come to Canada for a few years. He'd learn even more about automation, buy the machine, and go back to Jerusalem. Then the Six Day War broke out, he got a job at St. Mike's he liked, Canada allowed his mother and brother to join him, and those few years turned into a lifetime.

But before he and Penni married, Penni had something she needed to do. She could now see the possibilities of nursing that she hadn't been aware of when she'd applied to St. Mike's, that she couldn't realize with only her hospital diploma. She applied to McGill and was awarded a scholarship that would pay some of her way. The course lasted two years. She and John agreed to put off their wedding plans, and Penni arrived in Montreal in September 1970, at the same moment that Lynda and I did. John drove from Toronto to see her every second weekend, more than a thousand kilometres back and forth, and he helped her out when she ran short of money. In June 1972, she graduated with her degree in nursing. Before the month was over, they were married.

John's friends told him their marriage wouldn't last six months. He and Penni were just too different. On their honeymoon, they went to Europe—to the Netherlands, Belgium, Germany, and Switzerland. Penni had never been to Europe before. They had thought earlier that they might live in Montreal, but with the language tensions and political turmoil in the air, John knew that story too well. Toronto would be their future. Penni returned to St. Mike's and, with her degree, and now on a new path, she was soon a head nurse. Their first child, Marlene, was born in 1973, their second, Emile, a few years later. She and John bought a house in Leaside not much different than the one she had grown up in in Etobicoke, with money they didn't have, but with Toronto's ever-rising housing market, they felt they couldn't afford not to buy. Penni wanted a family very different from the one she'd grown up in. She wanted for her kids some steadiness, some certainty, so they didn't have to worry about what might be next. She didn't exactly know how to achieve that. Her own parents had been more a cautionary tale than role models. But sometimes will is enough until instinct settles in. Years passed.

In the late 1970s, Penni began to see another kind of future for herself in nursing. Historically, like her, most nurses had been trained in hospitals. As medicine advanced to offer more complex care, more nurses went to universities and colleges. Those already working in hospitals needed to upgrade their training. Penni had never taught before, but she'd had good teachers, and good theatre directors, and was asked to teach in the hospital's continuing education program. She loved it. When the program grew, she commuted to Brock University in St. Catharines two nights a week for two years to get her master's and upgrade her own skills. Later, she would also teach at Toronto East General, Mount Sinai, and Wellesley hospitals. Then, in the mid-nineties, she got sick. She recovered, and moved to the Ontario Ministry of Health, still involved in nursing education. But the Harris

government, seeking efficiencies, began bringing into nursing programs freshly redundant teachers trained in teaching, not nursing.
Frustrated, Penni left. It was 1999.

Sandie Barnard was the third of us to die. She had lived a full life
and then some in her fifty-one years. I didn't really know her in high
school. I wish I had.

I should have known there was something about her almost
from her first day in class in grade 12. Or if not then, surely after
she'd been willing to say what some of us were thinking and most
wouldn't even dare think, that we didn't need to give Mr. Hagerman
a present. It was the way she said it, a glint of mischief in her eyes.
This, among her new classmates who were not exactly lacking in self-
confidence. But Sandie had in her something more, a self-assuredness,
that didn't come from what others said, that had come from her alone.
In grade 13, alongside Penni, she had one of the lead roles in *Charley's
Aunt*, the school play. In a musical number at the end, a chorus line of
boys picked her up and raised her over their heads and carried her
off the stage. There she was, every eye on her, her arms extended in
the air, her head tossed back, a Sandie smile on her face. It's what the
playwright called for, what the character would do, but Sandie did it
her own way. Less a star's turn at a star's moment. Something deeper.
This is me. Live with it.

Everyone who came to know Sandie, at every age and stage of her
life, friends, co-workers, partners, asked themselves the same question: Where did this self-assurance come from? All they knew was
that it had come before them, as if it had been always there. Even
Sheila Goulet, who might have known Sandie better and longer than
anyone, didn't know. They had met at seventeen in cadets, both of
them training to be Brownie and Girl Guide leaders. They went to U
of T, travelled the world together for a year and a half, and were "life
partners," as Sheila would describe them years later. After drifting
apart, they spent the last more than twenty years of Sandie's life as best
friends. Sheila thinks Sandie's self-assurance might somehow have to

do with her home life, which wasn't at all *Leave It to Beaver*. Sandie's father had died before she was in high school, and her mother remarried. Her mother and her stepfather were a "rough and ready pair," Sheila recalls, who didn't seem happy together. Sandie grabbed her first chance to leave home in going to U of T, even deciding to board downtown with some elderly ladies, and act as their caregiver. "Sandie needed to take herself away from her family," Sheila says. "She needed to escape to her better self."

School had been that escape, just as it had been for Cheryl. But even more important for Sandie was Girl Guides. Her pack, about twenty-five girls, aged eleven to sixteen, met once a week at Park Lawn School, not far from her house. They wore their uniforms, recited pledges, marched, sang songs, worked on their badges, and did lots of different activities. For Sandie, Guides was a place to be—every Tuesday, for two hours, with twenty-four other girls, bonding, *belonging*. All the assumptions and expectations of adults, of culture, history, and the world got parked at the door. It was a chance to be a girl, and to be all a girl might be. At ECI, boys were student council president, girls were vice-president. Boys were treasurer, girls were secretary. Not here. In Guides, girls could be—girls *were*—the leaders.

Guide leaders were women and girls often not much older than the Guides themselves, and they didn't dominate their meetings the way a classroom teacher did a classroom. They "guided" and were role models for girls, many of whom had grown up short of role models. Guide leaders—one of Sandie's was a lawyer, another a publishing executive—might show them, as women, what they might do in the rest of their lives. And the very best thing about Guides? The Guide camps. One weekend during the school year, two weeks at a lake during the summer, where what happened during those two hours once a week had many more hours to blossom. Where, in Sandie's case, a simple introduction to the outdoors would grow into a lifelong need and love.

Also growing in her in those high school years was a love of English. Sandie loved stories, she loved being able to be other people in other places and other times, and in those different lives discover new feelings, ideas, beliefs. She also began to realize that these stories might be told in all sorts of ways, through literature, art, theatre, music, spoken language, and that if she had stories in her own life *she* wanted to tell, she needed the skills to tell them. She played major roles in the school play in both her years at ECI, she won the award as the school's top English student in grade 13, she took English language and literature at U of T and, in a world becoming ever more modern and proud of it, where nothing was more irrelevant than Chaucer, she specialized in medieval English, even joining a student society that staged productions of medieval plays. The society was an offshoot of Professor Leyerle's seminar in medieval drama, so, of course, some of its students decided it needed a name to reflect its origins, and, being students, and being in a pub one Saturday night, they turned what it literally was, Professor Leyerle's seminar, into an acronym, PLS, and, before the night was done, turned that back into words, in Latin of course, to reflect what they wanted their group to be, a "drinking and playing society," coming up with Poculi Ludique Societas, which they then turned into its own acronym, which in time, of course, got turned into other names: Perfectly Ludicrous Society, Parking Lot Sacrifices, Ph.D.s Lost in Space, Plays Larger than Shakespeare. Naturally, Sandie performed in those plays, because she found in medieval English, in the bigness of its themes of life and death and in the beauty and simplicity of its language, something pure, powerful, and unrestrained. And very funny, and very bawdy too, which also appealed to her. After graduation, she moved to Ottawa, to attend Carleton University, and got her master's in medieval poetry.

Then an unexpected twist—before she had a chance to head off to a new adventure, an English teacher at ECI got sick and she was asked to fill in. She had had no teacher training, she had left ECI only six years earlier, her students were not much younger than she was, and now her desk was at the front of the room. Yet what might have seemed weird to most wasn't to Sandie. This was an English class, her students were the same age as those she had been a leader to in

Guides, and she knew what they wanted and needed. During that year at ECI, she and Sheila also began to make plans.

Sheila recalls that it started with a conversation she and her mother and Sandie had, which somehow turned into a discussion about the "last frontier" and Sandie saying how she "wanted to go where no one had ever gone and see what they would never see," which in Sandie's mind, somehow, meant India. It was then, Sheila says, that she and Sandie began to "scheme and dream," and Sandie being Sandie, began to plan. "She read books about all the countries we might visit, about cheap travel and how we'd keep safe." And while almost every other North American in the early 1970s when they crossed an ocean went east, Sandie and Sheila went west, to San Francisco by bus, then by boat to Hong Kong. And not by ocean liner but by freighter, one that had room, as Sheila recalls, for "twelve passengers and a lot of freight." "Going by freighter was part of the allure," she recalls, "so was crossing the Pacific." It took them seventeen days, with land not once in sight, to reach Hong Kong. Then on to Singapore.

When they arrived, they opened a phone book, found the listing they were looking for, and stayed in a Girl Guide hostel. There they met other Guides from other countries, heard their stories, and made new plans, which came to be their new, ever-changing *plan*. "We didn't really know what we were doing or where we were going," Sheila says. And when they got to wherever they went, they knew what they would find because of the books Sandie had read beforehand, but had no idea how what they found would make them feel. Hong Kong and Singapore, with their old mouldy buildings, seemed so colonial to them. Burma (now Myanmar), after weeks on buses and trains in Malaysia and Thailand, was like stepping back centuries in time, yet with the whiplash of its disconnections—ancient Buddhist temples, kind and beautiful people, and a military so repressively everywhere. From Rangoon (now Yangon) they flew to Calcutta (now Kolkata). So crowded, colourful, so overwhelming, goods spilling out of the front doors of shops almost to the street. On the streets, every means of locomotion possible—transport trucks, smaller trucks, buses, cars, smaller cars, motorcycles, mopeds, rickshaws, bicycles, bicycle rickshaws—all swirling around them. And animals—cows, dogs—were everywhere. And people. Millions and millions of them. In Toronto or New York, most of those millions were out of sight in offices or homes; in Calcutta and Bombay (now Mumbai) they were all just there, in plain sight. Life was *everywhere*, and so was death. Life's sounds and smells, the food and the food markets, nothing bland, everything spicy. "It was the intensity of it all," Sheila says.

After four months in India they flew to Tel Aviv, where they got on a bus and for several more weeks travelled through Syria, Turkey, Bulgaria, Greece, and Hungary, finally meeting up with friends in Austria. Then it was back to Israel and to a kibbutz, where they worked for two months, spent the High Holy Days, and took in everything they could. Just before Christmas 1974, they flew home.

"Sandie could always see what others didn't want to look at," Sheila says of her and of their trip. "It was part of her gift." She had a sense of injustice, a capacity for outrage, and an unforgiving voice inside her that said, "That is not right," which made her deaf to excuse or explanation. Sandie didn't come home transformed. She came home more of what she was.

Sandie and Sheila soon after stopped being a couple. It didn't have to do with the trip. Now in their late twenties, they weren't the same people they had been. The pieces that had made up Sandie's life were coming to fit together in a different way. She had felt no great trauma years earlier when she realized she was gay. Not like when she had lost her father. She lived as she lived; she was who she was. She wasn't going to let anyone else define her. But sometime during the seventies, as feminism turned from being the fight of a relative few to the day-to-day existence of most every woman, she realized that being determined and smart wasn't enough to allow her to do what she wanted to do. Some barriers she couldn't break down, some fights she couldn't win herself. She needed others, and others needed her. Their lives were part of *her* life. Her life part of theirs. She'd need to use her voice to help them use *theirs*. Sheila wanted to live mostly the life they were living. Sandie needed to go where life was taking her.

In the mid-1970s, Sandie went back to the classroom, this time as a professor of English at Centennial College, in Scarborough, this time with students who were not like her. Many were children of immigrants, and they were in college to learn a trade, so they took English because they had to. But to Sandie, more important than language itself was *voice*—having something to say and the skills and the confidence to say it. To be who you are. She knew that to be successful as a plumber or carpenter, these students would need to deal with bosses and clients who, if they thought they weren't adept in English, would look down on them and take advantage of them. So for Sandie, if reading Shakespeare made her students feel stupid, she would teach them something that didn't. If writing essays made them feel the same, she would teach them to write smart, clear business letters. Don't ever dumb it down, but make it what they can do, and make it fun. She also introduced them to drama.

She had done the same in Guides. Guides had had an arts program that included music, dance, and crafts, and at Sandie's encouragement had introduced "creative drama" to their curriculum. She trained leaders across the country. National Guide camps in Nova Scotia and Alberta established drama programs, and Sandie ran them. In 1985, theatre and drama were at the centre of a big Guide event at Maple Leaf Gardens in Toronto to mark the seventy-fifth anniversary of Girl Guides in Canada. As the story is told, because Sandie knew Bill and Harold Ballard Jr. from ECI, and because their sister Mary Elizabeth was involved in Guides, Sandie sweet-talked their father, Harold Ballard, the owner of the Gardens and the Leafs, into giving her the arena for one night, free, for the celebration. She asked him because she knew that she was right to ask, and had every right to expect him to say yes because it would be unconscionable and incomprehensible for him to say no. Sandie created, wrote, and directed the show. It was two hours long and involved hundreds of Brownies and Guides.

Nobody remembers much about the night except that it began with a darkened Maple Leaf Gardens. Then, at centre ice, was a single spotlight on a four-poster bed, and under its bedcovers a child sleeping, her dreams represented by lights twinkling, dancing, all over the huge arena, reflections from a disco ball, and around the perimeter of the rink, on a walkway between the boards and the seats, hundreds of Brownies, each with one big round disc on her front and one on her back—giant Girl Guide cookies. It was magical. For Sandie, the night got done because it had to get done, because when it did, it was fabulous. It was girls who did it.

By this time, Sandie had also met Val Austin, a high school teacher who would become increasingly important in her life.

At Centennial, Sandie taught her required courses and created another. It was offered after spring term, lasted for a month, and was for students interested in the theatre—or for as many of them as could fit into two rented vans. Sandie organized everything. They might drive east, they might drive west, it depended on the year. They stopped in five or six small communities along the way, held workshops, performed a play, Sandie and her students billeted with local families. One year, they stopped in a Doukhobor community in Saskatchewan. Sandie wanted her students to experience the country, to take them "out of their comfort zone," as Val Austin put it, but into situations that Sandie carefully monitored, where she knew they would succeed—to gain confidence, to develop more of themselves, to give them more to say, to give them the skills they needed to say it. Again, it was all about voice. Val still remembers Sandie's mantra: "You can learn in a classroom, but you can learn better in life." When the students came back, Val relates, "They were totally changed." They were never going to go on in the theatre, that wasn't the point. But they would have a better chance to live who they are.

Sandie was all-in in everything she did, which meant that when she didn't need to be all-in, she needed to be all-out. She and Val bought a house in Stouffville, about an hour's drive east of Centennial on rolling farmland beyond the sprawl of Toronto. It offered the peace and calm that Sandie needed. At almost the same time, while canoeing on the South Magnetawan River near Parry Sound, she came upon a cottage that caught her attention. "Magnetawan," in the Ojibwa language, means "swiftly flowing waters," and on these waters, and anywhere, as one of her friends said, Sandie "could make a canoe dance." She stopped at the cottage, looked around, found out who owned it, and drove to meet him. His sons used it for hunting, the man told her, it wasn't for sale. Sandie persisted. It took some years, but eventually the man relented. She borrowed some money from a friend and bought it. The cottage had been built in 1906. It was on seven acres, on a peninsula, with water access only. It had no electricity or running water. It was a place to swim, canoe, get away, and be with nature, just what she was looking for. It was filled with beautiful old furniture, the name "Eaton's" stamped on many of the pieces, the legs of many of its chairs and tables cut shorter to bring the furniture closer to the floor to pick up the heat from the fireplace. The Mag, as she would come to call it, was her "heaven on earth."

The 1980s were eventful for Sandie. Her three-season life in Stouffville and at Centennial continued, hosting friends at her house, protesting twice on picket lines with colleagues at the college. Universities and colleges were the place every kid needed to go to have a chance at a future. High schools gave higher grades so students could meet their standards, governments turned a blind eye, parents were thrilled that their kids were so smart. And if governments chose not to spend the money to hire more faculty to teach all these kids, the professors would need to adapt. What's ten more students in a course that already has forty? While strikes that say they aren't about money are usually about money, the two at Centennial were at least as much about professors having time to teach properly. Sandie enjoyed the rightness of their fight, whether from behind a microphone offering her own voice or behind the scenes organizing, helping others to express theirs. Because once they find that voice, she knew, you can never know what will happen. Or whom it will happen to.

In 1984, the same year as the first of the strikes, Sandie decided it was time for her and some of her friends from Guides to go on an adventure. It would be like all those camping trips they had gone on as kids, only bigger. They would follow in the path of the Yukon gold miners of 1898: travel by ship from Seattle to Skagway, Alaska, hike the Chilkoot Pass, find their way to Whitehorse, then canoe the Yukon River the rest of the way to Dawson City. There were seven of them in all; the oldest, Marilyn Friesen, was forty-five, the youngest was eighteen. Sandie was thirty-seven. Marilyn, who was Sandie's first Guide leader, kept a diary.

The ship voyage from Seattle was a hoot, like Girl Guide camp all over again. The funny ones were funny, the organized ones organized, the not-so-organized hadn't changed a bit in twenty-five years. They were all excited, and anxious. The first two days of the hike were uneventful. Then came day three. They had all seen the photo of the miners, like ants, snaking their way up the snowy white section of the pass called the Golden Staircase. But without the snow, there was no staircase. Instead, a pile of giant boulders that over centuries had tumbled down the mountain and settled at odd jagged angles, which offered no obvious route to the top. This was no longer a hoot. At that moment, the women realized they weren't twenty-five years younger. When they finally reached the top that they'd had in their sights all day, it wasn't the top. There was another top, and if there was another, there might be others after that. When finally they did get to the Canadian side of the pass, they sang "O Canada." They had made it, and until they got there none of them had been sure they would. The campground was still some distance ahead. In the wind and rain, too tired to go on, they stopped for the night. When Marilyn climbed into her tent, she wrote in her diary, "Oh joy." The days after felt like a victory lap.

In Whitehorse, they picked up their rented canoes and started up the Yukon River, through Robert Service's Lake Laberge, then back onto the river. The sky was blue, the sun shone twenty hours a day, it was dusk for the rest. They saw eagles, beaver, and foxes. When they didn't paddle they strapped their two canoes together catamaran-style, put up a "sail," and let the current carry them. They sang songs, told stories, laughed, got caught up on years of feelings, the hardships of their lives nowhere within them. Sandie was in her element. As the waters pitched down the choppiest section of the river, as Marilyn recorded, Sandie "let out a 'Yahoo.'" Finally, they arrived in Dawson City. They had left Seattle six weeks earlier. These Girl Guides, now in the middle ages of their lives, had done it.

For most of them, this was the end of the story. For Marilyn Friesen, it was the beginning. She was married and had four kids. She loved her husband and their kids, but somewhere along the way, as she says, raising them, supporting everyone, "I lost Marilyn." In these six weeks, "Sandie gave me back who I am," she says. Over the next thirty years, Marilyn, her husband, and their kids went white-water canoeing in the Yukon and Northwest Territories. They went backpacking on Ellesmere Island and Baffin Island. "That trip was the beginning," she says. "Sandie proved to me I could do it."

In the late 1980s, Sandie left Centennial. She had written one book about public speaking and was about to write another. She wanted to reach an audience beyond her classroom and to help others get across what they had to say. Again, this was about *voice*, the chance to say what you need to say and to say it in a way that others take in. But Sandie also thought voice had to be more than that. It was about getting others to *act*. It was, as Nellie McClung put it, about "getting it done." And as a teacher, writer, speaker, organizer, activist, and conscience, she wasn't getting enough things done. She took a job with the Ontario government, on a project about sexual harassment in high schools.

A survey sponsored by the OSSTF, the high school teachers' union, and the Ontario government revealed that a high percentage of girls had been sexually harassed in school settings. Something needed to be done. Sandie needed school boards, principals, teachers, and students, both boys and girls, to understand that sexual harassment isn't just something adolescent boys did, but it is one person taking advantage of another, and that might be in all kinds of ways, and they do it because they are bigger, stronger, older, richer, white, most often male, because they think they are privileged and superior—because they believe they can. And if no one does anything about it, they're right—they can. And that's utterly, totally unfair. Sandie was in her wheelhouse. The project was called "The Joke's Over."

Sandie was fed up hearing "Hey, it was only a joke" from a guy who, when a girl stood up in class in front of him to answer a question, slid his hand up her skirt. Or after female students had to run a gauntlet of boys in the hallways, the boys having offered commentary on the girls' sex lives as they went by. Sandie knew all about jokes. She was hysterically funny. When she laughed, as one friend put it, "it was from the bottom of the soles of her feet." And she also knew that it isn't a joke if only the joke-teller laughs. It's only a joke if the *other* person laughs. And sexually harassing someone, female or male, is no joke.

Governments, companies, and individuals had been talking about bullying and harassment for years. Talk's done, the joke's over, it's time to get on with it.

She contacted schools, negotiated dates for workshops for staff. She travelled the province, to big places and small places, running the workshops, which were usually held on teachers' professional development days. They lasted about two hours. In that time, she had to find some way to engage her audience, and in such a way that, after she was gone, they would engage the principal and the rest of the staff just as fully, so the next time something inappropriate happened in their school, they recognized it, interrupted it, and addressed it. This was not going to happen easily.

She and the teachers also ran student workshops. From the students, they heard old familiar stories and new belly-twingeing ones. Not one to suffer fools in everything she did, Sandie had had to learn that sometimes to get things done she had to blunt her edge, slow her anger, and work harder than she should need to, to make her audience not-fools, so they would hear her. She also had to manage up. Her bosses had to be sure that the project would work, because their own bosses, the politicians, could not, must not, be embarrassed.

For Sandie, this chance was not going to come again soon. It had to succeed. The "That's not right" voice in her head never left her.

She was at it more than three years. Workshop after workshop, school after school. A package of print materials entitled "The Joke's Over/On a fini de rire," went to every high school in the province. They produced a video. They made up T-shirts. At the program's launch, the government ministers were there. In time, many sports organizations, especially hockey ones, picked up the program. It would become harder for bullies to be bullies. "The Joke's Over" was a beginning.

Often people who are forceful speakers, who know how to put words and thoughts together, and know they are right, run out of gas. They don't have the patience to deal with those who know only how to stand in their way. Advocates come and go. Sandie had the skills of an advocate, but she was also a community organizer, and community organizers know it takes a long, long time to change people's minds. As Karen Wheeler, Sandie's boss in the ministry that funded her work said, "You don't put your money on the megaphones, you put it on the slow-and-grow."

A few weeks before the program's launch, Sandie had been diagnosed with cancer. She had displayed no symptoms. She saw a doctor on a Friday and was operated on that Monday. It was the fall of 1996. The chemo knocked her flat. The cancer went into remission, the cancer returned, she tried massage therapy and aromatherapy, she tried to keep going, doing what she'd always done, living as she'd always lived, not wanting to talk about it, fighting like she'd fought other fights. Her new partner, Kathryn Mifflin, took a year off teaching to care for her. This time, when the cancer didn't go away, the person who had always turned anger into something more helpful sometimes got angry.

In early summer 1997, the doctor told Sandie the news, and she and Kathryn drove north to The Mag. She couldn't swim or canoe, but from her bed, or sometimes on the dock, she could watch the river, alongside her two dogs, Clover and Kodiak—Kodiak because she had always wanted to go to Kodiak Island to see the bears—and two cats, Wilf, for Wilfrid Laurier, and Shaganappi, for a character in a collection of Pauline Johnson short stories. Sandie was there until Thanksgiving, then returned home to Stouffville. In and out of hospital, she died two months later. After her funeral, many of her friends went to her house and stayed for hours, not wanting to leave. Out of many long silences, Kathryn recalls, one of the women finally said, "Well, there you go. Now we've got to do what she wanted us to do. We'd better be the people she wanted us to be." Nearby on the wall was Sandie's framed photo of Nellie McClung: "Never apologize. Never retreat. Never explain. Get the thing done and let them howl."

Later, some of Sandie's friends, Sheila, Marilyn, Val, and Kathryn included, went north to The Mag and scattered her ashes.

CHAPTER TWENTY-SIX

In 1979, I stopped playing for the Canadiens to do something else. I didn't know what that something would be, only that it wouldn't be hockey or law. At thirty-one, I had at least a few more good years of play in me, but that wasn't the point. I had made a lot of money, but not like stars today, not a lifetime's worth. I would need to continue to work, and I wanted to work. I still had decades of working life ahead of me. I had been good at the past, as it turned out, and I wanted to be at least as good at the future. I wanted those years to be just as thrilling and fulfilling. That might be unlikely, but why not, and why wouldn't I? But the clock was ticking. Not so much ticking away at the present as ticking away at the future, leaving me less and less time to make something of that future.

So now what?

First, I had a few loose ends I wanted to tie up. I had graduated from law school and done my year of articling, and I would need to pass a six-month-long bar course and get "called to the bar," as they say, to be able to practise. I wanted to finish what I'd started, and what for much of my life I'd imagined myself doing, even if I now knew I had no interest in being a lawyer. I had also got some advice from someone I barely knew, who had graduated from law school himself, gone into politics, risen to a high level, then when things went sideways had gone back into law, waiting for the right moment to make his return. Law is a great option, he said. It's a good and lucrative life, and at moments when people or circumstances at work get in the way of what you want to do, you can leave, or threaten to leave, to practise law, and the other person knows you can. It helps to set things right. In 1979, the bar course in Ontario was being offered for the first time in Ottawa, less than an hour and a half from our house.

When I had retired in July and was doing all the retrospective interviews, it had felt like it wasn't me doing them. It felt like I was watching other athletes I had seen retire. It felt poignant and sad, *and* happy, and then it was done. Only in September, after I'd started the bar course and the Canadiens were opening their training camp, when I was in Ottawa and not in Montreal, did it hit me. It was *me* who had retired, not someone else. Then I felt sad, and not at all happy.

As a kid I'd always wanted to be a sports announcer. (The only other thing I dreamed of being was a truck driver—being able to *drive* all day, and listen to the radio *all day*. Not Burt Reynolds and *Smokey and the Bandit*, they came years later, but Mike Malone and his driving sidekick, Jerry, on CBC's *Cannonball*—"Barrelin' down the highway, wheelin' right along, hear the tires hummin', hummin' out a song . . .") As other kids dreamed of being Mounties or firemen, I wanted to be Foster Hewitt or Curt Gowdy. To go everywhere, watch games, go to the World Series, the Stanley Cup finals, the Olympics, Wimbledon. Amazing! I knew by 1980 I didn't want to be a full-time announcer, but the Winter Olympics were in Lake Placid that year, only a few hours' drive from Ottawa, and I was hired by ABC to be a commentator for the U.S. men's hockey team's games and for the medal-round games after they had surely been eliminated. The bar course was divided into different subject areas. We'd start a subject on a Monday, get the materials only then, study, and write its exam that Friday or the Friday after that, depending on the subject, and start the cycle again the following Monday. I could commute to Ottawa to write the exams, then go back to Lake Placid and study there. Which is what I did. Except one week, the U.S. team was playing on a Thursday night and I had an exam the next morning. When the game was over, I hopped into the back seat of a car driven by an ABC staffer, crammed my way through a snowstorm, arrived in Ottawa in time for breakfast, wrote the three-hour exam, and got back in time for the next game. Like it had been all those years playing with the Canadiens, and in law school, the adrenaline of one generating adrenaline for the other. Perfect.

And in Lake Placid, the U.S. team was generating a lot of adrenaline. Each of its shocking wins led to bigger shocks until it led to the biggest shock of all—a team of college kids beating the Russians, at the time the best hockey team in the world. Then, for me, a different shock. After Al Michaels had delivered his timeless line—"Do you believe in miracles? YESS!!"—and I had delivered my less-than-timeless follow-up—"Unbelievable!"(and year after year hear our kids say to me: "Dad, all you could come up with was 'Unbelievable!'?")—and after the U.S. beat Finland two days later to win the gold medal, I was standing in our broadcast area, looking down at the American players about a hundred feet away jumping and hugging and rolling on the ice with a joy they had no idea how to express. I knew those players, I knew that team. I had followed them through the year. Al Michaels and I were about as close to them as any non-players were. And at the moment they won, I was really excited. Then about twenty seconds later, I felt something else. Still happiness, but, stronger than that, sadness. I realized then the difference between being on the ice and not being on the ice. A difference that was chasms and chasms wide. This was *their* team, not mine. I would never have that same big feeling again. Retiring from hockey was hard; retiring from that feeling was harder.

I passed the bar course and was called to the bar. Not to start down a new path, but to complete the one I was on.

One more loose end. I had read sports books all my life. From *Fullback Fuller*, *Penalty Shot*, and *Along Olympic Road* as a kid, to new bestsellers for plane rides and sleepless post-game nights in hotel rooms when I was with the Canadiens. The earlier books had offered me fantasies of what might be. The later ones were describing a life I was then living, and some things in them, it seemed to me, didn't read right. I wanted the chance someday to get down what I had seen, and felt, and thought. Like Bill Bradley, All-American, Princeton graduate, Rhodes Scholar, NBA star, future U.S. senator, had done in *Life on the Run*. Like Bill Russell, All-American, NBA superstar, activist, advocate, *champion*, did in *Second Wind*. Or had seemed to do. Until one moment in Russell's book when he was describing that rare, remarkable moment when a game feels suddenly not about the numbers on a scoreboard and takes off to some other place, where one player pushes another to do something more and better than he's ever done before, a player on your own team or one of your opponents, it doesn't matter, and that player pushes another, and that player another, until it's everybody, on both teams, and nobody has any idea what's coming next and nobody wants to know, they only know they have to be up to it and do it, and it's not them demanding that of themselves anymore, or their team or their opponent, but much more unforgivingly it's the game that demands it. When at that rare special moment, it's about, and only about, *the game*. As I was reading Russell's book and taking off with it, at some moment it lost me. Some words didn't read right. Russell hadn't written the book himself, I realized, but had worked with a ghostwriter. The ghostwriter had never been in that moment.

I wanted to write a book by myself, no ghostwriter. I wanted to try to get down what *I* had experienced.

I had never written a book before. I had written articles, but a book isn't a long article. For months, what I put on the paper in front of me looked nothing like what was in my head. I wanted to set before a reader a life, not just what happened on the ice but in all the hours and days between games as well. Almost every biography and autobiography I'd read about people in sports, entertainment, politics described lives that seemed entirely different from my own. They offered me this privileged, behind-the-curtain look at a world I'd never experienced and never would, a look at people who weren't like me. But from what I'd seen and lived, that didn't seem right. Behind *my* curtain was Etobicoke, it was Central Park, Central Arena, Humber Valley

Church, ECI. It was a family—parents, a brother, a sister—it was growing up, it was fantasies and hopes, it was succeeding, failing, learning,
trying. It was beating Burnhamthorpe and never being a prefect. It
was winning more often than we lost, and losing the big ones more
often than we won. It was going one place and ending up someplace
else. Sure, it was also the Forum and Luzhniki, Stanley Cups, money,
and millions of people watching. But to me, much more of my life was
the same than it was different. And what did seem different, winning
a Cup, which most people hadn't done, wasn't so much different, I
discovered, from winning a high school championship or some equiv-
alent in someone's life, which most people had done. I didn't want to
write a book about this *other* world because I didn't believe I had lived
an *other* life.

I thought I could write the book anywhere, and our kids were
young, so we moved to Cambridge, England, for a year, and we
loved it—the oldness of it, the university, the feeling of serious
learning everywhere, our daughter in a good school, with an instant
English accent.

We came back after a year as we'd planned, the book unfinished.
We returned to Toronto because I had no idea what I'd do once the
book was written, but whatever that was, it seemed more likely I would
do it in Toronto. We rented a house near U of T, and a year later,
when the book still wasn't done, we rented another. In the two and a
half years it took me to write the book, only slowly and only eventually did I see on my legal pad in front of me what I had in my head.
I also learned during this time something about writing that surprised
me. That writing mostly isn't about getting down what you know; it's
about what you didn't know you knew, and what you discover as you're
writing. That writing isn't this boring exercise of living day after day
with what you already know, and never learning, but is about *always*
learning. A sentence that comes to an end you didn't anticipate when
you began it. Still, to get through those years, I had to promise myself,
and felt I needed to promise everyone around me, that when I was
finished, I would never, ever do this again.

The book turned out. Instead of what a bestselling book for hockey fans might sell, *The Game* sold several multiples more. People who weren't hockey fans and felt they knew nothing about hockey, it seems, saw a little of their life in mine.

My hockey and law life were now at a close. My past was done, my future ahead. I was thirty-six.

I had worked for Ralph Nader and other public interest groups in the 1970s. Big companies and big governments did what they wanted to do, and citizens and consumers, too small to take them on, had to find a way to fight back. I wanted to do "public work." Not in politics, not then. (And I would never have used the word "politics." I would have said "government.") And not until I had done a lot more things, learned a lot more, been in more situations, been tested in more ways, had my beliefs challenged. Not until I had some more developed understanding of what Canada is, what the world is, how life works, where the future might go. An understanding that was deep enough to stand up to the moment-to-moment compromises, complications, trade-offs and tests of politics, where everything happens so fast you rarely have time to know what you need to know, and need some sense of what you think is right to keep yourself on your own path. In my mind, that wouldn't be until I was fifty.

I might have been elected easily after I retired from hockey, but that didn't seem the point. If I did get elected, I'd have all that extra time to learn to be a politician. Time also to make mistakes, time for those mistakes to be mostly forgotten, and time to live through the up-and-down cycles of politics where one party is in power until it's time for a change and the other gets its turn. Time, eventually, to ride the up cycle to something more. But I knew I wouldn't be very good if I got elected then. Why not come back later when I might be good enough. And public work can be lots of things besides politics. What I wanted to do at that moment was work for a few years as an assistant to some very interesting person who was doing some very interesting things. I got some advice in making up a list—the names on it, as it turned out, were mostly those who worked in energy, communications, and the environment. They were Arden Haynes at Imperial Oil; Bill Daniel at Shell; Jack Gallagher at Dome Petroleum, which was doing a lot of exploration in the Arctic; Conrad Black at Argus, a holding company that had large stakes in a who's who of Canadian companies; Doug Bassett at CTV; and Maurice Strong, a business and social entrepreneur who seemed to be involved in everything. I met with Haynes, Daniel, Bassett, and Black, talked by phone with Gallagher in some remote drilling location, and with someone in Strong's office— someone I pretty soon realized was the person whose job I wanted. It turned out it was John Ralston Saul, later a writer, public commentator, and husband of Adrienne Clarkson, the future governor general. As it also turned out, among other reasons, I'm sure, nobody was looking to hire an outsider as an assistant.

On to the next plan. I went to the CBC with two proposals. One was to change the approach and tone of its Sunday-night news program, to make it much more like the CBS show *Sunday Morning*, where, after a brief news summary, the rest of the ninety-minute program offered seven-to-ten-minute stories about people in different parts of the country who have in common only that they are doing something that fascinates them: growing giant zucchini, collecting and delivering books to shut-ins, operating a camp for whistlers, it didn't matter what. The idea was that after a week's worth of never-ending conflict, scandal, and disaster, for this one hour we could pause, take a moment to realize that not all was bad in the world or in Canada, and that individually and together we had made it through, allowing us to go to bed a little energized, and to wake up a little inspired, ready to take on the week ahead.

My other pitch was for a show that would be the reverse of what George Plimpton did. Plimpton was a prominent literary writer and editor who, though scrawny, aging, and unathletic (he used to play touch football with the Kennedys), had decided to take on the very physical and often dangerous jobs of well-known athletes and write about the experience. In real (exhibition) games against real opponents he was, among other things, the quarterback of the Detroit Lions (chronicled in his book *Paper Lion*) and the goalie of the Boston Bruins (which he described in *Open Net*). His books were hysterical and enlightening. By chronicling his own hopelessnesses, he helped the reader understand just how special the star is. In my reverse version, I would be the (relatively) well-known person, but also be the everyman doing regular jobs. I'd be a bricklayer, a postie, a fisherman, a salesclerk, to see how they did their jobs, to learn the tricks of their trade, and in doing so revealing how much more there is to those jobs, how inept this everyman (me), like Plimpton, was in doing them, and how special they are. I thought it would be interesting, and I knew I'd love to do it. And, as a grounding for a post-fifty life in politics (maybe), what could be more important to learn? The CBC said they couldn't figure out a way to make it work, and nothing happened.

I also thought about working in government, if not in politics. The federal government was about to pass freedom of information legislation and appoint its first information commissioner. I inquired about the job, but although there'd been no public announcement, someone had already been chosen. I said I would like to take the deputy's role if that was open. Lynda and I went to Ottawa, looked around, saw a house we liked, and put in an offer, which was rejected, happily, because I didn't get the deputy's job. In Ottawa, I also talked to some people at the Canadian International Development Agency, or CIDA. They were so excited about the work they were doing that they made me even more excited. What could be more useful than doing international work in countries struggling to make their way? I asked them what I might do. They brought out their org chart. CIDA has thousands of employees. There were big boxes and little boxes and medium-sized boxes, there were boxes everywhere. My box was hardly visible. I wasn't used to boxes.

It was 1984. At about the same time, I got a letter from Ontario's finance minister (then called the treasurer) saying he wanted to talk with me. We met. The recession of the early 1980s that had thrown Gord and Wood Gundy into a spin had driven not only markets lower but unemployment rates much higher, and youth unemployment to levels almost double that. The government decided to do more about youth unemployment, and be more visible doing it. It created the office of the youth commissioner, which would be responsible for the many new youth employment and training programs it would soon announce, and asked if I was interested in the job. I had lunch with the person in the ministry responsible. I tried to look calm, I thought I was calm, until I looked down and my tie was covered in blood, and the blood from my nose just kept gushing out. After that, I'm not sure I pulled off calm. I took the job. It wasn't my last bloody nose.

I was youth commissioner for two and half years, from 1984 to 1986. There were some telling moments. The first happened not long after I started. I was to give a speech at a conference—it would be my big coming-out moment—and I needed the speech to be right. The day before, I did a phone interview with a reporter at the *Globe and Mail*. She wouldn't be at the talk, she said, and wanted to know what I was going to say. I told her, she had some questions, and slowly it occurred to me that her questions seemed always about what I'd already answered, as if she hadn't heard. The interview, which was to have been half an hour, stretched on. I kept thinking that if I said what I said again, maybe a little differently, she'd understand. She didn't. Her tone was so disengaged and antagonistic. When the interview was over I realized she *had* heard what I'd said, she just didn't believe it. I had done hundreds of interviews before, some had gone well, some hadn't. In every other case, the person I'd spoken with believed that what I was saying was at least my best attempt at the truth. This was now government, not sports. She thought I was lying.

A few months later, another tough moment. All the programs had been announced, the money was flowing, we were beginning to do what we said we would do. But the youth unemployment rate remained largely unchanged. One day, I decided to do the math. At that time in Ontario about 140,000 youth, defined as aged fifteen to twenty-four, were unemployed. The budget for all our programs was $150 million a year. The cost of a program placement for each youth averaged a little more than $7,000. Which meant, I suddenly realized, that if we spent every dollar, and spent it wisely, and every youth emerged from their program with a job, we would've helped just twenty thousand youth. I was the youth commissioner. These were the province's programs. There were no more. The 140,000 unemployed youth hadn't done in their lives what they could have done, or their parents hadn't, or genetics hadn't, or the market hadn't. Whatever. They were out of school and unemployed at an age when they shouldn't be. We, in the Youth Commissioner's Office, were the hope, and we were 120,000 youth short. It wasn't a good day.

I never did get over it, but within a few weeks I tried to look at the problem from a different angle. Most of these kids were high school dropouts. If there was no more money, if we couldn't help any more kids get a job, maybe we could help more of them stay in school. In Ontario then, there was still grade 13. The percentage of students in 1985 that didn't graduate from grade 13 was a number I couldn't believe, and kept not believing even after it had been confirmed and reconfirmed. It was over 50 percent! I decided I should go into high schools and tell this story, and I created a presentation to give at assemblies.

At each school, I randomly selected twenty students from those in the auditorium, ten boys and ten girls, gave to each of them a name and a place card, which they would hold with that name printed on it, and also a backstory. Here, I said to the audience of students, was a typical grade 9 class in Ontario. And as you know, I said, grade 9 isn't easy. High school's a bit of a scary new place, but they're all doing fine. Or, well, maybe Fred isn't doing that well in algebra, and maybe not in English either, and Jenny's struggling a bit, but, after all, everybody learns at a different pace, they'll probably be fine. And sure enough, in grade 10, Jenny *is* doing better, but Fred isn't, and now he's finding it even harder to learn each new day's lesson because he still can't make sense of all those lessons he didn't understand before. And now he's showing up late more often, and his homework isn't done. And Joanne and Jamaal and Andrew aren't doing that well either. But again, in a month or two they'll probably be fine.

So the story continues. But in grade 11, things begin to change a lot. Now they're sixteen. Now they're old enough to drop out of school if they want. And Fred now is totally lost, and Jamaal and Angela and Mark too. Twenty percent of students drop out at age sixteen, statistics said, so I ask Fred, Joanne, Jamaal, and Angela to leave the stage. They're shocked, as are the other sixteen students, and those in the auditorium too. The story continues. The courses get harder, there's more homework, more students are falling behind, more aren't doing their homework, more aren't showing up to school, more are lost. More are dropping out, so I ask more to leave the stage. And the worst part, for those who do drop out, is that it all makes sense. In school, they aren't going anywhere and they know it. And they know *absolutely* that every next day they'll just be sitting there, understanding nothing, feeling stupid. But what they *don't* know, not for sure, even though they've been told, is what it would be like if they did drop out. They've never dropped out before. Sure, there aren't many jobs, but maybe they'd get one. Maybe, for them, at this moment, the devil they don't know—dropping out—is better than the devil they do—staying in school.

At the end of the presentation, nine out of twenty students remained. I looked out into the auditorium and said, "There you have it. The average high school class in Ontario. Jobs are hard to come by. The message is clear. Do yourselves a favour. Do what you're doing. Stay in school." The kids in the audience left stunned; the teachers did too.

The more I gave the presentation, the more invitations I received to give it. What I said was fair, it was honest, the students and teachers and officials needed to hear it. But gradually I got a feeling. It didn't matter that I was right. There was no mechanism, no big program that would help these kids keep up and want to stay in school. Nothing that would change things. Making the students more aware only made the teachers and officials and *me* feel better, it didn't make anything better for the students. What I was saying was a cheat. I stopped doing the talks.

I gave a lot of other speeches about unemployed kids, and drop-outs, to service clubs and at education conferences. Near the end of my term, I came across a story that is better known now but which wasn't often told then, and I ended each talk by telling it. The story had to do with an old man who every morning walked along a beach. This one day, starfish were strewn everywhere, having been washed up on the sand overnight. The old man saw a young boy ahead of him, and he was throwing the starfish back into the sea, one after another. The old man asked the boy what he was doing. The boy told him. The old man said, "But there are thousands of them. How can it matter?" The boy picked up another and threw it back into the sea. "It matters to this one," he said. I told that story as much for me as I did for the audience.

I think we did some good things, but what we did was much less than what the youth and the public were counting on, than what was needed, than what we were selling. Until those years as youth com-missioner, as a student in elementary school, high school, university, and law school, as a player, in summer and volunteer jobs, I'd had bad days, but I'd enjoyed what I was doing. As youth commissioner, I had good days, but I didn't enjoy what I was doing.

In 1985, my mother died. While I and others in our family seemed always to be looking for something, my mother wasn't. She had it, and she knew it. She was born Margaret Campbell in 1908. She had gone to the Toronto Normal School, to teachers' college, had taught kindergarten, and married my father, and then, like other women of her generation, was never "gainfully employed" outside the house after her first child, my brother, was born, except during the war years. She took care of the house, she took care of my father, she took care of Dave, Judy, and me. She understood that that was her job and that it was an important job, and she had no reason to think otherwise. It had been her mother's job, and her mother's mother's before that. It was the job of Mrs. Carpenter, Mrs. Mooney, Mrs. Gibson, and all the other mothers who lived around us, and all the mothers who were in the choir and in the Women's Missionary Society at the church and in bridge club. Mrs. Baird, the mother of a friend of Dave's, worked outside the home. She was a teacher, but her husband had died and she had no choice. If someone then had described my mother as "content," as they might do today, I'm sure she would've looked puzzled. Content was part of it, her look would say, but she had a purpose, and that was us, and day after day she was fulfilling that purpose. I think she was truly happy.

We didn't hear as much about her side of the family as we did our father's. Our family name was Dryden, so most of the stories we heard were about the Drydens, not the Campbells. The Dryden stories, at least to Dave and me, also seemed more worthy of telling. My father's cousin was Syl Apps, captain of the Toronto Maple Leafs in the 1940s, British Empire Games gold medallist in the pole vault, member of the Hockey Hall of Fame. Andrew Dryden Blair, or Andy Blair, played for the Leafs and Chicago, and Murray Murdoch, for decades, had held the record as the NHL's ironman, having played 508 consecutive games for the New York Rangers. They too were my father's cousins.

The names we heard on the Campbell side mattered to us only because they were our aunts or great-uncles. Bam, who lived with us all through our childhood and was almost like a second mother to us, was a Campbell, but what I remember most about the Campbells, maybe because I liked maps and imagining other places, were the names of the Franco-Anglo towns along the Ottawa River between Ottawa and Montreal where most of our branch of the Campbells had come from: Rockland, Hawkesbury, Thurso, Lachute, Brownsburg, and another that had a magical sound I never could quite make out, "Shootablondoh"—until after Lynda and I had moved to Montreal and I realized it was Chute-à-Blondeau. My grandfather, Alex Campbell, we knew had worked for American Comptometer and had been transferred from Montreal to Cleveland, where he died in the flu epidemic in 1920, leaving Bam a widow and single mother to my mother, then twelve, and my uncle, Alex, five. The next fifteen years of their lives

are less clear to me. There was a move to Ottawa, to live with one of
Bam's sisters and her family and another unmarried sister.

After my mother graduated from Glebe Collegiate, they moved to
Toronto, to a boarding house on Hawthorn Avenue in Rosedale, so my
mother could go to Normal School. The Normal School was where
most of Ontario's future teachers were trained, more than six hundred
each year, the great majority of them women. The school had three
divisions, two for the older grades, one for the younger, and my mother
chose Kindergarten Primary. She had played the piano for many years,
had sung in school choirs, and was physically active enough to enjoy
games. She was welcoming, patient, and not overpowering, the right
kind of person to introduce a five-year-old to school, to music, arts,
play, and friendships, to the pleasures and lessons of a five-year-old's
learning. Graduating one year later, she got a job teaching kindergarten at Prince of Wales School in Hamilton, where she remained
for seven years. Then, in 1934, she went back to her beloved Normal
School, to instruct in its Kindergarten Primary division and to teach
in its Model School. At about the same time, she and my father met.
He was living in Hamilton, still selling, still involved in all kinds of
things, still finding his way. In 1938, they were married. My mother
moved back to Hamilton, this time to teach at George R. Allan School,
which she did as Mrs. Dryden until my brother was born in 1941. As a
mother, normally she would have had to stop then. But this was wartime, and with Bam at home to take care of Dave, she received special
permission to continue.

I remember my mother as always there. She was there when I
woke up every morning, when I came home from school, right away
or after practice, whatever the time. She was there on weekends and
all summer. We didn't have a cottage (summer was my father's busiest
season), and if we went away at all we went together. The only time
I remember her not there was one weekend a year, when on a Friday
night we drove her to the Guild Inn in Scarborough, on the bluffs
overlooking Lake Ontario, and picked her up on Sunday afternoon.
Going away? From us? To Scarborough? None of that made any sense

to me. She would rarely get cross with us, as she put it, and I never heard her yell. And she always wore dresses, "house dresses" for every day around the house, proper dresses whenever she went outside our front door and for when my dad came home, and nice dresses for the rare night out for dinner or the theatre with my father. I saw her wear slacks once. It was for a family photo for our Christmas card. The theme of the card that year had to do with cutting our tree at my father's Christmas tree farm, Christmas trees having come to be another "line" for my father to sell. The rest of us were in our best woodsman's gear, Dave and me in our hockey jackets. In the attic, we had discovered an old ratty woollen *something* that billowed out at the hips—my mother's ski pants from the 1930s.

She spent her days, along with Bam, doing whatever was required in the house. Bam was the baker, Mom did the cooking. Taste wasn't my mother's first consideration. Bacteria had no chance of surviving her oven or stove. She manned the phones for my father's business, answering calls, placing orders. She lay down in the afternoon, the phone beside her on the bed, read *The Upper Room* magazine, short daily lessons from the Bible, and dozed. She didn't drive until she was sixty. When she went for her driver's test, the examiner said to her, "Well, you left that a little late, didn't you, lady?" She never made left-hand turns; a series of right ones would get her where she needed to go. She was tall for a woman of her time, but not physical or robust. I think she found me a handful. I wanted to do what I wanted to do, which is mostly the things Dave did, and he was six years older. My mother would be afraid I'd hurt myself, while my father would think, "Let him try." And when I did push things too much, which I would do, I can still hear her voice in my head: "Now Ken, don't ruin it." She never went to any of my games until finally, in Montreal, when Dave was with the Buffalo Sabres, and we played against each other, the first (and only) brother goalies in the NHL ever to do so, I think she felt she had to go. She would watch until the puck went into either Dave's or my end, look down, slowly peek upwards, raise her head when the coast seemed clear, then lower it again when it wasn't.

Until finally, she asked Dave and me if it was OK if she didn't come at all. She was afraid for us in a mother's hundred different ways. It just wasn't fun for her.

She wrote me every week once I'd moved away, when I was at Cornell, then in Winnipeg, then Montreal. Her letters were a slow recitation of her days—Bam and I did the wash today, had a nice chat with Mrs. Genova, was at choir practice last night, Tuesday was bridge club at the Roelofsens, "had punk cards." Through her letters, I could completely picture her days. If my father was the energy and the wings in our family, my mother was the calm and the roots.

The last few months of her life she was in the hospital, she had had a stroke, eventually she was on a ventilator. I would talk, she would nod, her eyes and face as expressive as always. When she had something she wanted to say, we had an Etch A Sketch–like device called a Magic Slate on which she could write her note, then erase it by lifting the cover, ready to use again. Just before she died, she asked me for the tablet and on it she wrote, "I've had 47 years of marriage with three great children and five grandchildren. I love you all."

I was nearly forty when my term as youth commissioner was up. I still wanted to do public work. The starfish story, corny as it is, I knew was true. Doing work like that isn't just throwing a pebble into the ocean, sending out ripples that get smaller and smaller until they disappear. *These* ripples *grow. One* person who stays in school and graduates: what might she be able to do now, might she be willing to try? What job might he get, and what job after that? Whom might she marry, what kids might he have? What view of the world will they pass on to those kids, and those kids to their kids? These ripples become giant waves. And one of those starfish *is* going to make it. That's what all those biographies and autobiographies tell us. So why not do more?

Women, I'm told, after having their first child, eventually get over their "never again" pain. I decided to get over mine from writing *The Game* by writing another book. I wanted it to be about Canada but seen through a very particular lens. I had thought for some time that if hockey was so tied to things Canadian, by looking at it up close it would tell a bigger, more widely accessible story about the country. Stories about kids and parents and growing up, hopes and dreams, big cities and small towns, stories about how we were, what we are, why we changed, where we're going. The book and the six-part CBC series that went with it were called *Home Game*. It did well. For the first time since I'd finished hockey and school, I could see a pattern and a path to my future. I would choose a subject that mattered to me, immerse myself in it, live it for a year, write about it the next year, publish the book, and repeat. All these years, I'd been asked about my life. Interesting to others, maybe, boring to me. This was my chance to live other lives, just as I'd wanted to do with the "jobs" series I had pitched to CBC. I would do it through writing books.

I decided next I wanted to write about an "average guy." Nobody writes about him, except in fiction. He's too average, too much like everyone else, to be interesting. Yet he, and she, is most of us. Surely we need to know more about them. They are our neighbours, our co-workers, us. Surely marketing people need to know more about them. Surely our politicians do—these are the people they supposedly set policies and make decisions for. But how would I even find this average guy? And what is "average" anyway? Statistically average? I would use statistics as a guide, but I also thought that most of us have in our minds an idea of what average is, someone about whom we say, "He's just an average guy." That's who I wanted to write about. To me, he or she was about forty, married, had at least one child, lived in a suburb, earned an average income, and had a high school education. Needing to make a choice, I decided my subject would be male. I thought I could write that story better. I went in search of a subject.

I contacted someone I knew at Imperial Oil, who got permission from his higher-ups to run employee record checks looking for a person with the background I described. My contact never mentioned any names to me. We talked by phone. When, eventually, he thought the person he saw on his screen might be the right one, he phoned him, told him about the project, and said if he was interested, here was my name and phone number. Which is how I came to meet Frank Bloye.

It turned out we are almost exactly the same age. Frank had grown up in Whitby, about an hour east of Toronto, then a town of about ten thousand. He was the second-youngest of eight children and the youngest boy. His father was a construction materials salesman, his mother a force—in the local Catholic church, in the family, with Frank. The family moved during his high school years to the Toronto suburb of Don Mills, a planned community much like Humber Valley. In school, he was just another kid in class, he didn't do poorly, he didn't do well. He finished grade 13, having taken two extra years to do it, and left with a clear understanding of himself. He wasn't a student, and he wasn't a learner. He got a job at Imperial Oil, did well, got promoted a few times, and continued doing well until, in order to advance to the next level, he would need to take some additional courses. When he saw the assigned books, he thought textbooks, he thought school, he thought learning, and he knew he couldn't learn because he wasn't a learner, hadn't been one in school, and he didn't take the courses.

By the time I got to know him, he was a credit card debt collector. He sat at his cubicle with a headset on, listened to the voices on the other end of the line, and looked at a screen in front of him, at the coded profile of the person he was speaking with. I sat beside him for two weeks as he did his job, with another headset on, looking at the same screen. The people on the other end of the line were anxious, defensive, sometimes aggressive, more often apologetic, and universally worried. Frank was unfailingly patient and polite. For a time, I stayed with him and his wife and their three kids in their small bungalow in Scarborough, as far east of Toronto's downtown as Etobicoke is west. They had a pool in their backyard; it was Frank's pride and joy.

The question was: How did Frank get here from there? Why was he so sure he couldn't learn? Why did he accept the hand that was dealt him? Why did he vote always for one of the always-governing parties? Why didn't he want to shake things up, demand that the deck be reshuffled? Why didn't he want change? History is written by the winners. Autobiographies and biographies are by and about the movers and shakers. I called the book *The Moved and the Shaken*.

It came out just before the federal election in 1993. The Progressive Conservatives had been in government for almost a decade. The public was ready for a change. I wanted to get the book into the hands of the Liberals. If they were going to campaign as they and every party always did—pitching themselves as the friend of the average Canadian—I wanted them to at least have a real average Canadian in mind as they shaped their platform and messages. Don't vote for the other guys, the fat cats, the party of the movers and shakers. Vote for us: *A better shake for the moved and the shaken.*

Nobody picked that up. The book had no effect. It did fine, it was on the bestseller list, but it sold multiples fewer than my other two books, *The Game* and *Home Game*. Some people loved it, some hated it, most didn't know what to make of it. It got a middling review in the *Globe and Mail* and a scathing one in the *Toronto Star*. I received that news on a Saturday morning in Halifax at the beginning of my book tour. I didn't have any events until the following night. I stayed in bed the rest of the day, and most of the next, often with the covers literally over my head. I was crushed.

I dealt with the feelings I had by jumping into my next book. It was 1993 and education was getting more and more attention. The personal and national stake Canadians had in it seemed ever higher. To make it in the future, we had to be a nation of learners. Instead of lobbing grenades from the sidelines at teachers and officials, I thought the debate needed a real-life reference point. A real-life school. I decided to go back to high school for a year, to sit in class day after day as the students did, to try to figure out who was learning, who wasn't, and why. Who was a good teacher, who wasn't, and why. To see what was going on. The school I chose was T.L. Kennedy, in Mississauga.

It may have been the most interesting year of my life. There, right in front of me, inside that public high school, was Canada: Canada of the present, Canada of the future. T.L. Kennedy had just over a thousand students, not much different from ECI in our grade 9 year more than three decades earlier. That, it seemed, was its only similarity. ECI had been a suburban school. Daryl, Ken, and Diana had talked of the open spaces just west of where they lived, where they explored and adventured—those open spaces continued on into Mississauga, and the kids who went to Kennedy in those same years were almost country kids. White kids. Now, at T.L. Kennedy, they were inner-city suburban kids of all different ethnicities.

The lunchroom in a high school is where the whole student population mingles. Except at Kennedy the kids didn't mix. The Sri Lankan kids sat with the Sri Lankan kids, the Jamaican kids with the Jamaican kids, the Hong Kong Chinese kids all together. The Canada that is, the Canada that will be, was right there in front of me. What a disaster. If I had been shooting a TV documentary, there a day or two to get my story and then gone, that's what I would have seen. But after a week or two, after a month, what I saw was different. In classrooms, you can't sit as blocks, you're side by side with who knows who, you might not talk with them, you might not become each other's best friends, but gradually, maybe even without your noticing, it starts to become no big deal that the other person is different. You get more used to difference, less uncomfortable with it. You might even learn something from it. And difference comes to matter less. This was the Canada of the moment, the Canada that might be.

Also right there in front of me in those classrooms were the kids who learned and the kids who didn't. The front-row kids, they were still there. Every day, on time, their homework done, their hands up, asking questions, answering them. So were the back-corner kids, taking in the front of the room as much as they had to, much more interested in each other. Yet it was the big, broad middle of the class that surprised me, which most interested me. The kids who are just there, because they have to be, and who, having to be, had learned how not to be noticed. Weeks and months pass without them ever saying a word. Sitting in class every day, that's what I saw.

For the individual futures of these kids, for the economy of the nation, this was a problem. The book was titled *In School*. That year I realized what I hadn't thought of before. The challenge with an unemployed youth, or a team, or an average guy is the same: How do you reach beyond the front row? (The book's working title, later rejected by the publisher, had been *Beyond the Front Row*.)

I hoped the book would deepen a conversation about education that had already begun in Canada. I was invited to speak at lots of teachers' conferences, and the response was good, but in the end not much changed. I wasn't "getting it done." Before, I had never thought of myself as a hockey player, but rather as someone who played hockey, and not as a lawyer, bureaucrat, or broadcaster, but as someone who had done all three. I'd never thought of myself as a writer, but as someone who writes. But now I was writing more. For a non-writer, I had become a good writer, but it wasn't clear to me whether I was a good writer *as a writer*. In any event, I wasn't as good as I wanted to be. I wasn't having as much of an impact as I wanted to have. I was also about to turn fifty, the age I'd always imagined I'd be when I went into politics. I had learned a lot in the nearly two decades since I retired from hockey, I had done many more things, been tested, challenged, had travelled to every province and territory. I had in me some things I believed about the country and the world, and had become whatever I was. Our daughter was at university outside Canada, our son would soon follow. My leading a life in public needn't limit their lives. I was as ready as I'd ever be to do what I was able to do.

But then I decided I didn't want to go into politics. Not then. Instead, I became president of the Toronto Maple Leafs.

Outside the highest jobs in politics, I thought I could have the most impact here, with this team. Probably the two best-known entities in Canada, not just in sports, were the Leafs and the Montreal Canadiens. Sports is an immense convex mirror. Everything you do in sports is reflected back at you, bigger and more exaggerated. Everything good is more amazing, everything bad more horrible. Until the late 1960s, the Canadiens and Leafs were almost equal in the number of Stanley Cups they had won. Then the Leafs crashed and the Canadiens soared. The Canadiens became the model of doing things right, the Leafs of all things wrong. Models, metaphors, matter. The Leafs needed to become what they should be. I said when I took the job that there were a lot of good teams in the NHL, many that were financially successful, but only two that were truly important: the Canadiens and Leafs. The NHL needed the Leafs to be good. Hockey needed them to be good too.

And the Leafs weren't. Off the ice, financially, they were fine. On the ice in the 1970s, they were pretty good, in the early 1990s better than that. At every other time, and off the ice in every other way, they were a mess. The Leafs needed to act like, and achieve like, one of the two most important hockey franchises in the world. This was the story that had to be written. I wasn't ready at the beginning. It took me a while to help write it.

It had to be a new story. The old glorious one was too many years in the past. And for twenty years, with Harold Ballard as the team's owner, that story had changed. Combative, addicted to the limelight, Ballard refused to be embarrassed when the team lost, he refused to be contrite. He had a need to act like a winner, and if the media and fans went at him, he'd treat them like losers. Win or lose, he said to them again and again, you just can't stop yourselves from filling my rink, you can't stop yourselves from filling my pockets. He laughed in their faces, he mocked them. Win or lose, he said, I still go to the bank.

The relationship between a team and its fans is like that between spouses. You have to give as much as you're given or it doesn't work. If the fans don't show up, the team doesn't need to give much. But if the fans give and give and give, their money, their time, their belief, their hope, their love, the team has to give back in kind. The Leafs fans were givers. The Leafs team were takers. Year after year, and because things didn't get better, they seemed to get worse. The fans didn't believe that the team wanted to win as much as they, the fans, did. So they loved the team, and they hated it.

We became a good team on the ice in the late 1990s and early 2000s. Among Eastern Conference teams only the New Jersey Devils won more playoff rounds; among Canadian teams, none. Off the ice, the Leafs became real and engaged members of the Toronto community. We made it to the conference final twice, but couldn't win the Cup. I loved watching us become good, I loved the spirit that came over the city during the playoffs. I learned, as I had at Cornell and in Montreal, that there's nothing like doing what you're doing where it matters. In Toronto, the Leafs, and hockey, mattered. In 2000, the team hosted the NHL All-Star Game. To end one century and one millennium and to begin another, the game needed to be played in its proper place.

The hardest challenge for me in those years came in the aftermath of an announcement that had been made three months before I began. Martin Kruze had been sexually abused as a youth at Maple Leaf Gardens. The team hadn't known what to do after he had come forward in 1997, and three months later I didn't either. The Catholic Church had floundered for decades to deal with the abuse within its ranks. So had schools, Cubs, Scouts, anywhere where vulnerable kids, or kids who could be made vulnerable, gathered. Each organization wanted not to believe, each wanted to protect itself from untold liability, each wanted the victim, who had often turned to alcohol or drugs in later years, to be the wrongdoer. Sometime that summer Martin Kruze wrote me a letter. The letter was still on my desk in October when he committed suicide.

I knew I had to go to his funeral, but I didn't know if the family would accept me being there. I contacted a family member, and she asked me to come. I remember walking to the church, which wasn't far from Maple Leaf Gardens. I remember the media asking me questions as I went that weren't the right questions for that day and that moment. I remember the sadness of his family and friends, I remember wondering what they were thinking when they saw me, wondering what they'd do. What became clearer and clearer through the service, what should've been clear to me earlier, was that Martin Kruze's father and mother and stepmother and brothers and friends, what they wanted more than anything wasn't revenge on the Leafs or on me as its representative. It was that something a little bit good come out of something so bad. Of course! Why hadn't I thought of that. There was a path now I didn't see before.

We started working with the Kruze family, with the other Gardens abuse survivors and their families, and other survivors as well. We opened Maple Leaf Gardens, and for two days, on the arena floor, in as much of the seating area as we needed, and in some of the rooms and dressing rooms below, community organizations put on information sessions and workshops. There were discussions, private conversations. Psychologists, therapists, and social workers were there in case they were needed. My wife, Lynda, organized it. We called the event Martin's Hope. High school students were bused in, members of the public walked in. The Leafs players participated. Tough guys like Darcy Tucker, who every person there, especially every kid, knew had never in his life been messed with because no one messed with Darcy Tucker, talked about times as a kid when he'd been taken advantage of, bullied, by someone older and stronger at school. One survivor who was there had made sure to tell me a few weeks earlier that he loved me and he hated me. Loved me because I had been his favourite player. Hated me because one morning when the Canadiens were in town and he was hanging around hoping to see us, a Gardens employee told him he could arrange for him to meet me. That was the beginning. I was the hook. Later, his parents bought him some new goalie equipment. Not long after, he threw it in a garbage pail and told them that someone had stolen it.

In those sessions, non-survivors, ordinary members of the public, learned how to protect their own kids. They also began to understand how the unthinkable happens, and how when it does, as with Cheryl, the effect can last and last and last. If the Gardens was where what should never have happened happened, as a message both to the survivors and to the Leafs, the Gardens would be where something a little bit good might happen too.

I began with the Leafs at the same time Wayne was retiring, as Sandie died, as Margaret was moving to the U.S., and Mary, Bruce, and the rest of the teachers were struggling with Mike Harris. Our careers, which were long past their beginnings and which had always seemed long from their ends, now didn't. At the decade's close, we were fifty-three or fifty-four. Soon the teachers would be adding up their numbers—age plus years of teaching, totalling ninety, meant retirement and full pension. For me, playing careers and sports management careers don't last forever. Something would be next.

VII

THE NEW MILLENNIUM

CHAPTER TWENTY-SEVEN

A new century. A new millennium.

Every person's story is a life *and* times. What happens in Canada, in the world, affects the way we as individuals live, the way we think. The way our kids live and think. In our lifetimes, the world, and Canada, had changed a lot.

In 1950, the world's population was 2.6 billion. Fifty years later, in 2000, it was 6.1 billion. Europe's population had increased by about one-third, North America's more than doubled, Asia's, South America's, and Africa's had increased by nearly three times or more. Sixty-one percent of the world's people were living in Asia. The great empires—British, French, Soviet—had disintegrated. The Iron Curtain had gone up and come down. China and India were beginning to stir.

On the other hand, the American Empire of 2000 seemed to be on unsettled ground. It wasn't only because of the Vietnam War and Watergate; it was because of all those things the U.S. had done, and was, inside its borders and outside them, that had made it no longer the America of the world's imagination, or even its own. Economically, militarily, in so many ways, for the U.S. there had always been another frontier, beyond the horizon, within its reach and no one else's. But as it turned out, not every country wanted to be like America, and wars, even small ones in Vietnam and Kuwait, soon in Afghanistan and Iraq, bogged down and ground down its mighty machine and began to take their toll. For the U.S., not every conflict now ended in glory. In 2000, American confidence should have been at its apex. Only a few years earlier the wall had come down and America had won its biggest ever war—the Cold War—over the Soviet Union, over communism, over misguided dictators whose people had been brought to see the light before they did. For the democratic way, the capitalist way, a final and forever victory. The end of history. Except, out from under the Soviet thumb, these countries had no interest in being under the thumb of another, if less malignant, one. They wanted to be different, better versions of themselves. By 2000, America had lost its sense of ceiling-less possibility.

Canada had also changed a lot. In 1951, according to the census, our population was 14 million. In 2000, despite John Largo's forecast in *Maclean's*, it was 30 million. Most provinces and the territories had hardly grown, while Quebec's population had almost doubled in size, Ontario's almost tripled, B.C.'s and Alberta's even more. The biggest growth was in our cities. Calgary was now oil-rich and oil-big, and Edmonton wasn't much smaller. Vancouver was no longer that mountain, ocean, and forest gem on the "left coast," away from Europe, away from exploration, settlement, and development, so cut off by distance, time, and topography as to be almost out of mind. Now it was our big city closest to Asia, and Asian economies were exploding. Canada was becoming a Pacific *and* an Atlantic nation in an increasingly Pacific *and* Atlantic world. Most of our population growth now wasn't from natural increase—births over deaths—but from immigration, and no longer primarily from Europe but, for the first time in our history, from Asia.

In 1951, less than 1 percent of our population had been visible minorities, defined as Canadians, other than Indigenous peoples, who were "non-Caucasian in race or non-white in colour." In 2001, that number was 13.4 percent. In 1951, just 32,528 people in Canada were of Chinese origin; in 2001, they numbered 1,029,395. For those the census described as "East Indian," or later "South Asian," the numbers were 2,148 and 917,075 respectively; for those "Negro," later "Black," 18,020 and 662,215. The most common birth countries of immigrants for almost all of Canada's history had been, in order, the U.K., Italy, Germany, Netherlands, Poland, and the U.S. Between 1991 and 2001, they were China, India, the Philippines, Hong Kong, Sri Lanka, and Pakistan. The Toronto and Canada that my classmates and I were born into had been almost entirely white—of ECI's more than one thousand students, only three had been visible minorities. Now over one-third of Toronto's and Vancouver's population were visible minorities.

Yet the more visible minority Canadians there were, the less *visible* they became. I remember walking down main streets in many of our big cities in the early nineties and I couldn't help but notice people of different nationalities, wearing different clothes. Ten years later, even in smaller towns, no double-takes. This is now just us. We had struggled with racial tensions as the U.S., U.K., France, and other multicultural countries had, but less so, it seemed. Maybe it's because we had always lived with division, English and French, because we'd had to learn to accommodate, because, smaller on the world scene, we'd always had to compromise, get along. Maybe too it was because, just as Canada's immigrants were being changed by Canada, the country was perhaps willing to be changed by them. All of us becoming something different than we'd been, not so much a multicultural mosaic as a *multiculture*, *all* of us with a hand in its making.

As the mix of immigrants to Canada changed, so did the mix of our religions. Throughout our history, astonishingly, the percentage of Catholics in Canada had remained almost the same—43.9 percent in 1871; 43.2 percent in 2001—even as Catholic families had become smaller. The number of Protestants had always been almost identical to that of Catholics, but by 2001 had dropped to less than 30 percent of the country's population. The largest increases were among Muslims, Hindus, Sikhs, and Buddhists, and even more so those who had checked the box for "No religion." In 1971, those accounted for 1 percent; in 2001, 16 percent. Every one of us in our high school class had been Protestant. Now, some of us may have checked "No religion" as well.

There were big changes, too, in how Canadians lived and worked. Between 1951 and 2001, marriage went down, from 64 percent to 49 percent, divorce went up, from 0.3 percent to 8 percent, and separation, not even a census category in 1951, was 3 percent. There were now more single-parent families, even more common-law families, and same-sex couples, a category that had also never been measured, now made up 0.5 percent of all couples. We lived more often in cities and worked city jobs. Twenty percent of Canadians now worked in manufacturing and construction, only 5 percent in agriculture. In 1951, the top five occupations for men had been farmers and stock raisers, labourers, farm labourers, office clerks, and truck drivers. Now only truck drivers still made it into the top five. For women in 2001, it was sales, as it had been office work in 1951—stenos and typists—and the number of child care workers had now risen sharply. So too had the percentage in computer-related jobs, for both men and women but particularly for men—analysts, programmers, software writers, website developers. The largest area of growth came under one category—no matter the field, it seemed everyone wanted to be, and to be called, a "manager." As for the jobs we had worked after university, many fewer Canadians now wanted to be teachers or nurses— just as Pat, Judy Tibert, Judy Clarke, Lisa, Cheryl, Joan Boody, Bruce, Mary, and Penni were soon to retire. (On the other hand, hockey was a growth field. In 1951, the NHL had six teams, only two in Canada; in 2001, of its thirty teams, seven were in Canada.)

But the two biggest changes in these fifty years, in our lifetimes, were in the growth of what the census called "highly skilled occupations," those that required a university education, and also in the number of women in the workplace. Our mothers had worked until they got married, usually in their early to mid-twenties. As a result, in 1951, only 24 percent of women over the age of fifteen were "gainfully employed." Fifty years later, that number was 60.5 percent. This was reflected in our own class's experience. Almost all the women in our high school class had left the workplace to have children, returned, and, now in their fifties, were still working. When we were growing up, only Daryl's and Cheryl's mothers were working at that age. In fact, in 2001, women made up 46.7 percent of the *entire* labour force, men 53.3 percent, and the number of women working was growing more than twice as fast as that for men. And, inconceivable when we were born, more women than men were now university and college graduates. This was also us. *Every* woman in our high school class graduated from university; not every man did.

Canada had changed a lot in non-statistical ways as well. The country felt different in 2000 than it had in 1950. In 1950, we were five years into a postwar world. There was the bomb, and Korea, and Cold War sabre-rattling, World War III was still a threat, but war was no longer at the centre of life. Nor had economic depression returned. Everything in the thirties and forties had been so urgent, so focused on getting through the moment. In the fifties, as if emerging from a long, long tunnel and suddenly bursting out into the open, there were possibilities everywhere.

But Canada in 2000, though we were so much better off in so many respects, didn't feel that way. Lister Sinclair's "Age of Science" had first turned into the "Age of the Common Man." More of us had become richer, better educated, and lived longer in nicer homes. The Toronto subway *had* been built, so too the St. Lawrence Seaway, and the bridge across the Strait of Canso, and TV did arrive, even in colour. But on Saturday, January 1, 2000, no voice in Ottawa spoke to the nation and said, "The 21st century . . . belongs to Canada," as Largo had imagined. In 1950, Canada was the thirtieth-biggest country in the world by population, ahead of South Africa, Democratic Republic of Congo, and Colombia. In 2000, though our population had doubled, we were the thirty-sixth-biggest, now behind South Africa, Democratic Republic of Congo, and Colombia. By almost every standard, we were better off than those countries, but after all these decades of growth, after all our possibilities, with a landmass unmatched by any country in the world except Russia, our ads didn't talk about "Canada Unlimited"

anymore. Our corporate messages didn't look to ride the coattails of
the country. We were never going to be *that* big, and now we knew it.
No longer the Age of Science or even of the Common Man, this was
the Age of Globalization. And in a global world, no country can dominate the world economically or militarily. Nobody, not even the U.S.,
can be the big guy. As the world had become smaller, it had become
a bigger presence in our lives, and Canada had come to seem smaller
still. In 1950, as a country, it had seemed we were what we were *going
to be*. In 2000, we were what we were.

As individuals, we had also changed a lot in these five decades.
We were in our fifties. We were married or not likely to be, divorced
or not likely to be, had kids or wouldn't. We were working where we
were going to be working for the rest of our working lives, living where
we were going to be living. It's not that things couldn't change—they
could—but it would take so much to change them. There would be
so many complications if they did change, if we tried. Something else
might be nicer but would bring with it too many unknowns. *This is
the life I have*, we thought. *I can live it. I can live it again tomorrow, and
maybe live it better. And that's not nothing.*

And how would things be different anyway? As Canadians, we
tried optimism and energy in the early postwar years, government and
a rising tide for all in the fifties, love and peace in the sixties, skepti-
cism and doubt in the seventies, business in the eighties and nineties.
Then, finding nothing bigger to believe in, we turned to ourselves,
individually, as the instruments of our own well-being. And who knew
where that would end up.

In those years before 2000, it seemed we were somewhere, we
were something, we had ideas in mind of what we might do, who
we might be. And now here we were. It was possible that now we were
exactly where we'd wanted to be, on the way to exactly where we'd
like to be—but probably not. We all have regrets, personal and otherwise. We all have our little dreams, as individuals, as Canadians, for
ourselves, for Canada—*If I do this, then that could happen, then maybe
this other* . . . But whereas there'd always been lots of time and lots of

opportunities for those dreams to be realized, there was less time now, and not so many opportunities.

We also knew people now who had had their lives turned upside down by illness. Others who'd lost their jobs, or were passed over for better ones because of age. That was different from before. Also different was where our own kids now fit in. In this new century, Lisa has a daughter who is thirty-three, Daryl a son who is two. Lisa also has a newborn granddaughter. I'm not sure many of us thought much about parenthood when we were young. Maybe most, like me, just assumed it would happen someday. We had grown up with a model of what a family was within our own families, what a mother and a father, and parents, should be. Some of us thought we had good models, some thought we had bad. Once we became fathers and mothers ourselves, sometimes we realized we were wrong about the good *and* the bad.

But right or wrong, for most of us, I think, what it was like to be a parent was a surprise. We just didn't know. Whether it was better or nicer or worse than we'd imagined, it was harder. It had been pretty straightforward at the beginning—here is someone to love, to care for, to make happy and healthy, and not a lot of that has to do with them and a lot has to do with us. As they got older, more *did* have to do with them, and with their teachers, leaders, coaches, friends. Less was in our hands. It also got harder for us not to see when things weren't right, harder not to think about what that might mean. Our kids began to look like grown-up people, still young enough that however and whatever they were and were doing, with a little effort, a special teacher, a wiser path, just by being older, just by the light going on, tomorrow could be, would be, better. But also, at the same time, old enough that we could now see in them their twenty-year-old and fifty-year-old selves, and a path that would be hard to change.

My classmates and I had lived busy lives in childhood. We had school, church, Scouts, Guides, teams, camps. To our parents, we and they seemed to be running from one to the next. It wasn't easy, but all of the pieces were meant to fit together and they did: school on weekdays, everything else after school, or on weekends, or during the summer. You couldn't go to school or play hockey in summer, or play baseball or go to camp in winter. They simply weren't offered. That changed for our kids. Now our kids and grandkids could play hockey or baseball and go to school and take courses all year round. In fact, to be good at them by today's standards, as good as they could be—the obligation of every parent to their kids—they had to, because everyone else was, and because the future was a competitive, unforgiving place. Childhood to us as parents now seemed a very complicated time, and just as our parents never shook off understandings that had been hardened by depression and war, we never shook off images of play, free time, and bike rides to who knows where. So our kids took lessons because lessons were there to take and that's what kids did, and as parents we hoped for some kind of sweet spot between raising a prodigy and raising a kid, hoped that somehow we'd find it, all the time worrying about what it would mean if we didn't.

By 2000, almost all our kids were on their way to or attending university or had graduated. For us as parents, we expected that the challenge of childhood would soon be over, our kids would soon be on their own. Instead, things got more complicated. What should they study? What would they do? Canada was going to be a very different place, the world even more so. For our kids, everything would be so much harder. We were the baby boomers, a historically privileged cohort. Jobs, homes in the suburbs, and university educations that most could afford, it had all been there for us. As for our kids, they were smart, we knew that, even thoughtful and capable at times, but they could also be head-shakingly irresponsible at times—we knew that too—and the world was tough. Soon they would be out of reach to us. With absolute clarity, we now knew what we hadn't known when we were their age. We knew this was a pivotal time for them—what job they took, whom they married or didn't mattered. (And good luck to us.)

Then they surprised us. Many didn't move away for university, and many who did came back. It was like that across the country.

In 2001 almost one-quarter of twenty-five- to twenty-nine-year-olds were still living at home, more than double the number of twenty years earlier. The cost of housing had skyrocketed, unemployment—youth unemployment especially—was high following the recession of the early 1990s. But mostly our kids were home because they were staying in school longer. Fifty years earlier, only 5 percent of kids between twenty and twenty-five had even attended university, let alone graduated—this was our parents' story. Fifty years later, in 2001, 28 percent of those between twenty-five and thirty-four—our kids' story—had *graduated* from university and 21 percent from college. They stayed longer because it's what society wanted, and what they wanted, and what we wanted, and so each of us adapted. Jobs were now harder to get, especially those that, to their parents (us) and to them, seemed the only ones appropriate to have after all the years they had put into school. In fact, better that our sons and daughters give themselves an even better chance by taking a few *more* courses, maybe getting a master's. Which all sounds very responsible, in fact, even wise. Keep pushing the future ahead. It's only failure if you try to get the job you want, and don't.

To support this life, more young adults had to keep living at home, which was often . . . awkward. Many in our class lived this experience. As parents, we tried to love that our kids were back, pretended to be bothered that they were, and weren't really quite sure. Before, we had lived as one family. Now, could two different stages of adulthood be accommodated under the same roof? Under whose rules? With this new life reality came a feeling that never quite went away: success for our kids—for us as parents, as it had been for our own parents—meant five (or four) years of high school without interruption, graduation, four years of university without interruption, graduation, a job, a place of their own, a life of their own. Anything else was failure, no matter that norms and economic realities had changed. Yet as parents with our kids still at home, try as we did, it was tough not to feel at least some failure, and tough for us not to make our kids feel at least a little like failures, which made living together often less fun. Which cast a shadow over the good, other years of their childhood and ours as parents, and over us as a family.

Once in the workplace, besides what the census told us, what jobs would our kids, especially our daughters, do? Would they do as their mothers had done—much as their own mothers had done, those who hadn't become secretaries—and be teachers and nurses, one generation with high school diplomas, the other with university degrees? Or would they become doctors instead of nurses, business executives instead of teachers? As parents, what did we expect of them? What did we put in their heads? How would we insist they be treated? They had the ability and training to do *anything*. No one had *any* right to stop them, to slow them down, to keep them from imagining and dreaming and being what they had in them to be, what *they* wanted to be. Yet because peak-achieving years coincide with peak child-bearing and child-raising years, what effect would biology continue to have on this? Our daughters were about to find out.

Much of how we felt in 2000, how our ECI class and our generation felt about the world and felt about Canada, depended on what the future of our daughters and sons would be.

CHAPTER TWENTY-EIGHT

Some big personal changes were still ahead for those from our class. First of all, Bruce.

In 2001, at fifty-three, Bruce retired as a math teacher, volleyball coach, and local rep for the teachers' union. He was still calling bingo, helping the local ambulance service, and doing whatever a small town needs done and doesn't have the resources to pay for. The kids were grown up and gone. He and Marion had sold their house. They knew that someday it would be too big for them, and its stairs would be too much, so years before they had to they moved into a smaller, single-storey home. They also had their cottage, which wasn't far away. It was pretty basic, but when their kids and grandkids returned for visits they could camp out there and make do. They were all good at that.

It was now 2009. Bruce and Marion had never had a lot of money. They had two kids, and kids of their generation were more expensive to raise—Bruce's university tuition had been about $400 dollars a year, and for his kids it was *$6,000* or more, and there was room and board for them if they went away, and living where they did, every university was "away," and who was going to pay for that? Still, on his teacher's salary, and Marion's as a social worker, they had enough to live the way they wanted to live, and in retirement Bruce had his teacher's pension, which was generous, not much less than his salary, and he also made a little extra money refereeing volleyball games.

His only real extravagance was the lottery tickets he bought with four of his teacher friends before he retired, and then by himself. Once they had won $2,000, which, split five ways, they said jokingly, was their retirement fund. Bruce kept buying tickets afterwards because he couldn't bear the thought of his buddies winning someday with number combinations he had come up with, or so he liked to say. He bought twenty-six weeks' worth of tickets at a time, two dollars for each ticket, two tickets a week, $208 a year, though as he preferred to think of it, $104 twice a year.

On Monday, June 29, 2009, he got the call. His numbers were 5, 15, 28, 31, 32, 45. The payoff: $4,184,965. And no five-way split.

On Friday, he and Marion took the train to Toronto. They walked into the lottery office, the people checked his ticket, made sure he was who he said he was, and handed him the cheque. He and Marion walked down the street to the nearest branch of his bank—he'd researched that ahead of time and notified the manager to expect him—deposited the cheque, and took the train home. Business class.

For Bruce, this win was life-transforming, and it wasn't. He was sixty-two years old. He'd had a lifetime of understandings and expectations drummed into him, by his parents, his teachers, his wife and kids and friends, by the students he taught and coached and refereed. From everything he'd experienced and learned himself. He was Bruce. What do you do when suddenly you're now four-times-a-millionaire Bruce—besides buy two business-class train tickets?

The first thing he did was pay off their debts. Then he bought the car he'd always wanted—a Lexus. More than $4 million to go. Marion retired. Otherwise, things didn't change that much for him, for them, things were just nicer. They spent four weeks in Portugal—they had never been away that long before. Later, they went to Scotland, England, and Wales, to Australia, to California in the wintertime, to Hong Kong several times when their son and his wife were living there. But the biggest part of nicer for him—the pressure was now off. At least financially.

He did have new feelings he had to live with. He couldn't get out of his mind that he hadn't exactly earned his windfall. There was no genius to his formula of numbers—a mix of family birthdays and other numbers that Bruce, the math teacher, describes as "mathematically significant," with some random numbers that had no pattern or connection to anything. Really, it had just been plain, old-fashioned "dumb luck," as he put it. He was a math teacher, for heaven's sakes. He had done the calculation. His odds of winning: 13.9 million to one! He came to say to people that with those odds he was glad he wasn't still teaching and having to explain to his Statistics and Probability students what kind of idiot would put down his money on something as nonsensical as this. He also came to feel a little pressure of a different kind, because coming this late in life when he should know well enough, he knew he had no right to blow it, and had no interest in being anybody's cautionary tale if he did.

Still, it was nice. He didn't need to worry anymore about most of the big things that can happen and send life into a spiral. He had been diagnosed with a serious illness less than two months before his lottery win. With his win, he knew he could now handle the money burdens of any end-of-life care for himself and Marion. And having the money, he didn't have to think about many other things he didn't want to have to think about. He could even buy lottery tickets. He could play golf—terribly, as it turned out, so maybe that one wasn't such a blessing. And he could actually buy that cottage he'd had his eye on, on the Rideau Canal. The cottage they had was small, accessible only by water, powered by propane they had to carry in and by a solar panel on its roof. It had a composting toilet. This one had electricity and a bathroom, and they could drive to it. Plus, it was beautiful. As Bruce says, it's "my happy place."

His sixty-two years had grounded him. He wouldn't let himself go off the deep end. Yet more than anything else, what winning the lottery did was give him the peace of mind to realize all the things he is lucky about.

—

Joan Boody also retired from teaching in 2001, but she didn't win the lottery. She and her husband, Gus, decided to open a B&B.

Every year Joan and Gus would go to the Shaw Festival, in Niagara-on-the-Lake. It was June, they were walking down the main street just before a performance or just after. It was a beautiful day. In the front window of a real estate office, they saw some pictures and thought, *what the heck*, went in, and inquired. By October, they were living in Niagara-on-the-Lake in a "perfect house" with cedar siding, a cedar shake roof, and gables. When the town's visitor season opened again in April, they welcomed their first guest. They called their place—what else—Cedar Gables.

Happily Joan, as the proprietor, was no Basil Fawlty, Gus no Sybil, and Cedar Gables wasn't big enough to afford a Polly or Manuel. It was just the two of them, and with Gus still working, mostly it was Joan who ran the B&B. The experience was not entirely what she'd expected. The town really was beautiful, the festival really was great, its productions routinely professional, all of which provided a completely reliable, year-after-year pipeline of guests. For many visitors, the town and the festival were the destination for an annual pilgrimage. The other B&B owners were also welcoming to them. They wanted the festival to grow even more, and for Niagara-on-the-Lake to be more than the festival. The town had few hotels, and they were expensive, it needed more B&Bs for everyone to succeed, so they supported each other. Joan also enjoyed being with people, and at Cedar Gables her guests might be from anywhere. They would sit at the communal tables in the breakfast room and talk with each other, and she could talk with them. She loved to travel, in winter she and Gus could do that, and the rest of the year the world could travel to her. And it was like this, and it wasn't.

They had three guest rooms and turned the downstairs into their own living quarters. Their guests were on vacation, so Joan didn't serve breakfast until nine. She was in the kitchen by six thirty, getting the cereals, juices, and yogurt ready, baking muffins and one hot dish a day, waffles, pancakes, quiche, eggs in all different forms. She'd talk with those who came down early—her kitchen door always open. By ten, breakfast was done, then cleanup, her guests checked out by noon, the rooms needing to be made up and ready by three for the new guests. There was also always someone looking for her guidance on the best places to see and eat in the area and the best routes to get there. Cedar Gables was never going to be fancy, but it was comfortable and nice, and Joan decided that she would think of everyone who stayed there as a guest in her home, that she was sharing it *with* them, and she wanted her guests to feel the same way. At times, they took her message a little too literally.

Once she woke up in the middle of the night to the smell of toast. She went to the kitchen and there was this very elderly man making toast (my home is your home). He told her that he'd had to search high and low to find the peanut butter. Joan took a deep breath, thought of how this might be her dad, and cut him a little slack. Another time, she and Gus, returning home from the theatre, found two of their female guests sitting in the living room. Having been unable to work the key to their room door, they had found the liquor cabinet. But most of her surprises were good ones. In time, she also came to learn some of the tricks of the trade—such as to close one day a week or else you never get a break. But as Niagara-on-the-Lake became more than a festival town, and more regular vacationers arrived at her door, with regular-vacationers' expectations that they could arrive anytime, eat anytime, and treat the help (her) as an invisible presence unless they needed something, all the time expecting a cozy, homey B&B experience, it ground her down. Happy she had done what she'd always imagined doing, after six years she was happy to stop.

Kathy McNab was still going. She had gone north when she was twenty-one, when young people in the north her age were going south. And why wouldn't they, and why would she? The north was definitely where it *wasn't* happening, and Toronto was where it was. Thanks to her father's job—his maps, his roads and highways, his stories—she had grown up with an awareness of the north no one else in our class had. To us, "the north" was a couple of hours away, Muskoka, Bracebridge, Huntsville, the Kawarthas. It was lake country, family cottages, summer camps. In our minds and imaginations, it extended to more distant places only through Robert Service, Jack London, and the Group of Seven, through stories of the fur trade, through Frobisher, Hudson, Franklin, and the search for the Northwest Passage. But in our real lives, the north pretty much stopped at Parry Sound. North Bay, another hour and a half farther, was too far. Sudbury was even farther.

Sudbury held a different place in our southern Ontario imaginations. It was mining country. Nickel, INCO, the Superstack, more than a thousand feet higher than the next-tallest structure in the city—*Isn't that the one that they built so high not to reduce its emissions but to spread them out over a bigger area? Ha ha.* Southern (Ontario) humour. Sudbury was its blighted landscape—*Isn't that where the Apollo astronauts trained, because its terrain was most like the moon? Ha ha.* To us, it was where people lived because someone had to get the stuff out of the ground. Probably nobody in our ECI class had ever been to Sudbury, unless they'd passed through it on their way west by road or rail. And why would they? In winter, it could be punishingly cold. Ten below is one thing, twenty below another.

But Kathy had gone there, and except for part of a year spent on the east coast of Vancouver Island in the mid-1980s, she has been there ever since. She went because she met her future husband, Bert, one summer at the Faculty of Education at Queen's, and Bert and a few generations of his family were from Sudbury and nearby. In Sudbury, she taught phys ed and coached some of the high school teams. Bert was a teacher, later a principal. Their jobs took them into the community, as did their involvement in their church. She worked as an on-air summer replacement at the city's CBC Radio affiliate, she edited academic works on outdoor education, social work, nursing, and Sudbury's labour history. She taught part-time in Laurentian University's History Department. She helped professors develop distance learning courses on subjects as varied as the women's movement, philosophy, nursing, and earth sciences, and worked with the university, the Canadian International Development Agency, and the University of Mauritius to bring distance learning, so crucial to the north, to Mauritius's far-flung islands in the Indian Ocean. She became immersed in all things Sudbury. She also worked as a photo editor on a bicentennial commemoration of the province's Ministry of Northern Affairs, a book entitled *A Vast and Magnificent Land: An Illustrated History of Northern Ontario*. It was a project that meant a lot to her because it expressed what she had come to feel and know. In the midst of all this, she and Bert had a daughter in 1981 and a son in 1986. But by this time, Sudbury was struggling.

By Toronto standards, Sudbury isn't much more than a blip on one of Kathy's father's maps. Yet it is the largest city in Ontario's north, with more people than North Bay, Sault Ste. Marie, or Thunder Bay. Ontario is *immense*. Not everything can be or should be run out of Toronto, not in government, business, health care, or education. Some place needs to be the local hub. A hub needs a university. Federal, provincial, and municipal governments need offices and people to fill them. Goods have to be distributed across the region, so there need to be service and distribution centres. People in smaller towns need to go somewhere to shop, to be entertained, to have some weekend fun. Shopping malls, a symphony, a Junior A hockey team, English and French theatres have to be somewhere. Sudbury became that place.

But in Sudbury, the underpinning of everything was mining. What happens, then, when mining shrinks? Would Sudbury become West Virginia or Wales? Sudbury had provided 80 percent of the world's nickel in 1915; by 1982, that was only 10 percent. In those years, extraction technologies had improved, metal prices had pinballed around, and global competition had increased dramatically. Employment in Sudbury was down. There were environmental problems too. Between 1971 and 1981, only a very few Canadian cities or suburbs shrunk in population, and Sudbury was one of them. Its story was a familiar one. A one-industry town, which for one reason or another—a resource runs out, increased competition, higher costs, a product that's had its day—begins to lose population, and with it its tax base, its infrastructure breaks down, then its spirit, until it continues to exist only because it does exist. Sudbury was on that path.

But there was one other big fact of Sudbury's life. Sudbury *is* good at mining. It is *expert* at it. It has bigger economic and environmental problems because it is bigger. Its answers would be harder to find, and Sudbury would need to work harder to find them, but if it did find them, it could pass on those answers to other mining towns, and there are mines and mining towns all over the world and always will be. Sudbury had a story to tell: it had made its mines more productive—here's how. Sudbury had reclaimed much of the land it had destroyed—here's how. The result: people from outside Canada and from across the country began to come to the city to learn, to its universities and colleges, to the Mineral Exploration Research Centre, the Centre for Excellence in Mining Innovation, the Northern Centre for Advanced Technology. And because it was now a centre of science, it built a science centre, Science North. Again those in the south who had never been to Sudbury laughed—*Sudbury, a place where people go to visit? Ha ha.*

Sudbury had to think of itself not as what it isn't, but as what it is, in every way. To make itself, in the world of mining in the broadest sense, too essential to fail. Most of the boom towns of our childhood, of our "Canada Unlimited" years—Arvida, Kitimat—are gone or going. Sudbury's still standing.

Kathy had reasons to go there, to be there, then more reasons. One thing led to the next. One year led to the next. Life happened.

CHAPTER TWENTY-NINE

In the 1990s, Murray's career in health care, and Gord's in business and finance, found new directions but continued mostly along the paths they had created. In the 2000s, for them, new interests took on more importance.

At Mount Sinai Hospital, Murray had a great job at a great place at a great time. The city was growing in size, status, wealth, and ambition. As the 1980s were ending, Murray's forties were beginning. If he was to move on to something else, this was the time. A friend, the head of North York General Hospital, told Murray he was leaving and suggested he apply for the job.

North York was the biggest of all Toronto's suburbs. It was similar to Etobicoke and Scarborough in the look of its houses and subdivisions, outdoor malls, low-slung apartments, factories and commercial buildings, nothing high enough or imposing enough to break the vista of sprawl. But if Toronto was growing, and its downtown couldn't accommodate the traffic of people and cars from all these suburbs and beyond, why not build another downtown, in North York?

North York's mayor at the time was Mel Lastman. Like my father and other fathers in our class, Lastman was a salesman. He had a chain of appliance stores he called Bad Boy, and in newspaper ads and TV commercials, dressed in black-and-white-striped prison-like garb, he was the "Bad Boy," loud, outrageous, the guy who was willing to undercut his competitors to give Torontonians the great, straight deal they deserved. To some, he was extremely funny, to others excruciatingly annoying. In other words, he was made for politics. By the time Murray arrived at North York General in 1989, Lastman had been mayor for sixteen years. The product he was selling was the *City* of North York.

To be a city, you need presence. You need high-rise buildings along your main thoroughfare for company head offices and big government departments. You need an imposing library, an arts centre, a central square with trees and gardens, a fountain, with a pool for summer that converts to a rink in winter. And you need an attitude: Toronto? Forget it! It's all built up, it has no room for new stadiums or arenas, Olympics or World's Fairs, or a papal mass for hundreds of thousands. *C'mon up here, we'll treat ya right*. A city also needs a big hospital, something that makes you proud. North York already did have a hospital, but not one befitting *this* North York.

It wasn't an easy decision for Murray to leave Mount Sinai. For sixteen years he'd been surrounded by lots of really talented people doing really exciting work, and Mount Sinai was in downtown Toronto, on University Avenue, on "hospital row," where major world-class hospitals are supposed to be. North York General was twenty kilometres and a million miles away. But, in 1989, Mount Sinai, a major Jewish institution, wasn't likely to hire a non-Jew to its top position.

It turned out to be a good time for North York General, in a way Murray didn't expect. The nineties were not the seventies. Then you dreamed dreams, now you lived realities. Governments were cutting back. In Ontario, Bob Rae's NDP government was constrained by economic downturns and deficit upturns. After Rae, Mike Harris's government by its own ideology. It said to voters that governments were taking too much of their hard-earned money and didn't have the instinct and drive or the efficiency and excellence citizens deserved.

Because Harris believed government *in general* was bad, not necessarily this part or that, cuts needed to be made across the board, including in health care, despite the fact that no fewer people got cancer, no fewer went to Emerg. The Harris government knew that for real cuts to happen in health care, the focus had to be on hospitals, because they spent the most money and as large institutions surely there were lots of efficiencies to be found. Some hospitals would need to be closed, others should join together. To Harris, this wouldn't be about cutting services—the public would never accept that—this it was about delivering those services smarter, better. Sure, the changes would cause immense disruption, but after decades of a status quo that had only brought about these problems, the government *wanted* to disrupt, shake things up a bit, just as it had done with the teachers. Hospitals, being at the centre of the health care system, established and highly respected, would be the hardest to disrupt, even if that were necessary. The big questions: How would it be done? And could the public and the health care sector trust those who were doing it?

Could we trust their motives? What was their real agenda? Canadians love, and hate, and mostly love our health care system. We are proud of its story. In 2004, in a CBC contest, the founding father of universal health care in this country, Saskatchewan premier Tommy Douglas, was named our "Greatest Canadian." We love that we have a health care system, that we did it, and that Americans don't and didn't. So when we hear the words "amalgamation," "restructuring," and "efficiency," especially when Conservative governments say them, we look down and count our fingers. What did Harris have in mind?

Some hospitals did need to come together, but from what the government was doing and the way they were doing it, Murray had no doubt about Harris's intent. "They were thinking, *Let's see how much we can reorganize hospitals and the hospital sector of health care in order to save money.* They were talking about saving money," Murray recalls. Which can be a good thing; disruption can be useful. The question is: Disrupt for what? To become what? "The problem was they had no vision of what an ideal type of health care system could look like," Murray says. "If they had taken a much broader vision of health care, if they had taken the Scandinavian model and focused not just on the provision of health care but on health in society generally, on the broad determinants of health, and put housing and social services into the mix, and tried to reorganize around primary care, that would have caused disruption too, and maybe more, but it would have been worth it." But they didn't.

Murray didn't have a vision for North York General, either, when he started. The hospital had about 3,400 staff, 900 physicians, and 1,200 volunteers—not much different than Toronto's big downtown hospitals, and Murray knew about big hospitals. But one thing stunned him: the number of patients NYG saw. "At Toronto General, there were about 30,000 visits in their Emerg each year, Mount Sinai slightly less, SickKids about 35,000. At North York, 115,000." This one fact made everything different. Who were all these people? What were they there for? What needs did they have? How could the hospital help them? Mount Sinai, SickKids, and Toronto General were amazing resources for people from all over Toronto, all over Ontario, even from other parts of Canada. North York General was a *community* hospital—as much like regional community hospitals in non-urban parts of Ontario as it was like the big guys downtown. It was a big community hospital for a big community. If most people, most of the time, need primary care, Murray believed, give them primary care, much of which can be handled by nurses or other health care providers, by social workers rather than doctors, by family physicians rather than surgeons. For Murray, here was the beginning of a vision.

Then, lo and behold, another discovery. North York General was a teaching hospital. Most of its staff had academic appointments at U of T. But just as their experience as doctors at NYG was somewhat different from those in the downtown hospitals, so too was their view of how health care could be and should be provided, which was part of the reason they had come to NYG in the first place, and which view was reflected in whom and how they taught. "By the early nineties," Murray recalls, "well over a thousand students went through North York General every year. We were a community teaching hospital but with a totally different model of care," teaching students who would then go out into the world to meet increasingly primary care needs.

The patients they were seeing at NYG were also different. The hospital stood at the junction of highways 401 and 404, two of the city's main arteries. A million and a half people lived within a twenty-minute drive of the hospital, and a lot more in fast-growing areas to the north and east, among them a large Muslim community and an even larger Chinese one. And among those communities were community leaders, high-achieving, highly respected, sometimes high-wealth individuals who were perfect candidates for the hospital's board and committees. Government money had gotten tighter; private giving now mattered more. "We were *their* hospital," Murray said. When he had left Mount Sinai for NYG in 1989, "Both in numbers and in terms of who Toronto was at that point, I went where the people were."

He was forty-two when he arrived. He was now fifty-five.

In the early 2000s, Murray attended a meeting of hospital presidents at which Stephen Lewis, Canada's former ambassador to the UN and at the time the UN's special envoy for HIV/AIDS in Africa, gave the address. A powerful, evangelical speaker, he appealed to an instinct he knew was there in his audience and challenged them: health care is about helping people, whoever they are, wherever they live, Lewis said. And at that time, one of the world's great needs had to do with Africa and HIV/AIDS.

At another time in his life, Murray might not have taken Lewis's challenge so personally, but North York General was now on a better path. It was on its way to being the big, important community hospital the Greater Toronto Area needed it to be, and feeling a little burned out after thirteen years, he was looking for new fascinations and new energy. He'd always talked about the value of public service, saying those two words not as a politician might, where they slide off the tongue and slide past the ear, but instead stressing each word and both together—*public service*. All his life he'd also heard the maxim

"To whom much is given, much will be required." He had said it often to his own kids, and meant it—he had been given a lot—and believed it. He had enough money now, he had a nice life, the kids were off, here was the test. Did he believe *enough* to do something?

Southern Africa had been hit the hardest by HIV/AIDS, and South Africa, Botswana, and Lesotho were the most affected countries. Murray and a group of other hospital presidents decided to focus on Lesotho. Funding was an issue, and they would need to cobble something together—from government, private donors, foundations, non-profit organizations—but they were well connected and had a powerful story to tell. They would need medical staff, nurses, pharmacists, and the support of the hospitals they worked in to grant them leaves of absence for a few months. Yet, still, there remained needs in their own hospitals, in their communities, and while it was easy to explain their desire to do something, it was much harder to justify taking resources from the system to enable them to do it. But as the head of the provincial nurses' association put it at the time, "Charity begins at home, but it doesn't end there." More than that, Murray and his group, and the hospitals and health care workers, knew that they would come back changed. This wasn't a vacation, it was about the furthest thing from it, but it was a break, the break of a lifetime. They would return better doctors and better people, with renewed pride and a fresh belief, in mid-career when they most needed it, that what they do matters.

Murray was involved for six years in the Lesotho project. It didn't take up all of his time, but a lot of it. For those in Lesotho involved in health care, and for the Lesotho people, this was a different kind of medicine, more urgent and immediate: if you've got a problem you solve it, and you solve it today. And finally they had the chance to do that. HIV/AIDS medicines had improved a lot in the previous years, and now, with more people and more resources, and being better organized, and seeing more people, in even more remote parts of the country, and treating them, and following up with them and their families in a more rigorous, systematic way, infection and death rates fell significantly. Murray was sixty-one.

—

After nineteen years at Wood Gundy and CIBC Wood Gundy, in 1990 Gord had left and started his own business as a consultant and advisor. It was a major change of life. In a big organization, working with clients, he was used to saying, *we* can do this, *we* can do that, then going back to the office and seeing that it was done. If there was something he didn't quite know, he had people around him who might know better and would help him find the answer he needed. Now it was just him and a secretary in an office in his house. Now if he said *we* can do it, he had to do it himself. "When you're on your own, you're talking to yourself," he said. Soon he decided to get some office space downtown.

What eased him through this transition were two big clients that he'd had almost from the first day he opened his doors. One was Bell Canada Enterprises. BCE had sold 50 percent of its real estate holdings to Brascan-Edper, which only a few years earlier had provided Wood Gundy with the financing that had allowed it to survive. As part of its deal with Brascan, BCE also agreed to manage all of the properties involved. But when the recession of the early 1990s hit and the real estate business suddenly got more complicated, BCE hired Gord to manage its interests in Toronto.

Gord's other big client was the government of Ontario. It hired him to help with the sale of the SkyDome (now the Rogers Centre), the home of the Toronto Blue Jays. The stadium had gotten built initially only through the complicated participation of many different parties—the city put up some money; the federal government provided the land through CN; there was money from the sale of concession rights and from contracts for Skyboxes and club seats—but the Province of Ontario owned the building itself, which meant that if there were any cost overruns, Ontario would be left holding a very expensive bag. Bob Rae's government had just been elected, and as the first NDP government in Ontario's history, it had things to prove, campaign promises to fulfill, and a rising deficit to cope with.

Across the table from Gord as the prospective buyer was a group led again by Brascan-Edper. The parties took six or seven months to negotiate a deal, and expected to take two or three months more to close it, except there were complications. There was a *draft* lease for the land under the SkyDome, but the lease had never been executed; there were memos and notes about easements with the city, but again, no legal document. McDonald's was the quick-service food provider, somebody else the full-service food provider, but there was no final contract that defined where quick-service ended and full-service began. These two or three months turned into two years. There were also problems on the revenue side. What the buyers were buying was less than what everyone thought was there. The result: a stadium that had been projected to cost $300 million, and which in fact cost over $600 million to build, sold for about $150 million.

Gord's work for BCE and on SkyDome carried him through the first few years he was on his own. He added other projects as he went along. He gave expert witness testimony for Imperial Oil on a legal problem, offered advice to AGF, Sherritt, and others on potential acquisitions. He also worked on some bigger contracts. The provincial government owned 25 percent of Suncor, the rest of it owned by Sun Company in the U.S., and it was seeking advice on whether to keep its share or sell it. The government hired Gord, and after it decided to take Suncor public, asked him to handle the sale. On and off, this all took a few years. Later in the 1990s, the new Harris government, seeing increased deregulation in the electricity sector in the U.S., hired Gord to advise it. Huge sums of money were involved, a lot was at stake for the province, Ontario Hydro, and investors. More years passed. By the time Ontario Hydro was finally restructured, into Hydro One and Ontario Power Generation, Gord had come to some conclusions of his own. He could see clearly now the limits of working by himself. He decided to put his own business to one side and become deputy chairman of Scotia Capital, the investment and corporate banking arm of Scotiabank.

At Scotiabank and Scotia Capital, his first few years were dominated by talk about mergers. As business was becoming even more global, the world's banks were growing larger. In merger discussions, the question was, were Canadian banks big enough to compete? The Royal Bank lined itself up with the Bank of Montreal, and the Toronto-Dominion Bank with CIBC, leaving Scotiabank without a dance partner. Scotiabank's CEO asked Gord to advise him on the bank's options. In the end, federal finance minister Paul Martin rejected the proposed mergers. The banks would need to find other answers.

At about the same time, Gord developed another interest. His oldest son, Chris, came home from school one day and said he had joined the robotics team. It was December 2000. Crescent School had participated in the Canadian robotics tournament the year before but had decided that year to go to the U.S. competition, called FIRST (For Inspiration and Recognition of Science and Technology) at the Epcot Center in Florida. There was a catch, Chris told his dad: you have to help raise the money to get us there. Lots of people volunteer to help with non-profit organizations, on events, policy, even administration, but please, anything but fundraising. Yet Gord knew that in his world people were much less short of money than they were of time, so in January he went about his job asking, and Chris went about his job—helping to build the robot.

Each robotics team had the same challenge to meet. On a certain date, every school would receive the same problem to solve and the same kit, or box of parts, out of which they'd have to build their robot to move this way, pick up that, and go around something else to solve the problem they'd been presented with faster than every other team. The schools each had six weeks to build their robots. As the deadline approached, Chris and his teammates were at the school working on it Saturdays and Sundays, eight, ten, twelve hours a day.

One Saturday, Gord dropped by. Not only were the kids applying the math equations they'd learned in class, he recalls, but they were "learning skills no longer taught in schools, like drilling, metalwork, using a lathe, soldering, wiring, electronics, pneumatics." It was like Hartree's Meccano set–differential analyzer, like his own punch cards and teletype machines, all over again. They were just trying to make something work. The kids were also learning what Gord had learned on a basketball court: how to work like a team. He saw how their teachers "were assigning different tasks to different students, developing and building a business plan, succeeding on some aspects and failing on others, only to try something different, managing with scarce resources, and uncertainty, and focusing on a 'drop dead' ship date for the robot. They were working with real-world constraints, uncertainties, and limitations." Just like Mr. Thom had taught him.

In April, the team travelled to Florida. Gord thought he'd play some rounds of golf at nearby Orlando courses and drop in for a few hours to see the event. "I was just blown away," he says. "It was in the parking lot at Epcot, they'd built these gigantic grandstands and had these huge tents where about a third of the space was for the competition and two-thirds, what they called 'the Pits,' where the kids were all roaming around talking to the other kids, swapping ideas, scouting the other teams." Gord never made it to the golf courses.

What happened next was no surprise: a teacher from Crescent, and one from another of the Canadian schools, and Gord started talking. They decided they should do a FIRST event in Canada. They met with the FIRST officials, who told them what to do: Raise the money, about $200,000, get twenty-five schools to take part, and find a venue. They would hold the event in Toronto. They thought they could get ten teams from nearby U.S. states, New York and Michigan, and the other fifteen from Canada, mostly Ontario. They pitched some companies, landed a few lead sponsors that would cover most of the money they needed, secured commitments from a number of Canadian and American schools, and contracted with Hershey Centre, a four-thousand-seat arena in Mississauga that was the home of a major junior hockey team. Two years later, a year longer than they had planned, a year shorter than they were told would be necessary, they held their first event. It became an annual competition.

A few years later, Gord invited me to see it. I was as blown away as he was. On the concrete floor of Hershey Centre were all kinds of ramps and various obstacles, and robots with wheels and appendages in configurations like you've never seen before, which the schools had cobbled together into something they thought could navigate its way through the course better than anyone else's. But stunning too were the flashing lights, the bright colours, the noise, the music. It was a carnival. Stuff going on everywhere. Even more than that, it was the kids. In their different-coloured T-shirts—their schools' uniforms— on the floor with their robots and teammates, in the seats with their parents, their brothers and sisters, with kids from their schools who had travelled to cheer them on. It was like a high school basketball tournament, except for one giveaway. Whenever a team finished their challenge and started to celebrate, jumping up and down, hugging, high-fiving, their hands would glance off their teammates' or miss them entirely. It was like they didn't quite know how to celebrate. These kids were geeks and nerds. Most had never been on a school team before, and never would be. Now others were cheering *them*. They were having the time of their lives.

Clearly, FIRST Robotics Canada had something. Now what would they do with it? They grew. Initially, the program was for high school students, so what about the younger kids? They started FIRST LEGO League for kids nine to fourteen, then FIRST LEGO League Junior for kids from kindergarten through grade 4. Because older students always dominated their high school teams, a program was created for those in the lower high school grades. Because some schools are smaller, poorer, or more distant, they created smaller, low-cost events, often holding them in high school gyms, so more schools could participate. Toronto had several strong teams—in 2013, Crescent would win the world championship in St. Louis—but Kincardine, St. Catharines, and Hamilton were also good, and so too North Bay, whose team initiated the formation of local Indigenous teams as well. At the same time, the federal government was trying to get girls more comfortable with science and technology. Coding became a priority, and FIRST was awarded a federal grant to set up a coding program across the country, and then was awarded another. More big companies got involved—Bombardier in Quebec, Microsoft in B.C. Some of their employees became FIRST mentors.

Yet there were also so many things FIRST wasn't doing. More than twenty thousand students, in more than 150 high schools, 700 middle schools, and 200 schools from junior kindergarten up to grade 4 were involved, which meant so many more weren't. And if 30 percent of the students were girls, why not more? There was lots more to do.

Gord chaired the FIRST Canada board through its initial ten years and was a member of its world counterpart as well. More than twenty years later, he remains on the Canadian board. For him, it had all begun with Chris coming home from school that day. It came at a time when he was looking, as he put it, to get involved in "more non-business stuff." To help build and grow something.

In 1998, Margaret Silvester was fifty-one when she and her husband, George, moved from Etobicoke to a small town in southwestern Illinois. Elsah, population 519, was in a very rural area about two hours south of Mark Twain's Hannibal, Missouri, an hour north of St. Louis, on a bluff above the tugboats and barges that wound up and down the wide, languid Mississippi River. They moved there because their oldest daughter, Caitlin, had finished her first year at Principia College, a Christian Science college in Elsah, and because George had heard that the school needed someone to teach photography and video production, and he had taken one of Mike Harris's retirement packages, and was ready for a change. He went there on his own to try it out first, to see if at this time in their lives it made sense to uproot the rest of the family. Margaret stayed home with the two younger girls, Bronwyn and Breanna, and did so until Bronwyn finished high school, the three of them joining George and Caitlin in Elsah on school breaks. They did that for two years, managing two households on one income, until in 1998, they all reunited in Elsah.

The college was very small, with fewer than five hundred students. It wasn't officially affiliated with the Christian Science church, yet the whole community seemed guided by the church's principles. Actor Robert Duvall, who had grown up in a Christian Science family, was the school's most famous graduate. It was a big move for Margaret and George at their stage of life, and Elsah was not Etobicoke. But George was quickly immersed in his job. As a first-time teacher he had more hours of preparation than he'd imagined, and extra courses to take in summers to get his master's, a condition of his being hired. Margaret began helping out at the Principia Museum, working with its artefacts, arranging displays, until the college, facing lower enrolment, needed to make cutbacks, and she was let go. She decided to go back to school, at nearby Southern Illinois University, to get her master's in English, then to teach English as a second language to the migrant workers and their families who worked farms in the area. She and George also found a new interest.

George had heard through the college grapevine about a course on sugar bush management given by a professor who had come from a college near Lake Placid, in the heart of Adirondack maple syrup country. George audited the course, then, near Christmas, asked the professor for advice on how he might start an operation of his own. The professor told him he'd better hurry. For maple sap to flow it needs cold nights and warm days, and while in Quebec and in neighbouring U.S. states that usually means March, in southern Illinois it meant January. The first year, George and Margaret collected two hundred gallons of sap. Boiling it down yielded five gallons of maple syrup. A very long run for a very short slide. Each year they produced a little bit more.

But whatever was different about Elsah, Margaret knew what she had known all her life: home is where you make it. It's where George and the kids are. It's where their church is. They lived as a Christian Science family, their church was a part of them, it moved with them. Christian Science has its odd-seeming beliefs and ways, as all churches do, yet fundamentally and day to day, Margaret and George lived lives not much different from those whose beliefs were rooted in more mainstream Christian denominations. They went to church on Sundays, and Margaret did her daily Bible readings. But unlike for most of us, Margaret's belief was at the core of her life.

Those outside the Christian Science church fixate on what they see as Christian Science's rejection of doctors, allowing that to define their understanding of the religion. Not Margaret. We are God's creation, she believes. God loves us unconditionally. It is God's love that Jesus relied on to heal sickness and overcome sin. It is Jesus' example we need to follow. It is God's love, through good and bad, sickness and health, we can rely on. This is what Christian Science was for her. This is how she saw life, and lived life.

My mother used to say about certain people, and only a rare few, that they had "nice expression." I didn't quite understand what she meant, it just seemed to me an old-fashioned way of saying that someone was good-looking. But now I think she was saying something else. It has to do with someone who has a face and a way not taken over by doubt or fear or sadness, but one that is open to the goodness of life. A face, a look, that is peaceful, kind, almost serene. Even in high school, Margaret had nice expression.

The kids grew up. Caitlin graduated and started teaching in Louisiana, in an impoverished area of the Gulf Coast far more remote than Elsah, living in an apartment built on stilts eight feet high to keep it above the storm waters. Later she moved to Houston—new destinations for family vacation drives, new opportunities for Margaret to help out. Bronwyn also graduated from Principia, got married, and travelled the world for a year before settling in California, where her husband's parents lived, teaching and having kids. Breanna graduated and moved to St. Louis, later to Dallas. More trips, and for Margaret more helping out.

Doug Little was the fourth of us to die. Even at ECI, there had always been in Doug's eyes something a little distant. It came across as wry, funny, and quirkily unknowable, as if in his head he was having a grand

old time taking in everything, all his friends and classmates, his teachers, and all our weirdnesses, and laughing his private laugh at what he
saw. Because everyone liked him so much, whatever he said or did he
was just Doug being Doug.

He got married, had two daughters, his wife left, their daughters
with her, and he got divorced. It knocked him off balance. His look
became more distant, his inside laugh less present, except with his
kids, later with his grandkids, and sometimes at the cottage when all
the family was around. But between those moments were days and
months and years when others weren't nearby. He moved to Shanty
Bay, on Lake Simcoe, then back to Toronto to a few different places,
then to Vancouver, then back to Toronto, all the time working for
Industry Canada and its Community Futures Program. Big cities were
growing, small towns were shrinking and needed help. He travelled to
these towns and worked with their businesses and governments, providing them seed money and advice to help get their economies going.
He liked his job. One wife and husband had a farm in the potato belt
south of Barrie and made potato chips for the local fair. With the help
of Community Futures, Miss Vickie's potato chips was born. Doug
was proud of that and of what he was doing. But his kids were hours
away, where his former wife and her husband lived, and because the
rest of the family was far enough away it became hard for any of them
to know for sure just how he was doing. There were always those good
moments, and Doug had always been a little distant anyway, so their
worries might be misplaced. It was all just so much easier to explain
everything away because you wanted to believe he was OK and didn't
want to hurt his feelings.

After twenty years with the federal government, Doug accepted a
buyout and moved to St. Catharines to continue his community development work with some of his former colleagues who'd also taken
their packages. Not long after, he moved north, near Huntsville, when
one of his daughters got sick, helping out with her kids, and after she
died, with his former wife, helped out more, the two of them even
attempting to gain custody of their grandkids. But years were passing.

He seemed never able to regain his balance. By the early 2000s, he was drinking more and was even more distant. Finally, Doug wasn't Doug. He died in 2011. He was sixty-three. We are what others remember, we are what we pass on. To this day, every time his brother, Tom, mentions Doug's name, warmly and with deep affection, it's with a giggle and a laugh.

We had reached an odd age. We were in our late fifties and early sixties. The paths we had chosen, the directions life had taken us, in retrospect all of them seemed possible, some even predictable, but so too would have been so many others. Life at any next moment could have gone this way or another or flipped back on itself and gone some new way entirely. It seemed everything could have been stopped, redirected. That felt less likely now. Whatever the mix of all the things that were in us was now finding its destination.

CHAPTER THIRTY

Time was up.

I had put it off for twenty-five years, since I'd retired from the Canadiens. I had wanted to do other things, even when I didn't know what they might be; now I'd done them. I had worked with many interesting people, in different places, been tested in lots of different ways, always with an ultimate test, an ultimate career, in mind: politics. It was 2004 and I was fifty-six. It was now or never.

It wasn't an easy moment. *Now* had consequences, and so did *never*. *Now* meant upending my life, and Lynda's life, to do something that ever-increasing numbers of people found nonsensical, even contempt-ible—"Why would anyone *ever* want to get involved in politics?" But *never* meant that unless I had absolutely changed my mind, and knew absolutely that I didn't want to go into politics, I'd live the rest of my life with regret hanging over everything I'd do in the future and over everything I'd done in the past. Because a lot of what I'd done in the past seemed only to make sense if I went into politics. I knew the consequences of regret because since I started playing with the Canadiens I'd met people who couldn't stop talking about the knee they'd injured, the coach who didn't like them, the choices they hadn't made, all that had led them to where they were now and not to the glory of the NHL. Many of them were very accomplished people who couldn't allow themselves to feel the satisfaction of what they had done, and could focus only on what they weren't, not on what they were. That was *not* going to be me.

Yet by 2004, my view of politics had changed. It wasn't just Estes Kefauver at the Democratic National Convention, or John Kennedy's "Ask not what your country can do for you . . . ," or Pierre Trudeau, or René Lévesque. It wasn't just headline-screaming, life-changing, future-changing stuff. Politics was also all the actions *not* taken, all the answers danced around and *not* given. Not just "what you can do for your country" but what *I* can do for *myself*. Yet some stars were still in my eyes, enough to say yes when no would've been easier.

I was parachuted into a safe Liberal riding just before the 2004 election was called. Less than three months later, I was a member of Parliament and the minister of social development in Paul Martin's government, and Lynda and I were moving to Ottawa. That first campaign told a lot about the next seven years of my life.

The riding was York Centre, in the heart of North York, Toronto's biggest suburb, which had been developed about the same time as Etobicoke, was a little less affluent, but otherwise not much different. Mel Lastman's avenue of civic monuments and Murray's hospital were just outside York Centre's boundaries. I remember knocking on doors on my first day of the campaign. We started in the west part of the riding, in an Italian neighbourhood, where Liberal support had always been unshakeably strong. Walking up the front steps to the first house, I asked the person with me, "What do I say when they answer the door?" He said, "Diefenbaker." I said, "Diefenbaker?!" John Diefenbaker had been the Conservative prime minister in the late 1950s, when most of the people in this neighbourhood had arrived as immigrants, when the Arrow was cancelled, when the economy turned down, when many of these new Canadians had lost their jobs, the men in construction, the women in factories. It turns out, they had never forgiven him, or the Conservatives. I said, "I'm not going to say 'Diefenbaker.'" The man shrugged. When the homeowner opened his door, I started into my "Liberals have always been strong on health care and on the social supports we all need at times . . ." spiel. The man with me, seeing I was getting nowhere, said, "Diefenbaker." The man at the door screamed, "Diefenbaker!!" The rest of his words I didn't know, but I understood.

Going door-to-door is the worst, and the best. The worst because you're looking for votes, and you know it and constituents know it, because at times other than during elections you might have been there but you weren't. The best because at the door people can see you and you can see them, because you can learn a lot at people's doors. First, the look of a street, its houses, in this part of York Centre small bungalows that many of the homeowners had built themselves fifty years earlier. The lawns cared for, the flowers, the shrubs; on driveways, a bike, some toys—likely those of the grandkids. In the backyards, the fruit trees, plums and pears, grapes winding up and around trellises. The vegetables—tomatoes, beans, zucchini, radicchio, peppers, eggplants—the herbs—rosemary, oregano, thyme— and more tomatoes. At the door, an older person, life weathered into their face. The clothes they wear, the smells from the kitchen, the crucifix on the wall, the family photos, the kids who've grown up and moved away, the grandkids. Everything immaculate. The words they say and mostly don't. Unimportant for laying bricks or washing floors, English words they'd never got around to learning. On other streets not far away, things not so immaculate, looking unsettled, not quite done, not quite redone, not quite in control, younger faces, worried, their voices hassled, unconfident. Behind each door a story—and in three or four minutes, what becomes clearest is whether life is basically OK or it isn't.

The incredible mix of the riding: 110,000 people. On its bigger streets, blocks of strip malls, low-slung apartments built in the 1960s, modern then, now stepping stones up or stepping stones down. To the east, a large Jewish community, one of the biggest in any constituency in Canada. The Jewish community, historically Liberal supporters, had been a major force in the creation of many of Canada's social programs. Now, because of what they perceive as the Liberals' less than total support for Israel, they're beginning to have a rethink. In the far northeast, a big Russian-speaking community, living mostly in large apartment blocks, often three generations of a family, having arrived in Canada a decade earlier after the collapse of the Soviet Union. Whereas most people in the riding are respectful at the doors, if not thrilled at what you are doing, and a few are disdainful, many Russian-speaking residents are hostile. In their life experience, government is evil or corrupt, so you must be too. When they speak to you, it's as if they're spitting on your shoes.

The campaign was going fine in the riding; we were going to win. Nationally, it was unclear. Six months earlier, the Liberals were on their way to a landslide. Then came the Gomery Commission inquiry in Quebec into the misuse of government funds that were supposed to promote Canada and counteract the PQ's message on Quebec independence but often weren't, the scandals it revealed only bringing back to mind other Liberal missteps, until the election now seemed up for grabs.

The national campaign thought I might help. I was asked to fly to New Brunswick on a Saturday night and give speeches in widely separated ridings the following day. I was pumped. I handwrote my speech on the plane, and on Sunday morning in Fredericton I delivered it. The audience was excited. I got more pumped. We drove a few hours along the Saint John River to Woodstock. Same speech, same reaction. We got back in the car and drove a few hours more. The next event was in a hockey rink. It was June, the ice was out. Portable chairs had been set up on its concrete floor. A small stage had been constructed. I got up to the podium and again I was rolling. I was Reverend Steed in the pulpit at Humber Valley Church, I was Kennedy and Trudeau. Then I got to the bottom of one page, moved that page to my left to see the next one, but the words at the bottom didn't match up with the words at the top. Worse, I'd neglected to handwrite the numbers on my pages.

I had been on such a roll I had no idea what I'd said or where I was going. I shifted my pages around, discreetly, so no one would notice—I couldn't find the right page. I ummed a few times, then a few more, then said a few things hoping that something came out that might sound right. The audience had been so with me they seemed not to notice—at first. Then I heard the beginning of a buzz. Finally someone in the front row, putting two and two together, whispered "It's under the chair." I looked down, and there in front of me, under a chair, was a sheet of paper. I kept talking and umming and, discreetly I thought, extended out my very long right leg, reaching for the paper with my shoe. My leg wasn't long enough. Finally, the audience couldn't not notice. I excused myself, walked to the chair, picked up the paper, and went back to the podium. I was no longer on a roll.

For the last big rally of the campaign, I was asked to travel to Thunder Bay to appear alongside Prime Minister Martin. Again, I was thrilled. When I'd been asked, I'd thought that "appear" meant "speak"; I was told by an event organizer that it instead meant I would *stand* with him, like *beside* him. I said that I had refused to be a ceremonial person in hockey and certainly didn't get into politics to be one now. I was told I'd have a few minutes to speak. The night was amazing. I couldn't believe the sound. When I had played, in front of much larger crowds, I was so absorbed in what I was doing I almost didn't hear the noise. That night the noise was everywhere. I didn't drop any pages. A few days later, we won. It was a minority government, not the majority we'd had, let alone a landslide, but I was too excited to notice and didn't understand enough to know what the difference between governing with a majority or with a minority would mean. Two weeks after that, Paul Martin called and asked if I'd be his minister of social development. What I'd had in the back of my mind all those decades had now come to be.

Social Development would've been a mid-level portfolio at most, except for one thing. In the party's platform, one of our biggest promises was that, if elected, after decades of failure, we'd create a system of early learning and child care across the country. I was asked, as minister of social development, to deliver that promise. It would be much harder than I knew at the time. Not many thought we could do it. Child care was under provincial jurisdiction, and the provinces lived with federal intrusions only when the feds put up the money and only after long, publicly rancorous bargaining, which this time, because several provinces had conservative governments and the federal Conservatives seemed ready to win the next election, would only be more rancorous. Also because after years of failure, the child care community didn't trust us. We would have to take it on as if on a mission. Lots of things in politics I wasn't trained for, but I knew how to go on a mission. That's what every season had been.

Critical to delivering the promise was how we understood the promise we had made. Was it to focus on the first part—to spend $5 billion over five years on child care—or on the second—to create a system of early learning and child care across the country? If it was on the first, if we spent the money wisely and honestly and brought child care as far as $5 billion could take us in five years, the promise was fulfilled. But if the focus was on the second part, and the real promise was to create a *system*, the $5 billion was only a down payment, and when five years were up more money would be spent, better approaches would be learned and introduced, until there was a system. This, we decided, was the promise.

That set everything in motion. We had an education *system* and a health care *system*. It was impossible to imagine Canada without them. Programs come and go, *systems* are forever. We needed to keep that always in mind. If one budget didn't deliver as much as was needed, if certain steps took seven years, not five, to achieve, that could be lived with, because a child care *system* once in place would never go away. This was about doing better in the present and winning the future. Child care advocates had fought small issue-by-issue fights in the past because they were the only ones on the table to fight. Now was the time to fight the big one.

As this was going on, scandal by scandal, revelation by revelation, the government was falling. The opposition parties saw our weakness, the media and public did too. Question Period was a daily angry forty-five-minute shambles. All the Liberal M.P.s except the prime minister and the minister of public works and government services,

Scott Brison, whom Martin had designated to answer the accusations that the opposition levelled about the Gomery inquiry, were spectators. I had one job the others didn't. I was Brison's seatmate. Every day for Question Period he brought in his notes and laid them on his side of our two-person desk. Then as the days got worse, he brought in more notes, and started to encroach on my side, then encroach some more. Every M.P. has an earpiece to hear the translation of what's being said in French or English, if needed, and more often just to hear anything in either language over the background noise. When Scott got up to answer, he'd take out his earpiece and put it on our desk, but with more and more notes there was less room to put it. Also the desktop was angled. I watched the earpiece each time as he spoke, and as it began to slide and got nearer and nearer to the edge I'd wait, and wait, until it began to fall, then grab it before it hit the floor, and, without him noticing, have it back on the desk when he needed it again. It got me through Question Period each day, and into the important hours after. We had a job we had to do.

Minority governments *can* work. Most countries have several political parties, and in their elections no one party wins a majority of the seats, ad hoc coalitions form, and parties govern together. Oftentimes in doing so, they offer a constructive mix of policies and priorities. Pierre Trudeau and the NDP's David Lewis had worked together in the early 1970s in what some consider Trudeau's most important years in office. But, with only Joe Clark's brief minority government in the late seventies, in the years since, Canada's parties had fallen out of practice. Even more so, in 2004 there was no will to come together. The Conservatives were rising, the Liberals falling. After twelve years of Liberal governments, the public and media were coming to feel, "It's time for a change." During the entire 498 days of our government, we campaigned more than we governed. It had never not seemed a matter of time. The noise in Ottawa got louder, then louder. We got hammered from every side. It wasn't fun. I said then, and I've said since, that in that year and a half I had the best job in government. I had what no other cabinet minister had: a mission to focus on. I was used to noise, I had dealt with noise most of my life, and knew that on the other side of noise was the prize, and it was my job never to stop seeing the prize, and to go over or around or through the noise to get to it. With a vote of non-confidence looming, I flew to P.E.I. one morning and to New Brunswick the same afternoon and signed the final child care agreements—ten provinces, ten deals. A week later, the government fell. We were into an election. The Conservatives won. The new prime minister, Stephen Harper, having different priorities, cancelled the child care deals. The price: one year's money that had already gone to the provinces, and one more year now that was owing as a cancellation fee. Two years out of five—a lot of money to advance child care in the provinces. But no system.

In the end, what had we done? What had we accomplished, *really*?

Fifteen years later, Justin Trudeau's government did bring in child care, did commit enough billions of dollars over enough years to create a *system*. Did begin spending that money, and continues to. In 2005, we lost the present, *politically*. But the public was changing. The way Canadians were living was changing. More and more parents were both in the workplace. More and more were needing, and using, child care. The appetite, and the clamour, for more and better, and more affordable, grew. Child care had become mainstream. It became the way we live. The way we are. In our eighteen months as government, we helped make child care mainstream. Governments and prime ministers come and go; the mainstream outlasts every decision maker. We lost the present, but we won the future. And the future lasts a whole lot longer than the present.

When I had thought of going into politics I had thought of governing. I never thought of being in opposition. It's not that I didn't know we could lose—I'd lost many times before—it's just I never thought of being in government and not governing. In the next five years, from 2006 to 2011, there were three more elections. We were never the government again. At the time those years in opposition seemed different, one from another, but really they were the same. Being in government defines the experience you have; not being in government defines it too. After we lost, there was disappointment and a lot more, but quickly there were things to move on to. Paul Martin resigned, there would be a new Liberal leader. Along with several others, I ran to replace him. When the race was over and I'd lost, one of my supporters said, "Well, at least we know we had the best candidate." I might or might not have made the best prime minister, but I was definitely not the best candidate. I had no idea how to run a campaign, or to support those who ran it for me. It was one price of starting into politics late. Another was that I didn't give myself time for a second chance, to lose, then win.

When a government is in power for twelve years, it, and you as an M.P., face so many things you never imagine, and act in so many ways you never considered, day to day, almost hour to hour, that you and it can lose your bearings. You know what you believed in when you started, but you become unsure. After hearing again and again about how useless government is and how stupid you are, you're also not sure you have the right any longer to feel excited or proud about anything. When you lose, however, you get a chance to take a step back, to refind your bearings, to rediscover what you believe in, to get re-energized and re-excited. The bad news about being on the wrong side of a minority government is that you're not in power. The good news is that in a few months you might be. But the really bad news is that when you don't stop campaigning, and don't take a step back, you don't refind and re-energize yourself, and you come back to the public with the same old you.

We thought we were different in 2008 going into the next election. We had a new leader, Stéphane Dion, but the public wasn't buying it. The Conservatives won even more seats, and we won even fewer. But again theirs was a minority government, again there might be an election any time, but again, for us, no stepping back, no refinding, no re-energizing.

Life in the opposition is lousy. The first time we lost, in 2006, I remember one prominent Liberal cabinet minister saying, "This is going to be great. It's going to be like shooting fish in a barrel."

Finally, us the shooters, them the target. And it was great—for about a week. After that, I realized it was a lot better to be the fish. As the government you can do things, important things; all you need is the ambition. You can affect people's lives. It's your job description to do so: *make things better for as many people as possible*. That's a pretty nice job description to have. To deliver on it, you need to know the country. What Canada was, and is, and how it has come to be. To know how we think, to know what's in us, what we can be and might be. To do that, you need to get out of Ottawa. What's the life of the Cape Bretoner, the Calgarian? The old, the young, the Indigenous person, the immigrant, the sick, the disabled, the high flyer, the addict in the Downtown Eastside of Vancouver, the ordinary guy? You need to know, and you can know, because you can go anywhere, because as an M.P. you have the right to talk to anyone and experience anything, and others want to talk to you because you're an M.P. As a kid I travelled in my mind in *Pirates and Pathfinders* and across the map on our kitchen wall. As a player, I travelled during seasons and more in summers. As a player you get invited to go anywhere, and after you retire, as a former player, it's the same. It never stops, and it's great that it never does. Maybe more than anything that I was doing in those twenty-five years between playing and becoming an M.P., I was learning about Canada.

Ottawa is beautiful. Its parks, the Ottawa River, skiing and hiking in the Gatineau, boating on the Rideau Lakes, each just a short drive away. The Rideau Canal in winter, frozen and maintained, becomes a skating rink that incredibly extends almost from Parliament Hill kilometre after kilometre to who knows where. But as an M.P., you don't experience much of this Ottawa. You arrive in the city on Sunday nights, and after Question Period on Fridays you leave to go back to your riding, for weekends there, for meetings, for events, always on call. People drop into your constituency office because they have a problem that they've tried to solve themselves, or with their families, friends, neighbours, or co-workers, and they can't. They think, they hope, desperately, you can help because you're the last resort, even if, as an M.P., you have no more power than a fire hydrant to force parents to let grandparents see their grandkids or to put up a stop sign or fix a pothole. Sometimes, maybe most times, all you can do is help them know where their desperately hoped-for answer isn't, or where it might be, or really that there isn't one, and for them just to go back to the rest of their lives, which, without this obsession, might be pretty good. Then, back in Ottawa, you go from early to late. You experience the life of intensely partisan politics, where the other guy is not only wrong but an idiot and you and your guys are not. "It's just politics," we say to ourselves, as in sports we're told that "it's just a game." But if you do something, it's not *just* anything. Not to voters or fans either.

I found Ottawa demoralizing, and de-energizing. If you're in government, everything you do is wrong. If you're not, everything the government does is wrong. It is the job of opposition parties to hold the government to account, to push them to govern better. It might also be their job to lay out alternatives for Canadians, to say what they would do if they were the government, but it doesn't work out that way. In opposition, you may be holding the government to account, but mostly you work to damage it. Make it weaker. You don't like to think so, but in opposition the line between holding to account and being treasonous is a fine one.

To the media, and most of the public, only the government matters. What the opposition, so far removed from governing, says is more irrelevant than a campaign promise. The media is interested only in what the opposition says about the government, not what it says about itself. The government is the one and only story. As opposition, you're a discretionary one. If you're to be heard, you'd better have something witty and wise to say, which is hard, or nasty and biting, which isn't. Day after day. And day after day, in opposition, as a party, as a person, you become *not them*, not you any longer. Opposition parties rarely win elections with the promise of what they will do, governments almost always lose them with what they have done.

I was somewhat effective in opposition the first few years, when facing only a minority government that might soon be toppled. It was interesting and useful to think about and plan for what we'd do differently and better with another chance. My last three years, after the 2008 loss, when the Conservatives held a strong minority, when our approach became even more critical, I wasn't good. You get sick of the government for what it's doing, and sick of your own voice and what you feel yourself becoming. You travel to other parts of the country to know them better, and you travel to get out of Ottawa. I went for the same reason I went door-to-door. Out of Ottawa, you see people in their own lives, trying hard to make them work. Trying to make their communities work. When people would say to me how difficult my travel was, I'd say, yes, it is, and every time I return to Ottawa I'm more physically drained than when I left. But I'd also say that every time I come back I'm more emotionally refreshed, with far more energy, and with a renewed reminder of why I'm doing what I'm doing.

It's more difficult for an M.P.'s family. It was less hard for us because Lynda and I were older, our kids were grown up and living their own lives. Other M.P.s had a big choice to make: go to Ottawa on their own, be alone for four days a week, then share three days a week with an airplane, your constituents, and your family; or move the whole family to Ottawa and reverse the sharing-time and the alone-time. Almost every M.P.'s family stayed home in the riding. Lynda came to Ottawa each week, drove back to Toronto on Fridays, then drove back on Mondays, four hours each way *when* the highways were snow-free. We rented places within walking distance of Parliament Hill and brought from home some stuff—sheets, towels, dishes, the basics—to make what very definitely wasn't home feel at least a little familiar. For our generation, for my ECI classmates, life has been more balanced—work and family not in a fifty-fifty balance, but close. But not in politics, not for many. Always some things *have to* be done, others *should be*, and the have-tos beat the should-bes every time. Politics is a *have to* life. Everyone else needs to adapt. It is a busy life. Often interesting-busy, at times really interesting-busy, sometimes worthwhile-busy. Often just busy.

After the 2008 election, again we had a new leader, Michael Ignatieff, again we faced a minority government, again there might be an election any time. And again, for us, no stepping back, no refinding, and from the public, no dice. The Conservatives won a majority, and we deserved to get hammered. The good news was that now the Conservatives had a majority there was no election right around the corner. There would finally be time to refind ourselves.

But not for me. I lost in York Centre. With each election my margin of victory had been comfortable but shrinking. I had never thought about losing, not because it couldn't happen—it just didn't enter my mind. It was only on election night, before the votes had been counted, when our campaign manager had come into my room and said, "You know you might not win," that I came to think about it. I'd always said, and believed, that in an election the public is always right. I still believe that. The public votes how they want to vote, and they get what they get. Even if one party or one candidate, by some objective standard that doesn't exist, is so vastly superior to another, the voter, at that particular moment, may want somebody else for reasons that make complete sense to them. The amazing thing to me is that one vote in one riding, for one candidate—Liberal, Conservative, NDP, Bloc Québécois, or Green—somehow, collectively, produces not only the party that wins the election but the scenario in which the voters want them to govern—a majority, a minority, big or small, Liberal or Conservative, and the messages that go with each: We like you [Liberals], but not too much, but we're not sure about the other guy [Conservatives]—2004 (Liberal minority); It's time for a change, but don't you [Conservatives] get too full of yourselves, and you other guys [Liberals], get your act together—2006 (Conservative minority); We told you [Liberals] to get your act together and you didn't—2008 (bigger Conservative minority); You [Liberals] will not listen!—2011 (Conservative majority, NDP second, Liberals distant third). It's as parties that we present ourselves, as if that's the only choice voters can make, and instead voters make their own choice, and vote for a scenario, and somehow get it, every time. The voters of York Centre were right. For their own good reasons, they wanted the Liberals, and me, out and the Conservatives in. They, and the country, got what they wanted.

I don't like to lose, but if I had won in 2011, facing four years of a majority Conservative government, I would've been miserable.

The question was: Now what? I was sixty-three years old. I wasn't going to run again in four years and hope things had changed enough for us and me to win. I'd also learned something from watching old hockey players and old M.P.s. Hockey lives and political lives are both consuming. They require you to jump in with both feet and more. And when you're in, you're totally in—you have to be. And when you're not in, you're totally out, and have to be that too. Old players and old M.P.s think they can stay a little bit in, so they keep doing stuff, making appearances, giving talks, not enough to be really doing something but enough to take up their time and energy so they can't be both feet into anything else. As of May 3, 2011, the morning after the night before, I was out.

What was I in?

VIII

GETTING
TO HERE

CHAPTER THIRTY-ONE

In 2011 and 2012, the thirty-one of us still alive turned sixty-five, Lisa first, Bruce last. It's a milestone that shouldn't have mattered to us much. Once upon a time the age of retirement had something to do with life expectancy, and by the late 1940s, when we were born, sixty-five was almost exactly the expected span of our lives. But by 2010, that span was more than a decade longer and getting longer by one or two months every year. Now there was no need for us to retire at sixty-five. We were healthy, for the most part. We could still do lots of things that would make almost any workplace better. Sure, some things we couldn't do—I couldn't move fast enough to stop a Bobby Hull slapshot (Hull, by then seventy-three, maybe I could), nor could Wayne finish with the leaders at the Boston Marathon (unless he had an hour's head start).

Yet those among us who were teachers could have kept teaching, our accountants could have kept accounting. We didn't because we didn't want to, because there were other things we wished to do, because we could afford not to, or because there were rules and regulations that stopped us, because society needed our kids, and soon our grandkids, to have a chance to get inside the job door and take over some of our corner offices as well. Now we'd have to find our possibilities someplace else, do something different. When I retired from the Canadiens and started playing weekly pickup games, I decided to be a defenceman, not a goalie, because I knew as a goalie I would only get worse, and as a defenceman, at least theoretically, I might get better. I didn't, not much anyway, but I might have. Better was a possibility. Possibility brought energy. At sixty-five, the question for us: Where does that possibility reside now?

These years were the first time in our lives when it seemed we could do what we wanted to do. We couldn't when we were kids, our parents wouldn't let us. At university, we could a little, but we had exams that hung over us, to say nothing of our parents, to say nothing of our own just-ahead ambitions. And after university, the future was looming. Then we got into a job, then we got married, then we had kids, then we were so far from doing whatever else we wanted to do that we lost some of our instinct, if not our appetite, to do it. Now we had all this free time in front of us. But now that we could do what we wanted to do, what did we want? What was worthy of this incredible opportunity?

Travel. Travel is the defiant, declarative message to ourselves and to everyone else that things are now different, that what all of our lives we couldn't do whenever we wanted, we now can. Travel is freedom. For the young rich of pre–twentieth century Europe, their rite of passage was the grand tour. This is *our* grand tour. We earned it, we deserve it, we're off to who knows where, and when we get back, and sometimes even before, we're thinking about where we'll go next. To London, Paris, Rome, not on any "If it's Tuesday, this must be Belgium" excursion, now it's for three weeks or four or longer. We'll go to places we have been to a hundred times in our minds that we thought we'd never get to. To St. Petersburg to see the Hermitage. Through the Rockies by train. To Florida by car, venturing off the interstates, taking our time, feeling the cold turn warm, watching the grey turn blue. And if not travel, other secret delights—golf, bridge, reading books in the middle of the afternoon. *Anything*, anytime. But then, eventually, as happens, it feels like it's time to go home. And retirement goes from being a milestone to a life. A life that will last many years.

Our parents, if they reached sixty-five, would live several years longer. But they never counted on it. As the Bible told them, "The days of our years are threescore years and ten"; anything more was God's blessing. Our reality is different. We will live almost one-quarter of our lives as seniors, most of those years in reasonably good health. Years we still can't count on, but ones we can plan for and imagine. Many, too many years just to play out the string. We want to be happy, every bit as much as we did in the earlier decades of our lives. We want to feel good, proud, fulfilled. Right up to the moment we retired we had a place to go, things to do, people who counted on us, people we counted on. It mattered to them if we were there, or if we weren't. We mattered to each other. We *belonged*. After I retired from the Canadiens, I realized that I didn't miss stopping pucks, or the money, I missed feeling special. Not *big*-world special, but *my*-world special. That I mattered in *my* world. I mattered to people with whom I shared a dressing room. I belonged. It's no different at this age. Recently, I was asked to thank a well-known person after a speech he had given, and to present to him one of my books. He was about a year older than me. He had been very involved in sports when he was younger, but his greatest accomplishments had come in other fields. What could I say to him that might be appropriate, that he might understand? I wrote in the book: "May your next game be your most important." We, all of us, no matter our age, still want something that gets us up in the morning and puts a spring in our step. What will it be now?

Wayne retired at forty-eight. He got a package. He'd had enough. After Wayne, en masse, were the teachers—Bruce, Joan Boody, Marilyn Adamson, Lorna, Judy Clarke, Mary, and eventually Lisa. Teachers are good at retiring. They know how. They have the means— they have good, sustainable pensions. They have the habits—they've lived modest economical lives. They have the state of mind—having done the same job for a long time, entering mid-career blahs if not a mid-life crisis, many are ready to leave. They have the incentive— approaching retirement age in the late 1990s, governments, looking to cut back, were handing out retirement packages. But even more, teachers aren't much afraid of retirement. They know what to do with free time. They've had decades of summers to develop other interests, to take once-in-a-lifetime trips more than once, and for whatever they weren't able to experience directly, they've had time to read. They can make retirement work and they know it.

As for our non-teachers, some continued on doing mostly what they had been doing. Wilf kept selling real estate—"the thrill of the deal" never not there. Steve did occasional acting gigs, and otherwise mostly did what he always liked to do, read and think. Gord left Scotia Capital and went back to his own business, and FIRST Robotics got bigger. At Mount Sinai and North York General, Murray had joined outside boards to learn about fields related to the hospital and to meet interesting people doing interesting things, and who might become friends. In retirement, he did the same, joining, among others, the board of Seeing Eye, the oldest guide dog school in the U.S. Marilyn Cade continued working every day in her accounting firm in the same low-rise building where her father, then her father and sister, had had their insurance office. She knew her clients—individuals, families, small businesses—often now more than one generation or iteration of them. She had lots of reasons to keep going, not many reasons to stop, and no rules or regulations to tell her she had to. Barbara continued as a physiotherapist, until the wear and tear on her shoulders became almost as bad as the aches and pains her patients were feeling. Roger still practised law with the same company, though less and less over time. Daryl, once the medical chief of child psychiatry for San Mateo County in the San Francisco area, continued on in his practice. At sixty-five, he was still finding the mind as fascinating as he had thirty years earlier.

I was teaching at McGill University. After losing in the 2011 election, I approached McGill with an idea for a course. As a member of Parliament, I had tried to understand the country, where we had been, how we got to where we are, where we are going, where better we might go. I thought the same challenge and experience might be interesting for students. I called the course Making the Future. I said to students that in your academic life you learn about the present and the past, but you'll live another sixty-plus years into the future. How do you want to live those lives? In what kind of Canada, in what kind of world? It's *your* life. And because "visions" are a dime a dozen, what steps do you need to take to get you there? Our own kids, and those of our ECI classmates, were fifteen years older than these students, our grandkids fifteen years younger. I thought about them, especially our grandkids, when I put the course together. What would I want them to know? What would I want them to think about to get ready for their futures?

At first I taught only at McGill, then after three years I was at McGill and the University of Calgary, and after that at Ryerson University (now Toronto Metropolitan University) and the University of Saskatchewan as well, the four together, same day, three hours in real time, connected by video screen—a Zoom class *before* the pandemic. Each week we focused on a different aspect of Canadian life—health care, the economy and jobs, religion, family, politics and government, Indigenous peoples, Canada in the world—each subject presented by an expert in the field who talked about the past and present of their specialty. In the second half of the class, the students, experts, and I discussed and debated the very unfamiliar, uncomfortable ground of the future, where none of us was an expert and we were all fellow puzzlers, and where students had the most skin in the game because they had the most years to live. In the third week each year, after the introductory class and one on health care, I invited a philosopher to speak about what philosophy has taught him or her, how human life has changed through history, and how many things are better than they'd been—we live longer and healthier—to help the students understand that even if every adult in their lives tells them the world is going to hell in a handbasket, they, as twenty-year-olds, have the right to believe they can make their lives better.

I taught the course for five years, until 2017, Canada's 150th anniversary. I stopped it to do a series for CBC TV, *We Are Canada*, which I saw as an extension of the course. The series focused on twenty or so Canadians under the age of thirty-five who were doing the kind of remarkable things that will help make our children's and our grandchildren's future. If 2017 was to be a year of celebration, I thought it should be celebrated by focusing on the future, not the past, because yesterday's Canada doesn't matter much if tomorrow's doesn't, just as what our parents and we have done doesn't matter much if what our kids do doesn't matter.

I also went back to writing, though I had never really stopped. I had written articles and op-eds if I hoped what I had to say might be useful somehow. Brain injuries in sports really bothered me. I was reading more often in newspapers about players I'd watched as a kid who died younger than they should have after having lived many years of their lives transformed by some form of dementia. In some cases, it was because of hits to the head they had received, sometimes accidental and unavoidable, often completely avoidable and unnecessary. We had grown up to believe that if something is bad and if decision makers can do something about it, they do it. And despite Vietnam and Watergate, most of us, most of the time, still believe that. Instead, the NHL and NFL, like tobacco companies, ignored, avoided, denied, and fought back with lies, fake science, and doubt as more and more players headed off into retirement with money, adulation, wonky brains, and a lousy life. It was really wrong.

I thought writing articles would be enough. This was a problem of awareness, surely. We, the public, the decision makers, the media, even the scientists, just didn't know. Now we will, so something, the right something, will be done. But that didn't happen. I decided to try again. To write better. To tell the story better. That didn't work either. I decided finally to tell it in an unmissable, impossible-to-ignore way. To tell the story of one player, one person, thoroughly, completely, of what it feels like, what life is like, with a young brain that doesn't work. A person who later died.

The book, *Game Change*, was about Steve Montador, a kid from Mississauga who loved to play hockey, was good at every level but never great, who hung in year after year when others didn't, made it to the NHL, played 571 games with six teams, scored a game-winning goal in overtime in the Stanley Cup playoffs for Calgary, suffered a number of head injuries, and died at thirty-five, with chronic traumatic encephalopathy in his brain. I wrote the book not as one more exercise in awareness, because as with tobacco or climate change, there was more than enough awareness to act. It was to get the NHL, and NHL commissioner Gary Bettman, to do not just *something*, because anybody can do *something*, but to do what is necessary, doable, and right. And because I knew that getting decision makers to make those right decisions often isn't a matter of "Where there's a will, there's a way," but the obverse—"Where there's a *way*, there's a *will*"—I laid out a thorough and doable way.

That didn't work either. I've written about brain injuries in sports for more than ten years. During that time, Gary Bettman and the NHL have done *something*, but they haven't done what is needed and possible. Not even close. I failed. But the game isn't over yet.

Go down to a local rink, watch the kids play. Not just the house leaguers, but those who someday might play in the NHL. Watch the U.S. college players, watch all the players at every age and every level in Europe. No hits to the head. And when, on the very rare occasion they happen, the players are thrown out of the game. Listen to the commentators, the guys who once played "old time hockey," as they like to call it, and are proud of it. Even they talk about "head hits," they distinguish them, they see them as different from the rest. Almost everywhere but the NHL, head hits have become unacceptable. On the way to becoming as unacceptable as smoking, as drinking and driving. The mainstream outlasts every decision maker. Just as in child care, losing the present isn't fun, winning the future is. And the future lasts a whole lot longer.

I also wrote a book about Scotty Bowman, our coach with the Canadiens and the greatest in hockey's history. Remarkably, and not coincidentally, he has also been witness, close up, to the best and worst of hockey, everywhere, at every level, from 1947 as a fourteen-year-old with a standing-room pass at the Montreal Forum, to the present as a ninety-year-old advisor to many, still going to games, still watching on TV. He saw Gordie Howe as a seventeen-year-old rookie, he sees Connor McDavid today. He also remembers everything, and maybe more amazingly, he watches the present with fresh eyes, as if what he's seeing he's never quite seen before. No one has ever lived a life like this, no one ever will again. This story, his story, how his mind works, how he thinks, had not to be lost.

In my book I also wanted to try to understand what makes someone the best, and how over several decades they can stay the best. In sports, in anything. How a coach, CEO, government leader, anyone does that. I had read Walter Isaacson's biography of Steve Jobs, who was also not an arm-around-the-shoulder guy and who won. Yet what Jobs and Scotty knew was that what those people who worked around them wanted most, more than the warmest smile or even the biggest paycheque, was to win. In Jobs's case, as he put it, "to change the world." In Scotty's, to win Stanley Cups.

I was now over seventy, and I'd had this book about our high school class in mind for some years. In the midst of writing it, something else came to mind that I had insisted to myself never would: to write a book about the fiftieth anniversary of the 1972 Canada–Soviet Union Summit Series. Where for its eighth and deciding game, on a Thursday in September, in the heart of the workday and school day all across the country, Canada stopped. Out of a population of 22 million, 16 million watched. It was the most shared moment in Canada's history. I wanted to find out what I remembered, what I felt and thought after all these years. To relive it for myself as a way to let others live it for the first time.

One of the many very nice things about writing is that there are no rules or regulations, there's nobody who tells you that you have to stop. If you like it, you can keep doing it. You don't need to retire if you don't want to. As age limits your mobility you can explore with your mind; as age limits your opportunity to affect things yourself, maybe you can do it through others who do have the power of position and authority. You can offer them at least some of the *way*, they offer the *will*. No coach told me to go home, so I kept playing. Then stopped. In *The Game*, I quoted Brigitte Bardot: "I leave before being left." If I keep writing I will face the same moment. I hope not soon.

—

After they retired, many of our classmates found new interests in old interests. Wilf and Gord played golf more often, then cut back when their backs and shoulders reminded them that they too were retired, and rebelled. Mary, Marilyn Adamson, and Murray also played more, Murray's tan-free gloved left hand maybe as ghostly as ever. Judy Clarke and Joan Boody turned what had been sideline interests most of their working years into something much more.

In 2003, Judy, a couple of years out of teaching, was ready for something. She had always loved to sing, but only when there were lots of others around so no one could hear her, or when she was young, at home and nobody noticed, except, at times, her father, who, when she'd sing along to the radio, not being a rock fan himself, would say, "Could you change the station?" Judy went online and searched for choirs. She knew she didn't want classical, she didn't want church. She also knew about herself that, all her life, when someone else would sing the melody of a song, for some reason she'd always sing harmony. "The part behind it," as she puts it. She joined a barbershop quartet, and later the Toronto Accolades, a women's chorus, singing baritone, singing harmony.

In high school, Judy had never been centre stage in any school activity or on any team or even in class. Later, as a teacher, she was, and she did love her red Mustang and her red Firebird with the spoilers she insisted on, but that was attention of a different sort. Here she would actually be on a stage, on a team, and only one of four. In barbershop, a tenor sings the highest part, a bass the lowest, the lead is the melody, a baritone sings a little high and a little low to fill in the spaces between to make their sounds connect. She recalls one rehearsal asking the chorus's director if he thought she should sing her part another way, and demonstrated. She wasn't expecting his answer. But it isn't as pretty that way, she said. "We don't need pretty," he said. "The melody does pretty. The lead does pretty. You do solid." The four parts also have to be perfectly in sync. Judy remembers the first time her quartet went onstage. It was at a competition. "There was this microphone, and you could hardly see the audience because of the spotlights glaring in your eyes." She was nervous, and she knew that when you're nervous you get out of breath faster and start taking extra breaths, which really doesn't work in barbershop because their sounds had to blend. "But then suddenly," she recalls, "I wasn't nervous. I just went, *Wow, my fantasy. My lifelong fantasy being a performer onstage.*"

The Accolades rehearsed every Thursday night for two and a half hours. They had a repertoire of about twenty songs and each year they would drop a few of them and add some others. Her favourite: Leonard Cohen's "Hallelujah." They performed about once a month, mostly at retirement residences, occasionally at community street fairs, and were especially busy around Christmas. One year they did twenty-four concerts in all. Between rehearsals, they practised on their own—Girl Scouts' honour—about half an hour a day. Though never one of the best groups, the Accolades did well enough in regional events to qualify for some international competitions. One year they went to Hershey, Pennsylvania, another to Orlando. Once they performed in front of two thousand people. "It was a whole different thrill to be onstage," Judy recalls, "when you're waiting for them to announce the winners. One time in Providence, when our name came up, I started to cry." She was sixty-three years old.

As Judy started with the Accolades, Joan Boody was moving to Niagara-on-the-Lake to open her B&B, leaving behind the North Metro Chorus, Canada's most famous barbershop group. The chorus had been world champions several times, and in the barbershop world, as Joan put it, "If people knew you were with North Metro, you were like a rock star."

There were 180 women in the chorus in all, 12 to 15 tenors, 30 to 40 leads, 50 to 60 baritones, and the rest were basses. Joan started as a lead, later she sang as a baritone. The chorus was known for its deep, resonant bass section and also for its choreography. Each of the twenty-four choruses that made it through the regional competitions to the big international events had fifteen minutes onstage to perform five songs. Complete with costumes and dance, it was like a mini musical, Joan says. In her first big competition, in Atlanta, the theme, or package as they called it, was "Anchors Away," and they all dressed up in red-and-white-striped tops, navy blue pants, white running shoes, and white sailor caps. In Orlando, the theme was Mary Poppins, the chorus director was Mary, the other 180 of them were chimney sweeps, black soot all over their faces.

The chorus didn't have a signature song but did have a signature style. As they'd come to the end of one of their upbeat songs, the tempo, everything, building and building, and the audience sensing the climax, "we'd always end with a *stomp*. You can imagine: a hundred and eighty feet stomping at exactly the same moment." Her favourite song of theirs, "Can You Hear the Love Tonight?" They didn't do it in competitions, but sang it in some of their shows. One nice thing about a cappella singing, she says, is that you can do it anywhere. Once a year, the chorus would go on a weekend retreat to the Nottawasaga Inn, about an hour north of Toronto. "It was lots of rehearsals and bonding time, and every weekend you could guarantee there'd be at least one wedding at the hotel. So often somebody from the chorus would speak to somebody with the wedding party, and without anyone else knowing, we'd file into the reception and circle the whole room and sing that song. It was *astounding*." One hundred and eighty of them. "I still get tears when I think of it."

Joan remembers especially the year the world championships were held in Nashville. Because it was Tennessee, they did a coal miners' package, all of them dressed as coal miners. She recalls the scene. "We got off the bus from the hotel and went into the green room in the arena and had our last little bit of water and a little pep talk. Then we lined up, and everyone, all hundred and eighty of us, knew our exact place in line to get onstage in the right position. Then we walked through all kinds of dark corridors, without a sound, nobody talking. When we got backstage, the chorus in front of us was just leaving with their applause, and the people in the audience all knew that North Metro was next. They started chanting as we were getting on the risers—the curtain was still closed. Then the announcer came out and said, 'And representing Region 16, from Toronto, Ontario, Canada . . . North Metro Chorus!' And the crowd just went crazy." This was Bridgestone Arena, where the Nashville Predators play. Jammed with twenty thousand people. "It was just like a hockey game. Really. I remember thinking, *This is me, I'm here. I just went to an audition. I'm not that great. The chorus is, but I'm not.*" Joan was fifty-five. She has kept singing since.

Cheryl's big moment didn't come in front of twenty thousand or two thousand people. In high school, she had been a cheerleader. After she received her first teacher's paycheque, she signed up for adult lessons at the National Ballet School, inspired by having seen a performance of its newly graduated students, one of them a young, regal Karen Kain. Thirty-six years later, in 2005, two years after she retired from teaching, she began a master's program in dance studies at York University. At the same time, her therapy had also been taking her in new-old directions, to where her mind had always gone. To art, to dance. She had heard Tchaikovsky's Sixth Symphony, *Pathétique*, not long before. More than ten years earlier, she had written a long poem about her childhood trauma. Suddenly, she could imagine a ballet emerging out of the music, against the backdrop of her words, that expressed the depth of what she had experienced. This was a way for her, finally, to integrate so many parts of her learning, her training, her teaching, her love of movement and dance, of images and patterns, her need to be creative, her need to express herself. Her trauma. Her*self*. As part of her master's program, she created her ballet, but instead of using the poem she had written, she replaced it with another that focused not on the trauma but on the physical, emotional, and spiritual releases she felt, when, as she put it, "I let my body dance." When she graduated with her master's, she started on her Ph.D.

She continued, not for the academic work itself, but as she put it, "because I could not bear to leave a community of dancers and an environment that focused on expressing emotions and ideas through the body." It felt like "I finally had found a place and a group where I belonged, and spoke the same language."

In 2018, she received her Ph.D. She had become what was in her to be. She was seventy-one. For her, as she puts it "it has been three steps forward, two steps back." Never not two steps back, never not three steps forward.

A few years before that, in 2012, Margaret and George decided to retire. Their kids were widely scattered, they had no real attachments to southern Illinois outside of their work, they still had some family in Toronto, but at that moment some different place that was new yet familiar was more interesting to them. That summer, they drove to Maine, found a house with a sugar bush, and bought it. They liked the rawness and freshness of Maine, the trees, the ocean, even the winter. And in Maine, after all the sap had been collected and boiled down, they would have lots more than five gallons of syrup to enjoy, maybe even enough to start their own business. But less than a year later Margaret got sick, and not many months after that, "passed on," as Christian Scientists believe and say. She was the fifth of us.

Her last months were hard; she didn't want her kids to know of her illness until they needed to. She had her faith, she knew from her faith that her body was material, but that her spirit was everlasting. Hoping to be healed, she went to a Christian Science practitioner. Later she asked the advice of some doctors, and when they told her they could do no more, she went back to what she knew, and continued to seek treatment in her faith. She wanted her kids not to dwell on her illness but to dwell on, to know *absolutely*, that her life was far more than the sadness of her passing. She was sixty-six. Her obituary read in part: "After a successful career in social work, Margaret dedicated much of her life to raising her three daughters and actively participating in her church community . . . Her passion for helping people made teaching ESL a perfect fit. Margaret's unconditional love and patience will be missed by all those who knew her."

—

In high school, we had the comfort of being in the same class, we wanted to fit in, and we also wanted to be different. Some more so, some less. After high school, discovering who we were, becoming whatever we became, we thought of ourselves as different from one another. We pursued different fields of study at different universities in different places, we developed different new interests and passions, we went into different jobs and lived different life timetables—marriage, kids—we had different experiences in the world and came to have different ways of seeing it, and took different paths into the future that seemed would hold more different paths still. We lived different lives.

But now, whether during those years we had more money or less, had big life ambitions, big life adventures or not, we are not so different. We are all aging. We are all looking for things that interest and excite us. Fantasies we've had that—what the heck, at this time in our lives, why not?—we at last pursue. But more than that, most of us have kids. For those who do, aging and kids have become the central facts of our lives. Aging and kids have brought us together.

CHAPTER THIRTY-TWO

Covid changed everything. Most of us were seventy-two years old when it hit in March 2020. Suddenly, we couldn't travel. We couldn't see our kids or grandkids. We couldn't golf, play bridge, go to lunch or the theatre. We couldn't be with the people we wanted to be with, or do many of the things that brought joy and purpose to our retirement. Our lives and the lives of families and friends were suddenly about food and toilet paper, unknown, unknowable, and complicated. Covid took over our time and energy, and did the same with our kids and grandkids, leaving them less time and energy for us. It turned life into survival. It shut us down.

Joan Boody and her husband had planned to go to Spitsbergen, an island north of the Norwegian coast, to kayak and look for polar bears. The trip was cancelled. Cancelled trips happen. You reschedule. But it's different when you're in your seventies. Biological time passes faster. When you're finally able to go, the testing, learning experiences you're looking for may be beyond you. Joan and Gus had had a taste of adventure travel a few years before Covid, when they went to Antarctica. They left Ushuaia, *el fin del mundo*, it calls itself, at the southernmost tip of South America, and sailed on a three-masted barque called the *Europa* across the Drake Passage into Antarctica's Weddell Sea until its waters began to ice over and they could go no farther—to a point, about two weeks into their excursion, where bucket list trips usually end. But theirs didn't. This was a learning *and* working "voyage," not a trip, the company's website said, and they and thirty-six others were "voyage passengers." They had "watch" to do, twice each day, four hours on, eight hours off, taking turns on the wheel, looking out for icebergs and floating debris, handling the sails if the captain wanted them set or taken down. They sailed from the Weddell Sea to South Georgia island, where a hundred years earlier Ernest Shackleton and a few others had set off across open waters in a lifeboat to find, and rescue, the rest of his crew. The *Europa* then sailed to Tristan da Cunha, one of the most remote places on Earth, more than four thousand kilometres from the Falkland Islands, almost three thousand from South Africa's Cape of Good Hope. They arrived Easter Day. For fourteen days, until Cape Town, they had no land in sight.

There were fifteen crew. The other passengers were from more than twenty countries, like Joan and Gus looking for a new and exciting experience. Joan was the second-oldest. She had always thought of herself as independent, and was proud of that. She had raised her kids after her marriage broke up, but on this voyage she realized that independent sometimes isn't enough, that at times you have to rely on each other, even on people you don't know. She thinks now how unadventurous she was as a kid. She didn't even have a bike, her mother so worried about Etobicoke's traffic. Maybe that's what happens when you have seven kids to care for, Joan thinks now. On the *Europa*, she was one of the solid, dependable ones ("Exemplary Party Member"), at least she hopes she was. She also earned another reputation. In her downtime, after her watch, after sleeping, eating, and attending the daily lectures, she knitted socks. It turned out that some of the others were knitters too, but had never knitted socks. After their stop on Tristan da Cunha, where there are very few people but lots of sheep, some of the women returned to the ship with wool. Joan taught them to knit socks.

They were gone fifty-two days. It was hard. Joan was sixty-eight years old. But whatever aches and pains of age the voyage brought, they were so much less than the exhilaration she felt. The adventure, the discovery, the challenge and the challenge met. It was like being a kid for the first time.

Covid took away more than time. It took away a feeling we had about ourselves. I had gone on an adventure of my own not long after Joan. Our son-in-law is from Alaska. When he was six and his sister was nine, with their parents they hiked the Chilkoot Pass, the route the Yukon gold seekers had taken in 1898, the one Sandie and her friends had gone on in the 1980s. When his and our daughter's own two kids were nine and six, they decided to replicate the hike, and invited his parents and Lynda and me to go. The hike lasted five days in all, two at the beginning and two at the end that the topographical maps said were flat, and weren't, and a day in between that was supposed to be straight up, and was. Each of us with our own backpacks, even the kids, step after uneven step, once in a while, which felt like once in forever, our son-in-law, our leader, saying, "Let's take a break," and seven seconds later, "Packs up!" When we arrived at the end at Lake Bennett, like Joan I was totally relieved and totally exhilarated. Given age, physical condition, and inexperience, I think it's the hardest thing I've ever done—game eight in Moscow in 1972? Piece of cake. I was sixty-nine.

Then Covid, and whatever next hikes and next adventures might have followed haven't. It seems we don't age a lot until we're about forty. Then it's as if we age less than a year each year until we're about sixty, then a year each year until we're seventy, then *BOOM*, every year is like five. In the mirror, in every aspect of our existence. Covid's two years were like ten. At our age, years we won't get back.

For the first time in our lives, *we* were the old and the vulnerable. Those in nursing homes, those over eighty, were most at risk, and we were next. We now thought about things we'd hardly ever thought about before. The only time I had thought about my own death was in the mid-1980s. It was after my term as youth commissioner and I was waiting for my final report to be printed and made public. I was in a village in India near the Pakistan border, by myself, and was bitten by a stray dog. The village had only a small clinic. I could hear rats scurrying across its floor. The doctor there had no treatment he could offer me, only one piece of guidance: whatever happens next, he told me, "It's God's will." I couldn't call home to talk with my family or to a doctor, or reach the Canadian High Commission in New Delhi— there was a telephone strike. All I knew about rabies was that death came within days, and was awful, and time was passing. I was shut off from everyone I loved. With Covid's arrival, thirty-four years later, it was different, but it didn't feel much different. Now if something happened, I'd have the best doctors around me, my family would be there, but I'd be on a ventilator and they'd be in another room as if still ten thousand kilometres away. In recent years I've come to feel claustrophobic. I've had a couple of incidences on airplanes and now in my mind I have a fear of getting stuck in a cave, able only to squirm and hope. This is what I imagined having Covid would be like. Cut off. All the things I'd want to say, and need to say, that I couldn't say. Life's not supposed to end this way.

At our age, some of us have had life-threatening illnesses, most of us live with life-worrying conditions, all of us have had people close to us die. None of this is a surprise, of course, we're in our seventies, but it is. Lisa's first partner, Henry; Mary's husband; Lorna's husband; Marilyn Adamson's partner—all died during Covid. And Penni. She was the sixth. I had tried to find her for more than a year, then one day I got a voice mail from an art school that had shown one of her paintings on its website. It was of the Old City of Jerusalem, where her husband, John, and his ancestors had come from. I didn't know that Penni was also a painter. Death, I knew, would never dare take Penni. But it did.

In his *Up* series of movies, Michael Apted told us, "Give me a child until he is seven, and I will give you the man." Maybe. But give me a child *under* the age of seven, and I'll give you the man or woman *over* the age of seventy. The same lesser capacity, the same lesser control, except one travelling one way, the other travelling the other. All this now is in our minds. Covid has given us more time to think, age has given us fewer things to do, to interest and distract us, both have given us more reason to wonder and *dwell*. About the future, and about the past. We're indoors more, surrounded by photos, by kids' and grand-kids' drawings, by objects on walls, tables, and shelves, by the past. Having the time now, we even go into our basements, into our deep pasts, and rummage around, examine, throw away, and mostly to see what we find. To get hints at what we're truly looking for: Who we were, who we are, what all *this* adds up to. What all *this* has been about.

Hard questions. Hard to answer, now harder to avoid. Before, we were too busy to think about stuff like this, or want to. Now we're not. Now we need to. Without some story, everything feels random, accident, chance. Religion is a story, it offers explanation, meaning. So does science. What *is* our story? What *have* all these years really been about? There's plenty in these years to make the case for almost anything. A life that's been happy, rewarding, fulfilling. All the things we've done, the challenges we've overcome, the things that absolutely never would have happened if not for us, at that moment, in that place, for somebody, for some thing. How we *did*, actually, make a difference. How we *were* the butterfly's wings.

But it would be just as easy to make a very different case. A life that's been unhappy, disappointing, one of promise unfulfilled. Every-one has regrets, almost every route is a route not travelled. We can travel only a few. And we were the Brain Class, the thirty-five best and brightest thirteen- and fourteen-year-olds in central Etobicoke in 1960. The first generation of kids that would grow up in suburbs, that would have the best schools, best teachers, the best and most of what the postwar Western world could offer. We were the first generation in all of human history for whom there was more to have—we had one specially designated parent, a father, whose job it was to bring home the most bacon he could, and another specially designated parent, a mother, whose job it was to support her kids in every way possible, both their jobs to prepare us for a future that was unimaginable in every way except that it would be better than any that had ever been

lived before. On top of all that, we were the first generation of kids
that could go to university in such large numbers. We'd then be able
to do what only rich, well-born kids had previously done, which would
give us, and our kids and our kids' kids, a chance at being rich and
well born too.

Further, the Board of Education of the Township of Etobicoke
had given us this gift, the chance to write a special test on May 11th,
1960. And on that Wednesday, maybe it was in the morning, maybe
in the afternoon, maybe it was because we were feeling rested and
well and enough of the other kids weren't, for whatever reason, we
did well enough and made it into the Selected Class, the chosen ones,
ahead of us five years of peer pressure of the most constructive kind.
We all graduated from high school when more than half of everyone
else in our grade didn't. And we all went to university, and we almost
all graduated from there, and when we went out into the world it
seemed it was there for the taking, and in it we could make a different
present and different future for us and for others.

By almost every measure, we were lucky (or "fortuitous," as Gord
likes to say). "Lucky" is not a word we use much now. Being lucky
seems too random, too much a matter of sheer chance, as if we haven't
earned what we have, as if whatever we've done has nothing to do
with us. How instead of making us feel proud, it makes us feel a little
unworthy, an imposter, a fraud. *Why me?* More often instead we say
now we are "blessed," as if we *have* done something, we are worthy
and have been blessed for it, by an employer, by God. A humble brag.
Why not *me?* We like this explanation better. We say in sports, "You
have to be good to be lucky." Maybe you have to be lucky to be good.
I was lucky. So why didn't we do better?

Those of us in the Brain Class haven't lived in traditional heroic
times. We fought no great wars, survived no Great Depressions.
Greatness wasn't asked of us or forced upon us. Greatness was an
option. Yet during our lifetimes, more people in the world have
become better educated, are healthier, and live longer. Maybe because
vast numbers still don't, and aren't, and because of the great injustices,

disparities, and power imbalances around us—white/not-white, rich/not-rich, male/not-male, educated/not-educated, climate-affected/not-climate-affected—things appear worse when in fact they've gotten better, but unacceptably, inexcusably, too slowly. Is there greatness in more and better? In many non-Western parts of the world, greatness hasn't been an option. They've had independence battles to fight, wars of poverty, and disease, famine, and drought to survive.

But whether or not things are empirically better now than when we were kids, how we feel about the world, about life, is not the same. We were younger, now we're older. That has a lot to do with it. We were born into the Age of Science, as Lister Sinclair told us in *Maclean's*. Then for most of our childhood years we lived in the Age of the Common Man, which then, in our young adult years, became the Age of Possibility, for each of us individually and all of us together. Then, as more became possible and more was expected, it became the Age of Expectation, and when that proved harder to realize, the Age of Distrust. And when we came no longer to be able to count on the village, it became a new Age of Possibility, but this time one of individual, *not* collective, possibility, where we'd have to do things ourselves.

Now it feels like a time of breakdown, not yet an *Age* of Breakdown, but still one where things might go in lots of directions. Again, maybe that's us. Maybe that's our age. But one thing does seem certain. Our kids and grandkids *will* face the dramatic, life-shifting effects of climate change. They *will* need to create a new relationship with the planet. One where more is only better if the Earth says so. Greatness for them will not be an option. As our Latin-educated hockey coach put it, "optional" will mean "be there."

There are lots of things in our lives each of us could've done and didn't, or did and could've done better. I could've done a lot better in math at ECI. I'm a pretty good problem solver, I can handle situations and scenarios and things unknown. I could've sat *way* in front of Peggy Clarke, but I get impatient with *x*'s and *y*'s. I could've stayed with the Canadiens in 1973 and not left to article in Toronto. I was stupid, the Canadiens' general manager, Sam Pollock, was stupid. We had a good thing going. He could've had a better team and I could've been a better goalie if I hadn't lost that year and much of the next finding my way again. Maybe we both needed to be stupid to appreciate what we had. After I retired, I could've stayed in Montreal. I think Lynda wanted to. But I didn't think I spoke French well enough to take in and understand everything around me. Always I'd be searching for clues, like trying to pick up a puck through a screen, never feeling sure enough to jump into the action, into the experience, with both feet. Never able to do all that might be in me to do. Afraid of embarrassing myself. I could've been a real point of connection, an *anglo* in Quebec, enough of a fish out of water to know what it's like to be a *franco* in the rest of the country. Maybe not to *do* all I could do, but to *be* all I could be. But I got it wrong.

I could've been a better player, a better TV person, writer, business executive, politician, teacher if I'd spent more time as any of them, but I never thought of myself as any of them, and I didn't want to be. I wanted to be an all-rounder. Live an all-round life. Back at ECI, I could've played that championship game against Don Mills. Our basketball team needed me more than our hockey team did. We might have won.

I could've been better in a hundred different ways, but I wasn't, and now, actually, at age seventy-six, I'm OK with that. And after talking with almost everyone from our class, over many hours, and knowing something about them from the five years we spent together, I think most of them are OK with that about themselves too.

And maybe, really, we didn't do better because why would we have done better? We were only thirty-five. There were 312 other grade 9s at ECI the year we entered high school, almost 21,000 other grade 9s in Toronto, almost 210,000 in Canada, almost 2.1 million in the U.S. There are only so many prime minister and president positions open, only so many Nobel Prize winners, Oscar winners, rock stars, CEOs, billionaires, and Mother Teresas around. Why *should* we have done better? And what's "better"?

Someone else is now doing the job I once did. They might even be doing it better. It's not about what we were, or are, we're not our CVs, it's what we pass on. To our kids, our grandkids, our friends, the people we worked with, to others we don't know and have never met whom we've somehow affected.

I wonder if Wayne knows how endearing he was. I wonder if Lisa knows how much someone like her in high school treating geeky guys like us so nicely mattered so much.

I didn't feel the same about myself, about my life, when I was twenty-five and fifty-five. I don't think many of us did. I had a script written in my head where I was going to be a lawyer, then go into government, and along the way play hockey until some coach told me, *No, not this year*, and I'd be done. But no coach did, and I didn't like law, and my script went all to hell. I think it did for most of us, even for those who wanted to be teachers and became teachers, or nurses, or engineers. How each of us got there, what it felt like when each of us did, what new directions opened up, what we learned, what we found we liked and didn't like, how we changed, what choices we made, what circumstances we were in, what came to matter and what didn't, what we became—not much is what we expected. Life is, life might be, life will be, life isn't, and finally, life is again. This has been the pattern of our lives, if there's been a pattern at all. ECI's motto, it turns out, was a good one—*Semper ad meliora*. I thought at the time it meant "Always towards the best." Instead it means "Always towards the better." "Better" relates to the times, to our circumstances, to what we know. "Better" we can do. "Best," untethered to a time, we can't know. We write our scripts, life intervenes, we rewrite. I don't think many of us, maybe any of us, had in mind to change the world. But I think we had in mind to make some things better. To be *useful*.

After all these minutes and hours and days and months of our lives, what we did doesn't seem like much. One of my favourite books is Bill Bryson's *A Short History of Nearly Everything*. I read it when it first came out, almost twenty years ago, and read it again recently.

The story he tells of how we—the universe, Earth, life, we as human beings—came to be is not impossible, or beyond imagining, because it happened. Because science says it did. Once there was nothing, *actually nothing*, and out of the Big Bang trillions of years ago, that nothing became something. In fact, it became everything that was needed, somehow, to become us. In further fact, some atoms from that very first instant, after bumping and colliding and forming as this and that and billions of other things, going wherever they were going, are in all of us. Those atoms will become part of something or someone else after us forever and ever until something becomes nothing again.

All of which can make not getting asked to the Sadie Hawkins seem not so existence-shattering. Or, depending on how you see things, can also make our seventy-five-plus years in this particular human configuration seem pretty significant. A speck of a speck of a speck to the almost infinite power, or as part of something to that same almost infinite power that is absolutely awesome. Ashes to ashes, dust to dust. I've heard those words since I was in Sunday school at Humber Valley and never understood their literal truth. I am not religious, but I find comfort in Bryson's story. I have been useful. My atoms have been useful, and will be again.

I wonder what our parents would think of the lives we've lived.

I don't know if the story I tell about myself is right. I don't know if the story anyone else tells about themselves is right either. In writing our stories, what we're looking for, I think, is something that connects this to that, that makes sense. That we can live with.

CHAPTER THIRTY-THREE

"In the end, during our brief moment in the sun, we are tasked with the noble charge of finding our own meaning."

Brian Greene, *Until the End of Time*

Covid or not, age or not, we have a lot more writing to do—we hope.

Most of our grandkids are now the same age as we were at ECI. If my mother were alive, she'd be 115, my father, 112. ECI is 95. Canada is 156. Etobicoke has disappeared into Toronto. Toronto is now the fifth-largest city in North America, after Mexico City, New York, L.A., and Chicago. Canada is the thirty-ninth-largest country in the world, our population just over 40 million (at Expo, fifty-six years earlier, we were 20 million "proud and free"), the world's population just over 8 billion, in both cases about three times what it was when those in our class were born. Among the class, we have sixty-two children (Ken Church has the most, four), eighty grandchildren, and no great-grandchildren. Several of our kids became teachers, almost none are nurses, work in government or in big companies. Instead, many work in hi-tech, some in start-ups, some in the arts, even one as a stand-up comic. We have ten grandkids who live in provinces outside Ontario. One of Cheryl's and one of Marilyn Adamson's live on the same street in Vancouver. We also have grandkids in Japan, Denmark, and Luxembourg, three in France, seven in the U.S. Yet in spite of all the travelling we did, that's only thirteen out of sixty-two who live outside Canada. In our lifetimes, the world may have come to live with us, but we haven't gone to live with it. Where will our kids' kids live? What work will they do?

Twenty-nine of us are left. Most of what will be in our end-of-life résumés is now already there, except for the number of grandkids (Marilyn Cade just had her first a few months ago) and maybe of great-grandkids we will have.

What we do now would seem very ho-hum to our fifty-year-old selves. We go for walks, we go for drives, we talk about the weather. We talk about our grandkids. To our younger selves, we've become our own worst nightmare. I never walked before *to walk*. I ran, or rode my bike, or got a ride, or drove. Walking was a long, slow way to get from A to B. I wanted to get to B as fast as I could, to start doing what made me want to get there in the first place. Who cares about the journey, it's the destination that matters. I don't think that way now. I like walking. It's moving, it's being outside, feeling the sun, the wind, even the cold. It's being in one place and, with each step, being in another. It's all the things that pop into your head along the way that don't pop into your head anywhere else, that get you thinking, until you're off in some other place you've never been.

As for drives, I used to think that was even worse than walking. My mother would always sound so cheery. "Why don't we go for a nice drive today?" she'd say to my father, and us. It would be a Sunday. I could think of a thousand reasons why not—I want to play baseball, I want to watch TV, I want to . . . do my homework, eat glass. But really, *why?* What was the point? *TGIAM*. Thank God It's Almost Monday. Now I love to go for drives. It started during Covid, as a way for Lynda and me to move from the safety of our house-bubble to the safety of our car-bubble and be somewhere else. With the border closed, we couldn't visit family, so it meant driving around southern Ontario, and with stops along the way a risky idea—motels, even gas station lavatories—it meant day-long trips, seven hours max, once a week, usually on Saturdays. We bought a lug-a-loo and put it in our back seat, and knowing it was there never had to use it. I thought I'd never last a month on these drives. More than two years later, we're still driving. I've become my mother.

We take secondary roads, and if we see something smaller, we take that. GPS, maps? Only if we're lost, and if you have no destination in mind, you're never lost. You just happen, *at that moment*, not to know where you are. We might, for example, start out with St. Thomas in mind. It's about three hours west and south of Toronto if you take Highway 401. We'd go on the 401 for a while, then set ourselves free from our tether cord and go who knows where. Much of the time we know only that we're going mostly west, but if some other road looks interesting and it's going north, we take it. Eventually, we know we'll take something else and something else that will bring us mostly southwest. And if we never get to St. Thomas that's OK because it means we found something along the way that interested us more, and someday we'll make it to St. Thomas anyway. But it's important to have St. Thomas, or some place, in our minds. Otherwise we'd never set out.

Ontario small towns are beautiful. They all have main streets that look important, that look like a main street should look. They all have their big, beautiful churches. If there's a Presbyterian church, there's an Anglican church nearby, and of course a Catholic church and a United church, and if it's old enough, the United church will have the name "Methodist" carved somewhere into it. In towns like these, three storeys high, church spires are like skyscrapers. In the late 1800s, when many of the churches were built, it seemed every man, woman, and child must've had to split themselves in five to fill even half their pews. I wonder who fills them now. Every small town also has its big old houses along either end of the main street, built by ancestors of the owners of the grist mills, lumber mills, or woollen mills who founded the towns around two centuries earlier. Towns, buildings constructed as if they were to last forever. One of those houses is now the funeral home. And everywhere, beautiful old trees. Towns you wanted nothing to do with as a modern suburban kid, towns you can now imagine yourself living in: Dundas, Guelph, the old downtown of Galt, now Cambridge, the river, its arena where Gordie Howe played with the

Galt Red Wings when he was sixteen, where my brother played and I watched, where Patsy Cline performed. Up the hill on the other side of the river, not one street but street after street of big old beautiful houses with big old beautiful porches, and at the end of one of the streets, the town's cemetery, where my ancestors, who arrived from Scotland in 1834, are buried. I didn't know they were there until one of our Saturday drives during Covid.

The rivers of these central Ontario towns, so community- and life-shaping, the Speed that runs through Guelph, the Grand that winds its way through Brantford, Paris, Cambridge, Kitchener, Waterloo, Elora, Fergus, from Lake Erie almost to Georgian Bay. The valleys they create in the gentle, rolling countryside, the uneven, ragged land they create beside them, no good for agriculture, but left to nature, to the trees, bushes, wildflowers, and later parks, good for everything else. Like Mimico Creek and the Humber.

We go on these drives through every season, watching the colours change: the drab grey of winter's land and sky, except for a few miracle days of blue and glistening white; in early spring, the brown and grey turning brown-green and grey-blue. Then week by week watching the corn grow, from snake's eye high to llama's eye high, until it's unmistakeably corn. Like watching a kettle boil—boring only if all you want is hot water. But if everything is your destination, everything is interesting. Then in the fall, oh my heavens, the fall. "Let's go for a drive to see the colours." I still hear my mother's voice. I still hear my own, in my head: *In Etobicoke, Mom, the colours also change. I see them change every day. Then the leaves fall, then we have a class party and rake them up, burn them, earn money for the United Way, and eat pizza. That's fun. Going for a drive to see them is not fun.* I thought everywhere had leaves like ours in the fall. They don't. Convoys of buses head north from the U.S., Caribbean cruise ships cruise the Gulf of St. Lawrence, just to see the colours. The rendered imaginations of our great painters aren't rendered from their imaginations at all. What they see and paint is real, every fall. I'm worse than my mother.

It's not because of the DNA we share. We become our parents because we get older too.

Now we take in the world more often through our car windshields, our TV screens, laptops, our kids and grandkids, their school plays, music nights, basketball games, and the stories they tell. And why not? We'll never be forty or twenty or eight again. We take in the world through what we're able to do, and what we have around to help us. Netflix and Zoom have been miracles. I watched TV a lot as a kid, and I watch even more now. Our big colour-popping screen on the wall is like my picture window on the world. The Great Wall of China—there it is. Lemurs in Madagascar, shattered apartment blocks in Mariupol, I used to think I'd be right there someday, live, taking it all in. Now Lisa can watch all the movies her mother, Adèle, watched and the movies and TV series Adèle would watch now if she were alive. She can watch tennis live from Australia and Spain and Italy, any time of the day or night, love Nadal, hate Djokovic, hate, love, wish redemption for the irredeemable Kyrgios. Gord and his wife, Ken and his wife, can play bridge with people they don't know. (For Ken, as it turned out, that first year of Queen's was good for something.) Pat can go on field trips and look under every rock, everywhere. All of it is virtual, but with age and Covid, what would otherwise be non-existent to us is almost real.

Covid may have taken away our last best years of adventuring, of actually being there, but it's given us a dress rehearsal, it's prepared us, for what is ahead.

Some of us, with age and Covid, have discovered, or rediscovered, baking, cooking, coffee, book clubs, milkshakes, a good night's sleep, dogs. Judy Tibert does jigsaw puzzles. Her kids are gone, with the pandemic she and her husband have no one to invite for dinner, she does the puzzles on their dining room table. About five a year, a thousand pieces in each. She organizes her pieces in small kitchen containers. She does the straight edges of the perimeter first, gets fed up sitting, goes away, comes back, and with fresh eyes attaches a piece here, another there. It takes her about three weeks to finish. Then she leaves the puzzle on the table for a day or two, glances at it, takes a picture of it—her own report card, evidence that she's done it (we *are* the Brain Class)—and puts it back in its box. She likes the concentration it requires, having to notice the little details and remember them. She likes watching the pieces come together and seeing the scene emerge in front of her. Not like real life, where pieces come together as *they* do, with no photo on the box as a guide. Still, even with Covid, this is something she can do.

Joan Boody and Judy Clarke are still waiting for their choirs to gather again. They can't do what they'd like to do. Choirs need everybody together, in one place, in person. Music is sound and connection, physics and chemistry. It's rehearsing once a week, and practising at home in between. Making music before the music is made. Until then they can rehearse in their minds.*

And Pat still has his animals. Not as many as before. Fred, the donkey, and many of the others have, as Pat says, "passed into the great sty in the sky," but he has a dog, Hedley, a cat, Felix, and a few box turtles none of which have names because they don't respond to names, except one, which doesn't respond either, but is called "Little Okie" because Pat found and captured him nearly forty years ago in Oklahoma. Pat also has his ball hockey. In 2014, he was diagnosed with Parkinson's. Every Christmas, the family played its annual game on the road in front of their house, with his daughters and their families, who live less than an hour away. When a car went by, which where they live wasn't often, they'd yell "Car!!" not out of any annoyance, but with the delight of a childhood memory. Then they'd move the nets, and move them back, and start up again. Pat played up until

---

* Joan's Chorus Niagara started up again in late 2022, re-finding their sound and each other. On March 5, 2023, along with the Orpheus Choir of Toronto, one hundred voices and thirty musicians in all, they performed Beethoven's soul-lifting *Missa Solemnis* in a full Metropolitan United Church in downtown Toronto. As she sang, Joan, one of the few still wearing a mask, so exuberant she looked like she was about to burst through her mask and swallow it.

2019, the game got weathered out the next year, his balance hasn't been good enough in the years since. But he watches, and yells "Car!!" when the others do, and still has his hockey stick, which, he says, has got to be twenty-five years old.

Of even greater importance to us now is *the cottage*. It held such meaning for so many in our class when we were kids. It has always been a place of generations—grandparents and grandkids—but now we're the grandparents. At the cottage, very different from our gatherings for special occasions in the city, there is time. We get to watch our kids and grandkids move, listen to their minds, see how they're doing. And when they aren't around, the cottage turns suddenly peaceful. It is a place to get outdoors, away from people, from disease, as everything else closes in, to feel space. Marilyn Adamson's cottage has been in her family for more than a hundred years. She always imagined writing a book about it. During Covid, she did. Bruce, Wayne, Cheryl, Ted, Mary, Gord, and Marilyn Cade now all spend more time at their cottages. Lorna and Kathy McNab, having moved north in their twenties, already live on a lake. Judy Tibert and her husband have a cottage near Ottawa, a long trip for them from Mississauga, but nearby for their kids. For Sandie, the cottage, The Mag, was her "heaven on earth." It's where her ashes are now scattered. For Doug, the cottage was his crucial point of contact with his family, and their touchstone with him, when little else was. When Roger, during Covid, needed to work from someplace other than his office, he worked at the cottage, then more and more often, until— why not?—he and his wife retired there. At the cottage there's always something to do, nothing needs to be perfect, and most of it can be done on *our* time, at *our* pace, a little today, a little tomorrow, in the way we can still do it. As for me, we never did get a cottage. But my brother, Dave, and sister-in-law, Sandra, have one, and they have shared it with us, and our kids and grandkids. And it's been fantastic. The cottage isn't about the north, or even about lakes and swimming. It's about being away, and together.

—

We think more about friends now, especially long-standing ones. My two oldest friends, we started in minor hockey together. I played with one longer than I did even anyone with the Canadiens, eleven years, from Humber Valley to the Etobicoke Indians, to Cornell. The other, after Humber Valley and Etobicoke, went to Princeton, where we played against each other, then played oldtimers hockey together back in Toronto. More than that, as kids, we both loved maps, thinking about different places in the world. We'd get on the phone and quiz each other—and argue—about world or state capitals. I still remember his phone number. We never did agree on whether Bhutan's capital was Punakha or Bumthang. (It was Punakha, now it's Thimphu. I bet he doesn't know that.)

And we think a lot more about our spouses now. We appreciate them more. Six in our class divorced, five never married, many of the rest have been together more than forty years, ten for over fifty. I've been married for fifty-three years. That's a long time. There have surely been moments for all of us when it seemed things wouldn't work, but for some simple or some very complicated mixture of reasons, we needed to make it, and we did. It all seems quite amazing now. That other person went through *a lot*. We have *shared* a life, our one and only. Now we know *inescapably* that one of us will survive the other. It's hard to think about that, about being the one who goes or the one who doesn't, who has to live with the consequences of death. Lorna's first husband died when she was twenty-seven, her second husband, Tom, during the pandemic, when she was seventy-four. They had known for months the end was coming. Before he died, they had "the talk." He told Lorna he didn't want her to be alone, he wanted her to find someone and be happy. Lorna found someone. She and her new partner, she says, feel "very fortunate" to have found each other.

And John Mansour, Penni's husband, came to deal with Penni's passing his way. They had been together more than fifty years, and had shared a part of almost every one of those days. They had created the family Penni never had and always wanted. Penni, never not at the centre, never not theatrical and over-the-top, especially at the family dinner table. Like Moira Rose, on CBC's *Schitt's Creek*, one of her kids remembers. Then she was gone. Now every morning, rain or shine or snow, John went to Tim Hortons, bought two coffees, one for him with four sugars and "time-and-a-half," one and a half, creams, as he put it, a double double for Penni, and went to her gravesite, where they had their coffees and talked. For more than a year. Until not many months ago, John died.

We think more about matters like this now, and even more we think about our kids and grandkids. We worry about them, we worry about their future. We hope for them. How we are these days is very much how they are. As parents and grandparents, we share one big overriding wish, one thing we most want to know, and can't know. That they will be OK.

And for us in the Brain Class: it's now fifty-eight years since we graduated from ECI. Few of us were each other's best friends then, none of us are today. I think what most of us feel now about each other is gratitude. It was very good to know each other.

Death, whenever it comes, will not be nice. It may be sudden, or not. It may be twenty years from now or later today. It will be sad. Life is all I know. But Margaret Silvester understood. She didn't want her kids to dwell on her passing. Death is a detail. Her life is what matters.

When our kids were living at home, we would go on family vacations, sometimes driving, sometimes flying and then renting a car. One time we went to Nova Scotia, New Brunswick, and Maine, other times to Manitoba and Saskatchewan, to Spain, France, and Italy, to Mississippi and Louisiana, to North Carolina and its Outer Banks. We would make some reservations ahead of time, usually for the first and the last night, but when we'd get back I'd always be surprised that our friends had hotel and restaurant vacation stories to tell and we didn't. We would eat when we got too hungry not to eat and stay at whatever we could find when it got too late to drive. I think it was our daughter, Sarah, who asked first, or it could've been our son, Michael: "Where are we going, Dad?" Cheerily, I'd tell them, but then several hours later, after I'd seen some name on a sign or billboard, something that seemed interesting, and I'd turned off, and then maybe saw something else, when we were nowhere near where I'd said we'd be, one of the kids would ask again, "Where are we going, Dad?" After several more days, and several more trips, I said finally, "We're going where we end up." Like Bryson's atoms. It's become our family joke.

From there to here. And now to who knows where.

ACKNOWLEDGEMENTS

I didn't think I would write this book, and once I started I wasn't sure I'd get very far.

It is the story of thirty-five, not twenty, not ten. I thought I could find most of us from the class who were still alive, and family members from many of those who had died. But I knew I needed not only their cooperation in writing this book, I needed their enthusiastic involvement. They would have to put in many hours on the phone with me talking about things they may never have talked about to family or friends, or even thought about, or wanted to think about, and to someone they hadn't known for fifty-five years, if they had known me even then. They would have to think about their life, one that's now not far from its end, and come to grips with the fact that this is what it is, and there's not much time left to change anything. I would have to do the same.

I don't think we thought much about big questions like this at the beginning. I don't think we could know what our conversations would be like, and how they would feel. And then Covid, and all that extra time we had to think and dwell, with so much less else to do to distract us. I remember a conversation with one classmate when, after about an hour and a half of our usual two-hour talk, she said, "Can we stop now?" And another, when after a time had opened up and I suggested we talk the following week rather than the normal two weeks later, said, "Oh, no, no, I can't do that." She always prepared for our talks, looked things up, made notes, thought long and hard. We talked three weeks later instead.

So, first of all, most of all, I want to thank the class of 9G (and those who joined the class after grade nine). Some things I surely heard wrong. Others I misunderstood. The mistakes are mine, not yours, and for that I'm sorry. But you really hung in. I hope you think it was worth it.

Every story about lives is a "life and times." The circumstances of a time, the ways of thinking, the possibilities. We had a chance to go to university, our ancestors did not. Our mothers had to stop work when we were born, the women in our class didn't. I want to thank *Maclean's* magazine for helping me understand the times we grew up in. The stories it ran each week during the forties, fifties, and sixties were not definitive, but they helped suggest what was on Canadians' minds, what we were talking about, as kids what we heard, what was in the air around us. I'd like to thank the librarians at the Toronto Reference Library who introduced me to the *Maclean's* archives. And also Denise Harris who, as a volunteer, assists the Etobicoke Historical Society in keeping Etobicoke's history alive. Librarians and archivists have to be among the most helpful people on Earth (something Daryl Browne learned much earlier, with Miss McKillop at ECI), maybe because they are genuinely interested in what they do and can't quite believe that non-librarians and non-archivists might be too.

I also want to thank Jared Bland, who was the publisher of McClelland & Stewart when I decided I wanted to write this book. Anybody who writes needs at least three very big things from a publisher: you need someone who understands what you're trying to do almost as well as you do, who feels almost the same need to do it, and who does so with almost the same excitement. Because so many days you're writing off into the unknown, where you don't know where you're going, or maybe even why, or why it matters. Jared always "gets it," gets those three very big "its."